THE PSYCHOLOGY OF THE RECESSION ON THE WORKPLACE

THE PSYCHOLOGY OF THE RECESSION ON THE WORKPLACE

Editor

Karissa Moris

Socialy PRESS
AN IMPRINT OF SCITUS ACADEMICS

The Psychology of the Recession on the Workplace
Edited by **Karissa Moris**

This Book is Printed on Acid-Free Paper. ♾

ISBN: 978-1-68117-750-2
Library of Congress Control Number: 2017938762

Socialy Press
(An Imprint of Scitus Academics),
616, Corporate Way, Suite 2, 4766,
Valley Cottage, NY 10989

www.scitusacademics.com

Notice

Printed in United States of America.

Preface

The impact of the economic recession has had a deep psychological effect on the health and wellbeing of people throughout the world. This has been particularly deceptive in the workplace, where there has been major downsizings, increasing levels of job insecurity, fewer employees meaning heavier workloads, longer working hours, a more robust and bottom-line management style and work spilling over into people's private lives creating work-life imbalance. An economic recession can lead people to feel more insecure about their financial situation. Financial insecurity is a form of chronic stress that increases risk for psychological distress. Managers need to be aware of how the larger world out there is affecting their staff, why they should be more attuned to employee conversations about money fears, separation and divorce, and how that has an impact on the organization. They should be extra vigilant, and able to identify red flags that someone is having personal difficulties. Managers can remind their team of the types of resources available to help them.

The Psychology of the Recession on the Workplace shows that accumulative job demands, inherent job insecurity and gradually more inadequate salaries make noteworthy contributions to psychological distress, family conflict and related behaviors. The contributors disclose that the recession has essentially changed the way employees observe their work and leaders. Little research has explored changes in workers' psychosocial hazard exposures, work-related stress and stress-related absence associated with the onset of unprecedented severe economic recession. Knowledge of these could inform psychosocial risk management measures appropriate to austere economic times. The text tries to emphasize the possibility of a crisis originating in the economic recession and affecting not only individual life but also the whole society. It demonstrates adverse changes in psychosocial hazard exposures, work-related stress prevalence and stress-related sickness absence associated with the onset of an unprecedented economic recession. Its findings indicate the need for a concerted focus on psychosocial risk management activities during austere economic times as a means by which to promote worker health and minimize sickness absence. This highly regarded and timely book shows a significant increase in the mean levels of distress and dissatisfaction in the work place in recent years. This hardcover will be valuable for students and experts in the fields of organizational behavior and human resource management.

Table of Contents

CHAPTER 1

Job Insecurity During Recessions: Effects on Survivors' Work Stress

Sepideh Modrek* and Mark R Cullen

General Medical Disciplines, Stanford University School of Medicine, Palo Alto, CA, USA

ABSTRACT

Background

Previous studies show a variety of negative health consequences for the remaining workforce after downsizing events. This study examined self-reported work stress from 2009–2012 in the context of a large multi-site aluminum manufacturing company that underwent severe downsizing in 2009.

Methods

This study examined the association between work stress and working at a work site that underwent severe downsizing. We assessed the level of downsizing across thirty plants in 2009 and categorized seven as having undergone severe downsizing. We linked plant-level downsizing information to individual workers' responses to an annual work engagement survey, which included three work stress questions. From 2009 to 2012 over 14, 000 employees were asked about their experience of work stress. Though the surveys were anonymous, the surveys captured employees' demographic and employment characteristic as well as plant location. We used hierarchical logistic regressions to compare responses of workers at severely downsized plants to workers at all other plant while controlling for demographic and plant characteristics. Responses to the work stress questions and one control question were examined.

Results

In all yearly surveys salaried workers consistently reported having more work stress than hourly workers. There was no differential in work stress for workers at severely downsized plants in 2009. In 2010 to 2012, salaried workers who remained at severely downsized plants reported significantly higher work stress than salaried workers at all other plants across multiple work stress questions. Examination of the 2006 survey confirmed that there were no pre-existing differences in work stress among salaried employees working at plants that would eventually experience severe downsizing. In addition, there was no difference in responses to the control question at severely downsized plants.

Conclusion

Salaried workers at plants with high layoffs experienced more work stress after 2009 than their counterparts at non-high layoff plants. Increased work stress is important to monitor and may be a mediating pathway through which the external economic environment leads to adverse health outcomes.

Keywords: Economic recession, Downsizing, Work stress

BACKGROUND

Throughout the economic recession of 2007–2009 organizations reduced personnel through downsizing and layoffs leading to widespread increase in job insecurity even for those who remain employed [1]. Previous research has found job insecurity to be associated with worse mental and physical health outcomes for the remaining workforce, hereafter referred to as survivors [2-4]. Many of these studies examined perceptions of work insecurity (as opposed to externally measured downsizing) and were undertaken in non-recessionary periods. During recessions when labor markets are weak and other work opportunities may be more limited, the sense of job insecurity may be particularly harmful. According to the American Life Panel survey conducted from 2008–2010, workers consistently overestimated their probability of losing their job in the upcoming year, suggesting persistent job insecurity was a prominent issue during the recent recession [5].

In addition to job insecurity, downsizing is likely to be accompanied by increased workload for the surviving workers. Studies of health care workers after downsizing suggest there is an association between downsizing and greater workload [6]. Both greater workload and job insecurity may in turn cause work stress [7], which previous studies have shown to have detrimental effects on health. Both stress at work and job strain, a related construct where employees have high work demands and low control, have been found to be associated with coronary heart disease [8,9], metabolic syndrome [10,11], and elevated blood pressure [12-14].

In this study, we examined workers' self-reported work stress at a large multi-site, geographically diverse, aluminum-manufacturing company, Alcoa. Our study leveraged large annual company wide work engagement surveys from 2009–2012, which included data during the height of and after the large layoffs in 2009. We exploited the variation in the timing and intensity of layoffs at thirty Alcoa plants to categorize each plant as either having high layoffs or not. We then examined the relationship between plant-level intensity of downsizing in 2009 and individual-level perceptions of work stress for surviving workers from 2009–2012.

Study context

As a consequence of rapidly declining demand for products in the construction, aerospace and automotive industries, Alcoa was forced to cut production broadly leading to layoffs at every level of the organization in 2009 [15]. However, not all worksites experienced similar levels layoffs. Some worksites let go of as much as 40% of their workforce while others lost only 5% — a turnover similar to that of normal times. We used the plant level variation in the severity of layoff to categorize plants by the intensity of the 2009 downsizing and evaluated perceptions of work stress for the remaining workforce from 2009 to 2012.

The outcome of interest, work stress, has been collected yearly through an anonymous survey of work engagement since 2006. The yearly surveys include three questions that deal specifically with work stress with identical wording and scales in all surveys. The survey is administered over a 20-day period between September and October of each year and employees are given time at work to complete it. Each survey is de-identified, but gender, race, tenure, employee type (hourly vs. salaried) and plant location are captured. The company encouraged employees to respond, providing them with paid time to respond to the survey, which contributed to the high response rates—exceeding 80% overall since 2008.

METHODS

Data

Independent variable of interest: external measure of job insecurity
To create a measure of downsizing, we used personnel data. For thirty fully functional US plants with greater than 100 employees in 2008, we calculated the proportion of the workforces that was laid off in 2009. For these same plants we noted dates in 2009 where more than forty workers had their contract of employment terminated on the same date and classify these dates as mass layoff events. The downsizing measure was then defined by two criteria: 1) the proportional change in size of the workforce at the plant in 2009 and 2) having experienced a mass termination event. Worksites with 20-40% reductions in the workforce and a mass termination event were categorized as high layoffs plants. Using this definition, seven plants were considered high layoff plants. The remaining twenty-three plants served as control plants though workers at control plants experienced some downsizing as well. These cut offs are similar to those used in previous studies of examining downsizing events [16,17].

Individual-level self-reported work stress

Alcoa conducts an anonymous annual survey of work engagement administered through a third party vendor. The company then receives department level scores for the 32-question survey. At the request of the research team the third party vendor has included three validated work stress questions derived from previous surveys of work organization [18]. Workers were asked how much they agreed or disagreed, on a 5-point Likert scale, to the follow questions: 1) I find my work stressful, 2) I find that I am worn out at the end of the day, and 3) I find that work issues frequently remain on my mind after hours. In our analyses responses to each question were dichotomized. Workers who reported that they agree or strongly agree with each statement were considered to have work stress in the analysis to follow and each question is analyzed individually (though the Cronbach internal consistently score for the three questions ranges from 0.78-0.84).

Figure 1 presents the response rate by year and plant type for the overall survey. The response rate was consistently over 70%, but response rates were substantially lower in 2006 (71%) and 2008 (75%). Data from the 2007 survey were not examined because plant identifiers could not be ascertained. From 2009 to 2012, response rates were relatively stable ranging from 83-87%. We excluded the 2008 surveys in the regression analyses and focused on the 2009–2012 surveys because 1) the response rate was lower and there were substantial differences in response rates by plant type, 2) the survey was conducted during the peak of the 2008 stock market crash and therefore responses may include ambient stressors and acute financial stressors outside of work, and 3) the layoffs in 2009 changed the composition of the work force dramatically from 2008. In supplemental analyses we examined the 2006 data to assess whether there were any pre-existing differences in reported work stress in plants that would eventually have high layoffs three years later. We present these analyses separately because the composition of the workforces who responded to the survey was different in 2006.

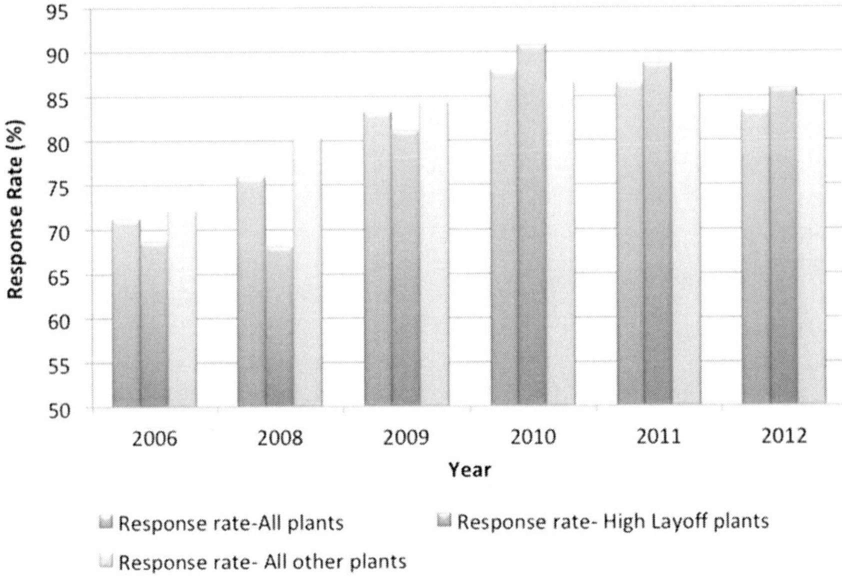

Figure 1. Work engagement survey response rate, by year and level of layoffs in 2009.

The responses to these surveys were anonymous. Though many of the same workers replied to the 2009–2012 surveys, we can not link individual responses from year to year, which precluded us from doing individual-level longitudinal analyses, i.e. panels. In the regression analyses detailed below, we examined the responses to three work stress questions controlling for basic demographic characteristics collected in each survey year. These characteristics included gender, race, hourly/salary status, and tenure. In addition we used the change in county-level unemployment rate in each prior year (compiled from Bureau of Labor Statistics data http://www.bls.gov) as an additional area-level control to capture the conditions of the local labor markets.

Statistical methods

For perceived work stress, the three work stress questions were individually examined. We first described patterns of responses to each of the work stress questions over time, from 2006 and 2008–2012 by demographic group. We employed hierarchical logistic regressions to assess the association of an employee working in a plant categorized as having a high level of layoffs in 2009 and reporting work stress. Since each observation corresponds to one worker's survey responses within a plant, the hierarchical model accounts for clustering of survey responses within a plant. For each of the three work stress questions we used the logistic function to model the binary outcomes. We estimated the following models:

Model 1

$$\begin{aligned}\text{Work Stress}_{p,i} = F_{logistic}\Big(&\alpha + \beta 1(\text{Sex}_i) + \beta 2(\text{Race}_i) \\ &+\beta 3(\text{Tenure}_i) + \beta 4(\text{Union}_p) \\ &+\beta 5\left(\Delta\text{Area Unemployment}_p\right) \\ &+\beta 6(\text{Salary}_i) + \beta 7\left(\text{High Layoff}_p\right) \\ &+\gamma_{pi}\Big)\end{aligned}$$

Model 2

$$\begin{aligned}\text{Work Stress}_{p,i} = F_{logistic}\Big(&\alpha + \beta 1(\text{Sex}_i) + \beta 2(\text{Race}_i) \\ &+\beta 3(\text{Tenure}_i) + \beta 4(\text{Union}_p) \\ &+\beta 5\left(\Delta\text{Area Unemployment}_p\right) \\ &+\beta 6(\text{Salary}_i) + \beta 7\left(\text{High Layoff}_p\right) \\ &+\beta 8\left(\text{Salary}_i{*}\text{High Layoff}_p\right) + \gamma_{pi}\Big)\end{aligned}$$

Model 2 is similar to Model 1 but allows for differential effects by worker type of working at a high layoff plant. Since each observation corresponds to one worker's survey responses within a plant, we modeled the overall error term, $\gamma pi = \alpha i + \epsilon pi$, using a random-effects at the plant-level to account for the interdependence of the observations within plants. In addition, we included all available individual-level covariate controls as well as a control for changes in county-level unemployment rates in each preceding year.

In addition to the three work stress questions, we also examined a fourth question throughout, "I am proud to work at Alcoa". Responses to this pride question were not correlated to the work stress question and are meant served as a control question in our analyses. The analysis of control question attempted to capture any systematic bias in employee responses. For example, there might have been some bias towards positive responses about the company in general after the 2009 downsizing from workers to exude an optimistic impression towards management, but these biases would lead to an underestimate of the effect of downsizing. On the other hand, if there were residual anger or disappointment towards the company for layoffs, then we would expect lower reports of pride in the company at high layoff plants. Overall, we expected less systematically positive or negative responses to the work stress questions because they were added to the survey by the research team and were not used in the third party vendor's assessment of work engagement.

In additional analyses we examined survey responses in the 2006 data. The composition of respondents to the 2006 survey was likely quite different than the respondents to the 2009–2012 surveys because of attrition, new hires and layoffs. Therefore, the two sets of analyses are not fully comparable. Nonetheless, the analysis of the 2006 data was conducted to assess pre-existing differences in work stress by plants that would eventually have high levels of layoffs. We also examined the control question in 2006.

Institutional review

The Stanford University Institutional Review Board approved this study's protocol, invoking the epidemiologic exemption waiving the requirement for individual consent.

RESULTS

Main analyses

Table 1 provides descriptive statistics for the analytic sample. For each year in 2006 and 2009–2012 the mean proportion who agree with the work stress questions, the pride question, as well as the sample characteristics collected in the survey are presented. For each individual work stress item, 37-55% of the sample report work stress. While these proportions are relatively stable from 2009–2012, reports of work stress are much lower for all the questions in 2006. For the control pride question, there is a notable increase in the proportion of the sample that report being proud to work at Alcoa from 45% in 2006, to 57% in 2009 to 79% by 2012. The demographic characteristics of this sample are comparable to the entire Alcoa workforces; predominately white (70%), male (79%), hourly workers (70%) who have been working at Alcoa for at least 6 years (75%) for 2009–2012. The sample of survey respondents in 2006 include workers with shorter tenure, more salaried workers, and more workers from plants that would eventually experience high layoffs. Due to these differences, we examine the 2006 survey data separately.

For 2009–2012, the years of the main analyses, these demographic characteristics of the sample remain stable, though there is some difference in worker tenure over the four survey years. In 2009 less than 1% and in 2010 about 3% of workers report working at Alcoa for less than 1 year. There is some more hiring in 2011–2012 as is evident by the 5-8% of workers who report work at Alcoa for less than one year. Overall, most workers in the sample are long tenured employees. A large proportion of these workers, 34%, work at the 7 plants that had high layoffs in 2009 and 37% of them work at plants with union contracts for hourly workers.

In Figure 2 we present the proportion of employees who agree/disagree with the three work stress questions and the pride question in the 2006, and 2008 to 2012 surveys. For each question we aggregated the mean responses over three factors, gender, employee type and race. While the composition of survey respondents changed in each survey year (the 2006 survey was conducted prior to any knowledge of layoffs or the upcoming recession and includes many workers who would be leave Alcoa before 2009 or be laid off in 2009, the 2008 survey was conducted before large layoffs but at the peak of the stock market crash and includes may workers who would be laid off in 2009, the 2009 survey was conducted after several rounds of layoffs but before all layoffs were completed, the 2010 to 2012 surveys were conducted after much of the workforce had stabilized), the figure indicates that regardless of survey

Table 1. Outcome means and sample characteristics

	Survey year				
	2006	2009	2010	2011	2012
Outcomes (% who agree or strongly agree)					
I find my work stressful.	40%	50%	49%	46%	46%
I find that I am worn out at the end of the day.	44%	55%	55%	53%	53%
I find that work issues frequently remain on my mind after hours.	37%	44%	44%	43%	41%
I am proud to work at Alcoa	45%	57%	64%	78%	79%
Demographic controls					
White	60%	70%	70%	70%	67%
Male	78%	79%	79%	79%	79%
Salary	30%	29%	25%	25%	25%
Tenure					
Less than 1 year	8%	1%	3%	9%	5%
1-2 years	13%	8%	4%	4%	10%
3-5 years	10%	17%	18%	15%	10%
6-10 years	19%	15%	17%	19%	20%
11-20 years	20%	26%	26%	24%	25%
Over 20 years	30%	33%	33%	30%	29%
Work at a plant with High Layoffs in 2009	39%	33%	34%	34%	34%
Observations	13980	14658	16144	15703	15667
Plants	30	30	30	30	30
Union plants	8	8	8	8	8
High layoff plants	7	7	7	7	7

Note: In this table the number of observations reflects the sample that responded to all the outcome questions. For any given individual outcome, the number of observations may be slightly higher.

year salaried workers were more likely to report more work stress. The figure also shows that regardless of the demographic group, workers reported much lower work stress in 2006. In contrast, there is no evidence of a marked difference in the proportion of workers that agree or strongly agree with the work stress statements between 2008–2012. Figure 2 also shows large increases in the proportion of employees who report that they are proud to work at Alcoa in 2010–2012 as compared to 2006 or 2008–2009 across all demographic groups; the largest increase in reporting pride in working at Alcoa was among hourly workers from 2006 to 2008.

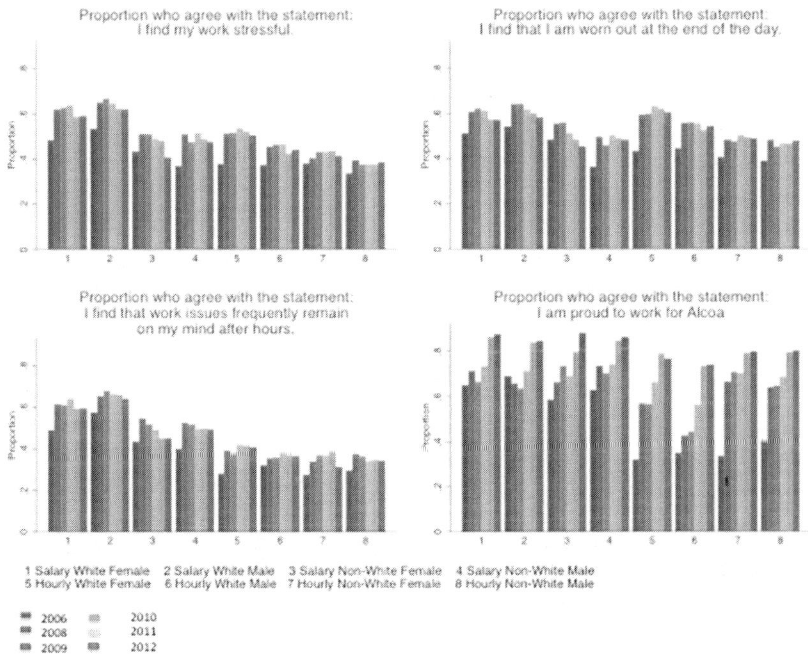

Figure 2. Work stress questions and control question 2008–2012 survey means for 2006 & 2008–2012 surveys, by demographic group.

Table 2 reports the association between working at a high layoff plant, the three work stress questions and the pride question from 2009–2012, our main analyses. The table presents both Model 1 and 2 for each question. In column one and two, we examine responses to the question, I find my work stressful. In 2009, we find that while more salaried workers report that they find their work to be stressful overall as compared to hourly workers (OR = 2.14; 95% CI 1.95 - 2.34), there is no difference for workers who work at high layoff plants. In contrast by 2010, more salaried workers at high layoff plants report that they find their work to be stressful compared to salaried workers at non-high layoff plants (OR = 1.30; CI = 1.11-1.53). This differential is found again in 2011 and 2012 and its magnitude and significance remain quite stable. Results for the second work stress question, I find that I am worn out at the end of the day, are presented in columns three and four. We find that salaried workers reported being worn out more than hourly workers in all the survey years. In addition, there is no differential for salaried workers at high layoff plants compared to salaried workers at other plants in 2009 or 2010. However, by 2011 more salaried workers at high layoff plants reported being worn out than salaried workers at all other plants (OR = 1.26; CI 1.068 - 1.486). This differential is observed again in the 2012 survey with very similar significance and magnitude to those found in 2011. Results for the final work stress question, I find that work issues frequently remain on my mind after hours, are presented in column five and six. Salaried workers reported higher rates of having work remain on their minds in all years. For this question there is no significant differential for salaried workers who worked at high layoff plants in any of the four years. In column seven and eight, we examined a control question, one not related to the work stress question but asked in the same survey, I am proud to work at Alcoa. Salaried workers consistently reported higher rates of pride in working at Alcoa as compared to hourly workers. However, for this question there was no differential at high layoff plants.

Table 2. Association between working at a high layoff plant and the work stress questions and the pride question from 2009–2012, odd ratios and 95% confidence internals

	I find my work stressful		I find that I am worn out at the end of the day		I find that work issues frequently remain on my mind after hours		I am proud to work at Alcoa	
2009 Survey								
	Model 1	*Model 2*	*Model 1*	*Model 2*	*Model 1*	*Model 2*	*Model 1*	*Model 2*
High layoff plant	0.895	0.901	0.92	0.943	1.009	1.048	1.139	1.097
	[0.666 - 1.201]	[0.669 - 1.215]	[0.665 - 1.273]	[0.679 - 1.309]	[0.834 - 1.221]	[0.860 - 1.275]	[0.734 - 1.766]	[0.706 - 1.704]
Salary	2.118***	2.136***	1.383***	1.422***	3.062***	3.193***	1.812***	1.739***
	[1.963 - 2.285]	[1.948 - 2.343]	[1.282 - 1.491]	[1.297 - 1.558]	[2.838 - 3.304]	[2.911 - 3.502]	[1.675 - 1.961]	[1.583 - 1.909]
Salaried * high layoff plants		0.975		0.918		0.88		1.149
		[0.831 - 1.143]		[0.784 - 1.076]		[0.750 - 1.032]		[0.969 - 1.362]
Observations	14760	14760	14748	14748	14762	14762	14776	14776
Number of locations	30	30	30	30	30	30	30	30
2010 Survey								
	Model 1	*Model 2*	*Model 1*	*Model 2*	*Model 1*	*Model 2*	*Model 1*	*Model 2*
High layoff plant	0.935	0.876	0.928	0.906	1.067	1.051	1.058	1.037
	[0.678 - 1.289]	[0.634 - 1.212]	[0.659 - 1.305]	[0.642 - 1.278]	[0.832 - 1.367]	[0.818 - 1.351]	[0.663 - 1.687]	[0.650 - 1.655]
Salary	1.929***	1.773***	1.230***	1.193***	2.656***	2.606***	1.763***	1.712***
	[1.789 - 2.081]	[1.619 - 1.943]	[1.141 - 1.326]	[1.089 - 1.306]	[2.463 - 2.865]	[2.379 - 2.856]	[1.624 - 1.915]	[1.550 - 1.890]
Salaried * high layoff plants		1.301***		1.101		1.061		1.097
		[1.107 - 1.528]		[0.940 - 1.291]		[0.904 - 1.246]		[0.921 - 1.306]
Observations	16185	16185	16187	16187	16184	16184	16169	16169
Number of locations	30	30	30	30	30	30	30	30
2011 Survey								
	Model 1	*Model 2*	*Model 1*	*Model 2*	*Model 1*	*Model 2*	*Model 1*	*Model 2*
High layoff plant	0.999	0.927	0.97	0.919	1.048	1.022	1.122	1.114
	[0.660 - 1.510]	[0.613 - 1.403]	[0.628 - 1.497]	[0.595 - 1.421]	[0.755 - 1.453]	[0.735 - 1.420]	[0.695 - 1.813]	[0.688 - 1.802]
Salary	1.974***	1.788***	1.240***	1.154***	2.685***	2.598***	1.859***	1.835***
	[1.826 - 2.134]	[1.628 - 1.962]	[1.148 - 1.339]	[1.052 - 1.266]	[2.464 - 2.902]	[2.367 - 2.853]	[1.680 - 2.058]	[1.622 - 2.075]
Salaried * high layoff plants		1.376***		1.260***		1.111		1.042
		[1.164 - 1.627]		[1.068 - 1.486]		[0.940 - 1.312]		[0.841 - 1.290]
Observations	15730	15730	15732	15732	15731	15731	15726	15726
Number of locations	30	30	30	30	30	30	30	30
2012 Survey								
	Model 1	*Model 2*	*Model 1*	*Model 2*	*Model 1*	*Model 2*	*Model 1*	*Model 2*
High layoff plant	1.002	0.941	0.979	0.934	1.093	1.078	1.032	1.019
	[0.671 - 1.496]	[0.630 - 1.405]	[0.624 - 1.537]	[0.594 - 1.466]	[0.783 - 1.527]	[0.771 - 1.509]	[0.608 - 1.750]	[0.600 - 1.732]
Salary	1.863***	1.712***	1.141***	1.068	2.701***	2.653***	2.000***	1.956***
	[1.723 - 2.016]	[1.558 - 1.881]	[1.055 - 1.233]	[0.972 - 1.173]	[2.496 - 2.923]	[2.413 - 2.918]	[1.799 - 2.224]	[1.722 - 2.222]
Salaried * high layoff plants		1.310***		1.231**		1.059		1.073
		[1.108 - 1.549]		[1.043 - 1.452]		[0.895 - 1.252]		[0.856 - 1.343]
Observations	15715	15715	15711	15711	15714	15714	15703	15703
Number of locations	30	30	30	30	30	30	30	30

95% Confidence intervals are in brackets.
Asterisk indicate significance level of estimated coefficient: *** $p < 0.01$, ** $p < 0.05$, * $p < 0.1$.
Note: Both model 1 & 2 include controls for worker's tenure, worker's race, worker's gender, whether the worker was employed at a union plant, and the change in the prior year's unemployment rate in the country of the plant. Model 2 incudes an additional interaction term between working at a high layoff plant and worker type to allow for a differential effect of working at a high layoff plant by worker type on stress outcomes.

Analyses of pre-existing trends

Table 3 reports the association between the same questions as above and working at a plant that would eventually have high layoffs in three years. Many respondents in the 2006 sample will have been laid off in the 2009 downsizing events. Nonetheless, the analysis was necessary to show whether there were any differences in reports of stress well before the onset of the recession and layoffs to come.

Table 3. Association between working at a high layoff plant and the work stress questions and the pride question from 2006, odd ratios and 95% confidence intervals

	I find my work stressful		I find that I am worn out at the end of the day		I find that work issues frequently remain on my mind after hours		I am proud to work at Alcoa	
	2006 Survey							
	Model 1	*Model 2*	*Model 1*	*Model 2*	*Model 1*	*Model 2*	*Model 1*	*Model 2*
High layoff plant	1.202	1.169	1.225	1.207	1.194	1.192	1.17	1.122
	[0.936 - 1.545]	[0.921 - 1.534]	[0.836 - 1.793]	[0.821 - 1.773]	[0.954 - 1.493]	[0.948 - 1.499]	[0.937 - 1.461]	[0.893 - 1.410]
Salary	1.408***	1.387***	0.927*	0.909*	1.692***	1.688***	2.586***	2.453***
	[1.299 - 1.527]	[1.253 - 1.535]	[0.852 - 1.009]	[0.816 - 1.011]	[1.560 - 1.835]	[1.524 - 1.870]	[2.381 - 2.809]	[2.211 - 2.723]
Salaried * high layoff plants		1.041		1.054		1.006		1.146
		[0.885 - 1.224]		[0.890 - 1.248]		[0.856 - 1.182]		[0.972 - 1.351]
Observations	14079	14079	14072	14072	14055	14055	14059	14059
Number of locations	30	30	30	30	30	30	30	30

95% Confidence intervals are in brackets.
Asterisk indicate significance level of estimated coefficient: *** $p < 0.01$, ** $p < 0.05$, * $p < 0.1$.
Note: Both model 1 & 2 include controls for worker's tenure, worker's race, worker's gender, whether the worker was employed at a union plant and the change in the prior year's unemployment rate in the country of the plant. Model 2 incudes an additional interaction term between working at a high layoff plant and worker type to allow for a differential effect of working at a high layoff plant by worker type on stress outcomes.

Though reports of work stress were much lower in 2006 overall (Figure 2), salaried workers reported more work stress even in the 2006 survey. Salaried worker reported significantly higher work stress for two of the three work stress questions, I find my work stressful (OR = 1.41; 95% CI 1.30- 1.53) and I find that work issues frequently remain on my mind after hours (OR = 1.69; 95% CI 1.52 – 1.87). They were also somewhat less likely to report being worn out at the end of the day compared to hourly workers (OR = 0.91; 95% CI 0.81-1.01). There was no difference in reports of work stress or workers' pride in Alcoa for workers who worked at plants that would have high layoffs in 2009.

Discussion

This study explored the consequences of downsizing on work stress for survivors of layoffs in the context of a severe recession at a large multi-site manufacturing company. The results show that salaried workers consistently report more work stress, but that by 2010 –one year after severe downsizing– salaried workers at plants with high layoffs reported that they experienced more work stress than their counterparts at non-high layoff plants. The differential increase in work stress was found in two of the three work questions, and was corroborated in all three independent surveys done in 2010, 2011, and 2012. In contrast, though we documented more variation over time in the control question we examined, we did not observe any difference in reports of worker pride in Alcoa in high layoff plants further corroborating that our results were not an artifact. We also showed that there were no pre-existing differences in reports of work stress or pride in Alcoa at plants that would eventually have high layoffs in 2009.

The results presented here are also in line with previous studies. A recent study using a population sample showed that among middle-aged, college-educated white men with full-time employment report increased stress from 2006 to 2009 [19]. This population would be very similar to the group that reported increased stress in our sample. In a more direct comparison, previous work in this workforces showed that employees who survive layoff but work at plants with severe downsizing, experience a higher incidence rate for hypertension than their counterparts in less affected plants [17]. Given the previously reported relations between work stress and health broadly, and previous findings within this workforce that remaining workers in high layoff plant after the 2009 layoffs had worse health outcome, we hypothesize that work stress may be a pathway linking the external economic forces with the health status change. In order to test such a hypothesis, that work stress mediated the adverse health outcomes previously found, we would need to examine whether including an individual's work stress would eliminate any association between health and working in a high layoff plant. However, we could not link individuals in the work engagement surveys to their health claims data, which was used in the previous analysis, to conduct a full mediation study.

Despite the inability to conduct mediation analyses, this study has several notable strengths. First we find convergence with regard to work-stress from three independent samples of the same workforce, which bolsters our confidence in the result. Second, we do not find that salaried workers at high layoff plants report more stress in either 2006 or 2009, suggesting that our results are not due to pre-existing plant differences. Third, our examination of the control question suggests that while some workers may have reported positive responses to please management, this practice was not systematic in high layoff plants. Had we found that workers in high layoff plant reported differential pride in working at Alcoa our interpretation of the results — that downsizing leads to higher work stress— would be undermined. Fourth, even though we are examining only one organization, the 30 plants studied cover 16 states and all census regions, suggesting that our results are unlikely due to localized effects.

The interpretation of results of this study in relation to previous studies of work stress, most notably from the cohort of civil servants in Whitehall II study [20], require an understanding of the differences in the aim and context of the current study. The present study aims to assess changes in workers' reported stress to a firm-level exogenous stressor, severe downsizing, as opposed to examining the role of a specific job on work stress. The finding that salaried workers within the manufacturing sector reported higher levels of stress after the layoffs, while initially unexpected, are consistent in the context of the study population for several reasons. First, salaried workers reported more work stress even before the recession, suggesting that even in normal times salaried workers bear more stress in this context. Second, we find evidence of increases in reported stress in high layoff plants for salaried workers in 2010–2012, after the 2009 layoffs. According to BLS data, productivity grew by 6% in 2010 for the manufacturing sector as a whole, yet we can imagine that in certain hourly jobs (assembly line, pot rooms, etc.) there is little room for speed up and increased productivity gains, whereas there is more leeway for productivity gains for administrative and technical jobs in the salaried portion of the workforce. It is likely that during downsizing salaried workers are more vulnerable to demands of increased effort or intensity without compensating rewards because hourly workers have union protection regulating any possible speed up and because any increase in work hours is directly compensated at the known hourly rate or through overtime. Hourly workers know their exact compensation for their efforts, whereas salaried workers may experience more effort-reward imbalance because their compensation is not directly tied to their efforts, especially in the short-run. Furthermore, salaried workers were at risk of having more uncompensated work demands and/or having the scope of their work duties expanded after the recession. Hourly workers were protected from such changes in scope of their work and any extra effort would have been compensated. Thus, the increase in work stress may be concentrated in the salaried part of the workforce because of increased workloads and job insecurity. While we cannot directly observe differential changes in work demands, there was some rehiring of hourly workers in 2010–2012, whereas staffing levels remained depressed in the salaried workforce.

CONCLUSION

The negative consequences of the recent recession among workers who have not themselves been displaced, but have experienced severe layoffs in their own firms have been underexplored. This study is an attempt to explore work stress as a proximal "outcome" for this population. Our results suggest that downsizing led to persistent work stress, which accumulated overtime and may in turn lead to other negative outcomes, particularly negative health outcomes as have been found previously [2-4,10-14,21]. Increased work stress is important to monitor and may be a mediating pathway through which the external economic environment leads to adverse health outcomes. Future studies will need to explore the links between persistent stress and health consequences after downsizing events.

ABBREVIATIONS

CI: Confidence interval; OR: Odds ratio.

Competing interest

Authors have no competing interest to declare. Dr. Cullen serves as a senior medical advisor to Alcoa under the terms of a research contract between Stanford University and Alcoa, Inc.

Authors' contributions

SM MC conceived of study. SM did data analysis. SM structured and wrote the manuscript. MC participated in the presentation of results and contributed to writing the manuscript. Both authors read and approved the final manuscript.

Pre-publication history
The pre-publication history for this paper can be accessed here:

http://www.biomedcentral.com/1471-2458/13/929/prepub

ACKNOWLEDGEMENTS

This research was funded by two grants from the National Institute on Aging (Disease, Disability and Death in an Aging Workforce, NIH/NIA, 1 R01 AG026291-06 and The Design of Social Insurance for the Elderly: Public Pensions and Health Insurance, NIH/NIA 1R01AG032449-01), as well as from Alcoa, Inc.

As an alternative to providing a de-identified data set to the public domain, we allow access for the purpose of re-analyses or appropriate follow-on analyses by any qualified investigator willing to sign a contractual covenant with the host Institution limiting use of data to a specific agreed upon purpose and observing the same restrictions as are limited in our contract with Alcoa, such as 60-day manuscript review for compliance purposes.

REFERENCES

1. In U.S., Worries About Job Cutbacks Return to Record Highs. http://www.gallup.com/poll/149261/worries-job-cutbacks-return-record-highs.aspx.
2. Burgard SA, Brand JE, House JS. Perceived job insecurity and worker health in the United States. Soc Sci Med. 2009;69(5):777–785.
3. Ferrie JE, Shipley MJ, Stansfeld SA, Marmot MG. Effects of chronic job insecurity and change in job security on self reported health, minor psychiatric morbidity, physiological measures, and health related behaviours in British civil

servants: the Whitehall II study. J Epidemiol Community Health. 2002;56(6):450–454.

4. Lee S, Colditz GA, Berkman LF, Kawachi I. Prospective study of job insecurity and coronary heart disease in US women. Ann Epidemiol. 2004;14(1):24–30.
5. Hurd MD, Rohwedder S. Effects of the Financial Crisis and Great Recession on American Households. Cambridge: National Bureau of Economic Research; 2010. p. 44. (NBER working paper series).
6. Hertting A, Nilsson K, Theorell T, Larsson US. Downsizing and reorganization: demands, challenges and ambiguity for registered nurses. J Adv Nurs. 2004;45(2):145–154.
7. Dragano N, Verde PE, Siegrist J. Organisational downsizing and work stress: testing synergistic health effects in employed men and women. J Epidemiol Community Health. 2005;59(8):694–699.
8. Rosengren A, Hawken S, Ounpuu S, Sliwa K, Zubaid M, Almahmeed WA, Blackett KN, Sitthi-amorn C, Sato H, Yusuf S. Association of psychosocial risk factors with risk of acute myocardial infarction in 11,119 cases and 13,648 controls from 52 countries (the INTERHEART study): case–control study. Lancet. 2004;364(9438):953–962.
9. Kivimaki M, Nyberg ST, Batty GD, Fransson EI, Heikkil K, Alfredsson L, Bjorner JB, Borritz M, Burr H, Casini A. et al. Job strain as a risk factor for coronary heart disease: a collaborative meta-analysis of individual participant data. Lancet. 2012;380(9852):1491–1497.
10. Chandola T, Brunner E, Marmot M. Chronic stress at work and the metabolic syndrome: prospective study. BMJ. 2006;332(7540):521–525.
11. Edwards EM, Stuver SO, Heeren TC, Fredman L. Job strain and incident metabolic syndrome over 5 years of follow-Up. J Occup Environ Med. 2012;54(12):1447–1452.
12. Kamarck TW, Janicki DL, Shiffman S, Polk DE, Muldoon MF, Liebenauer LL, Schwartz JE. Psychosocial demands and ambulatory blood pressure: a field assessment approach. Physiol Behav. 2002;77(4–5):699–704.
13. Schnall PL, Schwartz JE, Landsbergis PA, Warren K, Pickering TG. A longitudinal study of job strain and ambulatory blood pressure: results from a three-year follow-up. Psychosom Med. 1998;60(6):697–706.

14. Landsbergis PA, Dobson M, Koutsouras G, Schnall P. Job strain and ambulatory blood pressure: a meta-analysis and systematic review. Am J Public Health. 2013;103(3):e61–e71.
15. 10-K Annual Report. 2009. http://www.alcoa.com/global/en/investment/pdfs/2009_Annual_Report.pdf.
16. Kivimaki M, Honkonen T, Wahlbeck K, Elovainio M, Pentti J, Klaukka T, Virtanen M, Vahtera J. Organisational downsizing and increased use of psychotropic drugs among employees who remain in employment. J Epidemiol Community Health. 2007;61(2):154–158.
17. Modrek S, Cullen MR. Health consequences of the 'Great Recession' on the employed: evidence from an industrial cohort in aluminum manufacturing. Soc Sci Med. 2013. in press.
18. Sauter SL, Murphy LR, Hurrell JJ. Prevention of work-related psychological disorders - a national strategy proposed by the national-institute-for-occupational-safety-and-health (niosh) Am Psychol. 1990;45(10):1146–1158.
19. Cohen S, Janicki-Deverts D. Who's Stressed? distributions of psychological stress in the United States in probability samples from 1983, 2006, and 2009. J Appl Soc Psychol 2012;42(6):1320–1334.
20. Bosma H, Peter R, Siegrist J, Marmot M. Two alternative job stress models and the risk of coronary heart disease. Am J Public Health. 1998;88(1):68–74.
21. Ferrie JE. Is job insecurity harmful to health? J R Soc Med. 2001;94(2):71–76.

2

CHAPTER

Health Consequences of the 'Great Recession' on the Employed: Evidence from an Industrial Cohort in Aluminum Manufacturing

Sepideh Modrek, Mark R. Cullen

General Medical Disciplines, Stanford University, School of Medicine, 1070 Arastradero Road,Palo Alto

ABSTRACT

While the negative effects of unemployment have been well studied, the consequences of layoffs and downsizing for those who remain employed are less well understood. This study used human resources and health claims data from a large multi-site fully insured aluminum company to explore the health consequences of downsizing on the remaining workforce. We exploit the variation in the timing and intensity of layoff to categorize 30 plants as high or low layoff plants. Next, we select a stably employed cohort of workers with history of health insurance going back to 2006 to 1) describe the selection process into layoff and 2) explore the association between the severity of plant level layoffs and the incidence of four chronic conditions in the remaining workforce. We examined four health outcomes: incident hypertension, diabetes, asthma/COPD and depression for a cohort of approximately 13,000 employees. Results suggest that there was an increased risk of developing hypertension for workers that remain at the plants with the highest level of layoffs, and increased risk of developing diabetes for salaried workers that remain at the plants with the highest level of layoffs. The hypertension results were robust to a several specification tests. In addition, the study design selected only healthy workers, therefore our results are likely to be a lower bound and suggest that adverse health consequences of the current recession may affect a broader proportion of the population than previously expected.

Keywords: Economic recession, Health, Downsizing, Hypertension

INTRODUCTION

The 2007–2009 recession, dubbed "The Great Recession", has been most severe recession in the United States since the Great Depression of the 1930's with the fastest increase in unemployment rates—108% increase in two years—the longest duration, and the slowest recovery (Goodman & Mance, 2011). While there has been much interest in the experiences of those who lost their jobs during this period, there has been limited interest in those who remain employed after downsizing events, hereafter referred to as survivors. Though survivors have fared relatively well, their experience is of interest because this group represents the majority of the population— 79.3% of the labor force remained employed throughout the recession (Johnson & Butrica, 2012). Awareness of the rapidly changing unemployment rate may have increased all remaining workers' perceived job insecurity, but the risk may have been more salient at worksites that experienced layoff or downsizing events. In turn, this may have affected health or health related behaviors.

Indeed, the negative impacts of organizational downsizing and increased job insecurity on employee health have been highlighted in a series of recent reviews. Studies suggest increases in sickness absence, declining self-reported health, more self-reported job insecurity, and worse psychological well-being (Davis et al., 2003; Quinlan & Bohle, 2009). These reviews discuss studies done in many different countries (primarily in Scandinavia), which examine employed and unemployed populations, utilize both cross-sectional and longitudinal designs, and consider a variety of macroeconomic periods. However, neither the longitudinal pattern of change in relation to prior health status, nor long-term consequences have been well characterized.

While most studies suggest that organizational downsizing is bad for employee health, there have several notable limitations, thus making it difficult to draw general conclusions. First, many studies rely on self-reported job insecurity and health, which may inherently be biased (Hellgren & Sverke, 2003). Second, most studies of downsizing include those workers that are eventually laid off, but it has been documented that workers that are laid off are also generally at higher risk for adverse health or health related behavior to begin with (Bockerman & Ilmakunnas, 2009; Deb et al., 2009; Kivimäki et al., 2003). Third, studies often do not account for the macroeconomic condition. Yet during periods of heightened economic uncertainty the effects of organizational downsizing on health may be different than those occurring in a single sector, industry or firm. Finally, only a few studies have focused on the effects of downsizing and job insecurity on survivors (Dragano et al., 2005; Kivimäki et al., 2003; Martikainen et al., 2008; Vahtera et al., 2004).

Another salient issue for studies of survivors is selection in layoff events. An exceptional recent study of job insecurity on survivors used a population-level sampling strategy and examined the affects of an externally constructed measure of job insecurity (as opposed to self-reported) on excess mortality in an eight-year follow-up. This study was conducted during the deep recession in Finland of 1991–1993 (Martikainen et al., 2008), and it found no evidence of excess mortality among those remaining at downsized workplaces. However, the study did document that those who experienced the most severe downsizing at their worksite were actually protected in the eight-year mortality follow-up. The authors suggest that this was likely the result of selection—the survivors may well have been the healthiest workers. Thus, despite having an impressive sample, namely, a population registry, the authors could not account for the selection process into layoff. Our study intends to fill this remaining gap. There have been no studies in the United States of how survivors fared in the context of the 2007–2009 recession using external measure of job insecurity while accounting for previous health. Therefore in this paper, we first examine how survivors and those who were laid off differ, and then discuss the effects of organizational downsizing on survivors of mass layoffs in the context of the peak of the recent global recession.

We examine workers at Alcoa, a large multi-site, geographically diverse, aluminum manufacturing company with rich and uniform insurance benefits. Our study takes advantage of a large on-going cohort study dating back to 1996; therefore we have detailed data on the cohort before, during and after the recession at multiple worksites. Fortuitously we have significant variation on how worksites were affected by the global downturn. As a consequence of plummeting demand for its products, Alcoa was forced to cut production broadly, with layoffs and accelerated retirements at every level of the organization in 2009 (Alcoa, 2010). However, not all worksites experienced similar levels of layoffs. Some worksites let go of as much as 40% of workers while others let go of only 5% — a similar turnover to that in normal times. Unlike previous studies of downsizing in US manufacturing worksites in the auto and aircraft industries (Hamilton et al., 1993), the Alcoa worksites are distributed across 15 states with largely independent labor markets.

Accordingly for each plant, we categorize the severity of layoffs and/or their timing as an external measure of job insecurity and then evaluate subsequent health outcomes on the remaining workforce at each worksite. Based on the intensity of downsizing, our measure captures the extent to which downsizing induced job insecurity for the remaining workforce, but it cannot account for workers' own appraisal of how secure their job is. These attributes make our measure an imperfect proxy for perceived job insecurity, but also limit the potential for bias if the least healthy workers report the most job insecurity.

METHODS

Data Sources

This study relied on a series of administrative datasets including personnel data, health claims data, and earnings data, which have been made available to researchers through an ongoing collaboration between Alcoa and the study investigators. These data have been described in detail in previous publications where they have been used in a variety of studies ranging from validating the use of claims data to evaluate health to examining the association between job characteristics and health outcomes (Clougherty et al., 2009; DeSanto Iennaco et al., 2010; Pollack et al., 2007). The company's personnel dataset was used to construct the cohort of interest, extract basic demographic data, and define our exposure measure of interest, the intensity of downsizing at each plant. In addition to the personnel data, health claims data were used to administratively identify new cases of four health conditions and to control for previous health. We linked these data sources with available information on changes in area-level unemployment rate in our final analyses. Each dataset, its treatment, and linkages are detailed below.

Personnel data, demographic controls, cohort definition, and constructed downsizing measure

The central data set for this study was constructed from personnel data files. For each employee, this dataset included basic demographic variables (sex, race, age), employee type/job category (hourly or salary), employee tenure, plant information (location and union status), employment status (active or retired), and termination date. We used the personnel file to extract demographic control variables, define a cohort (detailed below), and construct external measure of intensity of downsizing as a measure of job insecurity (detailed below).

Cohort Definition

We used the personnel data to select a cohort of approximately 22,000 stably employed workers who were employed on January 1, 2006. Approximately 16,000 of these workers remained working at Alcoa on January 1, 2010. Of these 16,000 survivors of the 2009 layoffs, approximately 14,000 employees worked at plants for which we had a history of health insurance going back to 2006 to verify new onset of disease. Four plants were excluded. This cohort was further selected to exclude individuals who already had significant health issues before the recession (criteria based on risk scores which are detailed below) or for whom we did not have a measure of prior health status in 2008. Our final cohort included 13,393 employees. The cohort selection strategy is outlined in Table 1.

External measure of downsizing

To create an external measure of downsizing, as a proxy for job insecurity, we used two criteria: 1) the change in size of the workforce at each plant from January 1 to December 31, 2009 and 2) plants experiencing a mass termination event. For 30 fully functional US plants with >100 employees in 2008, we calculate the proportion of the workforces that was laid off in 2009. For these same plants we noted dates in 2009 where more than 40 workers had their contract of employment terminated on the same date and classified these dates as mass layoff events. Worksites with 20–40% reductions and at least one mass termination event were categorized as 'high layoff' plants. Using this definition, seven plants (five in sample) were considered high layoff plants. The ten plants (nine in sample) that fared the best, with less than 11% layoffs were categorized 'low layoff' plants. The remaining thirteen plants (twelve in sample) were categorized as 'moderate layoff' plants. These cutoffs were based on natural breaks in the data and selected to be comparable to those used in previous studies (Martikainen et al., 2008; Vahtera et al., 2004).

Table 1. Sample Selection

	Reasons for exclusion from analytical sample	
Reason	**Observations Excluded**	**Observation Left**
Workers at 30 plant on 1/1/2006		22164
No longer at Alcoa on 1/1/2010	6262	15902
Worked at four plant with high HMO coverage	1753	14149
Could not be matched in claims data	37	14112
Risk score in 2008 missing or >4	719	13393

Health claims data, health outcomes and risk score

As a self-insured firm, Alcoa provides identical health insurance benefits to employees through local preferred provider organization (PPO) subject to choice with respect to family coverage and deductible rates. The company contracts with a single firm to manage its claims data. With the exception of a small number of workers who select a Health Maintenance Organization (HMO), all claims are managed within this database.[1] We obtained claim files for all but four of the thirty plants where a sizable proportion of workers used HMOs. These data provided both a master list of eligible individuals, including spouses and children, and linkable detailed claims records for each inpatient/outpatient medical encounter and for each prescription filled. The claims data also provides both International Classification of Diseases, Ninth Revision (ICD9) and Current Procedural Terminology (CPT) codes.

Health Outcomes

We used the claims data to identify incident cases of four health conditions: hypertension, diabetes, asthma/COPD and depression. These chronic conditions are selected because they may be related to or exacerbated by stress or stress related behaviors. Individuals who had one or more inpatient claims with ICD9 diagnosis codes of 401-404 or two or more outpatient claims with the same ICD9 codes were designated as having hypertension. We used one or more inpatient claim with ICD9 diagnosis code of 250 or two or more outpatient claims with the same ICD9 codes to identify diabetes cases. We explicitly excluded cases of gestational diabetes using ICD9 codes 648 and 790. In addition, we included cases with only one outpatient diagnosis if it was accompanied by one or more prescription filled for glucose-lowering therapies (Sulfonylreas, Meglitinides, Thiazolidinediones, alpha-glucosidase inhibitors, and DPP-4 inhibitors). We identified workers with depression if they had one or more inpatient claim with ICD9 diagnosis codes of 296, 309, or 311 or one or more outpatient claims with the same ICD9 codes. Finally workers we designated as having COPD/Asthma if they had one or more inpatient claim with ICD9 diagnosis code of 493 or 496 or two or more outpatient claims with the same ICD9 codes. In addition, we included cases with only one outpatient diagnosis if it was accompanied by one or more prescriptions filled for inhaled Corticoids, mixed inhaled Corticoids, or Beta2-Antagonists.

For all of the four conditions, only outpatient claims with a face-to-face encounter were considered and a three-year run-in period (2006–2008) was used to find and exclude prevalent cases. That is, if an individual was identified as having been diagnosed with a hypertension via our definitions between 2006–2008, he/she could not be considered a new case; our analysis only included workers who were *at risk* of developing the specific condition.

Health Risk Scores

In addition to the health claims data themselves, we use a third-party algorithm to create a health-risk stratification score for each individual. This algorithm is based on a chronic disease model and inputs CPT codes, diagnostic codes, number of eligible months, and overall outpatient health expenditures derived from the claims data and outputs a continuous risk score (Verisk Health Inc, $D_xCG^{®}$ Software). A risk score of 1 indicates that the individual is predicted to have the median health expenditure in the following year. Each unit increase indicates a one-fold increase over the median. For example, a score of 3 indicates that the individual is expected to spend three fold over the median the following year. We use the 2008 lagged risk score (which predicts the health of the individual in 2009) and then categorized them into four groups as a summary measure to control for previous underlying health. The three groups were those with scores ranging from 0–1 (the omitted category-generally healthy individuals with predicted health expenditures less than the median), 1–2 (those who are predicted spend at or somewhat more than the median), and 2–4 (those who are predicted to spend at least twice the median but less than 4 times the median). Individual with risk scores greater than 4 were dropped from the analyses because they are likely to be quite unhealthy already and represent the sickest 2.1% of the sample.

Area Control Variables-Area Unemployment

To account for regional (state or county) unemployment and labor market conditions, we created an area-level unemployment rate variable for each plant based on the Bureau of Labor Statistics data. We weighted the unemployment rate of the county and adjacent counties by labor forces size in 2008 to avoid over counting unemployment related to plant layoffs. We then calculated the change in unemployment rate between 2008–2010 and used this measure as a control variable in all the analyses. This measure was included in the model because general unemployment rates may not be as relevant to an individual's sense of job insecurity or stress as the job losses within one's workplace. The latter effect is the one we wanted to isolate. While all the plants in the study were in areas that experienced an increase in the unemployment rate, some areas experienced more rapid changes in unemployment. We wanted to distinguish between the two distinct levels of effects particularly because in our data the counties that had the fastest rate of change of unemployment were not necessarily where the plant that had high layoffs were located.

Linkages

Figure 1 details the linkages of these different data sources in the final analyses. We first linked the extracted cohort to the claims data. In order to have a measure of previous health status, we select only members of the cohort who were insured in the 2008 and have a 2008 health risk score value. Our final sample included 13,393 workers who were actively employed between January 1, 2006 and who were still active as of January 1, 2010 and for whom we had basic demographic information. Despite their older age, the cohort *is selected* to be particularly healthy (still working, not terminated during the recession, not having a high risk score in 2008).

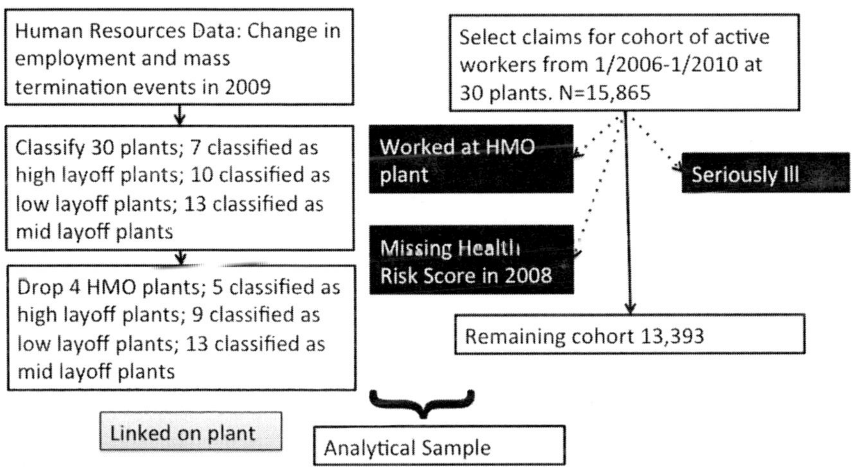

Figure 1. Sample selection and linkage

Statistical Analyses

We first characterized the exposure variable of interest. We graphed the layoff patterns and average hours worked by the three categories of plants layoffs using the longitudinal data. We then describe the selection process into layoffs by comparing the health status of those who survived and those who did not before the layoffs occurred. These descriptive analyses aid in the interpretation of our main result. Our main analyses explored whether working at a high layoff plant was associated with a new onset of one of the four chronic conditions. For the four outcomes, we had the advantage of being able to look longitudinally at health and establish a cohort for which we know the previous health status. After excluding prevalent cases (cases first identified between 2006–2008), we estimate the association between working at a high layoff plant and developing a new health condition using the following logistic regression model:

$$\text{New Diagnosis in 2009/2010}_{p,i} = F_{\text{logistic}}(\boldsymbol{\alpha} + \boldsymbol{\beta 1}(\text{High Layoff}_p) + \boldsymbol{\beta 2}(\text{Salary}_i) + \boldsymbol{\beta 3}(X_i) + \boldsymbol{\beta 4}(\text{Lagged Health Score}_{i,2008}) + \boldsymbol{\beta 5}(\Delta\text{Area Unemployment}_p) + \varepsilon_{pi}) \quad \text{(MODEL 1)}$$

(MODEL 1)

The vector of individual-level covariates, X_i, include gender, race, tenure and working at a union plant. The overall error term, $\varepsilon_{pi}=\alpha_i+\eta_{pi}$, is modeled using random-effects at the plant-level to account for the interdependence of the observations within plant.

We also explore whether hourly or salaried employees fared differently at high layoff plants. Hourly workers are almost exclusively production workers who are paid by the hour. Those at unionized facilities are, obligatorily, members of the union. Salaried workers represent a range of administrative and supervisory jobs and are compensated by regular salaries. Salaried workers are not represented by unions at any location. To understand the extent to which these differences mattered for health, we estimate models similar Model 1, but add an interaction term between working at a high layoff plant and employee type.

$$\text{New Diagnosis in 2009/2010}_{p,i} = F_{\text{logistic}}(\boldsymbol{\alpha} + \boldsymbol{\gamma}1(\text{High Layoff}_p) + \boldsymbol{\gamma}2(\text{Salary}_i) + \boldsymbol{\gamma}3(\text{Salary}_i * \text{High Layoff}_p) + \boldsymbol{\gamma 4}(X_i) + \boldsymbol{\gamma 5}(\text{Lagged Health Score}_{i,2008}) + \boldsymbol{\gamma 6}(\Delta\text{Area Unemployment}_p) + \varepsilon_{pi})$$

(MODEL 2)

In addition to the main analyses, we conducted a series of additional sensitivity analyses to test how robust our results were to alternate specifications. First, we limited our analyses to workers who worked at either low or high layoff plants, excluding the middle category. Based on news article counts, the overall uncertainty over the economy and economic policy in the United States was generally elevated compared to the recent years (Baker et al., 2013), thus even those employees not working in high layoff plants were likely to feel some work related stress or anxiety, and so the differential between high layoff plants and all others was likely to be an underestimate. Many workers, especially those working in the mid-level downsized plants, may also have felt elevated anxiety so may not be an appropriate comparison group. Therefore we compared those who experienced little downsizing compared to those who experienced relatively severe downsizing. We expected that this exclusion would strengthen the association between job insecurity and health outcomes if health is indeed related to the level of layoff in one's worksite. Second, we compared hourly workers with particularly long tenure to all the other workers because these workers were either protected completely by their union contracts or essentially irreplaceable because of their long experience. While some long tenured hourly workers were offered an incentive to leave during the recession—the so-called golden handshake— those who survived knew that they were unlikely to be laid off. We examined new onsets in this group versus all other workers. If we were to find an elevated risk of developing a new health condition in this group of relatively protected workers this would undermine our interpretation that job insecurity at high layoff plants has adverse consequences for health because these workers have contractual job security in the event of future layoffs. Third we looked at spouses. If we found a relationship for spouses whose partner was exposed to high layoffs, this could be due to area-level effects as opposed to plant specific effects. Even though spouses may experience excess stress and insecurity due to substantial layoffs at a spouses' worksite, the experience of stress is likely to be less acute or systematic, so we did not expect to find a relationship. Fourth, we altered the mix of plants categorized as high layoff plants and low layoff plants to examine how robust the results are to small changes in the exposure variable. Finally, we conducted a falsification test where we simulated for 2006 the layoff which later occurred then examined new onsets in 2007 and 2008-- prior to the actual layoff-- to see if we would find a differential in high versus low layoff plants merely as a consequence of the "culling" process at high layoff plants. If so, then this too would undermine our interpretation of any association found and would instead suggest that we were capturing a plant-level effect rather than the effect of job insecurity because there were minimal layoffs in 2007–2008 at these plants.

Institutional Review

The Stanford University's Institutional Review Board approved this study's protocol, invoking the epidemiologic exemption waiving the requirement for individual consent.

RESULTS

Job Insecurity Categories

In Figure 2 we present yearly headcounts from 2006–2011 by the three categories of plants. Of the initial 30 plants considered, 7 were categorized as having had a high level of layoff or severe downsizing, 13 as having a mid level of layoffs or moderate downsizing and 10 as having a low level of layoffs or limited downsizing. Figure 2 also shows that the dynamics of the downsizing process was somewhat different between the plants with mid-level layoff because these plants had changes in headcount between 2008 and 2009 and again between 2009 and 2010. In the high layoff plants, there was a dramatic decline in the number of employees between 2009 and 2010 and a stable number of employees in the three years prior. In the low layoff plants, we see that while there was a decline in employees between 2009 and 2010, the change was limited. In the 2010–2011 period there was little change in the number of employees across all the plant categories. In Figure 3 we present the average number of weekly hours worked in the 3 groups of plant in January of 2006–2010 for hourly workers. We find that between 2006–2008 the high and low layoff plants had a similar number of average hours worked. In the high layoff plants, there was a decline in hours between 2008 and 2009 of as much as 15%. While this results in a decline in wages for hourly workers—possibly a stressor—it also results in more leisure time, quite possibly a health buffer.

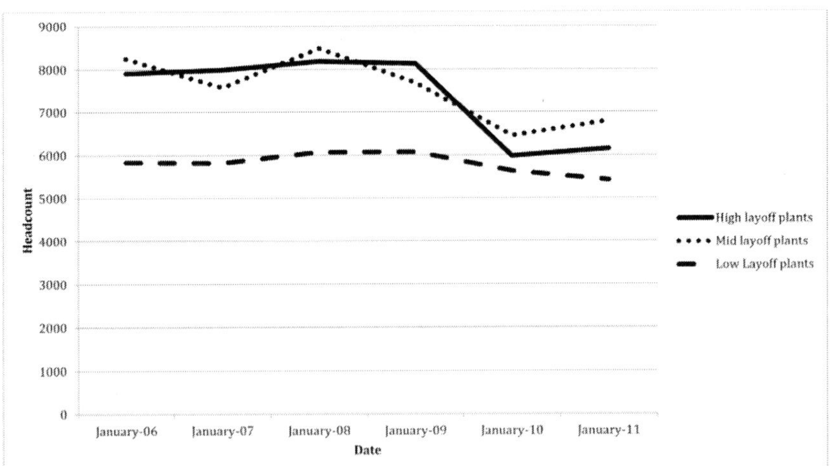

Figure 2. Number of Workers on January 1st from 2006–2011 by plant type

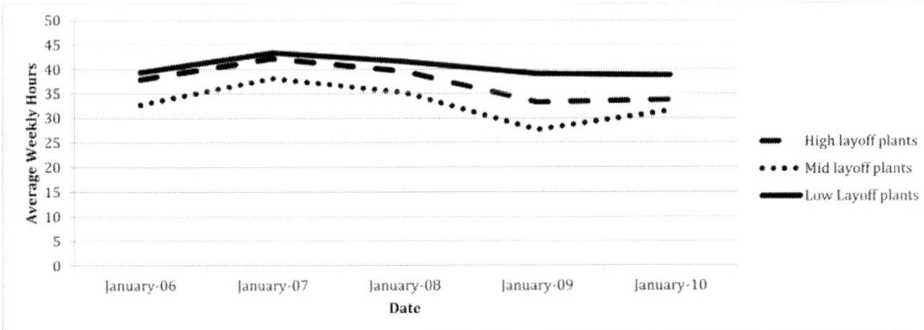

Figure 3. Average Number of Hours Worked by Hourly workers in January between 2006–2010, by plant type

Selection into layoff

We show descriptively that there was clear selection into the layoff category. Figure 4 presents the mean and 95% confidence intervals of the risk scores for member of the full cohort, those working on 1/1/2006, by whether or not they survived the layoffs. By 2007, two years before the layoffs, the health risk scores of those who were eventually laid off in 2009 were statistically different from those who survived the 2009 layoffs. More importantly, the health risk scores of those who were eventually laid off were rising faster than those who survived the 2009 layoffs and the difference in the rate of the rise was statistically significant. Appendix Figure A1 shows that there were also differences in wage growth in the period prior to the layoff events, such that survivors had higher wage growth prior to the onset of the recession [INSERT LINK TO ONLINE FILES]. We highlight this selection issue in order to put the subsequent observations into context. All the comparisons presented below include only those who survived layoffs, but the clear selection into layoff should make finding any result less likely.

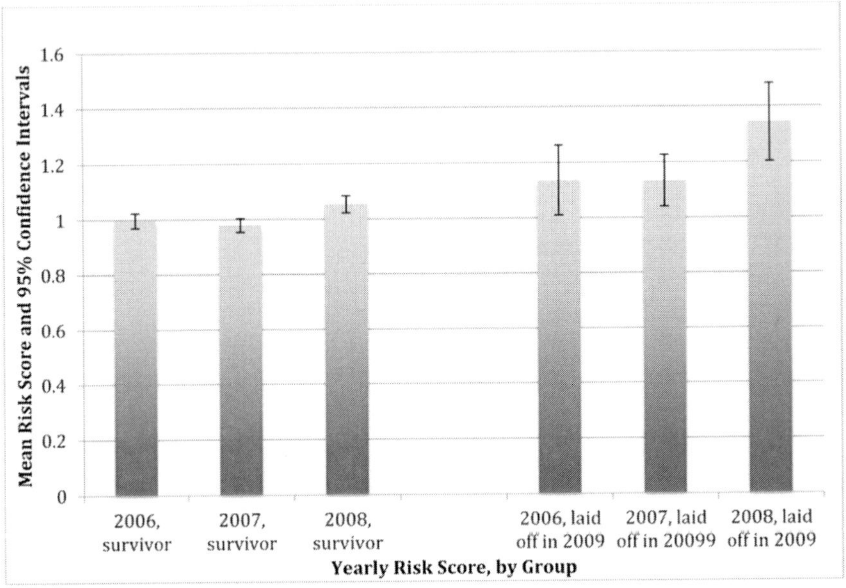

Figure 4. Risk Score for Cohort of Employees Working on 1/1/06*

Health condition results

We examined the new incidents of the four chronic conditions of interest. We limited our sample to only those individuals who were not previously diagnosed with the conditions throughout 2006–2008, thus only individual who are *at risk* were considered. Table 2 panel A presents the descriptive summary statistic for the cohort. The cohort includes predominately tenured white males who are on average 49 years old. Depending on the sample, either 38% or 64% work in high layoff plants.

Table 2 panel B provides the counts of the new incidents for each condition. We found that about 3.3% of the cohort was diagnosed with hypertension, 1.1% was diagnosis with diabetes, and 1.1% was diagnosed with depression and 0.6% was diagnosed with asthma/COPD in 2009 and 2010. These rates are largely consistent with reported incidence for this older age group of mostly men (Dannenberg et al., 1988; Fox et al., 2006; Murphy et al., 1988). In panel C we present the count of the new onsets by employee type. Salaried workers had lower rates of hypertension, diabetes and depression. Finally in panel D, we present the incidents for the spouses, which are used in the sensitivity analyses. Spouses had lower incidents of hypertension and diabetes, but a slightly higher incidence of depression. These raw percentages do not account for the gender mix, which affect the likelihood of a new incidence of these diseases and are accounted for in the regressions to follow.

Table 2. Summary Characteristics for Cohort and Counts of New Incidents of Health Outcomes

	Full Panel		High/Low Layoff plants	
Panel A: Individual-Level characteristics	**Observations**	**Mean**	**Observations**	**Mean**
Employee Category				
Salaried in a High Layoff Plant	955	7%	955	12%
Hourly in a High Layoff Plant	4142	31%	4142	52%
Salaried in non-High Layoff Plant	3311	25%	1843	23%
Hourly in a non-High Layoff Plant	4986	37%	977	12%
Risk Group (omitted 0–1)				
RS 0–1	8557	64%	4963	63%
RS 1–2	3509	26%	2171	27%
RS 2–4	1327	10%	783	10%
Gender				
Female	2756	21%	1285	16%
Race				
White	10949	82%	1582	83%
Union Plant	6121	46%	5494	69%
Tenure in 2009 (SD)	13393	19.08 (10.54)	7917	19.32(10.46)
Age in 2009 (SD)	13393	49.07 (8.90)	7917	49.29 (8.79)

	Full Panel		High/Low Layoff plants	
Panel B: Number of new onsets in 2009/2010	**Cases**	**Proportion of those at risk**	**Cases**	**Proportion of those at risk**
Hypertension	451	4.52%	283	4.89%
Diabetes	161	1.30%	103	1.42%
Depression	164	1.31%	93	1.25%
Asthma/COPD	86	0.67%	54	0.71%

Full Panel	Hourly		Salary	
Panel C: Number of new onsets in 2009/2010	**Cases**	**Proportion of those at risk**	**Cases**	**Proportion of those at risk**
Hypertension	354	4.80%	97	3.75%
Diabetes	137	1.48%	24	0.77%

Full Panel	Hourly		Salary	
Panel C: Number of new onsets in 2009/2010	Cases	Proportion of those at risk	Cases	Proportion of those at risk
Depression	134	1.43%	30	0.95%
Asthma/COPD	66	0.68%	20	0.63%

Full Panel	Spouses	
Panel D: Number of new onsets in 2009/2010, spouses	Cases	Proportion of those at risk
Hypertension	182	2.52%
Diabetes	80	0.97%
Depression	129	1.63%
Asthma/COPD	62	0.74%

Table 3 panel A presents the results of the association of working in a high layoff plant and the four conditions. Columns 1, 3, 5, and 7 present the association between working at a high layoff plant and developing a new condition for all workers (MODEL 1) while columns, 2, 4, 6, and 8, present the analyses with the interaction term which estimates the association of working in a high layoff plant separately for hourly or salaried workers (MODEL 2). We found that those who survived layoffs at high layoff plants did have an elevated risk of being diagnosed with hypertension, diabetes, and depression, but the estimated odds ratio nears statistically significant only for hypertension (OR=1.41, 95% CI=0.97–2.05). In addition, for these same conditions increases in area-level unemployment from 2008–2010 also led to higher risk of a new onset, though the odds ratios were not statistically significant. Comparing hourly or salaried workers, we find some evidence of a differential effect by job type. The overall association found between working at a high layoff plants and being diagnosed with hypertension was concentrated amongst hourly workers who survived layoffs (OR=1.48, 95% CI=1.00–2.19). We also found that while salaried workers were generally at a lower risk of developing diabetes (OR=0.355, 95% CI= 0.18–0.67), salaried worker at high layoff plants were more likely to have a new diagnosis of diabetes in 2009 and 2010 (OR=3.11, 95% CI=1.27–7.6).

Sensitivity Analysis

To ensure the robustness of the results, we conducted several sensitivity analyses. First we compare those who experienced little downsizing compared to those who experienced relatively severe

Table 3. Odds ratios and 95% confidence Interval from random-effects logistic regressions for the association of working in a high layoff plant and new onsets of health conditions

	Full Sample							
	Hypertension	**Hypertension**	**Diabetes**	**Diabetes**	**Asthma/COPD**	**Asthma/WCOPD**	**Depression**	**Depression**
High Layoff	1.412 [0.972 – 2.051]	1.483 * [1.004–2.191]	1.367 [0.815 – 2.292]	1.123 [0.653 – 1.931]	0.959 [0.541 – 1.700]	1.014 [0.543–1.891]	1.205 [0.686–2.117]	1.2 [0.668–2.156]
Salaried	0.816 [0.644 – 1.033]	0.874 [0.660 – 1.157]	0.563 * [0.362 – 0.876]	0.355 ** [0.189 – 0.668]	1.022 [0.613 – 1.701]	1.105 [0.597 – 2.046]	0.653 * [0.435 – 0.979]	0.649 [0.399 – 1.055]
High Layoff × Salaried		0.798 [0.478 – 1.334]		3.114 * [1.271 – 7.630]		0.789 [0.266 – 2.341]		1.02 [0.426 – 2.440]
Change in County Unemployment Rate&	1.193 [0.957 – 1.486]	1.196 [0.959 – 1.491]	1.36 [0.998 – 1.853]	1.354 [0.995 – 1.843]	0.868 [0.577 – 1.307]	0.869 [0.578 – 1.307]	1.144 [0.791 – 1.654]	1.143 [0.790 – 1.654]
Observations	10259	10259	12299	12299	12713	12713	12434	12434
Number of plants	26	26	26	26	26	26	26	26
	High Low Layoff Plant Sample							
	Hypertension	Hypertension	Diabetes	Diabetes	Asthma/COPD	Asthma/COPD	Depression	Depression
High Layoff	1.609 * [1.043 – 2.482]	1.693 * [1.069 – 2.680]	1.417 [0.629 – 3.188]	1.186 [0.513 – 2.745]	1.278 [0.527 – 3.100]	1.491 [0.568 – 3.919]	1.261 [0.659 – 2.403]	1.136 [0.561 – 2.300]
Salaried	0.779 [0.572 – 1.062]	0.867 [0.558 – 1.347]	0.781 [0.469 – 1.302]	0.483 [0.203 – 1.147]	1.054 [0.555 – 1.998]	1.398 [0.565 – 3.460]	0.514 * [0.283 – 0.936]	0.345 * [0.121 – 0.984]
High Layoff × Salaried		0.815 [0.441 – 1.508]		2.281 [0.777 – 6.694]		0.588 [0.165 – 2.101]		1.897 [0.533 – 6.751]
Change in County Unemployment Rate&	1.494 ** [1.110 – 2.011]	1.507 ** [1.118 – 2.032]	1.513 [0.825 – 2.775]	1.473 [0.805 – 2.698]	1.141 [0.584 – 2.228]	1.162 [0.594 – 2.276]	1.088 [0.652 – 1.817]	1.073 [0.642 – 1.792]
Observations	5980	5980	7246	7246	7524	7524	7354	7354
Number of plants	14	14	14	14	14	14	14	14

95% confidence intervals in brackets

** $p<0.01$,

* $p<0.05$

downsizing. We expected that excluding workers who experienced moderate layoffs, would strengthen the association between job insecurity and health outcomes if health is indeed related to the level of layoff in one's worksite. Table 3 panel B presents the results of the association of working in a high layoff plant and the four conditions described above. We found that those who survived layoffs at high layoff plants did have an elevated risk of being diagnosed with hypertension, diabetes, COPD and depression, but the estimated coefficients were only statistically significant for hypertension (OR=1.60, 95% CI–1.01–2.48). In addition, new increases in area-level unemployment were also associated with higher rate of new onset of hypertension. The diabetes result in Panel A, in which salaried workers at higher layoff plants developed excess diabetes, is no longer statistically significant.

Second, we examined long tenured hourly workers separately because they were less likely to be at risk of subsequent layoffs because of union protection and company policy. Given these protections, we would not expect tenured union workers to perceive substantial job instability even when there are massive layoffs. If we found an increased risk for these individuals, then that would suggest that our main results are likely an artifact. Table 4 columns 1–4 present the associations for tenured hourly workers and Table 4 columns 5–8 all other workers. Overall, Table 4 shows essentially no association between hypertension and experiencing high layoff for tenured hourly workers (OR=1.05; 95% CI=0.51–2.15), but a much higher magnitude for the association between hypertension and experiencing high layoff for all other workers (OR=1.91 95% CI=1.12–3.26). While the protected group differs from the remaining work force, particularly by being older, the magnitude of the coefficient on diabetes and depression is less than 1 for protected workers and higher than 1 for those workers not protected. Though none of these coefficients were statistically different from 1, they suggest that our designation of long tenured hourly workers as 'protected' is valid.

Table 4. Odds ratios and 95% confidence Interval from random-effects logistic regressions for the association of working in a high layoff plant and new onsets of health conditions, by worker type

	High Low Layoff Plant Sample (Protected Workers)				High Low Layoff Plant Sample (Unprotected Workers)			
	Hypertension	**Diabetes**	**Asthma/COPD**	**Depression**	**Hypertension**	**Diabetes**	**Asthma/COPD**	**Depression**
High layoff plant	1.05 [0.512 – 2.154]	0.768 [0.216 – 2.734]	2.726 [0.439 – 16.95]	0.784 [0.190 – 3.235]	1.907* [1.117 – 3.256]	2.007 [0.798 – 5.047]	0.97 [0.349 – 2.697]	1.484 [0.679 – 3.242]
Observations	1484	1931	2140	2121	4496	5315	5384	5233
Number of plants	13	13	13	13	14	14	14	14

95% confidence intervals in brackets

** $p<0.01$,

* $p<0.05$

All regressions include controls for risk score in 2008, gender, race (white/non-white), tenure, plant size, weighted area-level unemployment rate and plant union status.

If the results were driven solely by area-level or plant-level confounders, then we would expect to find a biased relationship for spouses whose partner is exposed to high layoff. While spouse may experience anxiety about their spouse's work prospects, the affect is likely to be less acute and we did not expect to find any *systematic* increases in health condition on spouses. For the 13,393 workers in our cohort, we were able to link spousal information for 8,909 partners, 67% (we would not expect to capture more than 85% since not all workers in the cohort were married between 2008–2010). Our spousal information comes from the claims data if a workers partner is enrolled in Alcoa's insurance benefits. While some partners were likely to take other insurance, perhaps through their own employer, the Alcoa benefits are quite generous, so we believe we capture a large proportion of eligible spouses.

In Table 5 we present the new onsets of the 4 conditions for spouses. Columns 1–4 include all 26 plants and compare spouses of workers in high layoff plants to all others, while columns 5–8 include only 14 plants and compares spouses of workers in high layoff plants to low layoff plants (Table 5). We found no association between plant layoff status and the 4 conditions considered in either sample.

Table 5. Odds ratios and 95% confidence Interval from random-effects logistic regressions for the association of working in a high layoff plant and new onsets of health conditions, spouse

	Full Sample				High Low Layoff Plant Sample			
	Hypertension	Diabetes	Asthma/COPD	Depression	Hypertension	Diabetes	Asthma/COPD	Depression
Spouse works at high layoff plant	1.052 [0.704 – 1.573]	1.04 [0.459 – 2.357]	1.633 [0.830 – 3.216]	1.234 [0.667 2.357]	0.010 [0.573 – 1.687]	0.97 [0.253 – 3.719]	2.318 [0.860 – 6.247]	0.798 [0.391 – 1.632]
Observations	7226	8243	8359	7930	4395	5088	5134	4857
Number of plants	26	26	26	26	14	14	14	14

95% confidence intervals in brackets

** $p<0.01$,

* $p<0.05$

All regressions include controls for risk score in 2008, gender, race (white/non-white), tenure, plant size, weighted area-level unemployment rate and plant union status.

Fourth, we altered the mix of plants categorized as high layoff plants and low layoff plants. When we changed the cut-offs and altered the plants that fell into each plant category, we did not change the magnitude of the association between working in a high-layoff plant and hypertension substantially (data not shown).

Finally, as a 'falsification test' we examined new onsets of chronic conditions in 2007 & 2008 in high layoff plants for survivors. While the recession started in December 2007, it was not widely publicized until late 2008 and in plants categorized as low or high there was limited layoff in 2008 (Figure 2). We examined those working at high layoff plants and compared them to those working at low layoff plants as in Panel B in Table 3, but instead used new onsets of the four conditions in 2007 or 2008. This changed both the population at risk (the denominator) and the identified cases (numerator). We did not find an association between plant layoff and new onsets (data not shown).

DISCUSSION

Our analysis examined the health consequences of downsizing events on the remaining workforce in the context of the 2009 recession. We found consistent evidence of an increased risk of developing hypertension for workers that remain working at plants where there was severe downsizing. The hypertension results were robust to several specification tests and a falsification test, suggesting that the association may be causal. We found some evidence of an elevated risk of developing diabetes for salaried workers at high layoff plants, but this result was statistically significant in only a subset of analyses. We found no association between working at a plant with high layoffs developing COPD or Asthma. Finally, we found no association between working at a high layoff plant and acquiring a new diagnosis of depression.

Though seemingly contradictory, the hypertension result found in this study is largely consistent with previous results. Particularly, Martikainen et al (2008), using a similar methodology during the severe recession in Finland found no adverse consequences on 8-year mortality. In contrast, in the UK a recent study found a small rise in self-reported poor health status not only for the unemployed, but also among people who remained employed (Astell-Burt & Feng, 2013). Our study found a modest increase in hypertension risk for survivors of layoffs, which is unlikely to affect mortality due to the wide availability of medication to control hypertension in the short run, but may affect self-reported health. Our results are consistent with these previous studies even though we found an association for increased incident hypertension. Other longitudinal studies of downsizing/restructuring or job insecurity have also found increases in blood pressure as workers transition from jobs perceived as secure to insecure (Ferrie et al., 2002; Pollard, 2001).

Surprisingly we did not find an association between downsizing and depression or physiological health as has been found elsewhere (Hellgren & Sverke, 2003; Hellgren et al., 1999; Kivimaki et al., 2007). While the magnitude of the odds ratios for depression at high layoff plants was generally elevated throughout many of the regressions, it is never statistically significant. One reason that we may not have found an association is that our measure of depression is a new diagnosis as compared to many other studies that rely on self-reported symptoms or depression scales. New diagnosis is a much more stringent measure because it excludes recurrent depression cases and requires workers to actively seek care for their symptoms using health resources—and co-pays— above and beyond the free employee assistance programs available at all sites. Given that we show that there was clear selection on health, many workers may have wanted to limit any sign of stigmatized mental health conditions. Finally, as noted above our exposure measure is based on the intensity of layoffs, as opposed to self-reported perceived job insecurity. From our data we have no way to identify workers who felt that their job was at risk and therefore may have had a physiological stress response. This too may have contributed to the lack of association with depression, our only mental health outcome. Future studies will need to assess this further, perhaps using a different marker for mental health.

The current study has several advantages over previous studies. First, the detailed timing of our data allowed us to examine only workers at risk for developing a new condition. Second, we used an external proxy of job security, the severity and observability of layoff events. Third, the analysis of new incidence of disease accounted for lagged baseline health in the year just before the layoffs. Fourth, we examined a population in which we know that on average their work hours were not changed substantially and if anything declined more in the high layoff plants, reinforcing the conservative nature of our inference. Most studies cannot account for these factors. Finally, we have reason to believe that our results are an under estimate of the true effect. Specifically, we selected healthy workers because of duration of employment (Tenure >4) and because they have lower overall health risk scores (risk score in 2008 <4). We also document the substantial selection on health into being a survivor of the layoff events. We also examined a well-insured population that has had ongoing access to care. Taken together these observations would make it even more unlikely for us to have found any health effect.

Nonetheless, interpretations of these results require caution and further analysis. Foremost, the population under study includes those in the heavy and light manufacturing industries, which were hit quite hard in the current recession. It could be that for different sectors of the economy, where job losses were not so substantial, the results may have been different. With regard to the health outcome variables, we provide evidence that workers in the high layoff plants were more likely to be diagnosed with hypertension in 2009 and 2010. In our analysis we were careful to control for previous health to try to mitigate the problem that those who are otherwise less healthy are also more likely to get a new diagnosis for common health conditions. Nonetheless, we may be attributing health utilization behaviors to manifestations of health outcomes. Another concern is that the selection process we document could induce an artificial association, similar to regression to the mean, between hypertension and working in a high layoff plant. If we assume that most workers will eventually get hypertension and that there was more culling of prevalent cases in high layoff plants, then we could have had a higher rate of diagnosis in high layoff plants. However, this issue should have shown up in the falsification test in which we simulated the selection impact of the (subsequent) layoff, so we do not believe this problem is driving our main result. Finally our most notable weakness is our measure of exposure to job insecurity, plant-level downsizing. In most analyses we used this measure as dichotomous exposure, which has limited variation. In addition, our measure may not capture perceived job insecurity, though results in the sensitivity analysis suggest that it may be a valid proxy.

All in all, our study provides evidence that even those who remained employed through the peak of the recession experienced some adverse health consequence. If the recent wave of downsizing in the recession increased the sense of job insecurity and/or altered health related behaviors of the remaining workforce even modestly, as is suggested by this study, then we may expect to find that the overall health impact of the global recession is much larger than previously anticipated.

Highlights

- Few studies have examined how survivors of layoffs fared in the 2007–2009 recession
- Analysis of longitudinal data shows that survivors of layoffs were healthier
- Survivors at plants with severe downsizing had higher incidence of hypertension
- Surviving salaried workers at downsized plants had higher incidence of diabetes
- Health effects of the 2007–2009 recession may be larger than previously expected

ACKNOWLEDGMENTS

This research was funded by two grants from the National Institute on Aging (Disease, Disability and Death in an Aging Workforce, NIH/NIA, 1 R01 AG026291-06 and The Design of Social Insurance for the Elderly: Public Pensions and Health Insurance, NIH/NIA 1R01AG032449-01).

FOOTNOTES

[1]While both PPOs and HMOs are a type of managed care, PPOs contracts with a network of "preferred" providers from which patients can choose to use at a discounted rate or patients can choose a provider outside the network without the discount. By contrast HMOs contract with a network of providers and patients receive all of their health care services from a provider within the network at discounted co-pay rates.

CONTRIBUTOR INFORMATION

Sepideh Modrek,

Mark R. Cullen,

REFERENCES

1. Alcoa 10-K Annual Report 2009 2010
2. Astell-Burt T, Feng X. Health and the 2008 Economic Recession: Evidence from the United Kingdom. PLoS ONE. 2013;8:e56674.
3. Baker SR, Bloom N, Davis SJ. Measuring Economic Policy Uncertainty. Social Science Research Network No 2198490 2013
4. Bockerman P, Ilmakunnas P. Unemployment and self-assessed health: evidence from panel data. Health economics. 2009;18:161–179.
5. Clougherty JE, Eisen EA, Slade MD, Kawachi I, Cullen MR. Workplace status and risk of hypertension among hourly and

salaried aluminum manufacturing employees. Social Science & Medicine. 2009;68:304–313.

6. Dannenberg AL, Garrison RJ, Kannel WB. Incidence of hypertension in the Framingham Study. American Journal of Public Health. 1988;78:676–679.

7. Davis JA, Savage G, Stewart RT. Organizational downsizing: a review of literature for planning and research. Journal of healthcare management/American College of Healthcare Executives. 2003;48:181.

8. Deb P, Gallo B, Ayyagari P, Fletcher JM, Sindelar JL. Job Loss: Eat, drink and try to be merry? NBER working paper w15122 2009

9. DeSanto Iennaco J, Cullen MR, Cantley L, Slade MD, Fiellin M, Kasl SV. Effects of externally rated job demand and control on depression diagnosis claims in an industrial cohort. American journal of epidemiology. 2010;171:303–311.

10. Dragano N, Verde PE, Siegrist J. Organisational downsizing and work stress: testing synergistic health effects in employed men and women. Journal of epidemiology and community health. 2005;59:694–699.

11. Ferrie JE, Shipley MJ, Stansfeld SA, Marmot MG. Effects of chronic job insecurity and change in job security on self reported health, minor psychiatric morbidity, physiological measures, and health related behaviours in British civil servants: the Whitehall II study. Journal of epidemiology and community health. 2002;56:450–454.

12. Fox CS, Pencina MJ, Meigs JB, Vasan RS, Levitzky YS, DÄôAgostino RB. Trends in the Incidence of Type 2 Diabetes Mellitus From the 1970s to the 1990s. Circulation. 2006;113:2914–2918

13. Goodman CJ, Mance SM. Employment loss and the 2007–09 recession: an overview. Monthly Labor Review. 2011;134

14. Hamilton VL, Hoffman WS, Broman CL, Rauma D. Unemployment, distress, and coping: a panel study of autoworkers. Journal of personality and social psychology. 1993;65:234–247.

15. Hellgren J, Sverke M. Does job insecurity lead to impaired well-being or vice versa? Estimation of cross-lagged effects using

latent variable modelling. Journal of Organizational Behavior. 2003;24:215–236.

16. Hellgren J, Sverke M, Isaksson K. A Two-dimensional Approach to Job Insecurity: Consequences for Employee Attitudes and Well-being. European Journal of Work and Organizational Psychology. 1999;8:179–195.

17. Johnson RW, Butrica BA. Age Disparities in Unemployment and Reemployment during the Great Recession and Recovery. Urban Institute Brief; Washington, DC: 2012.

18. Kivimaki M, Honkonen T, Wahlbeck K, Elovainio M, Pentti J, Klaukka T, et al. Organisational downsizing and increased use of psychotropic drugs among employees who remain in employment. Journal of epidemiology and community health. 2007;61:154–158.

19. Kivimäki M, Vahtera J, Elovainio M, Pentti J, Virtanen M. Human Costs of Organizational Downsizing: Comparing Health Trends Between Leavers and Stayers. American Journal of Community Psychology. 2003;32:57–67.

20. Martikainen P, Maki N, Jantti M. The effects of workplace downsizing on cause-specific mortality: a register-based follow-up study of Finnish men and women remaining in employment. Journal of epidemiology and community health. 2008;62:1008–1013.

21. Murphy J, Olivier D, Monson R, Sobol A, Leighton A. Incidence of depression and anxiety: the Stirling County Study. Am J Public Health. 1988;78:534–540.

22. Pollack KM, Agnew J, Slade MD, Cantley L, Taiwo O, Vegso S, et al. Use of employer administrative Databases to identify systematic causes of injury in aluminum manufacturing. American Journal of Industrial Medicine. 2007;50:676–686.

23. Pollard TM. Changes in mental well-being, blood pressure and total cholesterol levels during workplace reorganization: the impact of uncertainty. Work & Stress. 2001;15:14–28.

24. Quinlan M, Bohle P. Overstretched and unreciprocated commitment: Reviewing research on the occupational health and safety effects of downsizing and job

insecurity. International Journal of Health Services. 2009;39:1–44.

25. Vahtera J, Kivimaki M, Pentti J, Linna A, Virtanen M, Virtanen P, et al. Organisational downsizing, sickness absence, and mortality: 10-town prospective cohort study. BMJ. 2004;328:555

3

CHAPTER

Burnout and Its Association with Working Conditions among Greek Hospital Nurses in a Time of Financial Crisis

Asterios Skefales[1], Sotirios Plakas[2], Geórgia Fouka[2], Maria Goni[3], Maria Vassiliadou[4], Joanna-Despoina Bergiannaki[4]

[1]*Psychiatric Ward, Georgios Genimatas General District Hospital of Athens, Athens, Greece*

[2]*Department of Nursing, School of Health and Welfare, Technological Educational Institution (TEI) of Athens, Athens, Greece*

[3]*University of Athens, Eginition Hospital, Athens, Greece*

[4]*University of Athens, 1st Psychiatric Clinic, Eginition Hospital, Athens, Greece*

ABSTRACT

The recent global economic recession has affected nursing working conditions in terms of salary reductions, increased workload and staff shortages. Poor nursing working conditions are associated with higher levels of burnout. However in Greece this association has not yet been studied. The aim of this study was to explore financial crisis related changes in nurses' working conditions and their associations with burnout. A cross-sectional quantitative survey was conducted and data were collected through self-reported questionnaires from 299 Greek nurses from two Public Hospitals in 2012. Multiple linear regression analyses were used in order to find independent factors associated with burnout. The results showed that Greek nurses had high levels of burnout. Satisfaction from the job, quality of care and feeling equivalent with other professionals were independent predictors of lower emotional exhaustion. Workload increase and willingness to change career and work department were independent predictors of higher emotional exhaustion. Job satisfaction and satisfaction from care quality were independent predictors of lower depersonalization. Changes in working relationships and willingness to change career were independent predictors of higher depersonalization. Higher personal accomplishments were independently associated with more years in nursing, satisfaction from the salary prior to reductions, better quality of care, feeling suitable for the job and being anxious about future career. Influence on nurse efficiency by income reduction was an independent predictor of lower personal accomplishments. In conclusion, Greek nurses were suffering from high levels of burnout which was independently associated with crisis related working conditions. Interventions are needed in order to reduce the burden of burnout among Greek nurses.

Keywords: Burnout, Austerity, Nurse Practice Environment, Maslach Burnout Inventory

1. INTRODUCTION

The recent global economic recession has raised major concerns for the nursing workforce worldwide, concerning job losses and salary reductions that can lead to an unavoidable shortage of staff and increase in workload [1] [2] , thus affecting nurse's working conditions. Research evidence suggests that poor nursing working environments are associated with burnout [3] and especially work-life areas such as workload, control, reward, community, fairness and values [4] .

Greece in particular, since 2010, has imposed strict fiscal austerity measures in the public sector, part of the requirements of a bailout programme under the supervision of the so called "troika" (European Commission, the European Central Bank and the International Monetary Fund) due to large public deficit and debts that threatened the country with bankruptcy [5] . Health care systems in Greece have been largely affected as for 2011 the health budget was €1.4 billion decreased mainly through salary cuts and reductions in operating costs [5] [6] , while the plan is for a further reduction of €2.1 billion from health care budget until 2015 [7] .

Admissions in private hospitals have been reduced by 40% [7] . On the other hand there is higher demand for public hospital services. Admissions in public hospitals increased by 24% in 2010 compared to 2009 and by a further 8% in the first half of 2011 compared to the first half in 2010 [5] . Besides, 26,000 health professionals have been redundant including 9100 doctors [7] , while there is a plan for a further reduction of 150,000 jobs in the wider public sector between 2011 and 2015 [6] . Nonetheless, a 40% reduction in hospital budgets has caused shortage of pharmaceutical and medical supplies [8] .

As far as the nursing personnel are concerned, Greece had always a shortage of nurses. In 2009, before the onset of this crisis, there were only 3.3 nurses per 1000 population with the average in OECD countries at 8.4 [9] . During the crisis, new hiring in the public sector has frozen, while many nurses have chosen early retirement due to gross salary reductions and changes in the pensions scheme [10] . Unemployment rates tripled during the crisis from 8.6% in 2009 [11] , to 27.8% in 2013 [12] .

Salary reductions and increased taxation have severely diminished the income of public servants, including nurses. According to an OECD report, the gross salary earnings of the Greek population fell by 25.3% in 2011 [13] .

Other measures to reduce health budgets include elimination or merging of 370 specialist units and a reduction in public hospital beds from 35,000 to 33,000 [6] .

Under these circumstances the Greek public health care system is experiencing tremendous challenges to find a balance between diminished resources and increased demands for services. Greek nurses are at the core of the public health care system and are exposed to heavy workload and a number of other changes in their working conditions which remain unexplored and may increase their levels of burnout.

Burnout is a psychological syndrome entailing a long term reaction to job related stressors; it is quite common among nurses and nursing is one of the most extensively studied professions in this field [4] . The three dimensions of this syndrome, are emotional exhaustion, depersonalization and lack of personal accomplishments [4] . Emotional exhaustion refers to the state where the professionals are emotionally empty to care for other people, depersonalization means nurses treat patients as objects rather than human beings and is also called cynicism and lack of personal accomplishments means a feeling of inadequacy, accompanied by negative self perceptions [4] [14] -[17] .

Among the causes of burnout are: the long term stress at job, staff shortage, low rewards, high workload, and injustice [18] [19] . Morgan and Lynn [20] have pointed out that when the workload is high, nurses have fewer opportunities to receive intrinsic rewards from their work through the quality of nursing care they would be willing to provide to their patients.

According to an organizational model, 6 areas of the nurse worklife have been associated with burnout [4] . Among them work-load and control are key issues in the stress caused by the job demands. The other areas are the rewards that reflect both material rewards and rewards related to job satisfaction, social support and quality of interpersonal relationships, fairness and justice in relation to the other health care professionals and an ability to fulfill personal expectations and job targets [4] .

Burnout has been associated with depressive symptoms, chronic fatigue, psychosomatic symptoms and low satisfaction from personal and family life [21] . Furthermore burnout is a factor associated with reduced nurse productivity, diminished patient quality of care, job dissatisfaction and willingness to leave the job [4] [22] [23] .

However, other research evidence suggests that nursing working conditions can determine job satisfaction and intentions to leave the profession [24] -[27] and are related to poor quality of nursing care, and diminished patient safety [14] [28] -[31] . Jourdain and Chevevert [28] have indeed argued that professional commitment is a stronger predictor of nurse turnover than emotional exhaustion. Similarly Bartram et al. [32] found that perceived high performance work systems, which is a job resource for nurses, was the strongest predictor of intentions to leave the profession. Recent research by Kutney-Lee et al. [31] suggests that improvements in the working environments of nurses decreases not only burnout, but also their intentions to leave and their job dissatisfaction, while Van den Heede et al. [33] have found significant associations between staffing and work environment with intentions to leave the profession.

A recent survey in Greece to investigate the impact of job stress on satisfaction among nurses has reported that heavy workload and conflicts were related to work stress which in turn affected negatively all job satisfaction dimensions [34] .

In this study we aimed to investigate the associations between burnout and the new work related experiences of the Greek nurses during the crisis. In accordance to the research evidence mentioned above and bearing in mind the specific Greek context characterized by high unemployment rates and severe lack of new working opportunities, we considered intentions to leave the profession or change work department and job dissatisfaction to be work environment related experiences of the nurses rather than nurse outcomes and we wanted to explore their associations with burnout.

2. METHODS

2.1. Study Population

A cross sectional questionnaire survey was conducted with a convenient sample of 299 registered and associate nurses from 2 acute care District General Public Hospitals in Athens, Greece. All nurses with any educational background providing direct patient care in every ward of the hospitals were eligible to participate. The two hospitals have similar work environments and both have more than 400 beds.

2.2. Data Collection

Self reported questionnaires were distributed to the nurses by the principal investigator during repeated visits on the wards of the 2 hospitals on an early, late and night shift. Participants who agreed to participate completed the questionnaires when it was convenient for them and the researcher collected the completed questionnaires from the wards through repeated follow up visits. This strategy of repeated visits was deemed necessary in order to increase the response rate considering the high levels of workload for nurses and a lack of research culture in the public hospitals in Greece, i.e. lack of research officers, or research liaison nurses. Only a couple of nurses were very negative and refused to deliver the questionnaire at all. Approximately 10 - 15 nurses failed to complete or return the questionnaire they had received. Data collection took place between July-November 2012.

The questionnaire had two parts. The first part was about demographics, financial conditions and working related conditions. It had 27 single items with Likert type scales and yes/no questions and was developed by the authors based on the international literature.

The second part of the questionnaire was the Maslach Burnout Inventory for Human Services Survey (MBIHSS), by Maslach and Jackson [35] . This is one of the most widely used inventories of measuring burnout [19] . This is a self reported instrument consisting of 22 items on a seven point likert scale. There are 9 items for emotional exhaustion, 5 items for depersonalization and 8 items for personal accomplishments.

2.3. Ethical Considerations

Ethics approval was obtained from the research committees of the two hospitals and a Greek University. Questionnaires were accompanied by an information sheet explaining the purposes of the study and ensuring voluntarily participation, anonymity and confidentiality.

2.4. Data Analysis

Continuous variables are presented with mean and standard deviation (SD). Quantitative variables are presented with absolute and relative frequencies. Univariate linear regression analyses were performed in order to estimate association of burnout scales with demographics and work related characteristics. Multiple linear regression analyses were used in order to find independent factors associated with burnout scales using a stepwise method (p for removal was set at 0.1 and p for entry was set at 0.05). Regression coefficients and standard errors were computed from the results of the linear regression analyses. Variables that their responses were at a Likert scale were treated as ordinals in the regression models. All p values reported are two-tailed. Statistical significance was set at 0.05 and analyses were conducted using SPSS statistical software (Version 19.0).

2.5. Validity and Reliability

Reliability and validity for the Greek version of the Maslach Burnout Inventory have been established. In a randomly selected sample of 152 nurses content validity was confirmed and Cronbach's alpha was 0.83 for the emotional exhaustion subscale, 0.799 for the personal accomplishments subscale and 0.603 for the depersonalization subscale [36] . In this study overall Cronbach's alpha was 0.73 and for the subscales, Cronbach's alpha was 0.75 for emotional exhaustion, 0.75 for personal accomplishments and 0.72 for depersonalisation, indicating good internal consistency reliability.

3. RESULTS

Data from 299 participants were analyzed. Sample characteristics are presented in Table 1.

Most of the participants (80.9%) were women and the mean age of the sample was 37.8 years (SD = 7.3 years). Most of the nurses were on rotated shifts (81.8%) and 36.8% had a nursing specialty certificate. Almost one third (27.0%) were dissatisfied or very dissatisfied with their current job, 29.3% would like to change working department and 24.8% would like to change career. The work characteristics associated with crisis conditions are shown in Table 2.

Only 15.8% declared to have sufficient income, while most of the nurses (96.6%) were moderate to very much dissatisfied due to their income reduction. Almost half of the nurses (51.1%) stated that their efficiency has been influenced due to income reduction, 87.0% stated that their work load increased due to the current economical situation and 87.9% stated that the economical crisis affected their personal life. The majority of the nurses were moderate to very much satisfied from the care quality they provided in their last shift, while 58.2% believed that the care quality in their departments was reduced during the last year and 70.1% were moderate to very much anxious about their career in future. Also, 30.4% of the nurses stated that the working relationships with their seniors and their colleagues changed due to the economical crisis. The mean values for Emotional exhaustion scale was 27.5 (SD = 11.3) for Personal accomplishments scale was 32.6 (SD = 9.3) and for Depersonalization scale was 8.0 (SD = 6.1).

Univariate analysis for Emotional exhaustion (Table 3) showed that nurses from psychiatric departments had lower scores compared to all other departments.

Also, it was found that as "dissatisfaction due to income reduction", "influence on their efficiency by income reduction", the degree that the "work load increases due to the current economical situation" and "stress for their future career" become greater, the Emotional

Table 1. Demographic and work related characteristics.

	N (%)
Age, mean (SD)	37.8 (7.3)
Gender	
Male	57 (19.1)
Female	242 (80.9)
Married	
No	125 (41.8)
Yes	174 (58.2)
Work department	
Medical	58 (19.7)
Surgical	76 (25.8)
Urology	30 (10.2)
Psychiatric	36 (12.2)
Other	95 (32.2)
Do you work in rotated shifts	
No	54 (18.2)
Yes	242 (81.8)
Years in nursing, mean (SD)	13.3 (7.7)
Years in current department, mean (SD)	7.5 (6.2)
Work title	
Head nurse	22 (7.5)
Charge Nurse	64 (21.8)
Staff Nurse	207 (70.6)
Education	
Associate Nurses (Primary/secondary education)	80 (27)
Registered Nurses (Tertiary level)	216 (73)
Nurse specialty certificate	
No	165 (63.2)
Yes	96 (36.8)
Satisfied from your current job	
Very dissatisfied	10 (3.4)
Dissatisfied	70 (23.6)
Satisfied	178 (59.9)
Very satisfied	39 (13.1)
Do you want to change career	
No	221 (75.2)
Yes	73 (24.8)
Do you want to change your work department	
No	203 (70.7)
Yes	84 (29.3)
Annual family income (Euros)	
Lower than 10,000	18 (6.3)
10 - 15,000	78 (27.2)
15 - 20,000	70 (24.4)
20 - 25,000	44 (15.3)
25 - 30,000	38 (13.2)
More than 30,000	39 (13.6)

Table 2. Work characteristics associated with crisis conditions.

Very	78 (26.3)
Very much	33 (11.1)
Do you stress for your future career?	
Not at all	26 (8.6)
A bit	64 (21.3)
Moderate	67 (22.3)
Very	103 (34.2)
Very much	41 (13.6)
Do you feel suitable for this job?	
Not at all	3 (1)
A bit	7 (2.3)
Moderate	41 (13.7)
Very	153 (51.2)
Very much	95 (31.8)
Have the working relationships with your colleagues and seniors changed due to the economical crisis?	
Not at all	142 (47.5)
A bit	66 (22.1)
Moderate	58 (19.4)
Very	26 (8.7)
Very much	7 (2.3)
How would you describe your general health?	
Very bad	3 (1)
Bad	16 (5.4)
Moderate	66 (22.1)
Good	161 (53.8)
Very good	53 (17.7)

exhaustion increases. Additionally, the Emotional exhaustion decreases as the "satisfaction from your wage prior to the reduction" or from the "care quality they provided at last shift" increases. A similar pattern was found between Emotional exhaustion and the degree they feel "equivalent to the other health care professionals". Additionally, univariate analysis showed that subjects with better health, those that were satisfied from their current job, those declared that the care quality in their department during the last year improved and those with nurse specialty had lower levels of Emotional exhaustion. Greater scores on Emotional exhaustion were found in nurses that wanted to change career or their work department and in those that the economical crisis affected their personal life. When multiple analysis in

Table 3. Results from univariate and multiple linear regression analyses with dependent variable the Emotional exhaustion.

	$\beta^{*} \pm$ SE	P	$\beta^{**} \pm$ SE	P
Age	0.18 ± 0.1	0.079		
Gender, male (ref)				
Female	1.43 ± 1.79	0.426		
Married, no (ref)				
Yes	2.13 ± 1.45	0.144		
Work department, psychiatric (ref)				
Medical	5.94 ± 2.45	**0.016**		
Surgery	10.63 ± 2.37	**<0.001**		
Urology	10 ± 3.07	**0.001**		
Other	7.1 ± 2.28	**0.002**		
Do you work in shifts, no (ref)				
Yes	2.01 ± 1.91	0.294		
Years in nursing	0.16 ± 0.1	0.100		
Years in current department	0.11 ± 0.12	0.367		
Work title, staff nurse (ref)				
Head nurse	−4.39 ± 2.79	0.117		
Charge nurse	−2.61 ± 1.8	0.148		
Education, Associate nurse(ref)				
Registered nurse	−2.58 ± 1.69	0.128		
Nurse specialty, no (ref)				
Yes	−4.46 ± 1.58	**0.005**		
Satisfied from your current job	−7.27 ± 0.98	**<0.001**	−3.00 ± 1.20	**0.013**
Do you want to change career, no (ref)				
Yes	7.79 ± 1.57	**<0.001**	4.51 ± 1.59	**0.005**
Do you want to change your work department, no (ref)				
Yes	7.58 ± 1.53	**<0.001**	2.61 ± 0.81	**0.001**
How dissatisfied are you due to your income reduction?	4.18 ± 0.85	**<0.001**		
Were you satisfied with your wage prior to the reduction?	−1.85 ± 0.76	**0.015**		
How much influenced is your efficiency by your income reduction?	1.9 ± 0.58	**0.001**		
How much has your work load increased due to the current economical situation?	3.31 ± 0.64	**<0.001**	1.68 ± 0.64	**0.009**
Has the economical situation affected your personal life?, no (ref)				
Yes	6.09 ± 2.11	**0.004**		
Are you satisfied from the care quality you provided in your last shift?	−3.85 ± 0.86	**<0.001**	−2.19 ± 0.85	**0.011**
How would you describe the care quality in your department during the last year?, reduced (ref)				
Improved	−5.35 ± 1.46	**<0.001**		
Do you feel equivalent to the other health professionals?	−2.08 ± 0.55	**<0.001**	−1.1 ± 0.52	**0.037**
Do you stress for your future career?	1.37 ± 0.6	**0.024**		
Do you feel suitable for this job?	−1 ± 0.89	0.262		
Have the working relationships with your colleagues and seniors changed due to the economical crisis?	0.31 ± 0.69	0.656		
How would you describe your general health?	−4.17 ± 0.84	**<0.001**		

Ref = reference category; β = regression coefficient; SE = standard error. *unadjusted coefficients; **adjusted coefficients as derived from stepwise method.

a stepwise method was conducted (**Table 3**) it was found that satisfaction from the current job, the willingness to change work department and career, the work load increase due to the current economical situation, satisfaction from the care quality they provided at last shift and the degree they feel equivalent to the other health care professionals were independent predictors of Emotional exhaustion.

Univariate analysis for Personal accomplishments (Table 4) indicated a significantly greater score for Psychiatric and Surgical departments compared to Medical ones.

Also, Personal accomplishments were greater for those being satisfied from their current job or those declared that the care quality in their department during the last year improved. Personal accomplishments were lower for nurses working rotated shifts, for those that wanted to change career or their work department. Additionally, Personal accomplishments increases as the satisfaction from the wage prior to the reduction due to economical crisis or from the care quality they provided at last shift increases. The influence on their efficiency by income reduction and the degree that the working relationships with their seniors and their colleagues changed due to the economical crisis had a negative effect on Personal accomplishments. Years in nursing, the degree they feel suitable for their job or having stress for their future career were positively correlated with Personal accomplishments. Multiple analysis (**Table 4**) indicated that years in nursing, satisfaction from the wage prior to the reduction, the influence on their efficiency by income reduction, improvement of the care quality in their department during the last year, the degree they feel suitable for their job and being anxious for their future career were independently associated with Personal accomplishments.

As far as it concerns Depersonalization, univariate analysis (Table 5) showed lower levels for those that had Nurse Specialty, for those being satisfied from their current job or being more satisfied from the care quality they provided during their last shift, in those declared that the care quality in their department during the last year improved, in nurses feeling more equivalent to the other health care professionals or more suitable for their job and in those with better health.

Table 4. Results from univariate and multiple linear regression analyses with dependent variable the Personal accomplishments.

	$\beta^{*} \pm SE$	P	$\beta^{**} \pm SE$	P
Age	0.2 ± 0.08	**0.016**		
Gender, male (ref)				
Female	1.62 ± 1.46	0.268		
Married, no (ref)				
Yes	−1.06 ± 1.21	0.383		
Work department, Medical (ref)				
Surgery	7.07 ± 1.72	**<0.001**		
Urology	2.31 ± 2.23	0.301		
Psychiatric	6.61 ± 2.07	**0.002**		
Other	5.84 ± 1.63	**<0.001**		
Do you work in shifts, no (ref)				
Yes	−3.33 ± 1.54	**0.032**		
Years in nursing	0.2 ± 0.08	**0.013**	0.19 ± 0.08	**0.014**
Years in current departement	0.12 ± 0.1	0.208		
Work title, Staff nurse (ref)				
Head nurse	3.12 ± 2.24	0.165		
Charge nurse	−0.14 ± 1.53	0.927		
Education, Associate nurse (ref)				
Registered nurse	−0.95 ± 1.37	0.489		
Nurse specialty, no (ref)				
Yes	1.71 ± 1.34	0.204		
Satisfied from your current job	2.32 ± 0.87	**0.008**		
Do you want to change career, no (ref)				
Yes	−5.08 ± 1.36	**<0.001**		
How dissatisfied are you due to your income reduction?	0.7 ± 0.72	0.333		
Were you satisfied with your wage prior to the reduction?	1.31 ± 0.64	**0.042**	1.32 ± 0.58	**0.024**
How much influenced is your efficiency by your income reduction?	−1.27 ± 0.48	**0.009**	−1.01 ± 0.47	**0.033**
How much has your work load increased due to the current economical situation?	−0.44 ± 0.55	0.422		
Has the economical situation affected your personal life?, no (ref)				
Yes	−2.82 ± 1.77	0.114		
Are you satisfied from the care quality you provided in your last shift?	2.8 ± 0.71	**<0.001**		
How would you describe the care quality in your department during the last year?, reduced (ref)				
Improved	3.95 ± 1.2	**0.001**	1.76 ± 0.74	**0.018**
Do you feel equivalent to the other health professionals?	−0.27 ± 0.46	0.558		
Do you stress for your future career?	1.15 ± 0.5	**0.023**	1.19 ± 0.5	**0.018**
Do you feel suitable for this job?	4.76 ± 0.66	**<0.001**	4.04 ± 0.67	**<0.001**
Have the working relationships with your colleagues and seniors changed due to the economical crisis?	−1.15 ± 0.57	**0.043**		
How would you describe your health?	0.78 ± 0.72	0.281		

Ref = reference category; β = regression coefficient; SE = standard error. *unadjusted coefficients; **adjusted coefficients as derived from stepwise method.

In contrast, Depersonalization had greater scores in nurses working rotated shifts, in those that wanted to change career or their work department, in those that their efficiency was more influenced by income reduction and in those that the working relationships with their seniors and their colleagues had changed due to the economical crisis. Multiple analysis for Depersonalization (**Table 5**) indicated that satisfaction from their current job, satisfaction from the care quality they provided during their last shift were independently associated with less Depersonalization, while the degree that the working relationships with their seniors and their colleagues had changed due to the economical crisis and the willingness to change career were independently associated with greater Depersonalization.

4. DISCUSSION

This study investigated work environment related experiences in association with burnout during the economic crisis in Greece. Greek nurses suffered high emotional exhaustion, moderate levels of depersonalization and had moderate, but near low, personal accomplishments. As expected, in our study emotional exhaustion was higher in comparison to other studies in Greece before the crisis [36] -[39] . An unexpected finding was that depersonalization was lower in our study compared to other studies in Greece before the crisis [36] -[38] and similar with the findings of Kiekkas et al. [39] . This is probably a result of the particular situation in the country. During this crisis, the whole Greek society has experienced a lot of suffering and there is an increased solidarity among people during these difficult times. In addition research on nurse resilience suggests that the very demanding circumstances and psychological emptiness are contributing factors for nurse resilience [40] .

Personal accomplishments were also reduced in this study during the crisis in comparison with results from other Greek studies before the crisis [36] -[38] .

The findings of our study are congruent with the findings of a large European project (RN4CAST) where the Greek nurses had the higher levels of burnout among all 12 participating European countries [23] [41] , while at international level only in Japanese [22] , and Chinese nurses [42] have been reported higher levels of burnout.

Increased workload, self-reported quality of care, relationships with seniors and colleagues, job dissatisfaction and willingness to leave nursing or change work department, influence on efficiency by income reduction, feeling equivalent to other health professionals, were the main effects of the crisis on the working environment related experiences of the nurses that were also independent predictors of burnout.

Interestingly, we found that although for nearly 6 out of 10 nurses quality of care at their department had fallen during the last year, most of the nurses were satisfied with the quality of their care during their last shift. This can possibly be explained as a number of other factors may be considered responsible for a decline in quality of care on the wards, such as lack of resources, lack of medicines, lack of equipments, difficulties in performing laboratory tests, that have undermined quality of care in their departments and for which nurses cannot blame themselves. Before the crisis, only 27% of the Greek nurses had reported deterioration in quality of patient care during last year [29] . Considering that care quality in Greek hospitals was generally poor even before the crisis [29] it is alarming that quality of care during this crisis has been further deteriorated. Evidence shows that reduction of care quality is a consequence of the financial crisis as in the large European study in 2009-2010, 20% - 40% among the nurses of all countries reported a deterioration in quality of care during the preceding year [29] . Research confirms that quality of care rated by nurses themselves is a valid and reliable indicator of quality and is associated with mortality rates, failure to rescue rates and patient reported quality of care [43] .

In our study, satisfaction of the nurses from the care quality they provided in their last shift was an independent predictor of reduced emotional exhaustion and depersonalization, a finding that resembles the findings of other researchers [22] [30] [44] . In addition our study has shown that the better the quality of care in work department the higher the personal accomplishments for the Greek nurses, which also echoes the findings of Li et al. [23] and Poghosyan et al. [22] . In contrast, the reported reduced efficiency due to income reduction was an independent predictor of lower personal accomplishments. Maslach and Goldberg [45] have argued that low rewards diminish the value of the work and the value of the worker and a feeling of injustice is developed when other professions with less workload have better financial rewards. This finding is congruent with the findings of

Table 5. Results from univariate and multiple linear regression analyses with dependent variable the Depersonalization.

	β^{*} ± SE	P	β^{**} ± SE	P
Age	−0.01 ± 0.05	0.816		
Gender. male (ref)				
Female	−1.07 ± 0.94	0.255		
Married, no (ref)				
Yes	0.15 ± 0.76	0.843		
Work department, Medical (ref)				
Surgery	0.52 ± 1.12	0.643		
Urology	0.67 ± 1.47	0.648		
Psychiatric	−0.97 ± 1.35	0.472		
Other	−0.3 ± 1.08	0.781		
Do you work in shifts, no (ref)				
Yes	1.93 ± 0.97	**0.048**		
Years in nursing	−0.06 ± 0.05	0.190		
Years in current departement	0.02 ± 0.06	0.722		
Work title, Staff nurse (ref)				
Head nurse	−2.68 ± 1.41	0.058		
Charge nurse	−0.65 ± 0.93	0.484		
Education, Associate nurse (ref)				
Registered nurse	0.42 ± 0.86	0.625		
Nurse specialty, no (ref)				
Yes	−2.23 ± 0.83	**0.007**		
Satisfied from your current job	−2.8 ± 0.53	**<0.001**	−1.77 ± 0.57	**0.002**
Do you want to change career, no (ref)				
Yes	3.04 ± 0.85	**<0.001**	1.83 ± 0.86	**0.046**
Do you want to change your work department, no (ref)				
Yes	3.02 ± 0.81	**<0.001**		
How dissatisfied are you due to your income reduction?	0.31 ± 0.46	0.504		
Were you satisfied by your wage prior to the reduction?	−0.42 ± 0.4	0.295		
How much influenced is your efficiency by your income reduction?	1.11 ± 0.29	**<0.001**		
How much has your work load increased due to the current economical situation?	0.31 ± 0.34	0.369		
Has the economical situation affected your personal life?, no (ref)				
Yes	1.27 ± 1.14	0.264		
Are you satisfied from the care quality you provided in your last shift?	−2.46 ± 0.42	**<0.001**	−1.80 ± 0.44	**<0.001**
How would you describe the care quality in your department during the last year?, reduced (ref)				
Improved	−3.34 ± 0.74	**<0.001**		
Do you feel equivalent to the other health professionals?	−0.73 ± 0.29	**0.013**		
Do you stress for your future career?	0.02 ± 0.31	0.945		
Do you feel suitable for this job?	−1.89 ± 0.40	**<0.001**		
Have the working relationships with your colleagues and seniors changed due to the economical crisis?	0.99 ± 0.34	**0.004**	0.86 ± 0.33	**0.010**
How would you describe your health?	−1.19 ± 0.44	**0.008**		

Ref = reference category; β = regression coefficient; SE = standard error. *unadjusted coefficients; **adjusted coefficients as derived from stepwise method.

Karaniadou et al. [46] in Greece who also found an association between low income and low personal accomplishments.

That was the only observed effect of salary reductions on nurses' burnout. It was expected that the gross salary reductions in Greece over the last years could be a predictor of burnout for nurses. In our study almost all nurses were dissatisfied by their income reduction, however salary reduction per se was not found to be independently related with burnout. The intrinsic rewards such as the quality of care they provided during their last shift and the general quality of care on their wards and not monetary rewards were more important to Greek nurses during the crisis, a finding which is congruent with the findings of Morgan and Lynn [20] with British nurses.

The finding that job dissatisfaction and intentions to leave nursing or change work department were independent predictors of emotional exhaustion and depersonalization, resembles other reports showing similar relationships [16] [28] [47] .

Although some studies have shown relationships between job satisfaction and intentions to leave with emotional exhaustion only [3] [48] , other research [39] [49] has correlated job dissatisfaction with all 3 dimensions of burnout.

Another well established relationship in burnout research was verified in this study. The increased workload for the public hospital nurses during the crisis was an independent predictor of emotional exhaustion. Workload is a source of stress for nurses [50] and many other studies have identified workload as the main cause of emotional exhaustion [3] [4] [18] [28] [39] [51] -[53] .

In addition, feeling equivalent to the other health care professionals was also found to be an independent predictor of emotional exhaustion. This may mean equity in both terms of recognition, autonomy and rewards. Leiter and Maslach [4] have pointed out that organizational justice and respect and fair distribution of rewards, are related with burnout. Similarly Cho et al. [52] have found that lack of fairness was related to emotional exhaustion.

One more area in burnout research which are the relationships with seniors and colleagues and its relationship to burnout was also observed in our study. For those nurses who considered their working relationships with seniors and colleagues had changed, depersonalization was higher. As workload increases resulting in emotional stress, conflicts may arise between all health professionals and their superiors. Earlier research in Greece has shown that conflicts with doctors caused higher level of depersonalization between nurses [39] . Likewise, conflicts between nurses also caused depersonalization [49] . In other countries professional relationships have also been correlated with burnout [23] . In addition, it has been found that support among nurses and support from managers helps nurses be resilient and adapt to their work related stressors [40] .

Finally, the factors that were independently related with higher personal accomplishments such as years in nursing, suitability for the job, satisfaction with salary prior to reductions and being anxious about future career, seem to be interrelated. In the Greek context nurses with more experience and better salaries prior to reductions were the nurses in higher grades, performing roles such as charge nurses, sister assistants, clinical educators, or being placed in specialized units. Those nurses may also feel more suitable for this job. Although no other report was found in the literature to correlate nurses' anxiety for future career with personal accomplishments, anxiety for future career is probably a context specific finding in Greece where a lot of changes are happening in the health care sector with closures and merging of hospitals, hospital departments and special units, nurses mobility, reallocations of staff, privatizations and so on. This may have caused anxiety in those nurses who may think that their accomplishments through the years may be in jeopardy during the time of restructuring of the health care services.

In relation to age and personal accomplishments research evidence is conflicting with some studies showing that older age is related to lower personal accomplishments [54] and other studies finding that younger nurses had lower levels of personal accomplishments [16] [55] . This probably reflects cultural and context related influences. Research on personal accomplishment outcomes, agrees that those who were satisfied with their job had higher scores on personal accomplishments [16] . Nurses who feel they are suitable for nursing are obviously those nurses who are satisfied with their job. Other research in Greece [38] [39] has confirmed that the more suitable one feels for nursing, the higher the personal accomplishments.

5. LIMITATIONS

There are some limitations in this study. One limitation is the convenience sampling procedure for both hospitals and nurses which limits the generalization of the results. Although the questionnaire was distributed at various times during all three nursing shifts, nurses who participated in this study may have different characteristics from those not participating.

Another limitation lies in the validity of self-reported data. Perhaps many participants would like to express their unhappiness with the austerity measures and massive reductions on their salaries by the government during the crisis. However many months had elapsed since their income reductions thus this may have diminished the possibilities for biased results.

The study was conducted in only 2 hospitals in the capital city of Athens. Future research should include more hospitals from more geographical areas of Greece.

The cross-sectional design of this study does not allow to study associations between work environment related changes and burnout over time.

6. CONCLUSIONS

The new working conditions that have been created for the public hospital nurses in Greece during the years of strict austerity measures have raised their levels of burnout. In this first exploration of the associations between austerity related changes in nursing working environments and burnout we conclude that the factors found to be independently related with burnout belong to the six areas of nurse work life verifying this organizational model of burnout. Quality of care has been reduced during the crisis despite nurses' efforts who in vast majority were satisfied by their own quality of care offered. Quality of care was the only factor that was independently associated with all 3 dimensions of burnout. Income reduction per se was not an independent predictor of burnout. This finding is supportive of the notion that inner rewards rather than monetary rewards matter more for nurses. In this study the only financial related effect on burnout was a reduction in personal accomplishments for the nurses who reported diminished efficiency due to income reduction.

As the omens for the Greek economy are not optimistic for recovery and working conditions will continue to get worse as the austerity measures have not yet finalized and further structural reforms are underway, it is important to periodically evaluate nurses for burnout levels.

Deterioration of the quality of care is a negative consequence of the austerity measures and affects not only the patients but nurses' burnout levels. Those side effects of fiscal austerity measures could cause indirect health care costs that may exceed the amount of money saved now. Governmental officials ought to know that and take immediate interventions to improve the quality of care in the public Greek hospitals to protect the safety of the patients and preserve the wellbeing of the nurses.

There are some other low cost interventions to improve the working environment of Greek nurses during the crisis such as empowering professional relationships and adapting strategies to promote equity among health professionals.

Further studies on the effects of the financial crisis on the working conditions of the Greek nurses and their associations with burnout throughout the country to verify the findings of this study are needed.

FUNDING

This research has not received any funding.

CONFLICT OF INTEREST

No conflict of interest has been declared by the authors.

REFERENCES

1. Wray, J. (2013) The Impact of the Financial Crisis on Nurses and Nursing. Journal of Advanced Nursing, 69, 497-499.
2. Buchan, J., O'May, F. and Dussault, G. (2013) Nursing Workforce Policy and the Economic Crisis: A Global Overview. Journal of Nursing Scholarship, 45, 298-307.
3. Aiken, L.H., Clarke, S.P., Sloane, D.M., Sochalski, J. and Silber, J.H. (2002) Hospital Nurse Staffing and Patient Mortality, Nurse Burnout and Job Dissatisfaction. Journal of the American Medical Association, 288, 1987-1993.

4. Leiter, M.P. and Maslach C. (2009) Nurse Turnover: The Mediating Role of Burnout. Journal of Nursing Management, 17, 331-339.

5. Kaitelidou, D. and Kouli, E. (2012) The Health Sector in Greece Has Been Severely Affected by the Economic Crisis, Raising Concerns for the Future of the Greek Health System. http://blogs.lse.ac.uk/europpblog/2012/07/20/greek-health-system/

6. Karanikolos, M., Mladovsky, P., Cylus, J., Thomson, S., Basu, S., Stuckler, D., Mackenbach, J.P. and McKee, M. (2013) Financial Crisis, Austerity, and Health in Europe. Lancet, 381, 1323-1331.

7. Stuckler, D. and McKee, M. (2011) There Is an alternative: Public Health Professionals Must Not Remain Silent at a Time of Financial Crisis. European Journal of Public Health, 22, 2-3.

8. Kentikelenis, A., Karanikolos, M., Papanikolas, I., Basu, S., McKee, M. and Stuckler, D. (2011) Health Effects of Financial Crisis: Omens of a Greek Tragedy. Lancet, 378, 1457-1458.

9. OECD Health Data (2013) How Does Greece Compare. http://www.oecd.org/els/health-systems/Briefing-Note-GREECE-2013.pdf

10. Papathanassoglou, E. and Mpouzika, M. (2012) Critical Care in the Era of Global Economic Crisis: A Nursing Ethics Perspective. Nursing in Critical Care, 17, 275-278.

11. Notara, V., Koupidis, S., Vaga, E. and Grammatikopoulos, I. (2010) Economic Crisis and Challenges for the Greek Healthcare System: The Emergent Role of Nursing Management. Journal of Nursing Management, 18, 501-504.

12. OECD (2013) StatExtracts. http://stats.oecd.org/Index.aspx?DataSetCode=STLABOUR

13. Yannopoulos, D. (2012) Real Wages Tumble by 25% as Tax Burden Soars in 2011. http://archive.today/Ts1I4

14. Laschinger, H.K.S., Leiter, M.P., Day, A. and Gilin, D. (2009) Workplace Empowerment, Incivility, and Burnout: Impact on Staff Nurse Recruitment and Retention Outcomes. Journal of Nursing Management, 17, 302-311.

15. Kitaoka, K. and Masuda, S. (2012) Academic Report on Burnout among Japanese Nurses. Japan Journal of Nursing Science, 10, 273-279.

16. Colff, J.J. and Rothmann, S. (2012) Burnout of Registered Nurses in South Africa. Journal of Nursing Management, Early View.

17. Lee, H.F., Chien, T.W. and Yen, M. (2013) Examining Factor Structure of Maslach Burnout Inventory among Nurses in Taiwan. Journal of Nursing Management, 21, 648-656.

18. Jenkins, R. and Elliott, P. (2004) Stressors, Burnout and Social Support: Nurses in Acute Mental Health Settings. Journal of Advanced Nursing, 48, 622-631.

19. Glasberg, A.L., Eriksson, S. and Norberg, A. (2007) Burnout and 'Stress of Conscience' among Healthcare Personnel. Journal of Advanced Nursing, 57, 392-403.

20. Morgan, J.C. and Lynn, M.R. (2009) Satisfaction in Nursing in the Context of Shortage. Journal of Nursing Management, 17, 401-410.

21. Burke, R., Koyuncu, M. and Fiksenbaum, L. (2010) Burnout, Work Satisfactions and Psychological Well-Being among Nurses in Turkish Hospitals. Europe's Journal of Psychology, 6, 63-81.

22. Poghosyan, L., Clarke, S., Finlayson, M. and Aiken, L. (2010) Nurse Burnout and Quality of Care: Cross-National Investigation in Six Countries. Research in Nursing & Health, 33, 288-298.

23. Li, B., Bruyneel, L., Sermeus, W., Van den Heede, K., Matawie, K., Aiken, L. and Lesaffre, E. (2013) Group-Level Impact of Work Environment Dimensions on Burnout Experiences among Nurses: A Multivariate Multilevel Probit Model. International Journal of Nursing Studies, 50, 281-291.

24. Hasselhorn, H.M., Tackenberg, P., Kuemmerling, A., Wittenberg, J., Simon, M., Conway, P.M., et al. (2006) Nurses' Health, Age and the Wish to Leave the Profession—Findings from the European NEXT-Study. La Medicina del Lavoro, 97, 207-214.

25. Van Bogaert, P., Clarke, S., Roelant, E., Meulemans, H. and Heyning, P. (2010) Impacts of Unit-Level Nurse Practice Environment and Burnout on Nurse-Reported Outcomes: A Multilevel Modelling Approach. Journal of Clinical Nursing, 19, 1664-1674.

26. Estryn-Behar, M., Van Der Heijden, J.M., Fry, C. and Hasselhorn, H.M. (2010) Longitudinal Analysis of Personal and Work-Related Factors Associated with Turnover among Nurses. Nursing Research, 59, 166-177.

27. Aiken, L.H., Cimiotti, J.P., Sloane, D.M., Smith, H.L., Flynn, L. and Neff, D.F. (2011) Effects of Nurse Staffing and Nurse Education on Patient Deaths in Hospitals with Different Nurse Work Environments. Medical Care, 49, 1047-1053.

28. Jourdain, G. and Chênevert, D. (2010) Job Demands—Resources, Burnout and Intention to Leave the Nursing Profession: A Questionnaire Survey. International Journal of Nursing Studies, 47, 709-722.

29. Aiken, L.H., Sermeus, W., Van den Heede, K., Sloane, D.M., Busse, R., McKee, M., et al. (2012) Patient Safety, Satisfaction, and Quality of Hospital Care: Cross-Sectional Surveys of Nurses and Patients in 12 Countries in Europe and the United States. British Medical Journal, 344, Article ID: e1717.

30. Van Bogaert, P., Kowalski, C., Weeks, S.M., Van Heusden, D. and Clarke, S.P. (2013) The Relationship between Nurse Practice Environment, Nurse Work Characteristics, Burnout and Job Outcome and Quality of Nursing Care: A Cross-Sectional Survey. International Journal of Nursing Studies, 50, 1667-1677.

31. Kutney-Lee, A., Wu, E.S., Sloane, D.M. and Aiken, L.H. (2013) Changes in Hospital Nurse Work Environments and Nurse Job Outcomes: An Analysis of Panel Data. International Journal of Nursing Studies, 50, 195-201.

32. Bartram, T., Casimir, G., Djurkovic, N., Leggat, S.G. and Stanton, P. (2012) Do Perceived High Performance Work Systems Influence the Relationship between Emotional Labour, Burnout and Intention to Leave? A Study of Australian Nurses. Journal of Advanced Nursing, 68, 1567-1578.

33. Van den Heede, K., Florquin, M., Bruyneel, L., Aiken, L., Diya, L., Lesaffre, E. and Sermeus, W. (2013) Effective Strategies for Nurse Retention in Acute Hospitals: A Mixed Method Study. International Journal of Nursing Studies, 50, 185-194.

34. Trivellas, P., Reklitis, P. and Platis, C. (2013) The Effect of Job Related Stress on Employees' Satisfaction: A Survey in Health Care. Procedia-Social and Behavioral Sciences, 73, 718-726.

35. Maslach, C. and Jackson, S.E. (1986) Maslach Burnout Inventory Manual. 2nd Edition, Consulting Psychologists Press, Palo Alto, California.

36. Karanikola, M.N., Papathanassoglou, E.D., Mpouzika, M. and Lemonidou, C. (2012) Burnout Syndrome Indices in Greek Intensive Care Nursing Personnel. Dimensions of Critical Care Nursing, 31, 94-101.

37. Malliarou, M., Moustaka, E. and Konstantinidis, T. (2008) Burnout of Nursing Personnel in a Regional University Hospital. Health Science Journal, 2, 140-152.

38. Dilintas, A. (2010) Study of the Professional Burnout Syndrome in the Personnel of a University Hospital. Archives of Hellenic Medicine, 27, 498-508.

39. Kiekkas, P., Spyratos, F., Lampa, E., Aretha, D. and Sakellaropoulos, C.G. (2010) Level and Correlates of Burnout among Orthopaedic Nurses in Greece. Orthopaedic Nursing, 29, 203-209. [Citation Time(s):6]

40. Hart, P.L., Brannan, J.D. and Chesnay, M. (2012) Resilience in Nurses: An Integrative Review. Journal of Nursing Management, Early View.

41. Aiken, L.H., Sloane, D.M., Bruyneel, L., Van den Heede, K., Sermeus, W. for the RN4CAST Consortium (2013) Nurses' Reports of Working Conditions and Hospital Quality of Care in 12 Countries in Europe. International Journal of Nursing Studies, 50, 143-153.

42. Xie, Z.Y., Wang, A.L. and Chen, B. (2011) Nurse Burnout and Its Association with Occupational Stress in a Cross-Sectional Study in Shanghai. Journal of Advanced Nursing, 67, 1537-1546.

43. McHugh, M.D. and Stimpfel, A.W. (2012) Nurse Reported Quality of Care: A Measure of Hospital Quality. Research in Nursing & Health, 35, 566-575.

44. Liu, K., You, L.M., Chen, S.X., Hao, Y.T., Zhu, X.W., Zhang, L.F. and Aiken, L.H. (2012) The Relationship between Hospital Work Environment and Nurse Outcomes in Guangdong, China: A Nurse Questionnaire Survey. Journal of Clinical Nursing, 21, 1476-1485.

45. Maslach, C. and Goldberg, J. (1998) Prevention of Burnout: New Perspectives. Applied and Preventive Psychology, 7, 63-74.

46. Karaniadou, A., Anagnostopoulos, F. and Telioni, M. (2006) Sociodemographic, Labour and Administrative Factors Which Affect the Professional Exhaustion of the Doctors and Nurses. Nosileftiki, 45, 391-403.

47. Laschinger, H.K.S. (2012) Job and Career Satisfaction and Turnover Intentions of Newly Graduated Nurses. Journal of Nursing Management, 20, 472-484.

48. Chou, H.Y., Hecker, R. and Martin, A. (2012) Predicting Nurses' Well-Being from Job Demands and Resources: A Cross-Sectional Study of Emotional Labour. Journal of Nursing Management, 20, 502-511.

49. Piko, B.F. (2006) Burnout, Role Conflict, Job Satisfaction and Psychosocial Health among Hungarian Health Care Staff: A Questionnaire Survey. International Journal of Nursing Studies, 43, 311-318.

50. Happell, B., Dwyer, T., Reid-Searl, K., Burke, K.J., Caperchione, C.M. and Gaskin, C.J. (2013) Nurses and Stress: Recognizing Causes and Seeking Solutions. Journal of Nursing Management, 21, 638-647.

51. Sheward, L., Hunt, J., Hagen, S., Macleod, M. and Ball, J. (2005) The Relationship between UK Hospital Nurse Staffing and Emotional Exhaustion and Job Dissatisfaction. Journal of Nursing Management, 13, 51-60.

52. Cho, J., Laschinger, H.K.S. and Wong, C. (2006) Workplace Empowerment, Work Engagement and Organizational Commitment of New Graduate Nurses. Nursing Leadership, 19, 43-60.

53. You, L.M., Aiken, L.H., Sloane, D.M., Liu, K., He, G.P., Hu, Y., et al. (2013) Hospital Nursing, Care Quality, and Patient Satisfaction: Cross-Sectional Surveys of Nurses and Patients in Hospitals in China and Europe. International Journal of Nursing Studies, 50, 154-161.

54. Ross, J., Jones, J., Callaghan, P., Eales, S. and Ashman, N. (2009) A Survey of Stress, Job Satisfaction and Burnout among Haemodialysis Staff. Journal of Renal Care, 35, 127-133.

55. Lin, F., St John, W. and McVeigh, C. (2009) Burnout among Hospital Nurses in China. Journal of Nursing Management, 17, 294-301.

4
CHAPTER

The Impact of the Great Recession on Employment Polarization in Spain

Brindusa Anghe [1] · Sara De la Rica[1] · Aitor Lacuesta[2]

[1]*FEDEA, Madrid, Spain*

[2]*UPV/EHU, Bilbao, Spain*

[3]*Bank of Spain, Madrid, Spain*

ABSTRACT

This article analyzes changes in the occupational employment share in Spain for the period 1997–2012 and the way particular sociodemographic groups adapt to those changes. There seems to be clear evidence of employment polarization between 1997 and 2012 that accelerates over the recession. Changes in the composition of the labour supply cannot explain the increase in the share of occupations at the low end of the wage distribution. Sector reallocation may have partially contributed to explain the polarization process in Spain during the years of expansion (1997–2007) but it is a minor factor during the recession. The polarization of occupations within sectors observed, especially during the recession, appears to be related to a decline in routine tasks which is compensated by an increase in occupations with non-routine service contents, which are found both in the low and high end of the wage distribution. Instead, jobs with a higher degree of abstract contents do not appear to increase their share in total employment during these 15 years. The paper finds that this process has affected males more strongly than females because of their higher concentration in occupations more focused on routine tasks. Among males, for workers under 30 years old, we find a decrease in the share of occupations with more routine tasks which turns into increases in those with more abstract content and particularly with more non-routine service content. Instead, male workers over 30 years old seem to remain in declining occupations to a greater extent. Females of different ages are not affected by the abovementioned changes.

Keywords: Employment polarization Job tasks Routinization Business cycle

Authors are grateful to Juan Francisco Jimeno and to two anonymous referees for their comments and suggestions. We also gratefully acknowledge the support from the Ministry of Science and Technology through grants ECO2012-31985 and ECO2012-35820.

1 INTRODUCTION

Structural unemployment depends on a broad set of factors among which there are some institutional considerations which have to do with labour market regulation, product market regulation and the mismatch between occupations demanded by the market and the ability of different skill groups. This article analyzes the evolution of occupations in Spain for the period 1997–2012 identifying the structural part of this change. Moreover, it tests several hypotheses regarding the underlying factors of this structural change and the way particular sociodemographic groups adapt to it.

This question is relevant because one might want to use the observed changes in occupations over time to shed some light on the evolution of the demand for labour in the near future. However, it is not clear at first sight to what extent those changes arise as a result of structural variation in the demand for labour or as a result of other forces. On the one hand, one must take into account that the Spanish labour force has undergone a notable structural change over the last cycle. Indeed, there has been a substantial increase in the schooling attainment of the population, in female participation and in the supply of low-skilled immigrants which has affected the supply skill composition in the economy. On the other hand, the employment share of the Construction Sector changed enormously throughout the cycle. Total employment in that sector increased around 5 pp between 1994 and 2007 (from 8.7 to 13 %) and decreased by 7 pp from 2007 onwards (reaching 6 % of total employment by the first term of 2013—a level more in accordance with the share of this sector in other European economies). Since the beginning of the actual recession and as a consequence of the construction bust, this sector contributed to almost half of the 3.8 million jobs destroyed, and it is certainly not expected that in the future it will recover the same level of activity as in the recent past. The paper explores these issues in detail.

Recent evidence from a variety of countries has found a neat decline in the share of middle wage occupations which has been named the polarization process. Indeed, some authors, such as Autor and Dorn (2013) find that this process has accelerated during the great recession. This reallocation of workers has been mainly observed within different industries and this has led many scholars to relate this phenomenon to a change in technology motivated by a decrease in the price of capital goods. Indeed, Autor et al. (2003) and Goos et al. (2009) relate the abovementioned polarization process to a decrease in the demand for occupations performing routine job contents or tasks that workers in the middle-wage occupations perform and which can be easily mechanized. On the other hand, it has also been documented that occupations which perform jobs that are more difficult to be substituted by technology, such as abstract qualified occupations or unqualified jobs which require interpersonal skills, are rising in relative employment terms. This means that workers previously performing routine tasks have been reallocated to jobs requiring either more abstract or more interpersonal service job contents or tasks.

There is a growing literature that finds that allocation of skills into tasks might play an important role in explaining the difference in growth between the USA and Europe (Wasmer 2006), the higher unemployment rate in Europe than in the USA (Ljungqvist and Sargent 1998), the recent growth in wage inequality (Gavilán 2012; Autor et al. 2003) and jobless recoveries (Jamovich and Siu 2012). Although Goos et al. (2009) provide evidence of polarization for many European countries, including Spain, this paper is the first one to address, in detail, the polarization hypothesis for Spain at different moments of the business cycle as well as its different impact on different sociodemographic groups of workers.

To this end, the paper analyzes labour market changes over the last complete cycle (expansion and recession) to provide evidence of structural changes of the Spanish economy which might shape the way forward for its labour market. Indeed, since 1994, Spain has had 13 years of economic growth and 5 years of recession. By comparing changes from the starting to the end point of a whole economic cycle, we can distinguish structural movements from more cyclical ones. The paper focuses on labour market changes over the period 1997–2012 (ten years of expansion and five years of recession) instead of 1994–2012, which would delimit the whole business cycle better because it is only since 1997 that we have access to 3-digit level data on occupations in our database, which is highly recommended in order to perform the matching of tasks to occupations. As a consequence, we lose 3 years but that period is fairly similar to the period 1997–2012 in terms of labour force and employment composition.

Section 2 describes the important changes in the occupational distribution which Spain went through during these years. Whereas in the upper part of the wage distribution, the share of managers, professionals and technicians increased, in the lower part, the share of retail sales and services occupations and low-skilled occupations related to the service sector also increased. Instead, those jobs related to construction, agriculture or industry, regardless of their qualifications, declined in terms of relative employment. Interestingly, the increases even in the high end of the wage distribution are related to service tasks more than to abstract ones. All these changes over the cycle are documented in the second section of the paper.

Section 3 is devoted to confirm empirically that Spain also went through a polarization process over the 15 year interval. Potential changes in this process between the expansion and the recession period are accounted for. In addition, this section explores different hypotheses behind the polarization process such as changes in the labour supply, changes in the sectoral structure and changes in technology within sectors. It is found that neither of the first two hypotheses can explain the whole polarization process, whereas the latter one seems to fit the process better. To test for the latter, we distinguish between the already mentioned "routine tasks" from "abstract tasks" (job contents which require active learning, management of personal resources, deductive reasoning, speech clarity, or complex problem solving) and "Non-Routine Service tasks" (which entails activities that require caring for others, establishing and maintaining interpersonal relationships, selling and influencing others and active listening). In the United States, polarization has been driven by a growth in abstract tasks—usually at the upper part of the wage distribution, and low-skilled services—usually at the lower end of the wage distribution, coupled with a decrease in occupations with a high degree of routine tasks which lie around the middle of the wage distribution. However, it might not be possible to extrapolate this pattern to other countries, so we look at the connection between the polarization process and changes in the occupational distribution driven by changes in the tasks performed by workers in Spain.

Finally, Sect. 4 explores how changes in the demand for tasks over time cause different effects on different sociodemographic groups. Males and females at different stages of their life cycle are somehow segregated into different types of occupations and their ability to reallocate might differ because of their different capacity to readapt their accumulated human capital over time. Indeed, for the US, Autor and Dorn (2009) found that those in occupations more related to routine jobs have aged in the US, whereas workers in jobs which are closely related to abstract and service jobs have become younger.

2 CHANGES IN THE DISTRIBUTION OF EMPLOYMENT

During the last 15 years, employment growth in the private sector has been heterogeneously distributed among occupations. Figure 1 presents changes in the employment shares of seven major occupational groups for the private sector (including self-employed). Occupations are ranked according to average 1995 wages, from highest to lowest. The figure reveals that between 1997 and 2012 there were three broad occupational groups which expanded their share in private sector employment. These are, according to the expansion magnitude, managers, professionals and technicians, whose expansion reached 7.8 percentage points (henceforth pp); retail sales and service occupations, whose employment share increased in 3.91 pp and finally, low-skilled service occupations, with an almost negligible increase of 0.07 pp. The rest of the occupations declined in terms of relative employment. The occupational groups which declined most are production and craft occupations 5.9 pp, qualified workers in agriculture, which experienced a decrease of 3.7 pp, and machine operators and assemblers, with a decrease in 2.1 pp. Finally, clerical and civil servants declined very slightly, 0.09 pp.

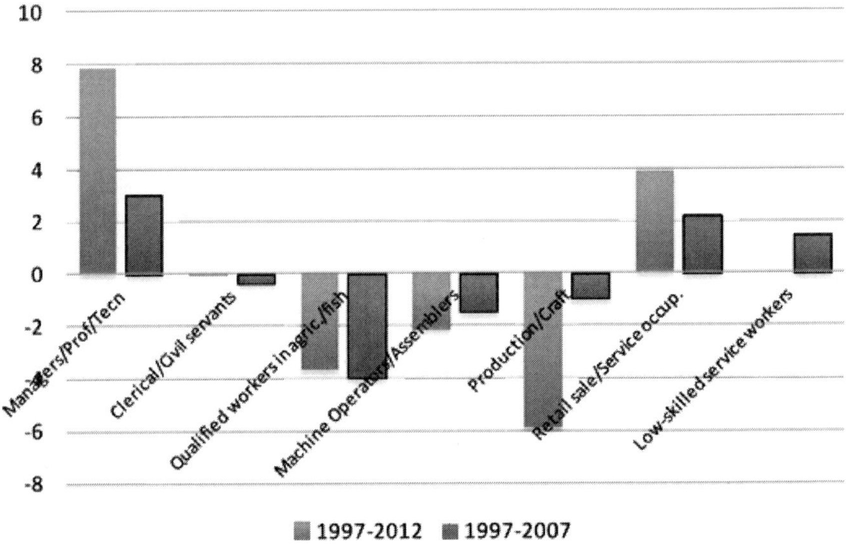

Figure 1. Changes in the share of private sector employment by occupation

Notice that the expanding occupations are precisely those whose contents have much to do with either abstract or service tasks. Indeed service tasks appear to be very related to the increase in the share of expanding occupations. More than half of the increase in managers, professionals and technicians is associated with increases in the share of administrative and business associate professionals; physicists, chemists and engineer professionals and technicians; and salespersons and restaurant service workers who are managers of their own business. The big increase in retail sales and service occupations is associated with an increase in personal services and the increase in low-skilled services is associated with an increase in domestic service occupations. Rather, the declining occupations seem to be much more associated with routine tasks. This will be further explored in Sect. 3.

It is also remarkable that expanding and declining occupations in the overall period remain as such when only the expansionary period (1997–2007) is taken into account. This provides an idea of the structural character of the employment composition changes across occupations in the Spanish economy regardless of the sizable housing boom that the Spanish economy experimented with during the expansionary period. From the comparison between the whole period and only the expansionary one, it looks like during the recession years (2007–2012), occupations related to managers, professionals and technicians expanded much more than those related to non-qualified services. Indeed, there is an important increase in the share of service sector managers between 2007 and 2012.

Given that gender segregation across occupations is high in Spain, it is interesting to present changes in the structure of employment by occupation separately for men and women. Again, this distinction might shed light on the structural character of the occupational changes since females were not affected as much by the housing boom and bust as males. Table 1 provides a static picture of the gender segregation of employment in 1997, the starting period of analysis. The evidence of the occupational segregation by gender is really high—males are much more concentrated in occupations related to machine operators, assemblers, craft and production whereas female jobs are basically associated with services of different types. The second interesting feature is that by 1997 males were overrepresented in declining occupations with respect to females.

Table 1. Share of private sector employment by occupation 1997

Occupational groups	Average wage	Overall	16–30		31–45		46–64	
			Males	Females	Males	Females	Males	Females
Managers/prof/tecn	26.450	24.88	16.4	22.21	27.58	29.74	27.03	27.62
Clerical/civil servants	13.895	9.09	6.4	20.47	6.77	14.28	5.36	6.88
Qualified workers in agric./fish		6.54	4.06	1.46	6.32	3.44	11.82	12.85
Machine operators/assemblers	13.418	11.8	13.91	6.03	15.37	6.08	14.98	4.22
Production/craft	12.945	19.64	26.84	4.06	27.68	4.13	26.98	4.26
Retail sale/service occup.	11.079	13.3	13.02	29.54	8.09	20.02	4.69	17.66
Low-skilled service workers	9.049	14.76	19.36	16.23	8.2	22.3	9.15	26.51

Source Spanish Labour Force Survey (LFS) and Wage Structure Survey (WSS) 1995

Figures 2 and 3 represent the change in the distribution of occupations by gender over the whole 15-year period, as well as only for the expansionary period. As for males, Fig. 2 reveals that over the 15-year interval the share of male employment increases to a greater extent in occupations related to managerial, technical and professional jobs; also, although to a lesser extent, in those related to sale and service occupations and finally, the increase is almost negligible in occupations related to machine operators and assemblers. On the contrary, male occupational shares decline sizably in production and craft (occupations related to the construction sector), qualified occupations in agriculture; and to a lesser extent, in clerical and civil servant jobs and low-skilled service workers (also related to the construction sector). If we focus only on the expansionary period, the most remarkable difference concerns the share of males working in occupations related to construction (production and craft and low-skilled primarily). Contrary to the overall period, where the share of those two major occupation groups decreased, during the expansion, they experienced a strong increase. Changes in the share of employment across the rest of the occupations do not differ much between the two year intervals.

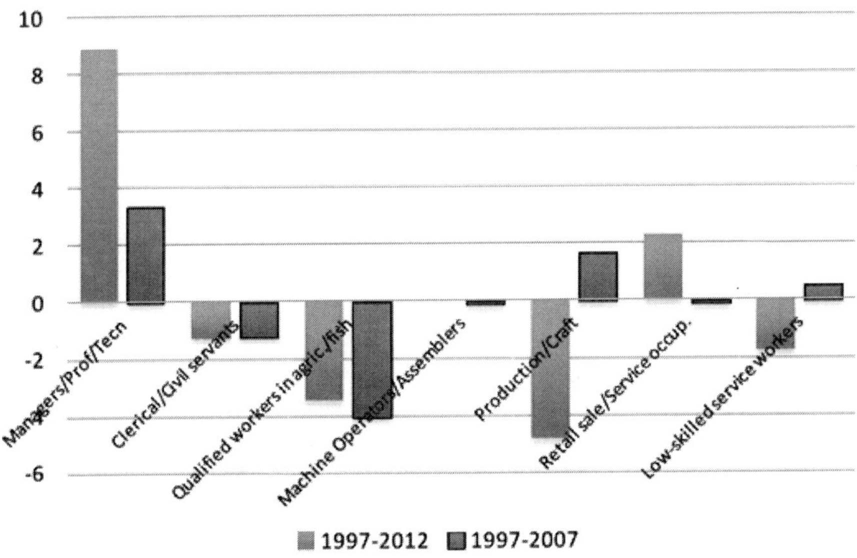

Figure 2. Changes in the share of private sector employment by occupation—males

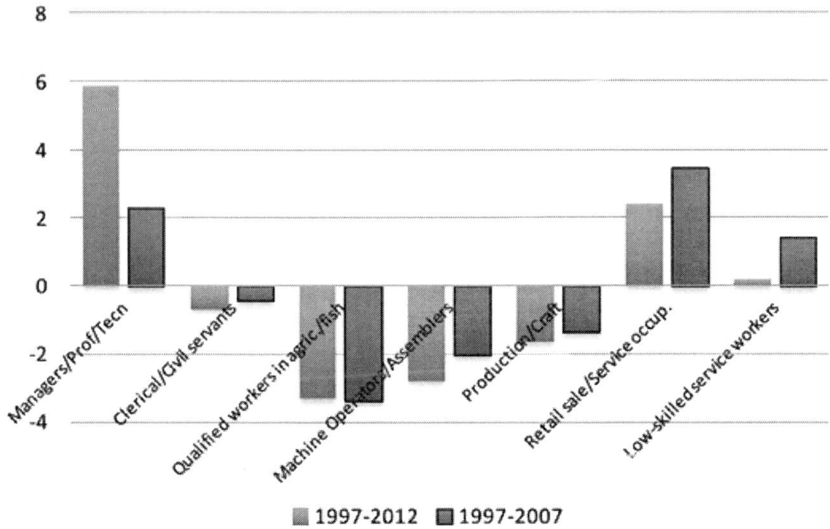

Figure 3. Changes in the share of private sector employment by occupation—females

With regards to women, changes observed for the overall period and for the expansionary period are very much the same with important increases in occupations related to managerial, professional and technical jobs and retail sales. This is very much related to the enormous entrance of women into employment from inactivity during the recession as a result of the "added worker" effect. Many of these women are directed into jobs related to sales and services either as managers or as employees. With regards to other occupations, the share of female employment decreases in manual occupations, such as production and craft and machine operators and assemblers and increases slightly in low service occupations.

To summarize, for both males and females and for the overall 15-year period, we observe increasing shares of employment in managerial, technical and professional jobs as well as retail sales and services occupations. On the other hand, we observe decreasing shares in manual occupations. In the following two sections, we analyze, with a higher degree of disaggregation, whether the above mentioned changes in occupations could be understood in a polarization framework. We also analyze different hypotheses behind this process at different moments of the cycle and how different sociodemographic groups adapt to these changes.

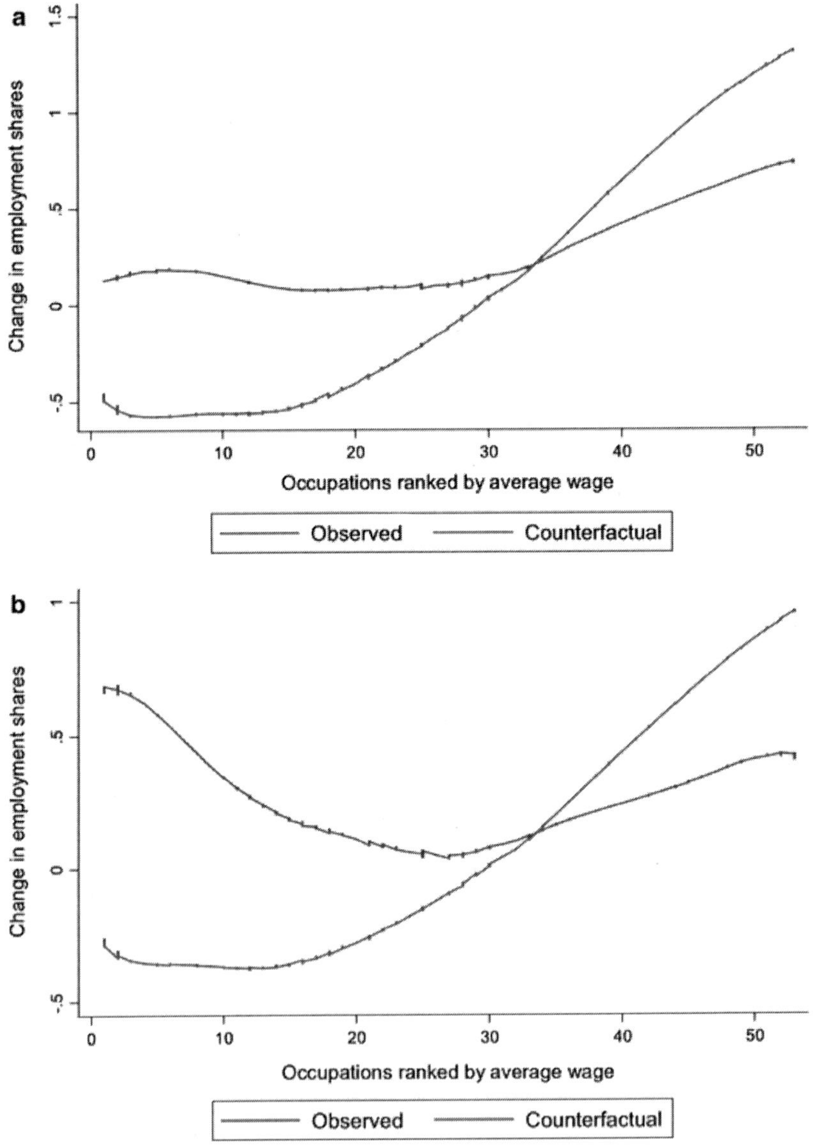

Figure 4.a Smoothed change in employment shares by occupations (1997–2012). **b** Smoothed change in employment shares by occupations (1997–2007)

3 POLARIZATION AND THE OBSERVED CHANGES IN EMPLOYMENT SHARES

3.1 Is there evidence of employment polarization in Spain?

Following Goos and Manning (2007) and Autor et al. (2006), we present some figures relating changes in the share of employment to the ranking of occupations in terms of average wages in Spain. We do so first for the entire period: 1997–2012 and then only for the expansionary period—1997–2007.

Figure 4a, b depict changes in the occupational share of employment following the National Classification of Occupations (1994—CNO-94) at a 2-digit level. Occupations are ranked according to average wages at the beginning of the period. The ranking of wages is obtained from the 1995 Wage Structure Survey (*Encuesta de Estructura Salarial* (EES)), which is the closest one to 1997, our initial period.[1] Unfortunately, this evidence must be presented at a 2-digit level occupational disaggregation and not at a higher one given that this is the maximum occupation disaggregation that is available from the different EES waves. The series titled "Observed" present changes in the share for the whole 15-year interval as well as only for the 1997–2007 expansionary period.

There seems to be clear evidence of polarization, both for the expansionary and for the overall 15-year interval. Nevertheless, the expansionary period presents a somewhat different pattern of polarization than the whole 15-year period. In particular, during the first 11 years and coinciding with the expansionary period, low-paying occupations expanded their employment shares relative to average-paying occupations but also with respect to high-paying occupations. These patterns are consistent with the occupational changes described in the previous section. During the expansionary period, high-paid jobs such as professionals and managers increased their share slightly, but the increase in the share was the strongest for the lowest-paid occupations, basically those related to low-skilled services. At least partially, this might reflect the effect of the housing boom in the demand for low skill jobs. Taking the whole 15-year period, high-paid jobs such as high-skilled services related to trade and sales and professionals and managers expand at a slightly higher pace than low-paid occupations such as low-skilled services or clerical jobs. This is overwhelmingly related to the increase in the share of managers of small businesses related to hotels, restaurants, retail and the service sector in general. Indeed, the increase in low-skilled service workers is marginal probably due to the effect of the housing bust on low-skilled services. The group of retail sale and service occupations is the only one whose share increases among those occupations which lay at the low end of the wage distribution. Rather, the increase is much stronger at the upper end.

3.2 Alternative explanations of the observed job polarization

3.2.1 Is job polarization explained by changes in labour supply?

One potential explanation for the observed job polarization is that it is driven by changes in the composition of the labour supply. The substantial increase in the schooling attainment of the population, the increase in female participation and the increase in the labour supply of low-skilled immigrants may have shaped the supply of skills, increasing it particularly at both ends of the wage distribution and eventually driving a polarization process over the business cycle. Additionally, we know that throughout the crisis, highly educated workers have performed better than low-skilled workers due to, among other things, the different incidence of temporary contracts in each of the groups. This factor might have biased the polarization process to the high end of the wage distribution during the recession.

Changes in the labour market activity during this 15-year interval are impressive. To give some examples, the number of active workers increased by 5.8 million—an average annual increase of 1.1 %—and the number of employed workers by 3.9 million—an average annual increase of 2 %. Furthermore, and as it has been documented by other studies (Izquierdo and Lacuesta 2012; Carrasco et al. 2012), these important employment changes have been unevenly distributed across particular groups of the population.

To test whether the observed changes in the labour composition may explain the observed job polarization, we split the working population into 22 cells (gender (2 groups), educational attainment (3 groups), age groups for natives (3 groups), and 4 groups of immigrants depending on their gender and whether they belong to OECD countries or not). We construct counterfactuals of the distribution of occupations (at a 2 digit level) in 2007 and 2012 keeping the 1997 structure of occupations constant within each cell and changing the relative weight of each cell.

The series titled "Counterfactual" in Fig. 4a, b show that changes in the composition of the labour force would have increased the share of occupations placed at the upper end of the wage distribution instead of the polarization process described above. During the recession, compositional changes, if anything, might have contributed even more to the expansion of occupations at the upper part of the wage distribution. Therefore, supply side changes cannot explain the increase in the share of occupations at the low end of the wage distribution and hence we require additional explanations to understand the observed polarization process.

3.2.2 Is job polarization explained by changes in the sectoral structure?

The Spanish economy has undergone a notable structural change over the last cycle. Indeed, the incidence of the Construction Sector in total employment increased around 5 pp between 1994 and 2007 (from 8.7 to 13 %) and decreased by 7 pp from 2007 onwards (reaching 6 % of total employment by 2013-Q1, a level more in accordance with the relative incidence of this sector in other European economies). Since the beginning of the actual recession and as a consequence of the construction bust, this sector contributed to almost half of the destruction of 3.8 million jobs. Therefore, it is likely that sector reallocation during the expansion affected the demand of certain occupations and hence changed their share in total employment. To test for this, we can decompose the observed changes in occupation shares into those which could be explained by changes in the sectoral structure of the Spanish economy (changes between sectors) and those changes which occurred within each of the sectors. Table 2 presents a shift share analysis for broader occupation groups ranked by average wages (as in Goos et al. 2009). Employment share changes across sectors can be attributed to demand changes, whereas those within sectors should be more as a result of technology changes. For each of the two periods, the first column shows the change (in pp) in the share of each occupational group. The second column reflects changes between industries and the third one changes within industries. When we consider the whole 15-year interval, changes within industries are the most important ones right after the observed changes in the distribution of occupations. Changes within sectors expanded the employment share of low-paying occupations and high-paying occupations relative to average-paying occupations. The reallocation of workers from craft and production occupations towards managers, professionals and technicians and sales and retail is crucial. On the other hand, during the expansionary period, changes between industries dominate both ends of the wage distribution. By broader occupational groups, those changes across sectors during the expansionary period expanded the employment share of low-paying occupations and high-paying occupations relative to average-paying occupations. Changes within sectors during this period point towards the same direction of the above mentioned changes between sectors but their importance is minor.

Table 2. Decomposition of the changes in the share of private sector employment by occupation

	1997–2012			1997–2007		
	Change ocup	Within	Between	Change ocup	Within	Between
Managers/prof/assoc	7.43	6.21	1.22	2.82	1.01	1.81
Clerical/civil servants	0.06	−0.26	0.32	−0.26	−0.47	0.21
Qualified workers in agric./fish	−3.80	−0.88	−2.91	−4.03	−1.01	−3.02
Machine operators/assemblers	−2.21	−0.09	−2.13	−1.64	−0.13	−1.51
Production/craft	−6.19	−8.74	2.55	−1.25	−1.32	0.08
Retail sale/service occup.	4.58	5.30	−0.72	2.62	0.99	1.63
Low-skilled service workers	0.13	−1.54	1.67	1.74	0.94	0.80

The first column corresponds to the average wage of each major occupation in WSS 1995. The rest of the table uses LFS. By sub period the first column corresponds to the change in the share of private sector employment by occupation, the second and the third are computed using a shift share analysis (Goos and Manning 2007)

The first column corresponds to the average wage of each major occupation in WSS 1995. The rest of the table uses LFS. By sub period the first column corresponds to the change in the share of private sector employment by occupation, the second and the third are computed using a shift share analysis (Goos and Manning 2007)

Overall, as opposed to evidence from other countries (Goos and Manning 2007), it appears that changes across sectors, potentially due to the housing boom, might have partially contributed to explain the polarization process in Spain especially during the period of expansion (1997–2007). Nevertheless, when considering the whole cycle (1997–2012), sector reallocation is less important in explaining the polarization process in Spain. We need an alternative explanation that could help us understand the polarization process from the point of view of technological changes within industries, especially for the crisis.

3.2.3 Is job polarization explained by the routinization process?

Autor et al. (2003) and more recently Acemoglu and Autor (2011) generalize the so-called canonical model for the labour market which includes two-skill groups of workers (high and low) who work in imperfectly substitutable occupations. Technology takes a factor-augmenting form, and thus may complement either high or low skill workers. Skill biased technical change is captured by changes in the factor-augmenting technology. The canonical model has proved to be conceptually tractable and empirically quite successful. However, it does not include a meaningful role for "tasks", or more precisely, impose a one-to-one mapping between skills and tasks.

Acemoglu and Autor (2011) distinguish very clearly the concept of task from that of skill. The latter is a worker's endowment of capabilities to perform different tasks, whereas a unit of task is a unit of work activity which produces output. This distinction is essential if we believe that workers of a given skill level can perform different tasks and furthermore, can change the combination of tasks they perform in response to changes in labour market conditions and technology. These authors develop a task assignment model where it is assumed that there is a continuum of tasks which together produce a final good.

Intuitively, each worker is endowed with either one of the following three types of skills—high, medium or low. Differences in comparative advantage among workers to perform different tasks together with the market prices of different tasks as well as wages for different skills, lead workers to endogenously decide the optimal allocation of skills to tasks. And in equilibrium, Acemoglu and Autor (2011) formally derive that the least complex set of tasks are supplied by the low-skilled workers, the intermediate set of tasks by the medium-skilled workers and finally the most complex tasks will be provided by the high-skilled workers.

One of the most attractive features of this model is that it can be used to investigate the implications of technological changes on worker displacement from previously performed tasks. In particular, routine tasks, which are mostly performed by medium-skilled workers, are those most subject to machine displacement, and therefore task-replacing technological changes can directly reduce wages of the medium-skilled group independent of changes in total output. As these workers lose comparative advantage in routine-intensive activities, they must be reallocated either to the highest or the lowest tails of the occupational distribution, leading to employment polarization.

Testing this theory requires matching occupations with particular job content measures. To this end, two American databases have been used in the literature: The version of the ONET database we use contains 96 variables which reveal the intensity of particular job contents. From these variables, Peri and Sparber (2009), Goos et al. (2010) and Amuedo and De la Rica (2011), make the next aggregation (by either computing the average or a principal component exercise) into abstract, routine and service contents and then match these tasks to 2 or 3-digit occupations. Instead of using the ONET database, one could use the DOT database as in Autor and Dorn (2013). As Autor (2013) argues, with either data sources, job content measures are often vague and are constructed using scales which may confuse respondents. DOT was first issued in 1939 and last revised in 1991. At the time of the last revision, DOT contained 44 objective and subjective job content measures. By 1998, DOT was replaced by ONET, which has been revised several times since then and the number of job content measures has increased substantially. With so many job content measures, researchers who need to use either of these databases must pick and choose among a large number of job content measures. We have decided to use the ONET dataset because it is a more recent one, it has been used to test for routinization in Europe (by Goos et al. 2010),[2] and in our view it is better suited to explicitly account for the degree of non-routine service content of each occupation.[3] The detailed description of the match between occupations and job contents can be found in the "Appendix".

Table 3 presents the abovementioned job contents for the 7 broad occupational groups used in Sect. 2, and as one might expect, high-skilled occupations, such as managers, professionals have the highest abstract and the lowest routine content. Rather, occupations such as production and craft or machine operators display the highest routine and the lowest service and abstract content.

Table 3. Intensity of different tasks by broad occupational categories

Occupational groups	Abstract intensity	Routine intensity	Service intensity
Managers/prof/tecn	0.39	0.26	0.35
Clerical/civil servants	0.28	0.33	0.38
Retail sale/service occup.	0.24	0.38	0.38
Qualified workers in agric./fish	0.30	0.49	0.21
Production/craft, non-constr.	0.27	0.57	0.16
Machine operators/assemblers	0.26	0.51	0.24
Low-skilled service workers	0.17	0.58	0.25

The intensities of the three tasks for each occupation sum up to one. They are relative task intensities

In order to check whether there is a correlation between changes in the employment shares by occupations and task intensities, we regress (separately) changes in the share of employment by occupation (3-digit ISCO88 occupations) on the following measures of job contents: (i) abstract intensity, (ii) service intensity and (iii) routine intensity. In addition, following (Goos et al. (2010), tables 6A, 6B and 7) and Autor and Dorn (2013), we also use a routinization index in a separate regression, which combines the previous three measures to create an index of routine task-intensity by occupation, which is defined as follows:

$$Routinization\ Index = Log(Routine\ Intensity) - log(Abstract\ Intensity) \\ -log(Service\ Intensity).$$

This index increases with the rise of routine intensity and declines with the rise of abstract and service intensity.

Table 4 presents the results of these estimations. The dependent variable is the change in the share of employment for each 3-digit ISCO88 occupation. We perform the estimations for the whole 15-year interval (1997–2012) and for the expansionary period (1997–2007). In the table, each coefficient is the result of a different OLS regression.

Table 4. The effect of task intensities on changes in share of employment

Independent variables	(1) 1997–2012	(2) 1997–2007	(3) Interacting effects
Abstract intensity	−0.446	−2.551	−2.551
	(3.599)	(2.851)	(2.855)
Abstract intensity* dummy period (2012–2007)			3.148
			(3.757)
Routine intensity	−1.850	1.733	1.733
	(1.582)	(1.838)	(1.840)
Routine intensity* dummy period (2012–2007)			−5.780**
			(2.586)
Service intensity	3.601**	−1.743	−1.743
	(1.549)	(2.381)	(2.384)
Service intensity* dummy period (2012–2007)			8.590***
			(3.199)
Routinization index	0.293	−0.290	0.250
	(0.296)	(0.250)	(0.181)
Routinization index* dummy period (2012–2007)			−0.908***
			(0.334)
Observations	70	86	156

Dependent variable: change in share of employment (% points)
Each coefficient corresponds to a separate OLS regression of the dependent variable on the control variables and a constant. Robust standard errors in parentheses. *** Significant at 1 % level, ** significant at 5 % level, * significant at 10 % level. Number of observations is the number of occupations at ISCO88 3 digits level. These estimations include also period time dummies not reported here. All estimations are weighted by the weight of employment of each ISCO88 3 digits occupation in total employment

Results suggest that when using the Routinization Index as the regressor, there seems to be a negative impact of the index on the change in the share of employment; this is only significant for the recession period. When separating out the different task intensities, there is no significant correlation between the change in the share of employment and the "Abstract Intensity" of occupations. This is true when considering the whole 15-year interval jointly and for separate regressions in each period. On the other hand, "Routine Intensity" of occupations exhibits a clearly negative correlation with the change in the share of employment in the recession period. Finally, "Non-routine Service Intensity" of occupations is positively and significantly correlated with the change in the share of employment. As before, the impact is particularly strong in the recession period.

In this regard, the evidence above shows that during the expansion period there was polarization but the routinization theory does not hold. This is consistent with results in the previous section that showed that polarization mainly came via a reallocation of sectors. Indeed, it is likely that the big expansion of the Spanish labour force coupled with the construction boom delayed the rapid mechanization of certain routine occupations that occurred in other countries in the pre-crisis period. During these years, there was a notable increase in the share of low-skilled service occupations, such as personal services and workers in restaurants and hotels, but also in the share of low-skilled routine tasks such as cleaners of buildings. On the other hand, middle-skilled occupations with higher routine content, high-skilled service occupations (such as professional services) and occupations requiring abstract tasks (support in the financial sector and administration) also increased their share, although at a slower pace. During the recession, however, it appears that there is a clear decrease in the share of the routine occupations that could easily be mechanized (especially related to the construction bust and the industry decline). This is compensated by non-routine services that move upward both low-paid (cleaners and personal services), and high-paid occupations (managers and professional services related to the service sectors as observed in Sect. 2). Instead, abstract tasks do not appear to increase their share during these 15 years.

4 THE EFFECT OF POLARIZATION FOR PARTICULAR DEMOGRAPHIC GROUPS

This section introduces the link developed by Autor and Dorn (2009) with regards to the implication of the routinization theory for the change in the distribution of employment by age. Routinization implies the displacement of occupations which are intensive in routine tasks to occupations more intensive in non-routine (service or abstract) job contents. This non-neutral occupational change may change the age composition of occupations if there are different incentives and/or abilities of workers to enter/exit from rising/declining occupations at different stages of their life cycle. In their paper, they find that older workers, regardless of their skills, moved from routine to non-routine low-skilled jobs, whereas the displacement of young workers from routine jobs increased the share of both low-skilled non-routine jobs and high-skilled abstract jobs.

In this fourth section, we look specifically at employed workers and analyze how their age structure changes in rising and declining occupations. To this end, we follow Autor and Dorn (2009) and estimate changes in the age composition of workers in each occupation for each of the intervals considered before, according to the three different job contents, as well as the routinization index. We do this separately by gender.

However, before looking at changes in the age structure in declining and expanding occupations over time, the distribution of males and females across occupations by age at the initial period deserves some attention. As Table 1 indicates, by 1997, males were overrepresented in declining occupations with respect to females. The percentage of young females in managerial and service occupations (52 %) was much higher in 1997 than the corresponding percentage for males (29 %). Interestingly, although not reported, at a further occupational disaggregation—at a 2-digit level, young males in managerial/technical/professional occupations are overwhelmingly concentrated in jobs such as chemistry/physics technicians, engineers or professionals in finance and trade, all of which are very intensive in abstract contents. On the contrary, their female counterparts are concentrated in occupations such as teaching professionals, health professionals and administrative associate professionals, which require more service intensive tasks. With respect to non-managerial/technical/professional jobs, young males are scattered along production occupations, low-skilled occupations (especially industry and construction pawns), machine operators and, to a lesser extent, retail and sales. All these occupations use quite intensively routine tasks. However, young females in non-managerial/technical/professional occupations are distributed among clerical, retail and sales occupations and, to a lesser extent, among low-skilled service occupations—in particular in personal services. All these occupations primarily require service rather than abstract or routine tasks.

Given this, if we think about the impact of polarization on the reallocation of males and females across job contents, we would expect a change in the distribution of tasks of young males as a consequence of the decrease in the demand for routine tasks and an increase of abstract and service tasks. Something similar would occur with older males given that they are over represented in routine occupations related to machine operators and production and craft. However, for male workers between 31 and 45 years of age in 2012, cohort effects must be taken into account when interpreting the changes over time, since in 1997 these workers belonged to the youngest group. These cohort effects are not expected to be important when analyzing the group of male workers over 45 years old since the distribution of occupations in 1997 was similar to the one of middle aged workers. With respect to female reallocation, we would not expect much change in task performance as a result of the polarization process since by 1997 females seemed to be very concentrated in occupations which did not require routine intensive tasks. These issues must be taken into account when interpreting the results.

In order to account for the changes in the age composition, we use two different measures: the change in the mean age of each occupation and the change in the share of workers in each occupation (i) less than 30 years old, (ii) between 31 and 45 years old, and (iii) more than 45 years old.

According to the regressions where average age is the dependent variable (Table 5), we observe that workers in occupations with more abstract content are becoming younger, as average age decreases. This is particularly so in the expansionary period. For the recession period, given the mass layoffs of younger workers with temporary contracts, this phenomenon is not observed. However, the recession does not overcome the effect of the expansionary periods and, taking into account the whole cycle (1997–2012), workers in abstract occupations also become younger. By gender, it appears that only for males do we observe the decrease in average age in occupations with more abstract content over the whole cycle. There is also a decrease in average age of females in abstract occupations in the expansionary period, but this is reversed in the recession. For the overall period, no significant change in average age is found for females.

In occupations with more routine content, we observe a slight aging of workers, as average age seems to increase. The effects by sub-periods are only marginally significant, but when the whole 15-year period is considered, we see a positive and stronger effect. When we disaggregate this by gender, we observe that if anything, the effect is driven by males, as we observed in occupations with higher abstract content.

Table 5. The effect of task intensities on changes in average age

	All			Males			Females		
	(1)	(2)	(3)	(1)	(2)	(3)	(1)	(2)	(3)
Independent variables	1997–2012	1997–2007	With time interactions	1997–2012	1997–2007	With time interactions	1997–2012	1997–2007	With time interactions
Abstract intensity	−8.713**	−11.025***	−11.025***	−6.900**	−10.513***	−10.513***	−3.049	−7.232**	−7.232**
	(3.410)	(2.561)	(2.564)	(3.454)	(3.150)	(3.153)	(4.159)	(3.466)	(3.471)
Abstract intensity* dummy period (2012–2007)			12.357***			13.285***			10.619**
			(3.234)			(3.889)			(4.483)
Routine intensity	5.149***	2.987	2.987	3.373**	0.989	0.989	4.679	3.055	3.055
	(1.739)	(1.963)	(1.965)	(1.452)	(1.751)	(1.753)	(3.324)	(2.551)	(2.555)
Routine intensity* dummy period (2012–2007)			−0.665			1.476			−2.372
			(2.463)			(2.487)			(3.734)
Service intensity	−4.673*	0.322	0.322	−2.420	3.553	3.553	−6.856	−1.684	−1.684
	(2.437)	(2.495)	(2.498)	(2.443)	(2.259)	(2.262)	(5.651)	(3.833)	(3.838)
Service intensity* dummy period (2012–2007)			−5.350*			−9.779***			−1.787
			(2.968)			(2.977)			(6.057)

Dependent variable: change in average age

Each coefficient corresponds to a separate OLS regression of the dependent variable on the control variables and a constant. Robust standard errors in parentheses. *** Significant at 1 % level, ** significant at 5 % level, * significant at 10 % level. Number of observations is the number of occupations at ISCO88 3 digits level. These estimations include also period time dummies not reported here. All estimations are weighted by the weight of employment of each ISCO88 3 digits occupation in total employment

In occupations with more non-routine service content, we observe a very similar feature to the one observed for occupations with abstract contents, but the effect seems to be smaller, namely, those workers in occupations with more service content are becoming younger. In this case, and differently from what happened with occupations with more abstract content, the effect is found to be significant in the recession period. As in the previous two cases, the effect is stronger for males. Indeed, for females the effect is not significant.

Regressions of the change in the share of workers by age provide more information on which age groups of workers are driving the previous results. Table 6 shows a process of rejuvenation motivated by an increase in the share of workers between 16 and 30 years old in occupations with more abstract and service contents. The former, which is especially intense, occurs during the expansion and the latter during the recession years. On the other hand, a clear aging effect is observed for occupations with more routine content. Again, there is no statistical effect for occupations with more abstract content.

Table 6. The effect of task intensities on changes in share of employment in 16–30 years age group

	All			Males			Females		
	(1)	(2)	(3)	(1)	(2)	(3)	(1)	(2)	(3)
Independent variables	1997–2012	1997–2007	With time interactions	1997–2012	1997–2007	With time interactions	1997–2012	1997–2007	With time interactions
Abstract intensity	37.053***	32.150***	32.150***	49.359***	44.199***	44.199***	7.538	−0.761	−0.761
	(13.785)	(10.192)	(10.207)	(9.579)	(11.120)	(11.134)	(17.837)	(12.673)	(12.692)
Abstract intensity* dummy period (2012–2007)			−28.936**			−42.819***			0.519
			(13.626)			(15.185)			(16.772)
Routine intensity	−21.590***	−4.450	−4.450	−27.413***	−5.172	−5.172	−11.402	−0.778	−0.778
	(7.019)	(6.846)	(6.855)	(5.042)	(7.052)	(7.061)	(14.514)	(11.839)	(11.856)
Routine intensity* dummy period (2012–2007)			−13.561			−17.179*			−5.097
			(10.003)			(10.241)			(18.598)
Service intensity	19.269	−8.376	−8.376	23.227**	−13.168	−13.168	16.620	1.764	1.764
	(11.633)	(8.931)	(8.943)	(10.391)	(8.270)	(8.280)	(24.724)	(20.720)	(20.751)
Service intensity* dummy period (2012–2007)			38.470***			52.225***			8.792
			(12.082)			(10.691)			(31.839)

Dep. variable: Change in share of workers in 16–30 years age group (% points)

Each coefficient corresponds to a separate OLS regression of the dependent variable on the control variables and a constant. Robust standard errors in parentheses. *** Significant at 1 % level, ** significant at 5 % level, * significant at 10 % level. Number of observations is the number of occupations at ISCO88 3 digits level. In the estimations for the pool of periods 1997–2007 and 2007–2012, period 1997–2007 is the reference period. These estimations include also period time dummies not reported here. All estimations are weighted by the weight of employment of each ISCO88 3 digits occupation in total employment

Table 7 indicates that the share of middle-aged workers in routine tasks has increased substantially with the corresponding decrease in the share of occupations with both abstract and service content. This is consistent with the hypothesis that cohort effects are playing a role. This is not observed for females (indeed the point estimate corroborates a decrease in occupations of routine content).

Table 7. The effect of task intensities on changes in share of employment in 31–45 years age group

	(1)	(2)	(3)	(1)	(2)	(3)	(1)	(2)	(3)
Independent variables	1997–2012	1997–2007	With time interactions	1997–2012	1997–2007	With time interactions	1997–2012	1997–2007	With time interactions
Abstract intensity	−27.423	−15.176*	−15.176*	−42.406**	−36.823***	−36.823***	−5.208	6.797	6.797
	(18.216)	(8.379)	(8.389)	(16.772)	(11.691)	(11.705)	(19.316)	(9.997)	(10.008)
Abstract intensity* dummy period (2012–2007)			11.957			41.759**			−8.324
			(14.588)			(18.796)			(20.452)
Routine intensity	14.413	0.806	0.806	26.632***	11.009*	11.009*	−1.716	−14.035	−14.035
	(9.910)	(4.530)	(4.536)	(8.986)	(6.489)	(6.497)	(16.463)	(9.704)	(9.715)
Routine intensity* dummy period (2012–2007)			11.384			3.945			25.859
			(9.238)			(10.925)			(17.153)
Service intensity	−11.447	6.212	6.212	−25.595*	−0.722	−0.722	5.919	21.267	21.267
	(14.517)	(5.008)	(5.014)	(13.999)	(6.499)	(6.507)	(26.248)	(16.550)	(16.568)
Service intensity* dummy period (2012–2007)			−25.903**			−29.258**			−41.498
			(11.326)			(11.499)			(25.863)

Dep. variable: change in share of workers in 31–45 years age group (% points)

Each coefficient corresponds to a separate OLS regression of the dependent variable on the control variables and a constant. Robust standard errors in parentheses. *** Significant at 1 % level, ** significant at 5 % level, * significant at 10 % level. Number of observations is the number of occupations at ISCO88 3 digits level. In the estimations for the pool of periods 1997–2007 and 2007–2012, period 1997–2007 is the reference period. These estimations include also period time dummies not reported here. All estimations are weighted by the weight of employment of each ISCO88 3 digits occupation in total employment

Table 8 provides evidence for older workers. This group should not be affected as much by cohort effects. The evidence points towards a group of workers who are stuck in routine tasks. This could be the case because of high firing costs for those over 45 years old, as most of them hold indefinite contracts. Again, females do not show any relevant effect. If any, there is a slight increase of female incidence in occupations which require more service intensive contents throughout the crisis. We must look at these results with caution. Further research is needed to disentangle cohort effects properly from the reallocation of particular groups of workers.

Table 8. The effect of task intensities on changes in share of employment in 46–64 years age group

	(1)	(2)	(3)	(1)	(2)	(3)	(1)	(2)	(3)
Routinization index	2.39*	0.116	0.116	4.225**	1.662*	1.662	−0.074	−2.198	−2.198
	(1.547)	(0.691)	(0.698)	(1.378)	(1.011)	(1.012)	(2.612)	(1.500)	(1.502)
Routinization index* dummy period (2012–2007)			1.923			0.799			4.210*
			(1.459)			(1.689)			(2.708)
Observations	70	86	156	70	86	156	65	78	144

Dep. variable: change in share of workers in 31–45 years age group (% points)

Each coefficient corresponds to a separate OLS regression of the dependent variable on the control variables and a constant. Robust standard errors in parentheses. *** Significant at 1% level, ** significant at 5% level. * significant at 10% level. Number of observations is the number of occupations at ISCO88 3 digits level. In the estimations for the pool of periods 1997–2007 and 2007–2012, period 1997–2007 is the reference period. These estimations include also period time dummies not reported here. All estimations are weighted by the weight of employment of each ISCO88 3 digits occupation in total employment

To summarize, the observed polarization process over the 15-year period under analysis seems to have reallocated young male workers from occupations with more routine tasks to others with more abstract and non-routine service content.[4] Young female workers who were already performing occupations with a high service content are not affected by this technological change. The fact that they are not working in abstract tasks is quite stunning and should be addressed carefully in further research. Instead, it looks like male workers over 30 are the ones who have stayed in the declining occupations more, especially those over 45. It is likely that this is the case because of the high severance payments that they have acquired during their lifetime.

5 CONCLUSIONS

This article analyzes changes in the employment share of occupations in Spain for the period 1997–2012 and the way particular sociodemographic groups adapt to them. We analyzed a whole cycle in order to find structural factors underlying such changes but we addressed the extent to which these occupational changes differed during the expansion and the recession years.

On the first hand, we addressed whether Spanish occupations experienced a process of polarization. That is, whether those occupations at the low and high end of the wage distribution expanded relative to the rest. We found clear evidence of polarization, both for the expansionary and for the recession period as well as for the whole 15-year interval. Nevertheless, there is a distinct pattern of polarization between 1997 and 2007 and the recession period. During the first 10 years and coinciding with the expansionary period, low-paying occupations expanded in employment terms relative to average-paying occupations but also with respect to high-paying occupations.

Next, we tested whether these changes follow from hypotheses such as changes in the composition of the labour supply or changes in sector allocation. We showed that changes in the composition of the labour force would have increased the share of occupations placed at the upper end of the wage distribution instead of the observed polarization process. During the recession, compositional changes, if anything, might have contributed even more to the expansion of occupations at the upper part of the wage distribution. Therefore, supply side changes cannot explain the increase in the share of occupations at the low end of the wage distribution. Regarding sector reallocation, we performed a shift share analysis of the changes to conclude that overall changes across sectors, potentially due to the housing boom, might have partially contributed to explain the polarization process in Spain especially during the period of expansion (1997–2007). Nevertheless, when considering the whole cycle (1997–2012), within sector changes are the major factor behind the observed occupational changes.

We then explored whether polarization arises as a result of a decrease in occupations which are intensive in routine contents. In this regard, we found that the observed polarization is indeed consistent with a decrease in occupations intensive in routine content and an increase in those intensive in non-routine services which are found both at the low and high end of the wage distribution. Instead, occupations with higher abstract tasks do not appear to have expanded during these 15 years.

Needless to say, these changes in the employment composition are not homogeneous across different sociodemographic groups. The paper finds that the observed decrease in routine occupations over the 15 years under analysis seems to have affected males more strongly than females as a result of their higher concentration in occupations which are intensive in routine tasks. Indeed, for male workers, the share of the unemployed in the population has increased notably, regardless of the age group. Young male workers decrease their share in occupations with more routine tasks and increase it in occupations with more abstract and, in particular, with more non-routine service content. Rather, male workers over 30 years of age tend to stay in the declining occupations. Females, given that they were not allocated to routine tasks during the expansionary period, are not affected as much by these changes, probably due to the fact that they were already more specialized in jobs with high service content.

FOOTNOTES

[1]When considering the whole cycle (between 1994 and 2012), the increase in aggregate unemployment is lower. During these years, the decrease in the inactive population (6.9 pp) was mainly absorbed by increases in employment (5.1 pp) and unemployment as a share of total population only grew by 1.8 pp. However, its concentration on particular sociodemographic groups is the same as in the period 1997–2012.

[2]In a more recent version of the Goos et al. (2010) paper, (see Goos et al. 2014), the authors use DOT measures instead of ONET ones and their results are almost the same.

[3]As a robustness check, we have used an alternative definition of routine-intensive jobs—only those whose content relate to Operation Monitoring and Operation and Control as Autor and Dorn (2013). The rest of job contents previously assigned as routine intensive by Goos et al. (2010) have been left aside (in their classification they also consider arm-hand steadiness, manual dexterity, finger dexterity and strength as routine job contents). Given that abstract, routine and service tasks are in relative terms, each of the measures has been redefined with respect to this alternative routine task measure. Results, although not reported and available upon request, are qualitatively identical to the ones found in the previous section, which suggests that the particular definition of routine-intensive tasks used in this paper is robust to alternative definitions of routine tasks used in other studies.

[4]We must not overcome the fact that young males have been hit by unemployment to a greater extent than their young female counterparts and than older males. Therefore, when we refer to reallocation of young males we restrict attention to employment shares, and to some extent ignore compositional changes due to exits from employment into unemployment.

[5]For the rest of the section on polarization, we will use the 3-digit ISCO-88 classification.

[6]In general, statistical significance of the regressions of females is low compared to that of males, but the signs coincide.

[7]They use version 11.0 of the survey, available at: http://www.onetcenter.org/.

[8]The *ONet* rates the importance of 99 job characteristics, including employee skills and employee activities—to which we refer to as task requirements or tasks in this paper—in each occupation in the Standard Occupation Classification (SOC). This information is continually updated by surveying a broad range of workers from each occupation in the US.

[9]See http://www.onetcenter.org/dl_files/paw/Products_at_Work.pdf for a summary of its many applications outside the US.

APPENDIX: OCCUPATIONS AND MEASURES OF JOB CONTENTS

To match occupations with particular job contents we rely on information on job task requirements assembled by Peri and Sparber (2009) for the US, Goos et al. (2010) for different European countries, and Amuedo and De la Rica (2011) for Spain, among others. The starting point is to merge data on job contents (or task requirements) based on the US Department of Labor's ONet survey[5] with Census occupation classifications to examine task specialization patterns of workers. ONet is a primary source of occupational information providing data on key attributes and characteristics of occupations. It replaces the Dictionary of Occupational Titles (DOT), which was used for earlier research, prominently by Autor et al. (2003). ONet data is collected for 812 occupations based on the 2000 Standard Occupational Code (SOC).

Through the development of careful crosswalks with the International Standard Classification of Occupations from 1988 at 3-digits level (ISCO88), ONet data has been increasingly used by a large number of researchers and institutions outside the United States.[6] We merge the ONet job skill data with the Spanish Labor Force Survey with occupations disaggregated at 3-digits level.[7] Like previous authors using the ONet dataset with European data,[8] we do so under the assumption that the occupations in the US and in Spain being examined herein are not that different with regards to the specified job contents.

ONet consists of around 100 variables related to the intensity of different job activities and abilities for each occupation. The original values range from 1 (very low intensity) to 5 (very high intensity). For comparability reasons, we use exactly the same variables as in Goos et al. (2010) to construct the job content measures we use for the analysis. Specifically, we make use of 96 of these variables and each of them is categorized into one of the following job contents: Abstract, Routine and non-Routine Service.

To give a broad idea of what type of content is included in each of the three measures, "Abstract Intensity" measures the extent to which each occupation entails activities such as: active learning, learning strategies, management of personal resources, management of material resources, deductive reasoning, speech clarity, complex problem solving, etc. "Routine Intensity" measures the extent to which each occupations entails activities such as: operation monitoring, operation and control, quality control analysis, arm-hand steadiness, manual and finger dexterity. Finally, "Non-Routine Service Intensity" measures the extent to which each occupation entails activities such as: assisting and caring for others, establishing and maintaining interpersonal relationships, selling and influencing others, active listening. The exact definition of each job content is detailed in (Goos et al. (2010), Table C1 (pp: 73)).

In order to construct the final measure of intensity in each of the described job contents, we must realize that the standard deviation varies to a great extent depending on the skill under consideration. This problem is also detected and accounted for by Peri and Sparber (2009), who tackle it by transforming the ONet job skill data to reflect the relative importance of each skill among all US workers in 2000. Like them, we transform the original job content data to reflect the relative importance of each skill among all workers in Spain during the time period under examination.

As in Peri and Sparber (2009), the final measures of Abstract, Routine and Non-Routine Service Job Contents are the weighted averages of the intensity of the activities included under each of the three measures.[9] In addition, given that our aim is to provide relative measures of intensity of abstract, routine and non-routine service job contents for each occupation, we normalize the intensity of each of these three job contents within occupations so that the sum of the intensities of the three of them is 1.

Table 2 displays the Abstract, Routine and Non-Routine Service Job Content values for each of the eight big occupational groups. This allows us to gauge the suitability of the ONet data in describing the distinct job content of the main Spanish occupational categories. As expected, high skill occupations, such as technical and professional occupations display a higher value of Abstract Content and a smaller value of Routine Content. The contrary is observed for low skill occupations, such as machine assemblers and low-qualified service occupations. With regards to the intensity of non-routine service jobs, higher values are observed for occupations at the two tails of the skill distribution.

REFERENCES

1. Acemoglu D, Autor DH (2011) Skills, tasks and technologies: implications for employment and earnings. In: Ashenfelter O, Card DE (eds) Handbook of labor economics, vol 4. Amsterdam, Elsevier
2. Amuedo C, De la Rica S (2011) Complements or substitutes: task specialization by gender and nativity in Spain. Labour Econ 18(5):697–707
3. Autor D (2013) The “task approach” to labor markets: an overview. J Labour Mark Res 1–15
4. Autor D, Dorn D (2009) This job is “Getting Old”: measuring changes in job opportunities using occupational age structure. Am Econ Rev Pap Proc 99(2):45–51
5. Autor D, Dorn D (2013) The growth of low-skill service jobs and the polarization of the U.S. Labor Market. Am Econ Rev 103(5):1553–1597
6. Autor D, Levy F, Murnane R (2003) The skill content of recent technological change: an empirical investigation. Q J Econ 118(4):1279–1333
7. Autor D, Katz L, Kearney M (2006) The polarization of the U.S. Labor Market. Am Econ Rev 96(2):189–194
8. Carrasco R, Jimeno JF, Ortega C (2012) Accounting for changes in the Spanish wage distribution: the role of employment composition effects. Banco de España Working papers 1120
9. Gavilán Á (2012) Wage inequality, segregation by skill and the price of capital in an assignment model. Eur Econ Rev 56(1):116–137

10. Goos M, Manning A (2007) Lousy and lovely jobs: the rising polarization of work in Britain. Rev Econ Stat 89(1):118–133

11. Goos M, Manning A, Salomons A (2009) Job polarization in Europe. Am Econ Rev Pap Proc 99(2):58–63

12. Goos M, Manning A, Salomons A (2010) Explaining job polarization in Europe: the roles of technology, globalization and institutions. CEP Discussion Paper No 1026, November

13. Goos M, Manning A, Salomon A (2014) Explaining job polarization: routine-biased technological change and offshoring. Am Econ Rev (forthcoming)

14. Izquierdo M, Lacuesta A (2012) The contribution of changes in employment composition and relative returns to the evolution of wage inequality: the case of Spain. J Popul Econ 25(2):511–543

15. Jamovich N, Siu HE (2012) The trend is the cycle: job polarization and jobless recoveries. NBER Working Paper 18334

16. Ljungqvist L, Sargent T (1998) The European unemployment dilemma. J Political Econ 106(3):514–550

17. Peri G, Sparber C (2009) Task specialization, immigration, and wages. Am Econ J Appl Econ 1(3):135–169

18. Wasmer E (2006) Interpreting Europe-US labor market differences: the specificity of human capital investments. Am Econ Rev 96(3):811–831

5
CHAPTER

The Great Recession, Unemployment and Suicide

Thor Norström, Hans Grönqvist

Swedish Institute for Social Research, Stockholm University, Stockholm, Sweden

ABSTRACT

Background How have suicide rates responded to the marked increase in unemployment spurred by the Great Recession? Our paper puts this issue into a wider perspective by assessing (1) whether the unemployment-suicide link is modified by the degree of unemployment protection, and (2) whether the effect on suicide of the present crisis differs from the effects of previous economic downturns.

Methods We analysed the unemployment-suicide link using time-series data for 30 countries spanning the period 1960–2012. Separate fixed-effects models were estimated for each of five welfare state regimes with different levels of unemployment protection (Eastern, Southern, Anglo-Saxon, Bismarckian and Scandinavian). We included an interaction term to capture the possible excess effect of unemployment during the Great Recession.

Results The largest unemployment increases occurred in the welfare state regimes with the least generous unemployment protection. The unemployment effect on male suicides was statistically significant in all welfare regimes, except the Scandinavian one. The effect on female suicides was significant only in the eastern European country group. There was a significant gradient in the effects, being stronger the less generous the unemployment protection. The interaction term capturing the possible excess effect of unemployment during the financial crisis was not significant.

Conclusions Our findings suggest that the more generous the unemployment protection the weaker the detrimental impact on suicide of the increasing unemployment during the Great Recession.

INTRODUCTION

Unemployment is a well-established risk factor of suicide, as indicated by studies at micro, as well as macro level.1 An urgent research question is thus to assess how suicide rates have responded to the marked increase in unemployment spurred by the Great Recession, considered to be the deepest global economic downturn since World War II. Marked suicide increases that seem to be linked to increasing unemployment have been reported for a large number of countries.2–5 However, the fragmentary character of these findings hampers any more general conclusions. To put the current crisis into a wider perspective, it seems feasible to consider a time period that is long enough to include previous economic downturns. Further, it can be expected that the impact of unemployment on population mental health is modified by the degree of unemployment protection offered by the social welfare system. The aim of the present paper is thus to address the topic at issue in a more encompassing manner by analysing time-series data spanning the period 1960–2012 for 30 countries which represent a wide spectrum of welfare regimes.

UNEMPLOYMENT AND SUICIDE

Job loss has several tangible and negative consequences that may adversely affect mental health. For instance, to lose one's job means that steady routines structuring everyday life dissipate, that social workplace relations vanish, and that the private economy becomes strained. It is therefore not surprising that unemployment is a well-established risk factor of suicide. Several prospective studies have thus documented an increased risk of suicide among those who become unemployed.6 ,7 The reported relative risk is typically in the range 2–38–10However, these estimates are probably inflated as unemployed people are likely to be selected on factors conducive to suicide; for example, depression increases the risk of both suicide and to become unemployed.11–13 An alternative strategy that should alleviate this problem is to analyse time-series data on the population level, that is, to look at how changes in the unemployment rate affect the suicide rate. Depression may increase the risk of unemployment at the individual level, but is less likely to do so at the aggregate level. It is worthy to note that analyses at the population level capture also the possible detrimental impact of unemployment on those who remain in unemployment, but fear losing their jobs (see1 and14 for more detailed discussions of differences between using micro and macro data in this context). Several aggregate level time-series studies report a significant relation between unemployment and suicide. The early studies in this tradition mostly rely on trend analyses (for reviews, see Platt6and Stack7) which compromises the validity of the findings. However, positive findings are also reported by researchers applying fixed-effects modelling of time-series data pertaining to a set of European countries,15 and to the US states.16 ,17

IS THE EFFECT OF UNEMPLOYMENT ON SUICIDE UNIFORM ACROSS TIME AND SPACE?

Welfare state regimes

In her review of the literature, Bartley18 identifies poverty and financial anxiety as especially important mechanisms linking unemployment to increased suicide risk (similar conclusions are drawn by Hamermesh and Soss19). This suggests a potentially modifying effect of a generous welfare system that can provide a safety net in precarious situations and mitigate the adverse effect of a job loss. The hypothesis that the health effect of economic downturns is contingent on the generosity of the social welfare system receives support from the few studies that have addressed this topic. Thus Stuckler *et al*,15 on the basis of time-series data for 26 European Union (EU) countries between 1970 and 2007, found that the unemployment effect on suicide was lower in countries with high labour market security, proxied by government spending on labour market programmes. Similar findings are reported on the basis of US state data.20Further, in their analyses of time-series data for 23 Organisation for Economic Co-operation and Development (OECD) countries for the period 1960–1997, Gerdtham and Ruhm21 found a modifying impact of social insurance spending on the association between unemployment and total mortality. However, the approach of using data on government expenditure on welfare provisions has some well-known limitations; social spending is in itself heavily influenced by structural changes reflecting business cycles, demographic trends or labour market transformation.[22] We will instead rely on an alternative approach that classifies welfare states on the basis of the content and nature of social citizenship rights, as indicated by legislated social insurance replacement rates. More specifically, we will apply a scheme that has been developed within comparative population health research,[23–25] and that has been used in comparative analyses of the association between unemployment and health.[23] In this scheme the countries are classified into five welfare state regimes, ranked from low (1) to high (5) levels of social and financial protection during unemployment: (1) Eastern European countries; (2) Southern European countries; (3) Anglo-Saxon countries; (4) Bismarckian; and (5) Scandinavian countries (see table 1). The ranking is based on the generosity of the unemployment protection system as indicated by four indicators: 'the generosity of benefits paid to the unemployed (replacement rates), the qualifying period and conditions, duration of benefit payments and the waiting period before entitlement is activated'.[23] The highest replacement rates (the most important indicator)[26] are thus found in the Scandinavian and Bismarckian countries, the lowest in the eastern and southern European countries, with the Anglo-Saxon countries in between (table 1).

Is the Great Recession worse than previous economic downturns?

An interesting research question is whether or not the effect on mental health of the present crisis differs from the effects of previous economic downturns. One hypothesis is that losing one's job would be particularly harmful when the national economy is seriously weakened. First, the poor prospects of finding a new job should bolster the feelings of hopelessness. Second, the austerities that have been implemented in several countries due to the recession have limited the access to social services and medical treatment.[27] As an alternative hypothesis it can be argued that a job loss be felt as less stigmatising when this situation is shared by many others in society.

Table 1. Descriptive statistics (period averages) for unemployment replacement rate, unemployment, male suicide rate per 100 000 (20–64 years), and female suicide rate per 100 000 (20–64 years)

	Observation period	Unemployment replacement rate* (%)	Unemployment (%)	Suicide rate per 100 000 (20–64 years)†	
				Females	Males
Eastern European countries					
Bulgaria	1990–2012		11.61	6.42	19.26
Croatia	1991–2012		12.93	9.31	32.73
Czech Republic	1993–2012		6.46	9.54	35.11
Estonia	1990–2012		8.86	11.00	61.80
Hungary	1992–2012		8.53	17.70	60.59
Latvia	1992–2012		11.68	11.31	64.02
Lithuania	1994–2010		12.91	14.08	88.94
Poland	1992–2011		13.36	5.25	31.14
Romania	1990–2011		7.45	4.62	25.60
Slovakia	1994–2010		14.49	4.06	27.78
Slovenia	1996–2010		6.61	12.62	51.61
Period average		56.10	10.45	9.92	44.64
Southern European countries					
Greece	1983–2010		9.83	1.95	6.01
Italy	1960–2010		8.31	3.76	10.35
Portugal	1974–2011		6.62	4.23	14.92
Spain	1972–2011		14.30	3.11	10.21
Period average		55.11	9.69	3.27	10.39
Anglo-Saxon countries					
Australia	1960–2011		5.45	9.01	25.16
Canada	1960–2009		7.53	7.99	25.1
Ireland	1960–2010		9.15	4.76	16.81
UK	1960–2010		5.79	6.17	14.84
USA	1960–2010		6.08	7.49	23.63
Period average		61.32	6.80	7.09	21.11
Bismarckian					
Austria	1960–2011		3.07	12.49	37.92
Belgium	1960–2009		7.40	12.31	29.46
France	1960–2010		6.51	10.67	30.87
Germany	1960–2012		5.30	11.13	28.22
Switzerland	1960–2010		1.64	13.05	34.61
The Netherlands	1960–2011		4.80	8.14	14.50
Period average		71.00	4.78	11.29	29.24
Scandinavian countries					
Denmark	1960–2011		5.38	16.25	32.79
Finland	1960–2011		6.25	13.27	50.89
Norway	1960–2012		2.81	7.86	21.92
Sweden	1960–2010		4.32	12.32	30.27
Period average		72.10	4.69	12.4	33.93

*The fraction of current wages which the social unemployment benefit system provides to a wage earner in the case of unemployment. Average for the period 1992–2009 for Eastern European countries, and 1971–2009 for other country groups.[26]

†Suicide data are missing 1997–1998 for Poland, 2004–2005 for Italy and 2000–2002 for Belgium.

DATA AND METHODS

The study comprises 30 countries, and the longest observation period is 1960–2012, though it is appreciably shorter for some countries (see table 1). Data on unemployment (% unemployed in the work force) were sourced from Eurostat. Age-specific mortality data for females and males were obtained from the WHO Mortality Data Base (Geneva). Gender specific age-standardised mortality rates (number of deaths per

100 000 population) were constructed (following WHO World Standard[28]) for the age-groups 20–64 years, and 65 years and above. Previous studies suggest that male suicide rates respond stronger than female suicide rates to economic downturns, which has been interpreted as a consequence of men's stronger work commitment and responsibility to be the main bread-winner.[7] However, some studies report social contagion effects from the job loser, particularly affecting the mental health of the spouse.[29,30] We expect any impact of unemployment on suicide to be confined to the age-group of the working population (20–64 years). We used the age-group 65 years and above as a placebo outcome where no or a minuscule effect is expected.

The association between unemployment and suicide was assessed by applying two different methodological techniques. The rationale for this is that triangulating findings from different methods should reduce the risk of obtaining method-bound results. The first method was fixed-effects modelling. To test the hypothesis that the unemployment effect may differ across welfare state regimes, the countries were sorted into five country groups ranging from low to high levels of unemployment protection, as described above and detailed in table 1. The other approach was to obtain country-specific estimates of the association at issue by means of time-series analyses of data for the individual countries; these estimates were then pooled into the five welfare state regimes. A brief description of the two methods follows below.

The first method involves analyses of pooled cross-sectional time-series data. When such data are used for estimating the relationship between two variables, there are two obvious sources of bias that may distort the outcome. One is the possible presence of unobserved country differences that are linked to the dependent as well as the independent variables. The other threat to validity of results is the possibility that X and Y variables have converging (or diverging) time trends that do not reflect a causal relationship, but rather the impact of other factors. We thus chose to analyse the differenced data because the differencing not only eliminated all trends in our data, but also means that only the intracountry covariation over time is explored (fixed-effects models), thus eliminating the first-mentioned source of bias as well. Further, the more conservative panel corrected SEs were used.[31] Finally, the models included panel-specific estimation of residual autocorrelation.

The time-series analysis was performed by applying the technique developed by Box and Jenkins,[32] often referred to as ARIMA-modelling (autoregressive integrated moving average). As noted above, a simple differencing was sufficient to remove trends to achieve the stationarity required for ARIMA-modelling. Further, the noise (error) term, which includes explanatory variables not considered in the model, is allowed to have a temporal structure that was modelled and estimated in terms of autoregressive and/or moving average parameters. All estimated ARIMA-models were satisfactory with respect to residual structure (which should not differ from white noise) according to the Box–Ljung Q statistics.31 The country-specific estimates of the unemployment effect were pooled within each of the five country groups (see Norström and Skog33 for a more detailed description of this approach.)

We included an interaction term to capture the possible excess effect of unemployment during the years of the financial crisis. The interaction term was constructed as follows: 1where Unemployment is the unemployment rate (%) and *Crisis* is a country specific variable that takes the value 0 in years with no recession, 0.25 in years with a 1-quarter recession, and so forth, and 1 in years with 4 quarters of recession. The common recession definition was used, that is, that a recession occurred when GDP has contracted at least two consecutive quarters. Data were obtained from Eurostat and OECD. Different International Classification of Diseases (ICD)-classifications have been used during the study period, from ICD-7 to ICD-10. Possible influences of revisions of ICD-classification were captured by dummy variables. Missing mortality data (table 1) were imputed through linear interpolation; dummy variables were created for these years.

One issue concerns the functional form of the relation between unemployment and suicide. Most previous studies have applied a semilog model, that is, with logged output. This assumes an accelerating risk function (convex downwards) which is far from obvious. As noted above, people who become unemployed tend to be selected on suicidogenic characteristics. The selection effect should be especially strong in periods of low unemployment, while the fraction of ordinary people among the unemployed is expected to increase with increasing unemployment rate. This should dampen the suicide response, suggesting a risk function that is concave downwards. This notion is supported by the study by Crawford, Kuforiji and Ghosh34 which on the basis of 54 published case control studies found a strong inverse relation between the prevalence of unemployment on the one hand, and the odds-ratio for suicide among the unemployed, on the other. A study based on data for Ireland35 reports findings consistent with this pattern. To test this empirically, we used the data for all study countries to estimate a fixed-effects model as described above, including unemployment and unemployment squared as predictors, and suicide (males 20–64 years) as output. The estimate obtained for unemployment was 1.181 (SE=0.214, p<0.001), and for unemployment squared −0.045 (SE=.010, p<0.001), which indicates a risk function that is concave downwards. However, this model specification would make comparisons across country groups awkward, and we thus chose a log–log model that can accommodate the suggested non-linear relationship, and that yields a single effect estimate in the form of an elasticity.

The following fixed-effects model was thus estimated for each of the five country groups (and for all countries together):

$$\nabla LnS_{it} = e_1 \nabla LnUnemployment_{it} + e_2 \nabla Uncrisis_{it} + \beta \nabla X_{it} + \varepsilon_{it} \qquad 2$$

where S is the suicide rate, Unemployment the unemployment rate (%), Uncrisis the interaction term as defined above, and X a vector of dummy variables capturing ICD-revisions and imputations of missing mortality data. The key parameters to be estimated are the elasticities denoted e_1 and e_2. Corresponding ARIMA-models were estimated for each of the 30 countries. For each of the five country groups we thus obtained two estimates of the unemployment effect on suicide, that is, one from the fixed-effects modelling and another from pooling the country specific ARIMA-estimates into country groups. We used F-tests to assess whether the estimated unemployment effects differed across country groups. We also used F-tests to assess whether the country specific ARIMA-estimates were homogenous within country groups.

We considered the option of controlling for GDP/capita. However, the obvious relation between unemployment and GDP (Okun's law) is best understood as a result of reduced labour input (increased unemployment) leading to decreased output (GDP).36 Controlling for GDP would thus potentially imply controlling for an intermediary variable, which is not recommended as this induces a bias towards the null.37 Thus, although controlling for GDP is not our preferred model we will investigate how such a specification affects the unemployment estimate because this gives a hint of how much of a possible unemployment effect on suicide that is mediated by reduced material resources.

All statistical analyses were performed with Stata, V.13 (StataCorp).

RESULTS

Table 1 displays descriptive statistics for the key variables. As shown in figure 1, unemployment increased after 2007 in all country groups except the Bismarckian; the increase was especially marked in the eastern and southern European country groups. (Although there is certainly a considerable heterogeneity within the country groups, unemployment increased in every single country, except Germany, where it decreased somewhat). It can also be seen that in some country groups (especially the Anglo-Saxon and the Scandinavian), unemployment increased at least as much during the 1990-crisis as during the current crisis. The male suicide rate increased markedly in the eastern European country group, but little or not at all in the other country groups. The female suicide rate was generally stable, or decreased. (2011 and 2012 are excluded in figure 1 due to missing suicide data for many countries, see table 1.) Generally, it seems clear that unemployment has a limited explanatory power with respect to trends in suicide. For instance, in three of the country groups (eastern Europe, Bismarckian and Scandinavia) there was a dramatic decline (35–40%) in male suicides during the study period that is obviously due to other factors than unemployment. This, of course, does not preclude that changes in the unemployment rate may impact on suicide, but we should not expect this impact to be very large. This expectation was borne out by the model estimations (table 2); a 1% increase in unemployment was associated with an increase in male suicides by 0.06% ($p<0.001$). However, this average effect for all countries conceals a great deal of heterogeneity. The estimated effect was thus strongest in the two country groups with the weakest unemployment protection, that is, eastern Europe (elasticity=0.128, $p<0.001$), and southern Europe (elasticity=0.166, $p=0.010$). In contrast, the weakest unemployment effect was found in the two groups with the strongest protection, that is, the Bismarckian (elasticity=0.038, $p<0.001$), and the Scandinavian countries (elasticity=0.030, $p=0.136$). This apparent gradient (figure 2) in the estimated effects on male suicides was statistically significant as suggested by the F-test that rejects the hypothesis that the five estimates are equal.

Table 2. Estimated effects (elasticities) of unemployment and Uncrisis on male suicide rate (20–64 years)

		Fixed-effects estimates						Pooled ARIMA-estimates							
		Unemployment			Uncrisis			Unemployment				Uncrisis			
Country group	N	Est	SE	p Value	Est	SE	p Value	Est	SE	p Value	F test†	Est	SE	p Value	F test†
1. Eastern European countries	210	0.128	0.028	<0.001	0.068	0.085	0.421	0.149	0.022	<0.001	1.658[NS]	−0.041	0.062	0.509	0.403[NS]
2. Southern European countries	153	0.166	0.065	0.010	0.000	0.062	0.997	0.133	0.053	0.013	0.071[NS]	0.009	0.047	0.842	0.012[NS]
3. Anglo-Saxon countries	250	0.085	0.034	0.013	−0.012	0.155	0.939	0.065	0.015	<0.001	0.169[NS]	−0.162	0.105	0.125	0.007[NS]
4. Bismarckian	303	0.038	0.009	<0.001	0.000	0.045	0.997	0.043	0.009	<0.001	0.957[NS]	−0.068	0.059	0.250	0.354[NS]
5. Scandinavian countries	204	0.030	0.020	0.136	−0.173	0.084	0.039	0.023	0.021	0.262	0.234[NS]	−0.114	0.108	0.294	0.391[NS]
F test for heterogeneity‡		2.535*			0.904[NS]			3.808*				0.672[NS]			
All countries	1120	0.062	0.011	<0.001	0.012	0.038	0.746								

Estimates from fixed-effects models, and pooled estimates from country-specific ARIMA-models.
*p<0.05; NS p≥0.05.
†F test for heterogeneity of estimates within country groups.
‡F test for heterogeneity of estimates between country groups.

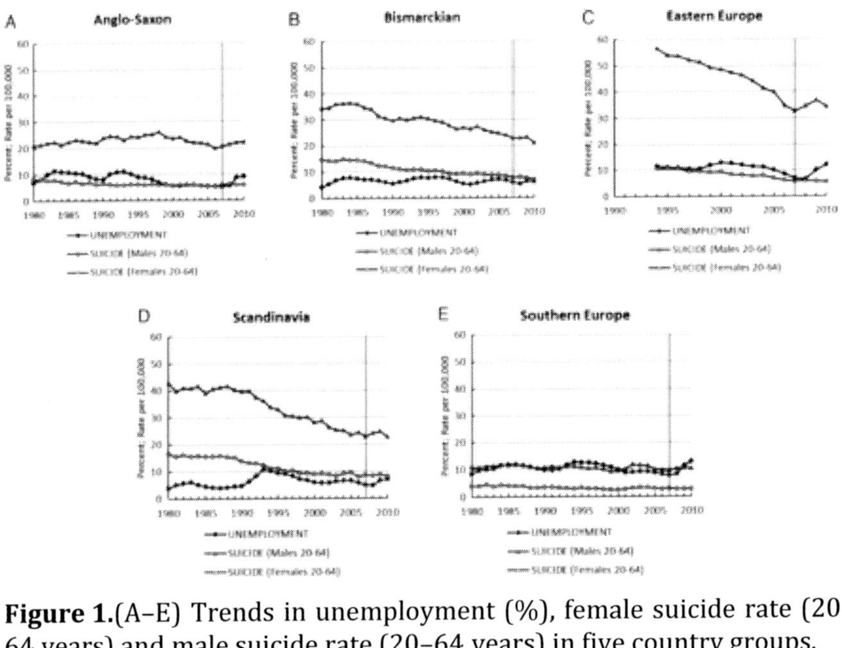

Figure 1.(A–E) Trends in unemployment (%), female suicide rate (20–64 years) and male suicide rate (20–64 years) in five country groups.

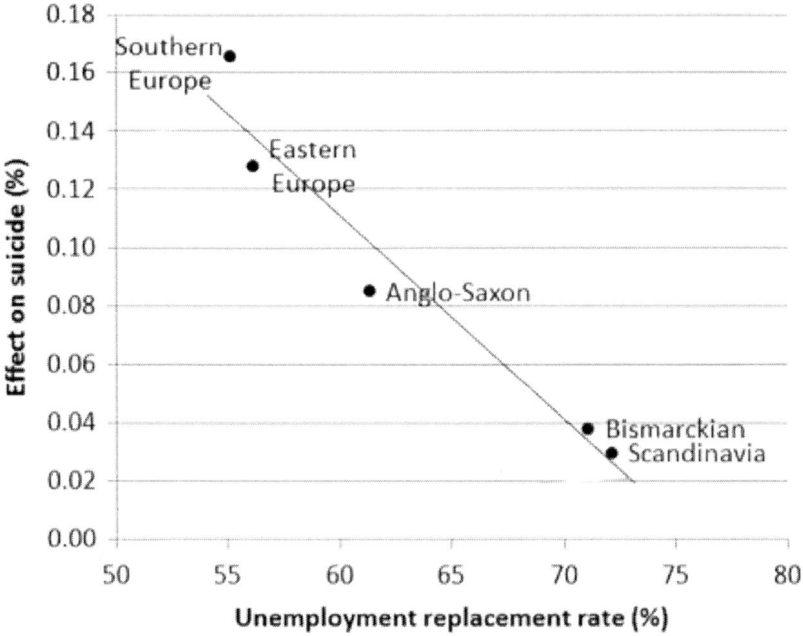

Figure 2. Estimated unemployment effects (FE-models shown in table 2) on suicide (males 20–64) plotted against unemployment replacement rates. See table 1 for definition of unemployment replacement rates and country groups.

The estimates from the fixed-effects models and the pooled ARIMA-estimates were fairly consistent with each other. Further, the F-tests indicate homogeneity of the ARIMA-estimates within each of the country groups. The estimated effect on female suicides (20–64 years) was significant only in the eastern European country group (table 3).

The interaction term (Uncrisis) capturing the possible excess effect of unemployment during the years of the financial crisis was clearly insignificant for all of the country groups. The dummy variables for changes in ICD-classifications were statistically insignificant (estimates not shown). The estimates on the placebo outcomes (female and male suicides 65 years and above) were also statistically insignificant (see online supplementary tables A1 and A2 in Web appendix). Including GDP/capita as control variable resulted in a lowering of the estimate and significance of the unemployment effect in the eastern and southern European country groups, while the estimates in the remaining country groups were unaffected (see online supplementary table A3 in Web appendix). This suggests that the unemployment effect on suicide in these country groups partly was mediated by reduced material resources.

Table 3. Estimated effects (elasticities) of unemployment and Uncrisis on female suicide rate (20–64 years)

		Fixed-effects estimates						Pooled ARIMA-estimates							
		Unemployment			Uncrisis			Unemployment				Uncrisis			
Country group	N	Est	SE	p Value	Est	SE	p Value	Est	SE	p Value	F test*	Est	SE	p Value	F test*
1. Eastern European countries	210	0.121	0.048	0.012	0.051	0.162	0.752	0.142	0.037	<0.001	0.338 NS	0.172	0.117	0.144	0.083 NS
2. Southern European countries	153	0.042	0.101	0.679	−0.109	0.109	0.315	0.024	0.066	0.719	3.940 NS	0.030	0.125	0.810	0.191 NS
3. Anglo-Saxon countries	250	0.084	0.059	0.151	−0.372	0.242	0.124	0.007	0.029	0.806	0.291 NS	−0.290	0.121	0.018	0.002 NS
4. Bismarckian	303	0.011	0.014	0.435	−0.055	0.066	0.404	0.023	0.019	0.228	0.888 NS	−0.033	0.097	0.734	0.001 NS
5. Scandinavian countries	204	0.017	0.030	0.570	−0.185	0.125	0.139	0.012	0.042	0.771	0.203 NS	−0.217	0.203	0.286	0.732 NS
F test for heterogeneity†		0.640 NS			1.079 NS			1.843 NS				1.847 NS			
All countries	1120	0.040	0.016	0.015	−0.097	0.056	0.081								

Estimates from fixed-effects models, and pooled estimates from country-specific ARIMA-models.
NS $p \geq 0.05$.
*F test for heterogeneity of estimates within country groups.
†F test for heterogeneity of estimates between country groups.

DISCUSSION

As noted in a recent *Lancet* article,38 remarkably little research has been devoted to the health effects of the economic crisis that bursted in the fall of 2007, and considered to be the deepest recession since the Great Depression. Suicide rates can be seen as a summary proxy for population mental health.39 From this perspective, it is of interest to analyse how this form of mortality is affected by the current crisis, and more specifically the ensuing surge in unemployment. This is an indicator that lies close to people's experience of economic turmoil, and which has proved to be the one that is most closely related to population health.40 In this paper we have put this issue into perspective by analysing time-series data that span a long period of time and cover countries representing welfare regimes with quite different degrees of unemployment protection. The data were analysed by two different methods that supplement each other.

The division of countries into the five welfare regimes unfolded a great deal of heterogeneity. First, our data show that some country groups are worse struck than others by the current crisis. Second, this uneven distribution of hardship is compounded by the marked gradient in the unemployment effect on suicide. Hence, the less generous the unemployment protection, the sharper the increase in unemployment, and, additionally, the stronger the unemployment effect on suicide. However, not to lose the perspective, it should be pointed out that in most country groups unemployment was at least as high during the crisis of the 1990s, and that the unemployment effect on suicide does not seem to be stronger during the Great Recession than during previous economic downturns during the study period. Our expectation, based on previous research, that the unemployment effect would be confined to males, was by and large borne out by our findings. The one exception from this pattern was the statistically significant effect on the female suicide rate that we obtained for the eastern European country group. However, some studies suggested contagion effects to spouses.29 ,30 Such effects may be particularly salient when the unemployment effect to a marked degree is mediated by material deprivation, affecting the whole household, which our analyses controlling for GDP suggested was the case for the eastern European country group.

There are some limitations of the study that deserve to be discussed. A potential concern is the quality of official suicide data. It is widely recognised that suicides are undercounted, and that this bias may vary across countries due to cultural and procedural differences. However, systematic examinations of the accuracy of suicide data at the national level suggest that they are reliable enough to be used in comparative research.41 ,42 Further, when the focus is on the temporal dimension, as in the present study, the evidence suggests that the variability in the quality of suicide statistics is less compelling than when the spatial dimension is in focus.43 The division of countries into the five welfare regimes seems to have been a fruitful approach, as it appeared that there was a substantial variation between, but not within the country groups with respect to the unemployment effect on suicide. However, it is clear that the scheme that we have applied conceals some heterogeneity within country groups, and in addition reflects the level of unemployment protection averaged over a long time period during which some countries have experienced marked changes in their social security systems. Our approach may thus be seen a compromise between two predominant approaches: (1) to analyse a shorter time period for a single country, which tends to yield low statistical power, and (2) to analyse data for all countries jointly, which is likely to conceal a good deal of heterogeneity. Another limitation is that there are no gender specific time-series data on unemployment covering our study period. This lowers the precision of our exposure measure which is likely to yield a downward bias of its estimated effect. Lastly, the risk of omitted variable bias can never be dismissed in the present kind of research. However, it should be noted that although there are numerous factors that affect the suicide rate, only omitted factors that also are synchronised with *changes* in suicide as well as unemployment would bias our outcomes.

To conclude, contextualising the unemployment increase spurred by the Great Recession, our findings suggest that its impact on suicide is not stronger than that of previous economic downturns, and that its impact is strongly modified by the level of unemployment protection.

What is already known on this subject?

- The Great Recession is considered to be the deepest economic downturn since World War II, but conspicuously little is known about its impact on population health. Previous research indicates that suicide rates tend to increase in economic downturns, the question is whether the current crisis is extra detrimental, and whether its impact might be buffered by welfare state provisions.

What this study adds?

- Our data indicate that unemployment rates increased most in country groups with the least developed unemployment protection (eastern and southern Europe). Our findings suggest that it was also in these country groups that increasing unemployment had the most detrimental impact on suicide. In contrast, the increase in unemployment in Scandinavia, with the highest level of unemployment protection had no noticeable effect on suicides. Our findings also suggest that the current crisis is not more harmful than previous economic downturns in the recent past.

Footnotes

- **Contributors** TN and HG conceived the design and drafted the paper. TN conducted the analyses. Both authors approved the final draft.

- **Funding** This research was funded by FORTE: Swedish Research Council for Health, Working Life and Welfare (2013–0376).

- **Competing interests** None.
- **Provenance and peer review** Not commissioned; externally peer reviewed.
- **Data sharing statement** All data sources are public and detailed in the paper.

REFERENCES

1. Goldman-Mellor SJ, Saxton KB, Catalano RC. Economic contraction and mental health. Int J Ment Health Nurs 2010;39:6–31.
2. Barr B, Taylor-Robinson D, Scott-Samuel A, et al. Suicides associated with the 2008– 10 economic recession in England: time trend analysis. BMJ 2012;345:e5142.
3. Reeves A, Stuckler D, McKee M, et al. Increase in state suicide rates in the USA during economic recession. Lancet 2012;380:1813–14.
4. De Vogli R, Marmot M, Stuckler D. Excess suicides and attempted suicides in Italy attributable to the great recession. J Epidemiol Community Health 2013;67:378–9.
5. Reeves A, McKee M, Stuckler D. Economic suicides in the Great Recession in Europe and North America. Br J Psychiatry 2014;205:246–7.
6. Platt S. Unemployment and suicidal behaviour: a review of the literature. Soc Sci Med 1984;19:93–115.
7. Stack S. Suicide: a 15-year review of the sociological literature part I: cultural and economic factors. Suicide Life Threat Behav 2000;30:145–62.
8. Blakely TA, Collings SCD, Atkinson J. Unemployment and suicide. Evidence for a causal association? J Epidemiol Community Health 2003;57:594–600.
9. Kposowa AJ. Unemployment and suicide: a cohort analysis of social factors predicting suicide in the US National Longitudinal Mortality Study. Psychol Med 2001;31:127–38.

10. Lewis G, Sloggett A. Suicide, deprivation, and unemployment: record linkage study. BMJ 1998;317:1283–86.

11. Thielen K, Nygaard E, Andersen I, et al. Employment consequences of depressive symptoms and work demands individually and combined. Eur J Public Health 2014;24:34–9.

12. Whooley MA, Kiefe CI, Chesney MA, et al. Depressive symptoms, unemployment, and loss of income: the CARDIA Study. Arch Intern Med 2002;162:2614–20.

13. van Rijn RM, Robroek SJW, Brouwer S, et al. Influence of poor health on exit from paid employment: a systematic review. Occup Environ Med 2014;71:295–301.

14. Norström T. Deriving relative risks from aggregate data. 1. Theory. J Epidemiol Community Health 1988;42:333–35.

15. Stuckler D, Basu S, Suhrcke M, et al. The public health effect of economic crises and alternative policy responses in Europe: an empirical analysis. Lancet 2009;374:315–23.

16. Mohseni-Cheraghlou A. Labor markets and mental wellbeing: labor market conditions and suicides in the United States (1979–2004). J Socio-Economics 2013;45:175–86.

17. Ruhm CJ. Are recessions good for your health? Q J Econ 2000;115:617–50.

18. Bartley M. Unemployment and ill health: understanding the relationship. J Epidemiol Community Health 1994;48:333–37.

19. Hamermesh DS, Soss NM. An economic theory of suicide. J Polit Econ 1974;82:83–98.

20. Cylus J, Glymour MM, Avendano M. Do generous unemployment benefit programs reduce suicide rates? A state fixed-effect analysis covering 1968–2008. Am J Epidemiol 2014;180:45–52.

21. Gerdtham U-G, Ruhm CJ. Deaths rise in good economic times: Evidence from the OECD. Econ Hum Biol 2006;4:298–316.

22. Korpi W. Power, politics, and state autonomy in the development of social citizenship: social rights during sickness in eighteen OECD Countries since 1930. Am Sociol Rev 1989;54:309–28.

23. Bambra C, Eikemo TA. Welfare state regimes, unemployment and health: a comparative study of the relationship between

unemployment and self-reported health in 23 European countries. J Epidemiol Community Health 2009;63:92–8.

24. Ferrera M. The 'Southern Model' of welfare in social Europe. J Eur Soc Policy 1996;6:17–37.

25. Bonoli G. Classifying welfare states: a two-dimension approach. J Soc Policy 1997;26:351–72.

26. Van Vliet O, Caminada K. Unemployment Replacement Rates Dataset Among 34 Welfare States, 1971–2009: An Update, Extension and Modification of the Scruggs' Welfare State Entitlements Data Set. NEUJOBS Special Report No 2, Leiden University, 2012.

27. Stuckler D, Basu S. The body economic: why austerity kills. UK: Penguin, 2013.

28. Ahmad OB, Boschi-Pinto C, Lopez AD, et al. Age standardization of rates: a new WHO standard. Geneva: World Health Organization, 2001.

29. Liem R, Liem JH. Psychological effects of unemployment on workers and their families. J Soc Issues 1988;44:87–105.

30. Rook K, Dooley D, Catalano R. Stress transmission: the effects of husbands' job stressors on the emotional health of their wives. J Marriage Fam 1991;53:165–77.

31. Beck N, Katz JN. What to do (and not to do) with time-series cross-section data. Am Polit Sci Rev 1995;89:634–47.

32. Box GEP, Jenkins GM, Reinsel GC. Time series analysis: forecasting and control. New York: Wiley, 2008.

33. Norström T, Skog OJ. Alcohol and mortality: methodological and analytical issues in aggregate analyses. Addiction 2001;96:5–17.

34. Crawford MJ, Kuforiji B, Ghosh P. The impact of social context on socio-demographic risk factors for suicide: a synthesis of data from case—control studies. J Epidemiol Community Health 2010;64:530–34.

35. Corcoran P, Arensman E. Suicide and employment status during Ireland's Celtic Tiger economy. Eur J Public Health 2010;21:209–14.

36. Prachowny MFJ. Okun's Law: theoretical foundations and revised estimates. Rev Econ Stat 1993;75:331–36.

37. Schisterman EF, Cole SR, Platt RW. Overadjustment bias and unnecessary adjustment in epidemiologic studies. Epidemiology 2009;20:488–95.

38. Karanikolos M, Mladovsky P, Cylus J, et al. Financial crisis, austerity, and health in Europe. Lancet 2013;381:1323–31.

39. Bray I, Gunnell D. Suicide rates, life satisfaction and happiness as markers for population mental health. Soc Psychiatry Psychiatr Epidemiol 2006;41:333–37.

40. Tapia Granados JA. Increasing mortality during the expansions of the US economy, 1900–1996. Int J Epidemiol 2005;34:1194–202.

41. Rockett IR, Thomas BM. Reliability and sensitivity of suicide certification in higher-income countries. Suicide Life Threat Behav 1999;29:141–49.

42. Sainsbury P, Jenkins JS. The accuracy of officially reported suicide statistics for purposes of epidemiological research. J Epidemiol Community Health 1982;36:43–8.

43. O'Carroll PW. A consideration of the validity and reliability of suicide mortality data. Suicide Life Threat Behav 1989;19:1–16.

6
CHAPTER

The Mental Health Consequences of the Recession: Economic Hardship and Employment of People with Mental Health Problems in 27 European Countries

Sara Evans-Lacko[1], Martin Knapp[1,2], Paul McCrone[1], Graham Thornicroft[1], Ramin Mojtabai[3]

[1] Health Service and Population Research Department, King's College London, Institute of Psychiatry, London, United Kingdom,

[2] London School of Economics and Political Science, London, United Kingdom,

[3] Department of Mental Health, Johns Hopkins Bloomberg School of Public Health, Baltimore, Maryland, United States of America

ABSTRACT

Objectives

A period of economic recession may be particularly difficult for people with mental health problems as they may be at higher risk of losing their jobs, and more competitive labour markets can also make it more difficult to find a new job. This study assesses unemployment rates among individuals with mental health problems before and during the current economic recession.

Methods

Using individual and aggregate level data collected from 27 EU countries in the Eurobarometer surveys of 2006 and 2010, we examined changes in unemployment rates over this period among individuals with and without mental health problems.

Results

Following the onset of the recession, the gap in unemployment rates between individuals with and without mental health problems significantly widened (odds ratio: 1.12, 95% confidence interval: 1.03, 1.34). This disparity became even greater for males, and individuals with low levels of education. Individuals with mental health problems living in countries with higher levels of stigmatizing attitudes regarding dangerousness of people with mental illness were more vulnerable to unemployment in 2010, but not 2006. Greater agreement that people with mental health problems have themselves to blame, was associated with lower likelihood of unemployment for individuals with and without mental health problems.

Conclusion

These findings study suggest that times of economic hardship may intensify social exclusion of people with mental health problems, especially males and individuals with lower education. Interventions to combat economic exclusion and to promote social participation of individuals with mental health problems are even more important during times of economic crisis, and these efforts should target support to the most vulnerable groups.

INTRODUCTION

Several studies have demonstrated large disparities in unemployment rates between people with and without mental illness. Although most people with mental illness want to work [1], they have higher unemployment rates than people without mental illness and compared to people with other chronic diseases [2]–[4]. High unemployment rates among individuals with mental illness are a major contributor to the substantial societal impact of these disorders [4]–[6]. Unemployment has an impact upon the course and outcome of mental illness [7] and excludes individuals from social participation. A period of macro-economic recession may be particularly difficult for people with mental health problems as they may be at higher risk of losing their jobs and more competitive labour market conditions may make it more difficult for them to find a new job in the first place [8]. This is especially important as research suggests that unemployment could present a specific barrier to recovery from mental illness [9], [10].

Unemployment among people with mental illness may be aggravated during times of economic hardship [7], [11], [12]. Negative attitudes towards marginalized groups (e.g., ethnic minorities or immigrant groups) which often increase during an economic recession [13] are one possible factor influencing this trend. Recent research from Germany suggests that the German public's unwillingness to recommend an individual with depression for a job increased between 2000 and 2011 (i.e., during the period of the economic recession) compared to 1990–2000 [14]. A synthesis of public attitude trends in the US between the 1950s and 1990s showed improvements and declines which mirrored the economic and employment context of the country [7]. Findings regarding the impact of economic recession on disparities [15] and the mechanisms involved, however, are mixed [15]–[18] and we need to better understand the complexity of this relationship. Interestingly, one study [16] did not show that individuals with severe mental illness were at earlier risk of unemployment during times of economic contraction; however, this study specifically investigated individuals with *severe* mental illness who received occupational rehabilitation services and these results may not be broadly generalizable to the wider population of people with mental illness. Furthermore, the effects of the recession since 2008 on disparities are yet to be determined.

In addition to research which suggests that mental health problems increase during times of economic recession, we investigate the impact of the economic recession on people with mental health problems and how this may be mediated by stigma. This paper investigates the impact of economic hardship on unemployment rates of people with mental health problems using Eurobarometer survey data collected from 27 EU countries in 2006 and 2010. We test the hypothesis that the European macro-economic crisis since 2008 has had a greater impact on employment of people with mental health problems compared to people without mental health problems. We also hypothesise that the impact on individuals with mental health problems is greater for people living in regions with greater public stigma towards people with mental illness, after controlling for regional unemployment rates. Additionally, as some research suggests that certain population subgroups, such as men or individuals with low levels of education [19], may be particularly vulnerable during times of economic recession, we investigate whether there is a differential impact of the recession on these subgroups in relation to unemployment.

MATERIALS AND METHODS

Data Source

Full details of the design and sampling for the Eurobarometer surveys *(Eurobarometer Mental Well-being 2006* and *Eurobarometer Mental Health 2010)* are given elsewhere [20], [21]. Data were collected via face-to-face interviews among European Union (EU) citizens (n=29,248 in 2006 and n=26,800 in 2010) residing in the 27 member states (approximately 1,000 individuals per country per year). For our analysis we restricted the sample to adults of working age (i.e., 18–64) (n=20,368 in 2006 and n=20,124 in 2010).

The initial mental health Eurobarometer survey was conducted in 2006 (fieldwork carried out between 7 December 2005 and 11 January 2006). A second survey assessing attitudes toward mental illness and treatment-seeking was administered to a new sample of respondents in 2010 (between 26 February and 17 March 2010). All participants were recruited via multistage random probability sampling. Participants were representative of residents aged 15 or older in the participating countries.

Assessments

Mental health problems were assessed via the Mental Health Inventory (MHI-5), a well-validated and reliable measure derived from the Short Form 36 (SF-36) [22], [23] As a validated cut-point has not been established for the MHI-5 [22], for the purposes of this study, individuals scoring one standard deviation higher than the standardised mean score were categorised as having mental health problems.

Stigmatising attitudes towards individuals with mental health problems were assessed in Eurobarometer 2006 using four questions about various stigmatizing beliefs: (1) People with psychological or emotional health problems constitute a danger to others; (2) People with psychological or emotional health problems are unpredictable; (3) People with psychological or emotional health problems have themselves to blame and (4) People with psychological or emotional health problems never recover. Participants were asked how much they agreed with each statement. Response options were on a 4-point Likert scale from 'totally disagree' to 'totally agree'. Participants who responded 'totally agree' or 'tend to agree' to each statement were considered as agreeing with that statement. Responses were aggregated within each country to obtain a country-level measure of stigmatizing attitudes.

Socio-demographic information included age band (18–29, 30–39, 40–49 and 50–64 years), gender, education level (age at which individuals finished full-time education), and urbanicity (i.e., size of locality of respondent residence: large town, small or middle sized town or rural area/village). Current employment was assessed via the question: 'What is your current occupation?' Individuals could endorse the following categories: (1) responsible for ordinary shopping and looking after the home, or without any current occupation, not working (referred to throughout the paper as 'home-maker'), (2) student, (3) unemployed or temporarily not working, (4) retired or unable to work through illness, or (5) in paid employment.

National level unemployment rates

National unemployment figures for the years 2006 and 2010 were taken from the Eurostat yearbook (http://epp.eurostat.ec.europa.eu/statistics_explained/index.php/Europe_in_figures_-_Eurostat_yearbook). Eurostat is a Directorate-General of the European Commission and the statistical office of the European Union. The Eurostat figures for 2006 were moderately highly correlated with the national unemployment rates calculated from the Eurobarometer data (r=0.76 and 0.70, respectively).

Statistical Analysis

Four separate multivariable logistic regression models were used to examine predictors of unemployment for individuals with and without mental health problems in 2006 and 2010. Independent variables included age, gender, urbanicity, country-level attitudes regarding dangerousness, recovery, blameworthiness, and unpredictability of people with mental illness. Country-level variables were computed as an average rating for each country and each variable was standardized. Eurobarometer post-stratification weights, based on sex, age, region and size of locality, were used in all analyses to estimate the country-level averages. We used generalized estimating equations (GEE) with the robust variance estimates to model within-country correlations. In the absence of theoretical reasons for specifying a correlation matrix structure, we used an unstructured correlation matrix [24]. In order to investigate whether individual unemployment status differed by population subgroups of interest (i.e., men, individuals with low levels of education and younger individuals) following the recession, we first tested the interaction between survey year and these variables and then tested a three-way interaction between survey year, mental health problems and these variables. All analyses were carried out using SAS version 9.3.

ETHICS STATEMENT

Ethical approval was not required as this was secondary data analysis.

RESULTS

Socio-demographic characteristics (Table 1)

Compared to individuals without mental health problems, individuals with mental health problems were disproportionately women (χ^2=125.2, df=1, p<0•001 in 2006 and χ^2=87.9, df=1, p<0•001 in 2010) and older (χ^2=316.9, df=3, p<0•001 in 2006 and χ^2=93.9, df=3, p<0•001 in 2010). The majority of people with and without mental health problems had completed education at least to 16 years of age; however, more of those without mental health problems finished education at age 20+ or were still studying (χ^2=210.1, df=1, p<0•001 in 2006 and χ^2=237.8, df=1, p<0•001 in 2010). A higher proportion of people with mental health problems had no formal education or only finished education at 15 years of age (χ^2=313.8, df=1, p=p<0•001 in 2006 and χ^2=213.7, df=1, p<•0001 in 2010). Individuals with mental health problems were less likely to be in paid employment or to be a student or home-makers and more likely to be unemployed or disabled/retired, (χ^2=452.6, df=4, p<0•0001 in 2006 and χ^2=109.4, df=4, p<0•0001 in 2010).

Trends in unemployment among people with mental health problems

Unemployment rates were higher among people with mental health problems compared to those without in both survey years (Table 1). Overall unemployment rates were also higher in 2010 compared to 2006. The gap in unemployment rates between individuals with and without mental health problems widened in 2010 compared to 2006 (Figure 1). The differential trend was statistically significant (odds ratio [OR] for the interaction term for mental health problems by year=1.12, 95% confidence interval [CI]: 1.03, 1.34. We performed several types of sensitivity analyses to test the robustness of this relationship. We investigated additional cutpoints for individuals scoring in the top ten and the top five percent of mental health problems and their likelihood of unemployment relative to the rest of the population. The differential trend was also statistically significant for these groups: the p-value for the interaction term for mental health problems by year for the top ten

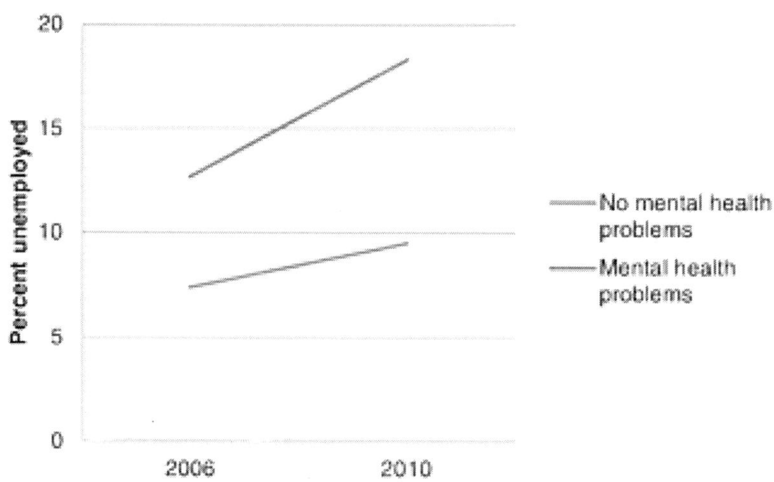

Figure 1. Average unemployment rates among individuals in Eurobarometer 2006 and 2010, stratified by presence of mental health problems (aged 18–65).

Table 1. Descriptive statistics among people with and without mental health problems in Eurobarometer 2006 and 2010.

	2006				2010			
	Individuals with mental health problems		Individuals without mental health problems		Individuals with mental health problems		Individuals without mental health problems	
	Freq	weighted % 95%CI	Freq	weighted % 95%CI	Freq	weighted % 95%CI	Freq	weighted % 95%CI
Gender								
Male	1183	40.4 (38.6, 42.2)	7728	51.3 (50.5, 52.1)	1668	42.9 (41.3, 44.5)	7759	51.3 (50.5, 52.1)
Female	2166	59.6 (57.8,61.4)	9224	48.7 (47.9, 49.5)	2343	57.1 (55.5, 58.7)	8453	48.7 (47.9, 49.5)
Age group								
18-29	465	16.8 (15.4, 18.3)	4127	28.5 (27.8, 29.3)	679	21.0 (19.6, 22.4)	3716	27.3 (26.6, 28.1)
30-39	622	20.6 (19.1, 22.1)	3828	24.6 (23.9, 25.3)	802	21.8 (20.5, 23.2)	3685	24.0 (23.3, 24.7)
40-49	783	24.7 (23.2, 26.3)	3689	21.9 (21.3, 22.6)	936	24.4 (23.0, 25.8)	3419	21.1 (20.5, 21.8)
50-64	1392	37.8 (36.2, 39.6)	4976	25.0 (24.3, 25.6)	1379	32.8 (31.3, 34.3)	5029	27.6 (26.9, 28.3)
Urbanicity								
Large town	1193	36.5 (34.8, 38.2)	4725	27.5 (26.8, 28.2)	1190	30.8 (29.3, 32.3)	4751	29.5 (28.7, 30.2)
Small or mid-sized town	1177	34.3 (32.6, 35.9)	6170	35.8 (35.1, 36.6)	1356	34.8 (33.3, 36.4)	5680	35.2 (34.4, 35.9)
Rural area	979	29.2 (27.6, 30.8)	6057	36.6 (35.8, 37.4)	1332	34.4 (32.8, 35.9)	5781	35.4 (34.6, 36.1)
Education								
No full time education	83	2.4 (1.9, 3.0)	278	1.61 (1.4, 1.8)	77	1.9 (1.5, 2.4)	171	1.0 (0.9, 1.2)
Education to 15	911	25.2 (24.5, 27.8)	2434	13.1 (12.6, 13.7)	789	19.6 (18.3, 20.8)	1929	11.3 (10.8, 11.8)
Education to 16-19	1574	47.8 (46.0,49.6)	7965	47.1 (46.3, 47.9)	1940	50.3 (48.7, 51.9)	7561	46.0 (45.2, 46.8)
Education to 20+ or still studying	781	24.6 (23.0, 26.1)	6275	38.1 (37.3, 38.9)	1035	28.2 (26.7, 29.7)	6481	41.7 (40.9, 42.5)
Employment								
Long term disabled/Retired	798	21.4 (20.0, 22.8)	1825	8.6 (8.2, 9.0)	663	15.5 (14.3, 16.6)	1869	9.6 (9.2, 10.1)
In paid employment	1584	49.6 (47.9, 51.4)	11042	67.2 (66.5, 67.9)	1862	48.8 (47.2, 50.4)	10200	63.4 (62.6, 64.2)
Student	124	4.5 (3.7, 5.3)	1264	8.6 (8.1, 9.1)	194	6.4 (5.5, 7.3)	1216	9.3 (8.8, 9.8)
Home maker	444	11.9 (10.8, 13.0)	1654	8.5 (8.1, 8.9)	467	11.1 (10.1, 12.1)	1395	7.9 (7.4, 8.3)
Unemployed	399	12.7 (11.4, 13.9)	1167	7.1 (6.7, 7.5)	692	18.2 (17.0, 19.5)	1532	9.8 (9.3, 10.3)

percent was 0.020 and the top five percent was 0.018. We also conducted additional sensitivity analyses applying an instrumental variable approach in which individual mental health problems were considered to be endogenous to the model and this also showed a significant relationship and the interaction term for year and mental health problems was also significant ($p<0.001$).

Relationship between unemployment and mental health status

In each of the survey years, local unemployment rates ascertained by Eurostat were strongly associated with the odds of being unemployed among participants both with and without mental health problems in Eurobarometer (Table 2). Among people with mental health problems, males were more likely to be unemployed than females in 2010 (OR: 1.58, 95% CI: 1.30, 1.92, $p<0.001$) and marginally more likely to be unemployed than females in 2006 (OR: 1.24, 95%CI: 0.99, 1.57, $p=0.067$). The interaction term for gender and year was statistically significant for the entire sample ($p<0.001$) and among individuals with mental health problems ($p<0.01$), but not among those without mental health problems. In 2010, 21.7% of men with mental health problems were unemployed, compared to 13.7% in 2006. For women with mental health problems, the difference in unemployment rate between 2010 (15.6%) and 2006 (11.9%) in 2006 was narrower.

Table 2. Results of multivariable logistic regression analyses for predictors of unemployment stratified by presence of mental health problems in Eurobarometer 2006 and 2010.

Predictors	2006 Individuals with mental health problems Adjusted GEE parameter estimates Odds Ratio (95% CI)	2006 Individuals without mental health problems Adjusted GEE parameter estimates Odds Ratio (95% CI)	2010 Individuals with mental health problems Adjusted GEE parameter estimates Odds Ratio (95% CI)	2010 Individuals without mental health problems Adjusted GEE parameter estimates Odds Ratio (95% CI)
Individual level variables				
Gender				
Male	1.24 (0.98, 1.57)	*0.85 (0.74, 0.99)	***1.58 (1.30, 1.92)	1.11 (0.91, 1.36)
Female	1.00 (ref.)	1.00 (ref.)	1.00 (ref.)	1.00 (ref.)
Age group				
18-29	*1.26 (1.05, 1.52)	***1.73 (1.48, 2.01)	*1.25 (1.00, 1.55)	***1.63 (1.42, 1.87)
30-39	1.09, (0.90, 1.32)	1.04 (0.94, 1.16)	*1.22 (1.04, 1.42)	*1.05 (1.00, 1.22)
40-49	1.12 (0.93, 1.34)	*0.86 (0.72, 0.99)	1.01 (0.87, 1.17)	*0.87 (0.77, 0.99)
50-64	1.00 (ref.)	1.00 (ref.)	1.00 (ref.)	1.00 (ref.)
Years of education	***0.73 (0.63, 0.85)	***0.65 (0.59, 0.72)	***0.68 (0.61, 0.75)	***0.55 (0.49, 0.62)
Urbanicity				
Large town	1.03 (0.71, 1.51)	0.93 (0.75, 1.17)	*1.27 (1.00, 1.62)	0.98 (0.84, 1.13)
Small or middle sized town	1.14 (0.85, 1.51)	1.02 (0.88, 1.20)	1.20 (0.95, 1.52)	1.05 (0.88, 1.25)
Rural area	1.00 (ref.)	1.00 (ref.)	1.00 (ref.)	1.00 (ref.)
Country level variable				
Dangerousness[a]	1.19 (0.93, 1.54)	1.17 (0.91, 1.51)	*1.41 (1.02, 2.04)	1.12 (0.87, 1.44)
Blame[b]	*0.72 (0.55, 0.93)	*0.78 (0.62, 0.98)	**0.66 (0.50, 0.88)	0.90 (0.71, 1.14)
Unpredictability[c]	1.12 (0.90, 1.40)	1.09 (0.87, 1.37)	0.93 (0.72, 1.20)	0.98 (0.78, 1.24)
Recovery[d]	1.22 (0.91, 1.65)	1.21 (0.97, 1.50)	1.22 (0.90, 1.66)	1.08 (0.81, 1.44)
Unemployment rate 2006	**1.10 (1.02, 1.19)	**1.09 (1.02, 1.16)	1.01 (0.93, 1.10)	0·99 (0.90, 1.08)
Unemployment rate 2010	NA	NA	***1.08 (1.04, 1.12)	***1·09 (1·06, 1.12)

[a]Average country-level agreeing with the statement: "People with psychological or emotional health problems constitute a danger to others".
[b]Average country-level agreeing with the statement: "People with psychological or emotional health problems have themselves to blame."
[c]Average country-level agreeing with the statement: "People with psychological or emotional health problems are unpredictable.
[d]Average country-level agreement with the statement: "People with psychological or emotional health problems never recover."
* = $p<0.05$, ** $p<0.01$ *** $p<0.005$.

In both 2006 and 2010 individuals in the youngest age band (18–29 years), with and without mental health problems, were more likely to be unemployed than individuals in the oldest age band (50–64 years). However, age patterns of unemployment in both survey years varied among those with and without mental health problems in that the younger age was more strongly associated with unemployment among those without mental health problems ($p<0.001$). Indeed, the unemployed with mental health problems were significantly older than those without mental health problems (mean age=4.3 vs. 36.1, t-test=10.16, $p=0.001$).

Fewer years of education was significantly associated with unemployment among individuals with and without mental health problems; however, education was more strongly associated with unemployment among individuals with mental health problems compared to those without these problems ($p=0.001$). The impact of education on employment was also more substantial during 2010 compared with 2006 among individuals with mental health problems only (p=0.010). This interaction was also significant among the entire sample (p=0.020), but not among those without mental health problems.

Urbanicity (i.e., size of the town where participants were recruited) did not play a major role in likelihood of unemployment except that individuals with mental health problems who lived in a large town relative to a rural area were more likely to be unemployed (Table 2), which could be interpreted as implying that a larger labour market disadvantages those with mental health problems.

During 2010, but not 2006, among individuals with mental health problems only, living in a country where a *higher* proportion of the general public agreed that people with mental health problems are dangerous was associated with a higher likelihood of being unemployed (Table 2). During 2006, individuals with mental health problems living in a country where a *lower* proportion of the general public agreed that people with mental health problems have themselves to blame were more likely to be unemployed. This relationship was maintained in 2010. Living in a country where a *higher* proportion of the general public agreed that people with mental health problems will never recover was associated with a marginally higher likelihood of being unemployed among individuals with mental health problems (p=0.097).

DISCUSSION

Economic recession has had enormous impacts across much of Europe; however, little information is available about the *specific* impact of the recession on groups who are already vulnerable to social exclusion, specifically individuals with mental illness. This is the first study to demonstrate that the European economic crisis had a greater impact on people with mental health problems, compared to people without mental health problems, as measured by exclusion from employment. Our study also identified important sub-groups which experienced greater impacts of the economic recession in terms of unemployment, specifically men and individuals with low levels of education. Overall, males and individuals with lower levels of education appear to have been affected disproportionately by the recession; both groups had a significantly greater increase in likelihood of being unemployed following the recession. Moreover, for individuals with mental health problems, gender and level of education were particularly important determinants of employment status as the recession seemed to have a disproportionately higher negative impact on their likelihood of being employed for men and those with less education. This may be due to shifts in labour markets: other studies have suggested that men may be more vulnerable to unemployment during the current recession in Europe as they are more likely to work in construction and manufacturing jobs which are more vulnerable to decreases in demand and job loss [25], while other research suggests that this disparity is only evident during the initial stages of a recession [11].

This study also showed that stigmatizing attitudes, specifically beliefs regarding dangerousness of individuals with mental health problems, could be an important mediator in the relationship between unemployment and mental health problems following the recession. Living in a country where a higher proportion of individuals believe that individuals with mental illness are dangerous was associated with a higher likelihood of unemployment for people with mental health problems, but did not influence employment rates for those *without* mental health problems. Moreover, this became significant in 2010, following the economic recession. Other studies have emphasised the persistence of attitudes related to dangerousness and their association with community rejection [26]. Research on racial discrimination suggests that stereotype amplification in relation to risk and fear of victimisation plays an important role in the persistence of racial inequalities and community segregation [27]. These attitudes may be internalised by the stigmatised group. Recent international work underscores the prevalence of experienced and anticipated discrimination among people with depression in relation to employment, suggesting that this is a critical barrier to achieving employment integration [28]. A recent analysis of trends in public attitudes toward people with mental health problems in England and older research from the U.S. also suggested that attitudes to people with mental health problems may harden during periods of economic crisis [7], [29]; however, there is a gap in research around this topic. Surprisingly, a higher proportion of the public endorsing blameworthiness was consistently associated with lower rates of unemployment among people with mental health problems. Previous research has found that stigmatizing attitudes are highly specific in their relation to impact on people with mental health problems. For example, living in a community with stronger beliefs about blameworthiness of individuals with mental illness is associated with lower rates of willingness to seek professional help [30] but also lower levels of perceived discrimination among people with mental health problems [31]. Other research has shown that world views such as stronger just world beliefs for self may be a double edged sword as they are associated with greater blameworthiness; but also lower self stigma among people with mental illness [32]. It could be that environments with greater endorsement of blame and controllability of symptoms and/or illness also engender a context where the guilt and blame associated with those who are not working is increased. Thus, any intervention would need to carefully consider the complexity of cultural factors and beliefs underlying individual and public attitudes.

Previous studies have demonstrated the impact of the recession on public health more generally [33]–[35], however, the selective impact of recession on people with mental health problems, especially males or individuals with lower levels of education, should be acknowledged through both research and policy. Analysis of general government policy responses in Europe following the crisis reveals deficiencies and problems and suggests that governments should allocate resources toward keeping and reintegrating people into employment in addition to initiating programmes that help people cope with the negative effects of job loss to counteract the adverse health effects of the recession [33]. Highlighting the population subgroups who are most vulnerable to economic shocks and identifying ways to mitigate the effects of these shocks is also important. It may be that investment in targeted programmes such as debt advice for people with mental health problems may improve their mental health and financial circumstances [36], [37]. Given the cuts in mental health services across Europe, the impact of the recession is likely to be felt among a growing number of individuals alongside dwindling resources. Lack of resources may strain mental health services during times of higher need leading to decreased access in the face of increased need. In Spain where the impact of the recent recession has been among the greatest, the prevalence of mental disorders diagnosed in primary care settings is increasing. These increases are associated with increases in unemployment and also present among individuals whose employment is threatened and also those who are struggling to make payments on their mortgage [38]. Recent findings from both England and Spain suggest that the recession is associated with a deterioration in population mental health [19], [38]. In addition to people with mental health problems generally, it is important to acknowledge specific subgroups with mental health problems, such as males and those with lower education. In addition to having a higher likelihood of unemployment, these subgroups have lower rates of help-seeking and more negative attitudes about mental illness [29], [39] and thus, may require specific forms of outreach.

LIMITATIONS

This study presents new and important information about the impact of macroeconomic downturn on people with and without mental health problems in Europe using nationally representative data from 27 countries in Europe surveyed over two time points, before and after the onset of the current recession. Nevertheless, the data were not collected with the specific aims of this study in mind and were not longitudinal in nature as the same individuals were not interviewed in the two surveys. Mental health status was determined via a brief self report measure and thus mental health problems were not verified by a clinician. Additionally, type and severity of problems were not assessed. Most previous research on employment of individuals with mental health problems and also on mental illness stigma has focused on those with severe mental disorders which could not be identified in the Eurobarometer data. Additionally, data on potentially important characteristics such as ethnicity and immigration status or survey response rates were not available. The investigation was limited to two time points only and although the impact of economic recession was clearly evident in 2010, long term effects could not be investigated. Relatedly, as these are observational data, our analyses could not rule out reverse causality, and the potential that people who were unemployed were more likely to develop mental health problems in 2010. Other research has suggested that a large proportion of the consequences of unemployment such as mortality are due to mental health related selection prior to becoming unemployed [40] suggesting that this is an important mechanism to investigate. Our main outcome of interest was unemployment; however, there may be other important effects of the economic crisis in terms of social exclusion which we were not able to examine. As Eurobarometer recruited individuals by household, we were not able to investigate individuals who may have transitioned into more extreme types of exclusion i.e., individuals who became homeless, were in care or hospital settings or were imprisoned. Finally, attitudes about people with mental illness were only collected at one time point in 2006 which precludes assessment of changes in public attitudes over time and its potential impact on unemployment trends. However, the assessment of attitudes preceded the economic crisis and so was not confounded by the effects of the recession.

Past research has consistently shown that people with mental health problems tend to be excluded from employment, housing and social relationships, and that this exclusion has negative social and economic consequences [8]. This study suggests that times of economic hardship are likely to heighten such exclusion for people with mental health problems. The study also provides some preliminary clues as to which groups of individuals with mental health problems are especially vulnerable during times of economic hardship, and what societal factors might moderate this adverse relationship. Use of both individual-level and aggregate-level data to explore this relationship provides new and important evidence about the impact of the macro-social context on individuals during times of economic recession and facilitates micro-macro research in relation to mental health and exclusion [41], [42]. Findings suggest that programmes to combat exclusion and to promote mental health may be more important during times of economic crisis. Future research should examine the long term effects of the economic recession on people with mental health problems and the relationship between different types of employment and social welfare policies and unemployment rates for people with mental health problems.

ACKNOWLEDGMENTS

We would like to thank J. Scheftlein, P. Hougron and F. Lefebvre from DG SANCO for kindly sharing the Eurobarometer data. The European Union has not gotten involved in analysis of this data and declines any responsibility stemming from such interpretation.

AUTHOR CONTRIBUTIONS

Conceived and designed the experiments: SEL MK PM GT RM. Analyzed the data: SEL. Wrote the paper: SEL MK PM GT RM. Wrote the original study design and protocol: SEL RM. Contributed to the original study design and protocol: GT PM. Initial drafting of the manuscript: SEL. Participated in interpretation of the analysis, editing and rewriting of the manuscript: PM MK GT RM. Approved the final version: SEL MK PM GT RM.

REFERENCES

1. Mechanic D, Blider S, McAlpine DD (2002) Employing persons with serious mental illness. Health Aff (Millwood) 21: 242–253.
2. Chatterji P, Alegria M, Lu M, Takeuchi D (2007) Psychiatric disorders and labor market outcomes: evidence from the National Latino and Asian American Study. Health Econ 16: 1069–1090.
3. Thomas C, Benzeval M, Stansfeld SA (2005) Employment transitions and mental health: an analysis from the British household panel survey. J Epidemiol Community Health 59: 243–249.
4. Zhang X, Zhao X, Harris A (2009) Chronic diseases and labour force participation in Australia. J Health Econ 28: 91–108.
5. **5.**Dewa CS, McDaid D, Ettner SL (2007) An international perspective on worker mental health problems: who bears the burden and how are costs addressed? Can J Psychiatry 52: 346–356.
6. Levinson D, Lakoma MD, Petukhova M, Schoenbaum M, Zaslavsky AM, et al. (2010) Associations of serious mental illness with earnings: results from the WHO World Mental Health surveys. Br J Psychiatry 197: 11
7. Warner R (2004) Recovery from schizophrenia: psychiatry and political economy. Routledge
8. Sharac J, McCrone P, Clement S, Thornicroft G (2010) The economic impact of mental health stigma and discrimination: a systematic review. Epidemiol Psichiatr Soc 19: 223–232.
9. Bush PW, Drake RE, Xie H, McHugo GJ, Haslett WR (2009) The long term impact of employment on mental health service use and costs for persons with severe mental illness. Psychiatr Serv 60: 1024–1031.
10. Drake RE, Bond GR, Thornicroft G, Knapp M, Goldman HH (2012) Mental Health Disability An International Perspective. Journal of Disability Policy Studies 23: 110–120.
11. Viinamaki H, Hintikka J, Kontula O, Niskanen L, Koskela K (2000) Mental health at population level during an economic recession in Finland. Nordic Journal of Psychiatry 54: 177–182.

12. Wahlbeck K, McDaid D (2012) Actions to alleviate the mental health impact of the economic crisis. World Psychiatry 11: 139–145.

13. Burns P, Gimpel J (2000) Economic Insecurity, Prejudicial Stereotypes, and Public Opinion on Immigration Policy. Political Science Quarterly 115: 201–225.

14. Angermeyer MC, Matschinger H, Schomerus G (2012) Public attitudes towards people with depression in times of uncertainty: results from three population surveys in Germany. Soc Psychiatry Psychiatr Epidemiol

15. Hong J, Knapp M, McGuire A (2011) Income-related inequalities in the prevalence of depression and suicidal behaviour: a 10-year trend following economic crisis. World Psychiatry 10: 40–44.

16. Catalano R, Drake RE, Becker DR, Clark RE (1999) Labor market conditions and employment of the mentally ill. J Ment Health Policy Econ 2: 51–54.

17. Kondo N, Subramanian SV, Kawachi I, Takeda Y, Yamagata Z (2008) Economic recession and health inequalities in Japan: analysis with a national sample, 1986–2001. J Epidemiol Community Health 62: 869–875 62/10/869

18. Valkonen T, Martikainen P, Jalovaara M, Koskinen S, Marrtelin T, et al. (2000) Changes in socioeconomic inequalities in mortality during an economic boom and recession among middle-aged men and women in Finland. European Journal of Public Health 10: 274–280.

19. Katikireddi SV, Niedzwiedz CL, Popham F (2012) Trends in population mental health before and after the 2008 recession: a repeat cross-sectional analysis of the 1991–2010 Health Surveys of England. BMJ Open 2 bmjopen-2012-001790

20. European Union (2006) Mental well-being:soecuak Eurobarometer 248/Wave 64.4. Available: http://ec.europa.eu/health/ph_information/documents/ebs_248_en.pdf. Accessed 2013 Jun 1.

21. European Union (2010) Mental Health: Special Eurobarometer 345/Wave 73.2. Available: http://ec.europa.eu/health/mental_health/docs/ebs_345_en.pdf. Accessed 2013 Jun 1.

22. Kelly MJ, Dunstan FD, Lloyd K, Fone DL (2008) Evaluating cutpoints for the MHI-5 and MCS using the GHQ-12: a comparison of five different methods. BMC Psychiatry 8: 10.

23. Ware JE Jr, Gandek B (1998) Overview of the SF-36 Health Survey and the International Quality of Life Assessment (IQOLA) Project. J Clin Epidemiol 51: 903–912.

24. Zeger SL, Liang KY, Albert PS (1988) Models for longitudinal data: a generalized estimating equation approach. Biometrics 44: 1049–1060.

25. Seguino S (2009) The global economic crisis its gender implications, and policy responses.

26. Pescosolido BA, Martin JK, Long JS, Medina TR, Phelan JC, et al. (2010) "A disease like any other"? A decade of change in public reactions to schizophrenia, depression, and alcohol dependence. Am J Psychiatry 167: 1321–1330.

27. Quillian L, Pager D (2010) Estimating Risk: Stereotype Amplification and the Perceived Risk of Criminal Victimization. Soc Psychol Q 73: 79–104

28. Lasalvia A, Zoppei S, Van BT, Bonetto C, Cristofalo D, et al. (2012) Global pattern of experienced and anticipated discrimination reported by people with major depressive disorder: a cross-sectional survey. Lancet

29. Evans-Lacko S, Henderson C, Thornicroft G (2013) Public knowledge, attitudes and behaviour regarding people with mental illness in England 2009–2012. British Journal of Psychiatry

30. Mojtabai R (2010) Mental illness stigma and willingness to seek mental health care in the European Union. Soc Psychiatry Psychiatr Epidemiol 45: 705–712.

31. Evans-Lacko S, Brohan E, Mojtabai R, Thornicroft G (2012) Association between public views of mental illness and self-stigma among individuals with mental illness in 14 European countries. Psychol Med 42: 1741–1752.

32. Rüsch N, Todd AR, Bodenhausen GV, Corrigan PW (2010) Do people with mental illness deserve what they get? Links between meritocratic worldviews and implicit versus explicit stigma. Eur Arch Psychiatry Clin Neurosci 260: 617–625

33. Stuckler D, Basu S, Suhrcke M, Coutts A, McKee M (2009) The public health effect of economic crises and alternative policy responses in Europe: an empirical analysis. Lancet 374: 315–323.

34. Stuckler D, Basu S, Suhrcke M, McKee M (2009) The health implications of financial crisis: a review of the evidence. Ulster Med J 78: 142–145.

35. Stuckler D, Basu S, Suhrcke M, Coutts A, McKee M (2011) Effects of the 2008 recession on health: a first look at European data. Lancet 378: 124–125.

36. Fitch C, Hamilton S, Bassett P, Davey R (2011) The relationship between personal debt and mental health: a systematic review. Mental Health Review Journal 16: 153–166.

37. Knapp M, McDaid D, Evans-Lacko S, Fitch C, King D (2011) Debt and Mental Health. In: Mental health promotion and prevention: the economic case. London, UK: Personal Social Services Research Unit, London School of Economics and Political Science.

38. Gili M, Roca M, Basu S, McKee M, Stuckler D (2013) The mental health risks of economic crisis in Spain: evidence from primary care centres, 2006 and 2010. Eur J Public Health 23: 103–108 cks035

39. Rüsch N, Evans-Lacko SE, Henderson C, Flach C, Thornicroft G (2011) Knowledge and attitudes as predictors of intentions to seek help for and disclose a mental illness. Psychiatr Serv 62: 675–678 62/6/675

40. Lundin A, Lundberg I, Hallsten L, Ottosson J, Hemmingsson T (2010) Unemployment and mortality–a longitudinal prospective study on selection and causation in 49321 Swedish middle-aged men. J Epidemiol Community Health 64: 22–28 jech.2008.079269

41. Coleman JS (1986) Social theory, social research and a theory of action. American Journal of Sociology 91: 1309–1335.

42. Wray M, Colen C, Pescosolido BA (2011) The sociology of suicide. Annual Reviews of Sociology 37: 505–528.

7

CHAPTER

What Factors Contributed to Changes in Employment During and after the Great Recession?

Ammar Farooq[1] and Adriana D Kugler[2]

[1]Georgetown University, Intercultural Center 580, 37th and O Streets, NW, Washington, DC 20057-1036, USA.

[2] Georgetown University, NBER, CEPR and IZA, Old North 311, 37th and O Streets, NW, Washington, DC 20057-1036, USA.

ABSTRACT

Unemployment increased drastically over the course of the Great Recession from 4.5 percent prior to the recession to 10 percent at its peak in October 2009. Since then, the unemployment rate has come down steadily, and it stood at 5.8 percent in November 2014. Based on existing analyses and some new evidence, this paper establishes that much of the change in unemployment during the Great Recession and during the recovery can be attributed to cyclical factors rather than structural factors. The paper then presents new suggestive evidence to quantify the employment impacts of various counter-cyclical policies introduced during this time. We conduct a counter-factual and find that employment would have been between 4.2 percent and 4.5 percent lower had it not been because of the spending in Medicaid injected in local economies by the Recovery Act. In addition, we conduct a differences-in-differences and triple difference analysis, which suggests that the Work Opportunity Tax Credits increased the likelihood of employment by about 4.7 percent for disconnected youth but had no effect on disabled and unemployed veterans. Finally, we also find evidence that suggests that the Hiring Incentive to Restore Employment (HIRE) Act increased employment of the unemployed by 2.6 percent and that the reemployment reforms introduced in 2012 as part of the UI extensions increased employment by 6 percent for the long-term unemployed.

Keywords: Employment Labor demand Unemployment incidence Job search Unemployment insurance Tax credits Hiring subsidies

1 INTRODUCTION

In December 2007, the US economy entered into the deepest recession since the Great Depression. Like other recessions precipitated by financial crises, the Great Recession was accompanied by a substantial contraction in aggregate demand. Following the crisis, there were sharp drops in consumer spending and to a lesser extent in investment. This translated into a drastic fall in output, which hit a low point in the fourth quarter of 2008 with a contraction of real GDP of 8.3 percent. Figure 1 shows that by the beginning of 2010, the economy had turned around in terms of GDP, consumption and investment, though these remain low by historical standards.

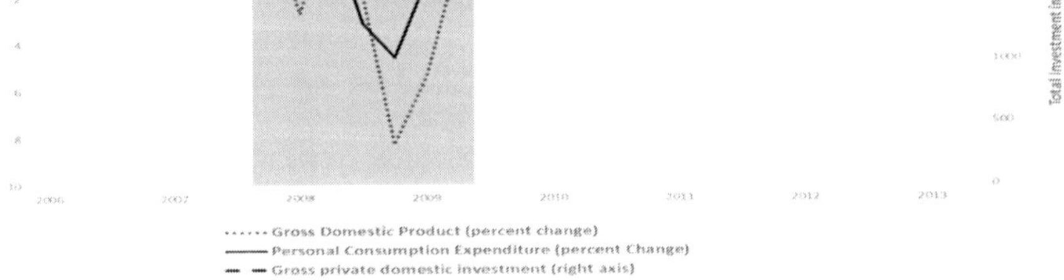

Figure 1. US GDP, Investment and personal consumption, 2006 (quarter 1)-2013 (quarter IV). Source: Bureau of Economic Analysis.

Just as the goods, services, financial, credit, and housing markets were all affected by the Great Recession, so was the labor market. The sharp contraction in demand generated massive layoffs, a sharp drop in employment and a rise in unemployment. While total employment and private sector employment have been growing steadily by 178,000 jobs per month and 188,000 jobs per month on average, respectively, since February 2010,[1] the loss of jobs during the Great Recession was so great that the economy only recently (in May 2014) recovered the 8.7 million jobs it lost. Unemployment reached a peak of 10 percent in October 2010 and has been declining steadily since. Indeed, the share of the short-term unemployed has returned to pre-recession levels, so the continued high unemployment reflects the larger share of long-term unemployed during the recovery. As explained below, the large share of long-term unemployed has important implications in terms of the speed at which the unemployment rate can continue to fall.

In Section 2, we discuss the severity of the labor market downturn during the Great Recession. In Section 3, we review past evidence and present some new evidence on the extent to which unemployment during the Great Recession and the recovery can be attributed to cyclical or structural factors. In Section 4, we explain the policy tools used during this period and present some evidence of their employment impacts during the recession and later during the recovery. We conclude in Section 5.

2 THE LABOR MARKET DURING THE GREAT RECESSION AND RECOVERY

As the Great Recession evolved, the unemployment rate rose sharply from a low of 4.5 percent the year prior to the recession in June 2007 to a peak of 10 percent in October 2009. As Table 1 shows, this rise of 5.5 percentage points in the unemployment rate between the 2007 low and the 2009 high is unprecedented for any post-WWII recession period. However, this table shows that the drop of 4.2 percent after the recession is higher than the average drop of 2.75 percent over the last nine previous recessions. While it is argued that this recovery has been particularly slow, this is not apparent from the drops in unemployment after previous recessions shown in Table 1 and in Figure 2. In fact, the fall in the unemployment rate has been greater during this most recent recovery than during the recovery of the early and late 1950s, the late 1960s, the early 1970s, the early 1990s, and the early 2000's.

Table 1. Changes in unemployment rates during each post-war recession and recovery

Recession	Lowest unemployment rate in the year before start of recession	Highest unemployment rate during or after the official end of recession	Difference from trough to peak
Nov-48	3.7	7	3.3
Jul-53	2.6	6	3.4
Aug-57	4	7.4	3.4
Apr-60	5.2	7	1.8
Dec-69	3.4	6	2.6
Nov-73	4.8	8.9	4.1
Jan-80	5.9	10.7	4.8
Jul-90	5.3	7.6	2.3
Mar-01	3.9	6.2	2.3
Dec-07	4.5	10.0	5.5
Recession	**Highest unemployment rate during or after the official end of recession**	**Lowest unemployment rate in the recovery (up to 6 years after the recession)**	**Difference from peak to trough**
Nov-48	7	2.6	4.4
Jul-53	6	4	2
Aug-57	7.4	5.1	2.3
Apr-60	7	3.7	3.3
Dec-69	6	4.8	1.2
Nov-73	8.9	5.7	3.2
Jan-80	10.7	6.6	4.1
Jul-90	7.6	5	2.6
Mar-01	6.2	4.5	1.7
Dec-07	10.0	5.8	4.2

Figure 2. U.S. Unemployment rate, 1965-2013 (Dec). Source: Bureau of Labor Statistics-Current Population Survey.

What has been atypical relative to all other recoveries going back to the early 1970s is that government jobs have not contributed to this recovery. In fact, the fall in government jobs has held back the economy from a healthier employment recovery. Figure 3 shows government employment changes during recoveries of the 1970s, 1980s, 1990s, and 2000s as well as during the most recent recovery. This figure shows that every other recovery has been accompanied by government job growth, with the exception of the recovery from the Great Recession. While the role of government jobs on employment during previous recoveries had always been positive, the role of government jobs has been declining over the past decades since the 1970s. By contrast, the recent recovery has seen a large decline in government jobs, with the exception of the few months surrounding the hiring for the 2010 Census. In fact, close to 600,000 government jobs have been shed during this recovery.

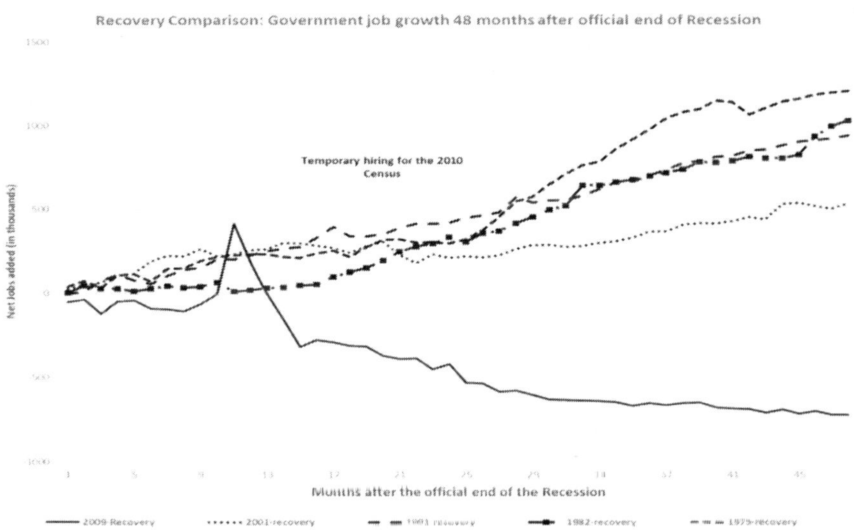

Figure 3. Government job creation in current and previous recoveries, 1975-2009. Source: Bureau of Labor Statistics-Current Employment Statistics survey.

Much of the rise and sustained unemployment can be explained by private sector job losses during the recession and public sector job losses during the recovery. In addition, a big part of the sustained unemployment can be explained by the inability of people to exit unemployment as private sector employers have not been creating enough jobs, and public sector employers have not created jobs on net during this period.

Figure 4 shows the drastic increase in layoffs during this time, with layoffs increasing by over 50 percent during the Great Recession. The vast majority of these discharges were the result of mass layoffs of more than 50 individuals. At the height of the recession, all dismissals were due to mass layoffs. Yet, there were also many experiencing individual layoffs before the peak of the recession. Since then, employers have substantially reduced mass and individual layoffs, and these are currently below the pre-recession levels in 2006. As shown in Figure 5, because there were so many individuals losing their jobs and so few new jobs created, the ratio of the number of unemployed to job vacancies reached a high of close to 7 unemployed per vacancy in July 2009 – the highest ratio since JOLTS data has been collected. As fewer people entered into unemployment and more jobs have been added, this has now dropped to about 3 unemployed per vacancy.

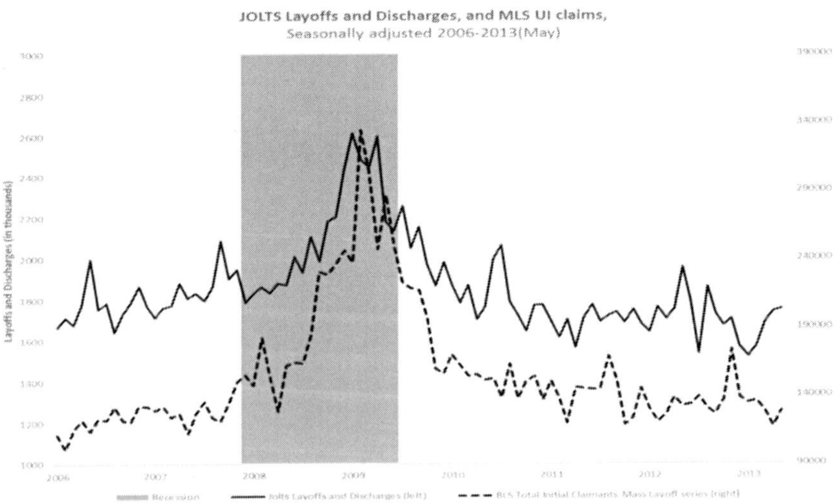

Figure 4. Layoffs and discharges and mass layoffs, 2006–2013. Source: Bureau of Labor Statistics- Job Openings and Labor Turnover Survey & Mass Layoff Statistics.

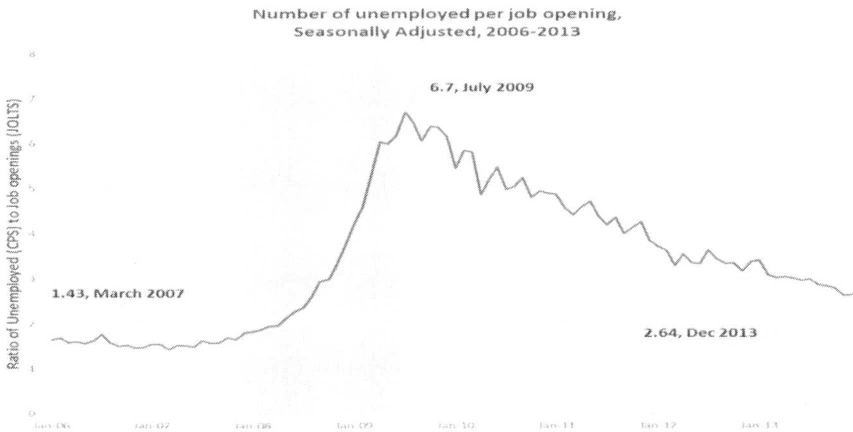

Figure 5. Ratio of unemployed-to-job openings, 2006–2013. Source: Bureau of Labor Statistics- Job Openings and Labor Turnover Survey & Current Population Survey.

Figure 6 shows that the chances of finding a job within the last month for an individual who has been unemployed for less than 6 months is over 20 percent, and the chances of finding a job within the last month for an individual who has been unemployed for more than 6 months is a little over 10 percent. This is because while job-to-job turnover substantially declined during the recession, there are still many employed looking for work that enter new jobs directly from other employment.[2] For example, even today, there are still 6.9 million part-time workers who would rather be working full time and who continue to look for full-time work. In addition, there are many individuals among those classified as out of the labor force that would like a job and would enter directly into jobs. There are 2.1 million marginally attached workers who are willing and available for work but did not look for work during the past month, which means that many workers entering new jobs come directly from the pool of individuals out of the labor force.[3]

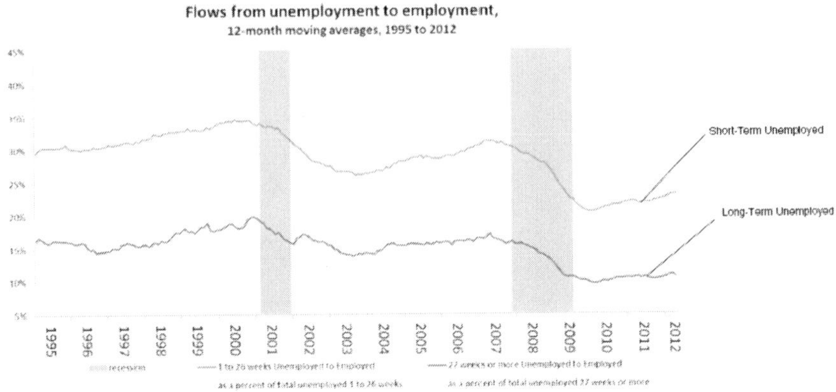

Figure 6. Flows from unemployment to employment for short- and long-term unemployed, 1995–2012. Source: Bureau of Labor Statistics-Current Population Survey.

The evidence above shows that the short- and long-term unemployed are not equally likely to find jobs, and the unemployed, and in particular the long-term unemployed, may have to compete for jobs with currently employed workers and even with workers who have been out of the labor force. Indeed, there is evidence of duration dependence, which implies that it is harder to exit unemployment the longer an individual has been unemployed. Kroft et al. (2014) indeed find that duration dependence can account for much of the increase in long-term unemployment. The share of the long-term unemployed increased sharply during the Great Recession. While the long-term unemployed comprised less than 15 percent of all the unemployed prior to the recession, by April 2010, 44 percent of the unemployed had been unemployed for more than 6 months. Figure 7 does show a slow decline in the share of the long-term unemployed in the past two years, with this share now standing at 30.7 percent – still high by pre-recession standards.

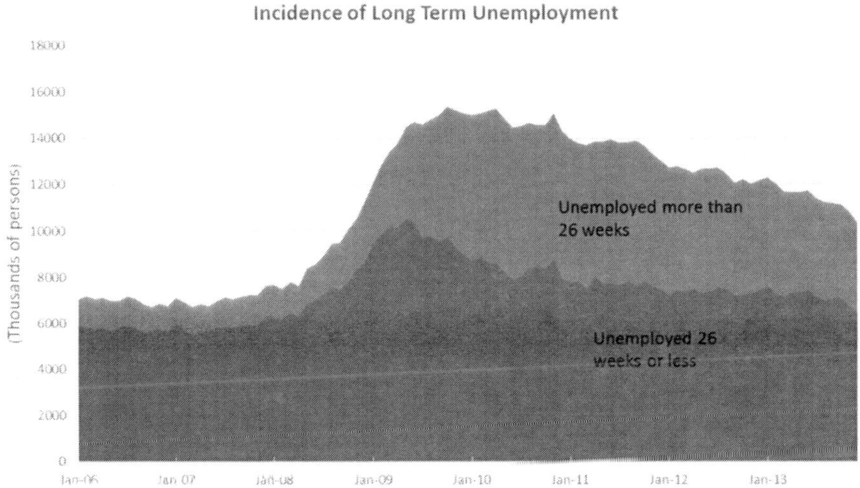

Figure 7. Incidence of long-term unemployment, 2006–2013. Source: Bureau of Labor Statistics-Current Population Survey.

There are a number of reasons why the long-term unemployed may find it harder to find jobs than the short-term unemployed and contribute to keeping the share of the long-term unemployed and overall unemployment high. First, employers may simply take employment status or duration of unemployment as a signal of worker quality. Even though the extent of mass layoffs suggests that employment status and unemployment duration were probably relatively bad signals of quality during the Great Recession,[4] in their audit study, Kroft et al. (2012) find evidence of substantial statistical discrimination against the long-term unemployed. Second, the unemployed, and in particular the long-term unemployed, may find it much more difficult to find a job because individuals may lose their skills and motivation as they remain longer in unemployment. This may be because they are either less skilled or less desirable to hire as their spells of unemployment prolong. Third, the unemployed, may have less access to information about jobs because those in their networks may also be unemployed, and many jobs are filled through informal channels. There is anecdotal evidence that many employers turned to using informal channels during the recovery as a way to save on recruiting costs given the abundance of potential applicants. In fact, the share of individuals searching for work through family and friends grew from 19.7 percent in 2006 to 26.4 percent in 2007, then to 28 percent in 2008, and has stayed at over 32 percent since 2009.[5] This increased reliance on family and friends as a way to find jobs has occurred even though networks are likely less effective in generating job offers on average given the higher unemployment today.[6] Finally, as the financial assets of the unemployed deplete the longer they have been in unemployment, it becomes harder to pay for transportation, to move to take a job and to pay for other costs associated with looking for jobs.

This section shows that the Great Recession was atypical in terms of the drastic impact it had on the labor market. All measures show large losses for workers, including extensive mass layoffs, widespread drops in employment, a steep rise in unemployment, and greater difficulty in finding employment. In addition, this section shows that the recovery after the Great Recession was different in that government jobs have delayed rather than sped up the recovery of the labor market, as in past recessions. Finally, even though the labor market is back to where it was in terms of most indicators, the Great Recession has been different in that it has had a long-lasting impact in the labor market because of its effect on long-term unemployment. The share of long-term unemployed is twice the pre-recession share, and the long-term unemployed face numerous difficulties finding employment even as the economy has continued to recover.

3 CYCLICAL VS. STRUCTURAL UNEMPLOYMENT DURING THE GREAT RECESSION AND BEYOND

In this section, we explore how much of the unemployment during the Great Recession and beyond was cyclical and how much reflected mismatches and other structural challenges faced by the economy. Below, we review the large body of past evidence and present some new evidence pointing to the unemployment problem being largely driven by cyclical factors during this period. Yet, the evidence also indicates that some new problems have emerged in the labor market which could potentially turn into structural factors if they persist over the years to come.

3.1 Evidence from Okun's law

A number of previous studies have re-estimated Okun's Law during the Great Recession and recovery. These studies show that much of the change in unemployment is due to changes in GDP and that the persistent high unemployment is due to a slow recovery in GDP. Arteta et al. (2011) show that the majority of movements in unemployment since the Great Recession were due to changes in output. According to this study, the drop in GDP can explain 63 percent of the rise in unemployment during the recession. Similarly, about 57 percent of the drop in unemployment during the recovery can be explained by the rise in GDP. This indicates that both during the recession and during the recovery, cyclical factors were key in explaining changes in unemployment and that cyclical factors have remained important during the recovery. Importantly, Ball et al. (2012) find that the relation between the change in unemployment and the change in GDP has been stable over the periods 1990–91, 2001, and 2007–09. Rather, they conclude that the strength of economic growth relative to the trend is what has been different during these periods.

In Okun's law, the rest of the changes in unemployment are considered as unexplained or explained by factors not included in the regression. These could be factors such as skill, sectoral, or regional mismatches.[7] Thus, an extension of Okun's Law would include measures of mismatches in the regression. Estevão and Tsounta (2011) estimate a relation of changes in unemployment at the state level on changes in gross state product (GSP), a measure of skill mismatches in the state, and a measure of geographical immobility. This study finds that much of the change in state unemployment can be explained by GSP and that only about 0.5 percentage points of the increase in the NAIRU can be explained by skill gaps.

3.2 Evidence from the Beveridge curve

The Beveridge Curve, which establishes the relation between the job openings rate and the unemployment rate, is yet another way to disentangle how much of the change in unemployment is due to cyclical factors and how much is due to other factors. The Beveridge Curve, estimated by the Bureau of Labor Statistics over the last decade,[8] shows that during the early 2000s, unemployment increased and the job openings declined starting in November 2001 until around November 2007. These movements along the Beveridge Curve are consistent with cyclical factors driving the changes in unemployment during this period. In December 2007, the unemployment rate increased rapidly together with much slower drops in the job openings rate. These movements since 2007 are also consistent with cyclical factors driving these changes. In October 2009, the unemployment rate started to drop and the job openings rate started to rise. The backward movement to the Northwest points to a decline in cyclical unemployment. Yet, the fall in unemployment has not been fast enough to match the rise in the job openings rate. This indicates that for a given job openings rate, the unemployment rate is higher than it used to be, pointing potentially to the rise in the importance of structural factors.

A number of studies have examined and explained this shift in detail. Diamond (2013) explains that the Beveridge Curve may be using proxies rather than the correct measures of those searching for work and the right measure of job openings. Indeed, the unemployment rate may not capture everyone looking for work. Diamond (2013) does a thorough analysis of flows from and to employment, unemployment, and out of the labor force and finds transitions of similar magnitudes from non-employment to employment and back as from unemployment to employment and back. This is indicative that many of those classified as out of the labor force may be actively looking for work. In addition, Davis et al. (2012) have found that the speed of filling vacancies and the proportion of hiring varies by industry and over the business cycle. For instance, the industry composition of job openings has been changing over time, with many fewer job openings in construction, which have short durations, and many more job openings in health and education, which have longer durations. Given that long durations imply low closing rates of vacancies or high job opening rates, then one may worry that changes in the composition of vacancies may be accounting for the high opening rate associated with the same unemployment rate as before.

Ghayad and Dickens (2012) disaggregate the unemployment-vacancy relationship by industry, age, education, and duration of unemployment and by blue- and white-collar groups to understand if the shifts in the aggregate Beveridge Curve are driven by particular groups. They find that the outward shift in the Beveridge Curve was common among all major industries, all age groups, all education groups and among blue- and white-collar workers. What is noteworthy is that the outward shift in the Beveridge Curve is only evident for the long-term unemployed. Thus, whether this shift becomes a structural problem will depend on how permanent the obstacles faced by the long-term unemployed become and on how effective the policies to help the long-term unemployed, discussed in the following section, have been.

Finally, Daly et al. (2012) indicate that a longer series to estimate the Beveridge Curve, like the one they construct using the Help-Wanted

Index to go back to the 1960s, shows that the shift in the Beveridge Curve observed in the current cycle is within the range of what occurred in past business cycles. Moreover, when they combine the Beveridge Curve with the Job Creation Curve, they estimate an increase in the natural rate of unemployment of between 0.4 and 1.4 percentage points, or between 7 percent and 25 percent of the rise in unemployment during the last recession.

3.3 Evidence of mismatches

Lazear and Spletzer (2012) conduct a rigorous quantification of the extent of mismatches and find that changes in industrial mismatch are cyclical. They construct an industrial mismatch index using JOLTS and CPS data and they find that the index was the same in 2011 as prior to the Great Recession. Instead, they find that industrial mismatches increased sharply because unemployment went up in every industry, exceeding the number of vacancies in every industry. Much of the increase in the gap between unemployment and vacancies during the recession and the subsequent decline during the recovery can be explained by four industries: health services, government, construction and manufacturing. Lazear and Spletzer (2012) also estimate an occupational mismatch index and find that this is much higher than the industrial mismatch index, but, like the industrial mismatch, it is pro-cyclical, and the occupational mismatch index has already returned to its pre-recession level. Importantly, they point out that mismatch indices were higher during this period because unemployment was higher in all industries and occupations and not because the skills desired by employers are less in line with what they desired in the past.

In fact, this is exactly what is borne out when employers are asked about their ability to find workers qualified to fill their vacancies. Only 6 percent of employers in 2012 and 5 percent of employers in 2013 reported the low quality of labor as a major concern for their businesses. Moreover, finding qualified applicants was less of a concern during the recovery than it was before the recession. In 2013, 36 percent of employers reported that there were too few or no qualified applicants, compared to 41 percent in 2012 and 48 percent in 2007.[9] By contrast, employers continue to report poor sales as one of their top concerns. In 2012, about 21 percent of employers reported poor sales as their most important challenge, and around 17 percent of employers continue to report poor sales as a major challenge in 2013. This suggests that aggregate demand problems are more prominent in employers' decisions than skill gaps problems. It also suggests that skill gaps were there before the recession and after the recession, but do not appear to have become more pronounced in the view of employers.

Another approach towards estimating the extent of mismatches is to directly estimate the efficiency of matching in the economy instead of estimating the relation between the unemployment rate and measures of mismatches. Estimating matching functions of employment on the number of unemployed and the number of vacancies allows for estimating the parameters of the matching function and the efficiency of matching parameter. Sahin et al. (2014) estimate matching functions using recent data from the Current Population Survey, the Job Openings and Labor Turnover Survey (JOLTS), and the Conference Board's Help Wanted Online (HWOL) which covers the universe of online U.S. job advertisements. They find that mismatches across industries and 3-digit occupations can only explain a third of the total observed increase in the recent rise in the unemployment rate.

Barlevi (2011) also estimates matching functions using a Cobb-Douglas specification and using data on unemployment from Haver analytics and vacancy data from JOLTS for the period from 2000 to 2011. He finds that the reduced matching productivity from normal times (defined as 2000-August 2008) to the end of 2011 can explain an increase in unemployment to 7.1 percent. Given that the rise in unemployment from his defined normal times was 5.3 percent and 9.3 during the period after, then mismatches could explain 45 percent of the rise in unemployment, and 55 percent would be explained by other factors. However, Barlevi (2011) acknowledges that his assumption of a fixed ratio of the value of a job to the cost of filling a vacancy leads to an over-estimate of the effect of mismatches and, thus, provides an upper bound of the impact. Given these two studies, the impact of mismatch ranges between 33 percent and 45 percent (with the latter being an upper bound), while the impact of other factors (including slack demand) account for between 67 percent and 55 percent of the rise in unemployment during the Great Recession.

In contrast to industry and occupational mismatches, the study by Dickens (2010), which looks at geographic mismatch, finds no evidence at all of mismatches in this dimension. This study and others (Lazear and Spletzer, 2012; Elsby et al., 2011) provide support to the broadly accepted view that housing lock and the inability to move to look for jobs due to the lackluster housing market cannot account for any of the increase in unemployment.

Overall, this section shows that regardless of the method used to identify the relative importance of demand and structural factors in explaining the rise in unemployment, the answer is always the same – the majority of the increase in unemployment can be explained by cyclical factors rather than structural factors.[10] Nonetheless, the evidence does provide a range of estimates of the importance of structural factors ranging from 25 percent for estimates from the Beveridge Curve, to 33 percent using the most credible mismatch function estimates, and to 40 percent when relying on Okun's law.

4 POLICIES TO ADDRESS THE UNEMPLOYMENT PROBLEM

It is clear from the previous sections that there were two key factors contributing to unemployment that needed to be addressed during the recession and recovery. The most important challenge facing employers and workers during the Great Recession, and even through the recovery, was slack demand. In addition, labor markets are now facing new problems during the recovery which were not present prior to the Great Recession. In particular, the large rise in the fraction of long-term unemployed made it more difficult to bring down the unemployment rate during this time period. The majority of measures introduced to address unemployment during this period, thus, focused on different policies to stimulate labor demand. Later, during the recovery, policy measures focused on how to aid the long-term unemployed.

4.1 Impact of fiscal spending on employment: American recovery and reinvestment act

In 2009, the American Recovery and Reinvestment Act (ARRA) generated a large fiscal stimulus. The Recovery Act introduced $840 billion in government spending directed towards tax benefits; contracts, grants and loans; and entitlements. The initial spending was divided into $290.7 billion for tax benefits including individual tax credits, tax incentives for businesses, energy incentives, and manufacturing incentives. Another $261.2 billion was spent on contracts, grants, and loans for education, transportation, infrastructure, energy and the environment, research and development, housing, health, and job training. Finally, a total of $264.4 billion was spent in entitlements, including $105.7 billion, which was spent on Medicaid and Medicare, mostly for Medicaid Grants to States, another $61.3 billion was spent on unemployment insurance programs and the rest on family services and energy and housing subsidies.[11] The economic rationale behind this spending was based on the evidence on fiscal multipliers and the idea that public spending would spur economic activity in the private sector. The implication for the labor market was that government spending would have an impact on direct job creation and, at the same time, induce hiring in the private sector. In December 2010, the government passed the Middle Class Tax Relief Act of 2010, introducing another large packet of fiscal spending of close to $700 billion that also financed tax cuts and income support programs.

The time-series evidence suggests that fiscal spending was effective. Employment losses quickly lessened after the passing for the Recovery Act, and employment growth started a year later. In fact, employment reignited again 7 months after GDP picked up. Indeed, this is in line with the usual lag between GDP and employment growth.[12]Likewise, employment appears to have grown at a faster pace after the additional fiscal stimulus was introduced in December 2010. A problem with this evidence is that it is not possible to distinguish if that employment growth would have taken place even without the stimulus.

Thus, panel data evidence is more useful to disentangle the causal effect of the stimulus. Feyrer and Sacerdote (2011) indeed present evidence from panel data that exploits the fact that different states and localities received different amounts of stimulus funds over that time period. Their study finds a broad range of fiscal multipliers from 0, for expenditures on education, to 2, for support programs for low-income households and infrastructure. More importantly, Feyrer and Sacerdote (2011) find that regions of the country that received more recovery funds experienced faster employment growth during the recession and recovery. They found that a state's receipt of $100,000 generated between half a job and one job. Another study by Chodorow-Reich et al. (2012) finds that recovery fund outlays in Medicaid expenditures had substantial impacts on job creation. By focusing on Medicaid outlays, they are able to address the endogeneity of state receipt by instrumenting the Recovery Act funds for Medicaid with previous expenditures in Medicaid in the state. They find that a state's receipt of a marginal $100,000 in Medicaid outlays generates 3.8 additional job-years, with 84 percent of those new job-years created outside of government, health, and education.

We use the Feyrer and Sacerdote (2011) and the Chodorow-Reich et al. (2012) estimates to construct counter-factuals of the employment impact of the fiscal expenditures and the multiplier effects introduced by the Recovery Act. To conduct this counter-factual exercise we take the lower bound of the Feyrer and Sacerdote (2011) study and assume that the entire amount of $840 billion of expenditures from the Recovery Act was evenly distributed over the course of the Recovery Act. We then determine what employment would have been if the Recovery Act was not passed. Although this is not a perfect counter-factual exercise, it provides an estimate on the effectiveness of the various fiscal programs on employment creation. We find that employment would have been, on average, 72,000 lower per month without the Recovery Act or about 63% to 67% lower. However, since Recovery Act resources may have gone to those states which were ready to start investments and support contracts, or by contrast the federal government may have distributed entitlements to those places that needed them the most, the Feyrer and Sacerdote (2011) multiplier may be biased up or down.

The counter-factual employment using the Chodorow-Reich et al. (2012) multiplier is smaller. While Chodorow-Reich et al. (2012) found a bigger multiplier, the amounts spent in Medicaid were much smaller. This multiplier is credible since their estimation strategy takes into account the potential endogeneity of the distribution of resources to different states. Applying the $88 billion allocated to Medicaid funds in the original Recovery Act, the counter-factual shows much smaller reductions in employment of 5,000 jobs per month, on average, or between 4.2 percent and 4.5 percent had the Recovery Act not spent resources in Medicaid. While these results are smaller, these effects are more reliable.

4.2 Impacts of tax credits and subsidies for employers

4.2.1 Impact of the work opportunity tax credits (WOTC)

Work Opportunity Tax Credits (WOTC) were first introduced in 1996. These were tax credits to employers hiring workers in specific target groups. Work Opportunity Tax Credits were introduced to incentivize employers to hire people from groups generally considered to have low skill levels and, thus, less likely to find employment. The target groups covered by WOTC have been expanded or changed a few times since 1996. More recently, these credits were expanded during the period covering the recession. The passage of the U.S. Troops Readiness, Veteran's Care, Katrina Recovery and Iraq Accountability Act of 2007 expanded the tax credits until August 21, 2011 to cover disabled veterans who were discharged from active duty in the past year. Before this, WOTC credits covered members of families receiving TANF, veterans who were members of families receiving food stamps, 18–39 year olds who were members of families receiving food stamps, ex-felons, SSI recipients and those in communities designated as empowerment zones, enterprise communities, and renewal communities.

The Recovery Act further included $32.6 billion in tax credits to provide incentives for employers to hire members of two additional groups until December 31, 2010. The two groups for which WOTC was expanded included: unemployed veterans who were discharged in the past 5 years and who had collected unemployment insurance payments for at least 4 weeks in the past 12 months, and disconnected youth aged 16–24 years old who had neither regularly worked nor attended school in the past 6 months. While these credits expired in December 31, 2010, on November 21, 2011, Congress passed the VOW to Hire Heroes Act, which extended tax credits for unemployed veterans who first benefited from the Recovery Act WOTCs. The VOW act expired on December 31, 2012. The timeline below describes the introduction and expiration of these credits and the reforms, which are discussed in more detailed in the next two sections (Figure 8).

4.2.2 Impact of the work opportunity tax credits (WOTC) on veterans

To examine the impact of these credits, we do a difference-in-difference analysis to compare the treatment groups to non-treated veterans. For veterans there are two treatment groups. The first is the group of disabled veterans who were discharged in the last year. The second is the group of unemployed veterans who have received UI for at least 4 weeks in the past year and who were discharged from active duty in the past 5 years. Since the Current Population Survey, which we use for our analysis, does not allow us to identify collection of UI in the past year, we can only identify those that were unemployed for at least 4 weeks in the past year. Given that not all of the unemployed qualify for UI benefits, this group will include some who would not have qualified for the credits, but this is the best that can be done with CPS data. Similarly, we cannot identify disabled veterans discharged in the past year or unemployed veterans discharged in the past 5 years. The best we can do with the CPS is identify those discharged from active duty since 2001. In this case too, we may be including some individuals in the treatment group who would not have qualified for WOTC. We then focus on the years 2008, 2009, 2010 and 2011 for disabled veterans and on the years 2009, 2010, and 2012 for the group of unemployed veterans. The analysis leaves out TANF and SNAP recipients to avoid including in the comparison group individuals who continued to benefit from the earlier tax credits introduced before the 2007 U.S. Troops Readiness Act and the 2009 Recovery Act. Unfortunately, we cannot identify ex-felons, those receiving SSI, or those in designated communities, so the comparison group will have some who may have still benefited from WOTCs. We also do a difference-in-difference-in-difference analysis in which we also use non-veterans (disabled non-veterans and unemployed non-veterans) as comparison groups.

Table 2 presents descriptive statistics using CPS data for those affected by WOTCs. The table shows that disabled veterans and unemployed veterans have lower employment than other veterans and the population as a whole, and they are more likely to be male and more educated than the population as a whole. Since the treated groups are different from the control groups, for the DD and triple difference strategies to be valid, it has to be the case that the treatment and comparison groups had similar pre-treatment trends. Figure 9 shows that the pre-treatment employment trends of disabled veterans and disabled non-veterans move roughly in tandem for the two groups. Figure 10 similarly shows that pre-treatment employment of unemployed veterans and non-veterans moved roughly similarly for these two groups.

Table 2. Descriptive statistics for different WOTC eligible groups

	Full sample	Veterans	Disabled veterans	Disabled Veterans Before WOTC Eligibility (Pre-2008)	Disabled veterans during WOTC eligibility (Post-2008)	Unemployed veterans	Unemployed Veterans Before WOTC eligibility (Pre- 2010)	Unemployed veterans during WOTC eligibility (Post-2010)	Youths (16-24 year olds)	Disconnected youth	Disconnected youth before WOTC eligibility (Pre- 2010)	Disconnected youth after WOTC eligibility (Post- 2010)
Employed	0.729	0.730	0.546	[illegible]	[illegible]	[illegible]	0.643	0.504	0.485	0.340	0.350	0.326
	(0.444)	(0.444)	(0.498)	(0.496)	(0.498)	(0.484)	(0.479)	(0.499)	(0.500)	(0.474)	(0.477)	(0.469)
Weeks looking for work	1.405	1.364	1.244	1.057	1.310	20.50	19.68	[illegible]	1.597	4.706	4.151	[illegible]
	(6.162)	(6.076)	(5.803)	(5.163)	(6.512)	(12.66)	(12.77)	(11.02)	(6.330)	(12.05)	(11.32)	(13.08)
Male	0.480	0.909	0.896	0.905	0.891	0.894	0.896	0.892	0.506	0.472	0.452	0.502
	(0.500)	(0.298)	(0.306)	(0.293)	(0.312)	(0.306)	(0.306)	(0.311)	(0.500)	(0.499)	(0.498)	(0.500)
Less than H.S.	0.117	0.0373	0.0826	0.0427	0.0276	0.0390	0.0435	0.0322	0.431	0.306	0.341	0.259
	(0.321)	(0.198)	(0.178)	(0.202)	(0.164)	(0.194)	(0.204)	(0.176)	(0.495)	(0.462)	(0.474)	(0.438)
H.S. diploma	0.299	0.329	0.264	0.268	0.260	0.370	0.374	0.364	0.210	0.432	0.426	0.442
	(0.458)	(0.470)	(0.441)	(0.443)	(0.439)	(0.483)	(0.484)	(0.481)	(0.407)	(0.495)	(0.495)	(0.497)
Some college	0.294	0.380	0.444	0.448	0.442	0.418	0.415	0.423	0.299	0.180	0.167	[illegible]
	(0.456)	(0.485)	(0.497)	(0.497)	(0.497)	(0.493)	(0.493)	(0.494)	(0.458)	(0.384)	(0.368)	(0.404)
Bachelor's and higher	0.290	0.253	0.266	0.241	0.271	0.173	0.167	0.181	0.0600	0.0799	0.0709	0.0937
	(0.454)	(0.435)	(0.439)	(0.428)	(0.444)	(0.378)	(0.373)	(0.385)	(0.237)	(0.271)	(0.257)	(0.291)
White	0.795	0.809	0.793	0.808	0.797	0.793	[illegible]	0.782	0.796	0.753	0.711	0.747
	(0.404)	(0.393)	(0.405)	(0.394)	(0.402)	(0.405)	(0.399)	(0.413)	(0.403)	(0.432)	(0.436)	(0.435)
Black	0.115	0.128	0.140	0.127	0.144	0.136	0.132	0.142	0.108	0.143	0.145	0.141
	(0.318)	(0.334)	(0.347)	(0.333)	(0.351)	(0.342)	(0.338)	(0.349)	(0.310)	(0.350)	(0.352)	(0.348)
No. Observations	141,3820	100,591	8,223	3,140	5,733	6,517	3,906	2,611	260,842	32,656	19,766	12,890

Notes. Mean coefficients; SD in parentheses. Unemployed Veterans are defined as veterans who had searched for more than 4 weeks for work during the last year. Disconnected Youth are defined as 16-24 year olds who are not enrolled in school and who worked less than 26 weeks in the previous year. Data is from Annual Social and Economic (ASEC) supplement of the Current Population Survey spanning the years 2003–2013.

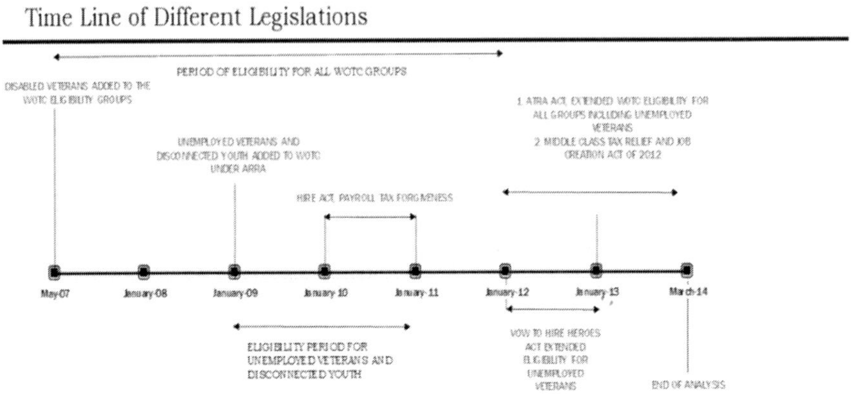

Figure 8. WOTC legislation history. Source: Congressional Research Service, http://fas.org/sgp/crs/misc/RL30089.pdf.

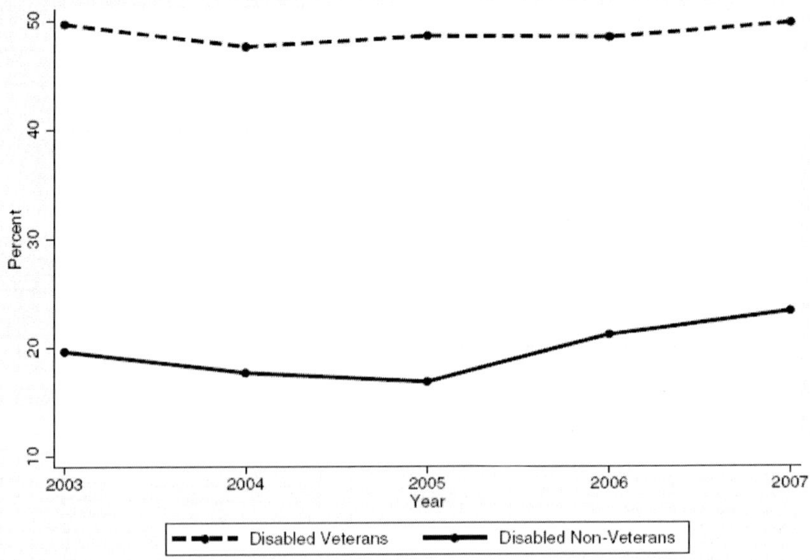

Figure 9. **Employment rates of disabled veterans and non-veterans.**

Table 3 shows the difference-in-difference estimates for disabled and unemployed workers. Columns (1) and (2) show the results for all veterans and Columns (5) and (6) show the results for those discharged after 2001. All specifications control for age, a quadratic term for age, education indicators, gender, and race. Columns (2) and (6) include state and year fixed effects. When we focus on all veterans, the results show an increase in the likelihood of employment after exposure to WOTC of 0.05. However, the impact disappears when focusing on those discharged since 2001. Columns (3), (4), (7) and (8) show results for unemployed veterans. As for disabled veterans, the result on all unemployed veterans suggests an increase in the likelihood of employment of close to 0.02 due to WOTC, but the effect disappears when focusing on those recently discharged from active duty.

Table 3. Difference-in-difference (DD) effects of work opportunity tax credits (WOTC) on disabled veterans and unemployed veterans

	All veterans				Recent veterans only			
	(1)	(2)	(3)	(4)	(5)	(6)	(7)	(8)
Disabled veteran X WOTC eligibility period for disabled veterans	0.0491***	0.0471***	0.0499***	0.0501***	-0.0127	-0.0115	-0.0043	0.0003
	(5.57)	(4.83)	(5.66)	(5.72)	(-0.30)	(-0.30)	(-0.10)	(0.01)
Disabled veteran dummy	-0.237***	-0.212***	-0.239***	-0.242***	-0.0643	-0.0635*	-0.0706	-0.0801*
	(-24.95)	(-27.84)	(-25.13)	(-25.31)	(-1.48)	(-1.72)	(-1.62)	(-1.81)
WOTC eligibility period for disabled veterans	-0.0416***	-0.0393***	-0.0204***	-0.0129*	-0.0634***	-0.0397**	-0.0182	-0.0105
	(-13.96)	(-5.23)	(-5.00)	(-1.69)	(-5.53)	(-1.97)	(-1.18)	(-0.48)
Unemployed veterans X WOTC eligibility period for unemployed veterans			0.0308**	0.0181*			0.0208	0.0186
			(1.97)	(1.75)			(0.76)	(0.68)
Unemployed veterans dummy			-0.167***	-0.163***			-0.128***	-0.121***
			(-20.06)	(-19.58)			(-4.32)	(-4.11)
WOTC eligibility period for unemployed veterans			-0.0308***	-0.0285***			-0.0609***	-0.0484***
			(-7.15)	(-3.55)			(-5.36)	(-2.65)
State fixed effects	No	Yes	No	Yes	No	Yes	No	Yes
Time fixed effects	No	Yes	No	Yes	No	Yes	No	Yes
Demographic controls	Yes	Yes	Yes	Yes	Yes	Yes	Yes	Yes
N	100,584	100,591	100,584	100,584	9,505	9,514	9,508	9,505

Notes: The table above reports marginal effects from probit models. Demographic controls include age, a quadratic in age, dummies for education attainment, and gender and race dummies. Unemployed Veterans are defined as veterans who had searched for more than 4 weeks for work during the last year. Data for this table was restricted to veterans only. Data is from Annual Social and Economic (ASEC) supplement of the Current Population Survey spanning the years 2003-2013.
t statistics in parenthesis.
*p < 0.10, **p < 0.05, ***p < 0.01

Table 4 uses the non-veterans also as potential comparison groups by doing a triple difference analysis which controls for veteran status, disabled status, unemployment status, post-treatment indicator, interactions of veteran with disabled and veteran with unemployment, and interaction of each of these with the post-treatment indicator to allow for the possibility that veterans, the disabled, or the unemployment faced different situations after WOTCs were introduced. These results, like the double difference results, suggest an impact of WOTC on disabled veterans, but the impacts disappear when focusing on those recently discharged. Also, in this case, the impact of unemployed veterans disappears altogether.

Table 4. Difference-in-difference-in-difference (DDD) effects of work opportunity tax credits (WOTC) on disabled veterans and unemployed veterans

	All veterans eligible for WOTC based on employment history				Only recent veterans eligible for WOTC based on employment history			
	(1)	(2)	(3)	(4)	(5)	(6)	(7)	(8)
Disabled X veteran X WOTC eligibility period for disabled veterans	0.0472***	0.0465***	0.0471***	0.0480***	-0.0193	-0.0180	-0.00910	-0.0084
	(4.06)	(4.30)	(4.06)	(4.16)	(-0.45)	(-0.43)	(-0.22)	(-0.20)
Disabled X WOTC eligibility period for disabled veterans	0.00847	0.00766	0.00962	0.00870	0.0169***	0.0164***	0.0166***	0.0162***
	(0.86)	(0.78)	(0.97)	(0.88)	(2.71)	(2.63)	(2.66)	(2.59)
Veteran X WOTC eligibility period for disabled veterans	-0.0162***	-0.0185***	-0.0139***	-0.0144***	-0.0402***	-0.0310**	-0.00807	-0.0005
	(-5.71)	(-5.81)	(-3.39)	(-3.39)	(-2.65)	(-2.06)	(-0.47)	(-0.03)
Disabled X veteran	0.154***	0.152***	0.154***	0.152***	0.174***	0.172***	0.171***	0.169***
	(33.90)	(32.99)	(34.11)	(33.23)	(13.00)	(12.71)	(12.40)	(12.13)
Disabled dummy	-0.560***	-0.559***	-0.567***	-0.562***	-0.442***	-0.442***	-0.444***	-0.445***
	(-77.57)	(-76.79)	(-78.36)	(-77.58)	(-76.49)	(-76.30)	(-77.06)	(-76.91)
Veteran dummy	-0.0137***	-0.0145***	-0.0114***	-0.0121***	0.00567	-0.00208	0.00948	0.00236
	(-5.85)	(-6.17)	(-4.77)	(-5.29)	(0.45)	(-0.16)	(0.74)	(0.19)
WOTC eligibility period for disabled veterans	-0.0168***	-0.0147***	-0.0100***	-0.0266***	-0.0174***	-0.0151***	-0.0107***	-0.0271***
	(-21.24)	(-7.12)	(-9.07)	(-14.66)	(-22.69)	(-7.39)	(-9.97)	(-15.14)
Unemployed X veterans X WOTC eligibility period for unemployed veterans			0.0118	0.0105			0.0155	0.0130
			(0.95)	(0.84)			(0.48)	(0.40)
Unemployed X veterans			-0.0295***	-0.0296***			-0.0199	-0.0175
			(-3.86)	(-3.89)			(-0.72)	(-0.64)
Veterans X WOTC eligibility period for unemployed veterans			-0.00888**	-0.00824*			-0.0442***	-0.0442***
			(-2.04)	(-1.89)			(-3.23)	(-3.22)
Unemployed X WOTC eligibility period for unemployed veterans			0.00983***	0.0093***			0.0109***	0.0103***
			(3.00)	(2.82)			(3.43)	(3.24)
WOTC eligibility period for unemployed veterans			-0.0102***	0.0111***			-0.0103***	0.0110***
			(-8.83)	(5.41)			(-9.21)	(5.41)
Unemployed dummy			-0.119***	-0.117***			-0.122***	-0.120***
			(-48.30)	(-47.60)			(-51.18)	(-50.46)
State fixed effects	No	Yes	No	Yes	No	Yes	No	Yes
Time fixed effects	No	Yes	No	Yes	No	Yes	No	Yes
Demographic controls	Yes	Yes	Yes	Yes	Yes	Yes	Yes	Yes
N	1,285,543	1,285,543	1285543	1,285,543	1,285,543	1285543	1,285,543	1,285,543

Notes: The table above reports marginal effects from a probit model. Demographic controls include age, a quadratic in age, dummies for educational attainment, and dummies for gender and race. Unemployed Veterans are defined as veterans who had searched for more than 4 weeks for work during the last year. Unemployed dummy refers to all individuals in the sample who had searched for more than 4 weeks during the last year. Data for this table leaves out individuals who could have qualified for WOTC, including SNAP and TANF recipients. Data is from Annual Social and Economic (ASEC) supplement of the Current Population Survey spanning the years 2003–2013.

t statistics in parenthesis.

*p < 0.10, **p < 0.05, ***p < 0.01.

Heaton (2012) has done similar analysis using the American Community Survey (ACS) and double and triple difference specifications. Our results are remarkably similar to those of Heaton (2012) when focusing on all veterans even though he uses a different source of data. However, Heaton (2012) fails to take into account that one of the requirements to qualify for WOTC was to have been recently discharged. While we cannot perfectly identify those discharged 1 and 5 years ago, we can at least identify those discharged since 2001. This makes a big difference – the impact of WOTC on veterans disappears.

4.2.3 Impact of the work opportunity tax credits (WOTC) on disconnected youth

As explained above, the Recovery Act not only extended credits for unemployed veterans but also for disconnected youth. Disconnected youth are defined as those between 16 and 24 years of age who are not working or have not been in school in the past year. Table 2 shows that disconnected youth have lower employment, have been looking for work longer, and are more likely to have dropped out of high school or to have only a high school degree. Thus, it is clear that disconnected youth and other youth groups are likely to be different. Figure 11 directly compares pre-treatment trends of disconnected and non-disconnected youth between 16–24 years of age. The figure shows that the trends move roughly together for the two groups.

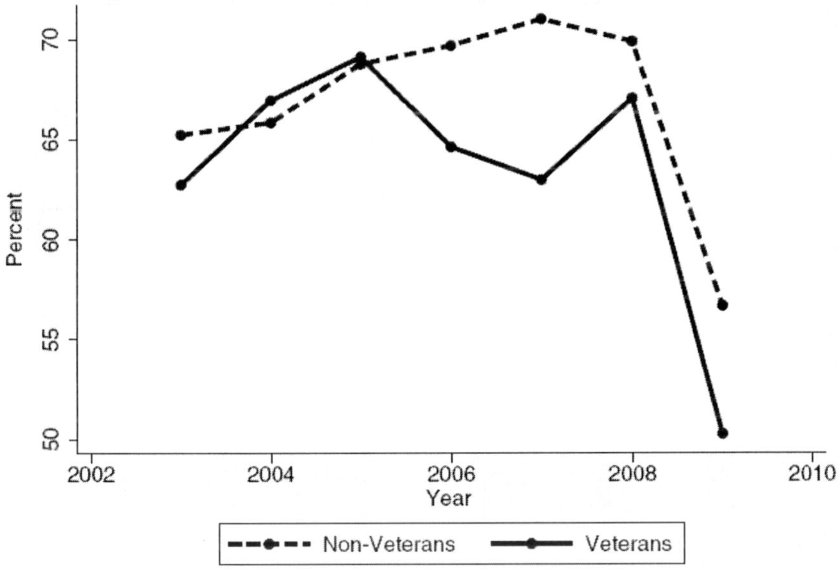

Figure 10. Employment rates of unemployed veterans & non-veterans.

Table 5 shows results of the double difference regressions for disconnected youth. Columns (1) and (2) both include the demographic controls, but Column (2) also includes state and time fixed effects. The results are similar with or without state and time fixed effects and show that the likelihood of employment of disconnected youth increased by 0.015, or an increase of 4.7 percent, relative to the pre-treatment employment for this group.

Table 5. Difference-in-difference (DD) effects of work opportunity tax credits (WOTC) on disconnected youth under the ARRA

	(1)	(2)
Disconnected youth X WOTC eligibility period	0.0152* (1.83)	0.0157* (1.88)
Disconnected youth	−0.289*** (−101.09)	−0.285*** (−98.47)
WOTC eligibility period (Under ARRA)	−0.0688*** (−22.97)	−0.0236*** (−4.00)
State fixed effects	No	Yes
Time fixed effects	No	Yes
Demographic controls	Yes	Yes
N	260,841	260,841

Notes: The table above reports marginal effects from a probit model. Demographic controls include age, a quadratic in age, dummies for educational attainment, and gender and race dummies. Disconnected Youth are defined as 16–24 year olds who are not enrolled in school and who worked less than 26 weeks in the previous year. Data for this table is restricted to 16 to 24-year-olds and leaves out individuals who could have qualified for WOTC, including SNAP and TANF recipients. Data is from Annual Social and Economic (ASEC) supplement of the Current Population Survey spanning the years 2003–2013.
t statistics in parenthesis.
*$p < 0.10$, **$p < 0.05$, ***$p < 0.01$.

We find mixed results of targeted tax credits on employment. While we find a positive and non-trivial impact on the employment of disconnected youth, we do not find evidence of an impact on veterans. Previous evidence on tax credits is also mixed. Katz (1998) finds that the Targeted Jobs Tax Credit, a major wage subsidy program for the economically disadvantaged introduced between 1979 and 1991 had modest but positive employment effects. Hamersma (2008) argues that the WOTC had minimal effects on the employment of targeted groups because of low take-up of the credits. Burtless' (1985) analysis of a randomized targeted wage subsidy program in Dayton, Ohio suggests that vouchers may have even hurt the targeted groups by stigmatizing them. Our results are a little smaller than the ones reported by Katz (1998) for disadvantaged youth of a reduction in employment of 7.7 percent due to the discontinuation of the Targeted Jobs Tax Credit, though the TJTC applied to an older age group of 23 to 24-year-olds, who Katz (1998) argues are more attached to the labor force and, thus, more likely to benefit from the credits[13].

4.2.4 Impact of the Hiring Incentives to Restore Employment (HIRE) Act

An alternative to tax credits attached to individual groups are tax credits provided to employers hiring any workers, which would avoid the problem of stigmatization. In March 18, 2010 the Hiring Incentives to Restore Employment (HIRE) Act was passed, which instead gave a direct payroll tax exemption of 6.2 percent to employers hiring unemployed individuals who had been unemployed for at least 60 days or who worked less than 40 hours (part-time workers) in the last 60 days. The HIRE Act expired on December 31, 2010. While there has been no evaluation of this program, at the time, the Treasury Department indicated that there were 3.2 million jobs created which, in principle, qualified for these credits over the time period during which the credits were effective. Here we attempt to quantify the impact of the HIRE Act.

Table 6 presents descriptive statistics for those who qualified for the HIRE Act. We define these as those who have been unemployed for at least 60 days in the past year. Those who qualify have lower employment and have searched more. They are also more likely to be male and African American, and they are more likely to be high school drop outs or to have only a high school degree. The first row in Table 7 reports the interaction between eligibility for the HIRE Act and an indicator for 2011, since the CPS reports employment in March for the previous past year. The specification controls for demographic characteristics, an indicator of whether the person is eligible, and state and time fixed effects. The results show that the HIRE increased employment by 1.6 percentage points or 2.6 percent relative to the employment for this group pre-HIRE Act.

Grijalva and Neumark (2013) similarly find that state tax credits increased employment for the unemployed, but that the effects were not large. By contrast, evaluations of similar tax credits in other countries suggest that these credits have been effective in encouraging hiring. Kugler (2011) presents an extensive literature review with evidence on the effectiveness of payroll tax cuts for employers from a number of natural experiments around the world as well as from cross-country panel data studies. While there is no data on take-up of credits from the HIRE Act, there was a perception that take-up of the hiring credits was low, and this may be one reason why the impact was not bigger.

Table 6. Descriptive statistics for different unemployed groups

	Full sample	HIRE act eligible	HIRE act eligible pre-2011	HIRE act eligible post-2012	Long term unemployed	Long term unemployed pre-2013	Long term unemployed 2013 & 2014
Employed	0.729	0.609	0.605	0.623	0.540	0.536	0.563
	(0.444)	(0.488)	(0.489)	(0.485)	(0.498)	(0.499)	(0.496)
Weeks looking for work	1.405	23.62	22.96	24.62	34.08	34.04	34.30
	(6.162)	(11.77)	(11.57)	(12.00)	(7.984)	(7.961)	(8.100)
Male	0.480	0.544	0.541	0.540	0.533	0.534	0.529
	(0.500)	(0.498)	(0.498)	(0.498)	(0.499)	(0.499)	(0.499)
Less than H.S.	0.117	0.173	0.181	0.156	0.184	0.188	0.164
	(0.321)	(0.378)	(0.385)	(0.363)	(0.388)	(0.391)	(0.370)
H.S. degree	0.299	0.349	0.356	0.334	0.360	0.362	0.346
	(0.458)	(0.477)	(0.479)	(0.472)	(0.480)	(0.481)	(0.476)
Some college	0.294	0.287	0.278	0.308	0.281	0.277	0.304
	(0.456)	(0.452)	(0.448)	(0.462)	(0.450)	(0.447)	(0.460)
Bachelor's and higher	0.290	0.191	0.185	0.202	0.175	0.173	0.186
	(0.454)	(0.393)	(0.388)	(0.402)	(0.380)	(0.378)	(0.389)
White	0.795	0.761	0.763	0.750	0.729	0.729	0.727
	(0.404)	(0.427)	(0.425)	(0.433)	(0.444)	(0.444)	(0.446)
Black	0.115	0.145	0.142	0.155	0.168	0.167	0.174
	(0.319)	(0.352)	(0.349)	(0.362)	(0.374)	(0.373)	(0.380)
No. Observations	1,413,820	74,985	48,004	18,839	35,368	29,687	5,681

Notes: Mean coefficients; SD in parentheses. HIRE eligible are defined as workers who searched for at least 60 days in the past year. Long Term Unemployed (LTU) are defined as unemployed who were unemployed for six month or more in the last year. Data is from Annual Social and Economic (ASEC) supplement of the Current Population Survey spanning the years 2003–2013.

4.3 Employment impacts of policies to get the long-term unemployed back to work

As shown in Figure 7, those unemployed for more than six months are about half as likely to find a job as those who have been unemployed for less than six months. Yet, the share of long-term unemployed increased sharply during the Great Recession and remains twice as high as before the recession.

Yet, under most states' unemployment systems, individuals are entitled to unemployment benefits for up to 26 weeks, and the replacement rate is close to 50%. Given that long-term unemployment rises during recessions, over the past several decades, emergency unemployment compensation has been extended 8 times to provide additional unemployment benefits to the long-term unemployed.

Table 7. Difference-in-difference (DD) effects of unemployment assistance programs on the employment of the long-term unemployed

	(1)	(2)
HIRE eligible X 2011	0.0184*** (3.57)	0.0159*** (3.07)
HIRE eligible	−0.0894*** (−33.62)	−0.0875*** (−32.98)
2011 Year dummy	−0.0174*** (−11.49)	
LTU X LTU assistance period	0.0327*** (5.39)	0.0304*** (4.97)
Long Term Unemployed (LTU)	−0.106*** (−26.47)	−0.102*** (−25.53)
LTU assistance period (2013,2014)	−0.00895*** (−7.66)	0.0106*** (5.02)
State fixed effects	No	Yes
Time fixed effects	No	Yes
Demographic controls	Yes	Yes
N	1,199,947	1,199,947

Notes: The table above reports marginal effects from probit models. Demographic controls include age, a quadratic of age, dummies for educational attainment, and gender and race dummies. HIRE eligible are defined as workers who searched for at least 60 days in the past year. Long Term Unemployed (LTU) are defined as unemployed who were unemployed for six months or more in the last year. Data for this table leaves out any individuals eligible for WOTC, including SNAP and TANF recipients. Data is from Annual Social and Economic (ASEC) supplement of the Current Population Survey spanning the years 2003–2013.
t statistics in parenthesis.
*$p < 0.10$, **$p < 0.05$, ***$p < 0.01$.

During this last recession, emergency unemployment compensation (EUC) was first introduced in June 2008, then extended in February and November of 2009, and again in December 2010, February 2012, and January 2013. The initial program introduced two 'tiers' of additional weeks of benefits. In November of 2009, the program was expanded to include two additional tiers. While the exact weeks and qualification for each tier has changed with each new extension, the current four tiers have been in place since 2009. The latest extension of EUC in January 2013 provided 14 additional weeks of benefits in the first tier to all states. The second tier provided 14 additional weeks for states with unemployment rates over 6 percent. Tier 3 provided 9 additional weeks if the unemployment rate is above 7 percent, and tier 4 provided 10 additional weeks if the unemployment rate is above 9 percent. The rationale in providing more weeks of benefits in those states with higher unemployment is that those are precisely the places where the long-term unemployed will be facing the biggest hurdles in getting jobs. In addition to emergency unemployment compensation, extended benefits (EB) trigger in for up to 20 weeks in states where the unemployment rate is above 6% and remains above what it was in the past three years.

These extensions have provided income support to close to 25 million workers and their families since the beginning of the recession and have helped many of these families from falling into poverty. However, one concern with unemployment benefits extensions is that they may generate a moral hazard and cause people to search less and to lower their acceptance of jobs. Yet, there are a number of reasons why extending unemployment benefits may be beneficial on economic grounds. First, unemployment benefits are an automatic stabilizer and avoid big consumption drops by households facing unemployment. Gruber (1997) finds that consumption drops by 22% for those without unemployment benefits while only dropping by 7% among those receiving unemployment benefits. Also, Vroman (2010) finds a multiplier of 2 for unemployment insurance. This means that the economies of entire regions and states where the long-term unemployed received benefits grew by twice as much as the benefits received in those states.[14] Second, Krueger and Mueller (in progress) find that unemployment benefits help the unemployed stay attached to the labor force rather than going into disability insurance. Both Rothstein (2011) and Farber and Valletta (2013) find that the unemployment insurance extensions reduced exits from unemployment but that this was largely due to reductions in exits from the labor force rather than a decrease in exits to employment. This is particularly important given the decline in labor force participation which started in 2000 and which has continued during the recession and also given the rise in disability insurance enrollments since the 1980s. These studies suggest that while the UI extensions may prolong unemployment, this is not because the unemployed are turning down job offers but because they are staying attached to the labor force rather than going into disability or stopping their job searches.[15] Also, Chetty (2008) shows evidence that unemployment benefits may also provide liquidity to individuals during periods of unemployment, which may improve the quality of the jobs they get. Finally, Farooq and Kugler (2013) find that public insurance programs increase labor mobility by increasing occupational and industry mobility but also mobility into self-employment and wage employment.

In addition to extending the period of time for which individuals can receive unemployment benefits, the Middle Class Tax Relief and Job Creation Act of 2012 introduced important reforms to help the long-term unemployed get back to work. First, the 2012 act introduced reemployment assistance and eligibility assessments (REAs) for those getting additional unemployment insurance. The REAs required in-person check-ins in UI offices, skill assessments, and job search counseling during those visits for the long-term unemployed. This proposal was based on a number of studies of randomized trials in Nevada, Minnesota, Illinois and Florida showing substantial reemployment effects. Michaelides et al. (2012) showed that UI recipients who were randomly assigned to REA's were 15 percent less likely to exhaust benefits, reduced the period for which they received benefits by 3 weeks, and increased their earnings by 18% in the 6 quarters following participation in REAs. Second, the reform introduced a self-employment assistance (SEA) program which allows the long-term unemployed to continue using UI benefits while setting up their own business. Benus (2009) evaluated a similar program, the Growing America through Entrepreneurship (GATE) program introduced in Pennsylvania, Minnesota, and Maine, which randomly assigned half of the people to training and business counseling and provided assistance in applying for business financing, and found that those assigned to the program were 6 percent more likely to own a business, were likely to start their business sooner, and their businesses had greater longevity. They also found that the program was most effective among those receiving UI. Benus et al. (1994) and Benus et al. (1995) also show positive employment impacts from the Self Employment Enterprise Demonstration (SEED) and the Massachusetts Enterprise Program, which allowed the unemployed to continue claiming benefits while receiving entrepreneurial training and setting up a new business.

Table 6 shows descriptive statistics for the long-term unemployed and other groups. The long term unemployed are less likely to be employed and to have searched longer for work. They are also more likely to be male and African American and to have dropped out of high school or to have only a high school degree. Figure 12 shows the pre-treatment employment for the long term unemployed and those unemployed for less than six months. While the short-term unemployed have higher employment throughout, the trends are similar, except that the long-term unemployed experienced much sharper drops in employment both in the 2001 and 2009 recessions. Table 7 shows the results from a regression that interacts the long-term unemployment dummy for those unemployed for more than 6 months with the 2012 and 2013 dummies, after the WOTC and HIRE Act were no longer in effect, but when the REAs where already in effect. The results are reported in row 4 of Columns (1) and (2), and they suggest that the introduction of REAs increased employment by 3 percentage points or 6 percent for the long-term unemployed. While the effect is not directly comparable with the studies cited above, the effect seems somewhat weaker compared to the randomized trial states which spent similar amounts on eligibility assessments and reemployment ($85 vs. $200 per long-term unemployed). Given evidence of duration dependence and evidence on statistical discrimination against the long-term unemployed, this is an important step towards avoiding hystereses in the U.S. labor market.

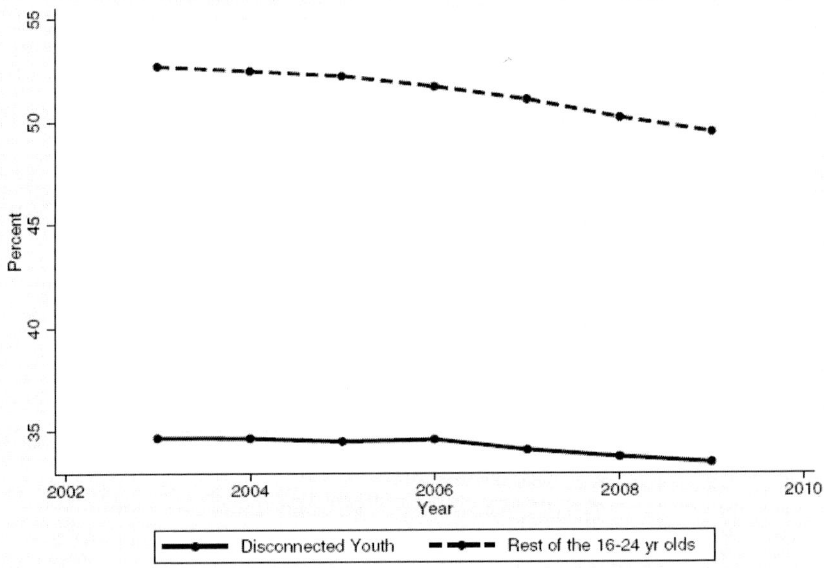

Figure 11. Employment rates of disconnected youth & rest of 16-24 yr olds.

5 CONCLUSION

This paper documents the severity of the Great Recession on the labor market and presents evidence that the majority of the sharp rise in unemployment during the Great Recession was generated by cyclical as opposed to structural factors. This paper also presents new evidence on whether different policies introduced to help address the cyclical unemployment problem helped to increase employment. The tools

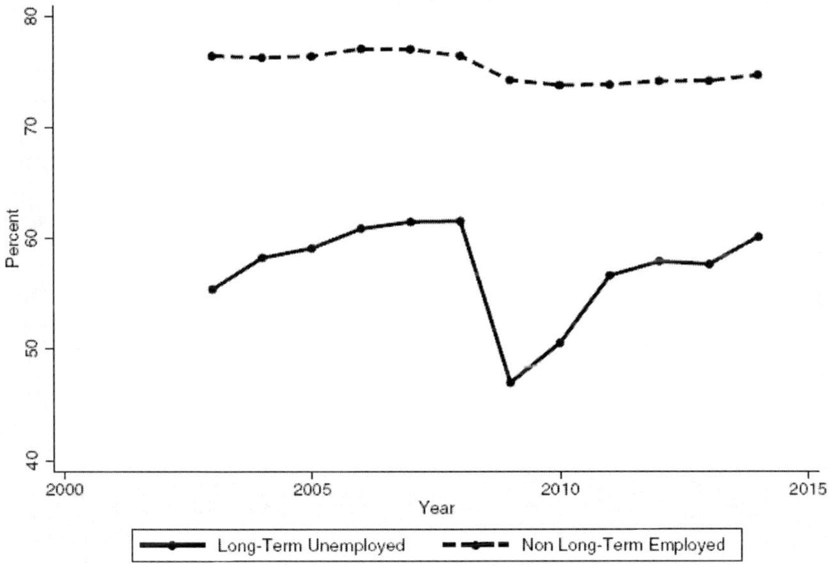

Figure 12. Employment rates of unemployed with longer & shorter durations.

included direct fiscal spending as well as broad and targeted hiring tax credits. The most reliable results from a counter-factual exercise show that employment would have been 4.5% lower had it not been for the spending on Medicaid from the Recovery Act. In addition, the results suggest that the targeted Work Opportunity Tax Credits increased employment for disconnected youth by 4.7 percent. However, the credits seemed to have been ineffective for disabled and unemployed veterans, which could be due to lack of take-up since employers appeared to have been increasing the hiring of all veteran groups during this time. Finally, measures targeted toward the long-term unemployed seemed to have been somewhat effective. The HIRE Act appears to have increased employment by 2.6 percent for those unemployed for more than 2 months; though, take up was low probably due to the complicated rules to qualify for the hiring credit. The Reemployment and Eligibility Assessments introduced in 2012 as part of the extension of unemployment benefits appear to have had greater impacts on those unemployed for more than six months. The REAs appear to have helped to boost employment for the long-term unemployed by 6 percent. All in all, the reduction of the unemployment rate from the high of 10 percent in October 2009 to the current rate of 5.8 percent probably was helped by the various measures taken to help boost labor demand and support the long-term unemployed get back to work.

6 ENDNOTES

[1]These average job growth numbers refer to growth during the period from February 2010 to November 2014.

[2]See Hyatt and McEntarfer (2012).

[3]See BLS's The Employment Situation (November 2014). Also, Hyatt and McEntarfer (2012) report a sizable flow from employment to out of the labor force and back to employment.

[4]See Kugler and Saint-Paul (2004) for a model that shows why employers would want to use employment status as a signal of worker quality. Kugler and Saint-Paul (2004) also present evidence that employers in the U.S. prefer hiring out of the pool of the employed, rather than out of the pool of unemployed, when it is costly to hire and dismiss workers.

[5]Shares of unemployed using friends as a search method come from the Bureau of Labor Statistics' Labor Force statistics calculated from the Current Population Survey: http://www.bls.gov/cps/tables.html.

[6]One reason why employers may prefer using informal channels is to save on monitoring and screening costs. Kugler (2003) shows that while informal channels may generate fewer offers and applicants, they generate access to high paying jobs, and they save employers on monitoring costs.

[7]If mismatches were correlated with GDP growth, this would bias upwards the estimate in Okun's Law. However, since sectoral and skill mismatches are most likely to be a drag on growth, this means that mismatches are likely negatively related to GDP growth and are, thus, likely to bias downwards the estimates in Okun's Law relation.

[8]See the following link from BLS: http://www.bls.gov/opub/ted/2013/ted_20130612.htm.

[9]Various reports from the National Federation of Independent Businesses.

[10]Others instead argue that the increase in unemployment is due to a decrease in the incentives to work due to extended unemployment benefits and other programs introduced by the Recovery Act (Mulligan 2014). If this story was correct, this should reduce labor supply and push up wages, but Rothstein (2011) presents evidence showing that wages fell rather than increased during the Great Recession and recovery. Moreover, there is no evidence that the increased unemployment largely results from decreased desire to work. Instead, the increase in the number of people out of the labor force is driven by individuals who indicate they are available for work and would like to get a job but who are unable to. The number of marginally attached workers more than doubled during the Great Recession and recovery, increasing from 1.3 million in December of 2007 and hitting a high of 2.8 million as late as January 2011 (Employment Situation BLS releases: http://www.bls.gov/schedule/archives/empsit_nr.htm). Moreover, close to half of the marginally attached were discouraged workers who had given up looking for a job because they believed no jobs were available. Likewise, the number of part-timers for economic reasons (those who work part-time but would prefer to work full time) was 4.7 million at the time of the official start of the recession and almost doubled, hitting a high of 9.3 million, in October 2009 (Employment Situation BLS releases: http://www.bls.gov /schedule/archives/empsit_nr.htm).

[11]Information on the amounts spent on various programs by the ARRA comes from http://www.recovery.gov/arra/Transparency/Recovery Data/Pages/JobSummary.aspx.

[12]Hamermesh (1993) surveys the literature on GDP and employment and shows that employment typically lags GDP by about two quarters.

[13]Neumark (2011) provides a good summary of the research in this area.

[14]The fact that those who receive UI are less likely to reduce their consumption and that UI disbursements have big multiplier effects are inconsistent with Mulligan's hypothesis that UI generates both a voluntary reduction in effort and consumption by households that causes both longer unemployment durations and lower propensity to consume.

[15]The fact that more generous UI receipts are not associated with lower exits out of unemployment due to greater attachment to the labor force is also inconsistent with the hypothesis that UI prolongs unemployment due to lower search effort.

DECLARATIONS

Acknowledgements

We are grateful to George Akerlof, Bill Gale, Ed Montgomery, Casey Mulligan, David Neumark, Coen Teulings, and Robert Valletta for helpful comments and conversations as well as participants at the IZA Workshop on Labor Market Reforms during the Great Recession for helpful conversations and comments. The authors would like to thank the anonymous referee.

Responsible editor: David Neumark

Competing interests

The IZA Journal of Labor Policy is committed to the IZA Guiding Principles of Research Integrity. The authors declare that they have observed these principles.

REFERENCES

1. Arteta C, Fischer S, Klein M (2011) Breaking Okun's Law? A Cross Country Comparison, 2009-2011. Department of the Treasury, Mimeo, U.S.
2. Ball L, Daniel L, Prakash L (2012) Is Okun's Law Fit at 50? Paper presented at the 13th Jacques Polak Research Conference, IMF, D.C., November 8–9, 2012
3. Barlevi G (2011). Evaluating the Role of Labor market Mismatch in Rising Unemployment. *Economic Perspectives*, Vol. 35, No. 2011–3
4. Benus J, Johnson T, Wood M (1994) First impact analysis of the Washington State self-employment and enterprise development (SEED) demonstration. Unemployment Insurance Occasional Paper 94–1, Washington D.C
5. Benus J, Johnson T, Wood M, Grover N, Shen T (1995) Final impact analysis of the Washington and Massachusetts self-employment demonstrations. Unemployment Insurance

Occasional Paper 95–4, Washington, D.C, DOL/ETA/UIS Final Report

6. Benus J, Shen T, Zhang S, Chan M, Hansen B (2009). Growing America Through Entrepreneurship: Final Evaluation of Project GATE. IMPAQ International

7. Burtless G (1985) Are targeted wage subsidies harmful – evidence from a wage voucher experiment. Indust Labor Relat Rev 39(1):105

8. Chetty R (2008) Moral Hazard versus Liquidity and Optimal Unemployment Insurance. J Polit Econ 116(2):173–234

9. Chodorow-Reich G, Feiveson L, Liscow Z, Coolston WG (2012) Does state fiscal relief during recessions increase employment? Evidence from the American recovery and reinvestment act. Am Econ J 4(3):118–145

10. Daly M, Hobijn B, Sahin A, Valleta R (2012) A Rising natural rate of unemployment: transitory or permanent? J Econ Perspect 26(3):3–26

11. Davis S, Jason F, John H (2012) Recruiting Intensity During and After the Great Recession: National and Industry Evidence. NBER Working Paper No. 17762

12. Diamond P (2013) Cyclical unemployment, structural unemployment. IMF Econ Rev 61(3):410–45

13. Dickens WT (2010) Has the Recession Increased the NAIRU? In academic advisory meeting of the Federal Reserve Board of Governors, vol. 12

14. Elsby MWL, Hobijn B, Şahin A, Valletta RG, Stevenson B, Langan A (2011) The Labor Market in the Great Recession—An Update to September 2011 [with Comment and Discussion]. Brookings Papers on Econ Act 353-384

15. Estevão M, Tsounta E (2011) Has the Great Recession raised US structural unemployment? International Monetary Fund, Washington, DC

16. Farber H, Valletta R (2013) Do Extended Unemployment Benefits Lengthen Unemployment Spells? Evidence from Recent Cycles in the US Labor Market. National Bureau of Economic Research No. w19048

17. Farooq A, Kugler A (2013) The Impact of Tax and Transfer Programs on Labor Mobility. Mimeo

18. Feyrer J, Sacerdote B (2011) Did the stimulus stimulate? Real time estimates of the effects of the American Recovery and Reinvestment. National Bureau of Economic Research Act. No. w16759

19. Ghayad R, Dickens W (2012) What can we learn by disaggregating the unemployment-vacancy relationship? Public Policy Briefs 12-13

20. Grijalva D, Neumark D (2013) The Employment Effects of State Hiring Credits During and After the Great Recession. Mimeo

21. Gruber J (1997) The consumption smoothing benefits of unemployment insurance. Am Econ Rev 87(1):192–205

22. Hamersma S (2008) The effects of an employer subsidy on employment outcomes: a study of the work opportunity and welfare-to-work tax credits. J Policy Anal Manage 27(3):498–520

23. Heaton P (2012). The Effects of Hiring Tax Credits on Employment of Disabled Veterans. RAND, National Defense Research Institute, Occasional Paper

24. Hyatt H, McEntarfer E (2012) Job-to-Job Flows in the Great Recession. The Am Econ Rev 102(3):580–583

25. Katz L (1998) Wage Subsidies for the Disadvantaged. In: Freeman R, Gottchalk P (eds) Generating Jobs. Russell Sage, New York, pp 21–53

26. Kroft K, Lange F, Notowidigdo MJ, Katz LF (2014) Long-term unemployment and the Great Recession: the role of composition, duration dependence, and non-participation. Working Paper

27. Kroft K, Lange F, Notowidigdo M (2012) Duration Dependence and Labor Market Conditions: Theory and Evidence from a Field Experiment. Q J Econ 128(3):1123–1167

28. Krueger A, Mueller A. Applications for Disability Insurance and the Extension of UI Benefits: New Evidence from a Survey of Unemployed Workers. in progress

29. Kugler A (2003) Employee Referrals and Efficiency Wages. Labour Econ 10(5):531–556

30. Kugler A (2011) Is there an Anti-labor bias of Taxes? A Survey of the Evidence from Latin America and Around the World. Inter-American Development Bank

31. Kugler A, Saint-Paul G (2004) How do Firing Costs affect Workers Flows in a World with Adverse Selection? J Labor Econ 22(3):553–584

32. Lazear EP, Spletzer JR (2012) The United States labor market: Status quo or a new normal? National Bureau of Economic Research No. w18386

33. Michaelides M, Poe-Yanagata E, Benus J, Turancharetti D (2012) Impact of the Reemployment Eligibility Assessment (REA) Initiative in Nevada. IMPAQ

34. Mulligan CB (2014) Uncertainty, redistribution, and the labor market since 2007. IZA J Labor Policy 3(1):8

35. Neumark D (2011) Policies to Encourage Job Creation: Hiring Credits vs. Worker Subsidies. National Bureau of Economic Research, NBER Working Paper 16866, Cambridge Mass

36. Rothstein J (2011) Unemployment Insurance and Job Search in the Great Recession. Brookings Papers Econ Act Fall 43(2):143–213

37. Sahin A, Song J, Topa G, Violante G (2014) Mismatch Unemployment. Am Econ Rev 104(11):3529–3564

38. Vroman W (2010) Role of Unemployment Insurance as an Automatic Stabilizer During a Recession. DIANE Publishing

8
CHAPTER

Changes in Labour Market Transitions in Ireland Over the Great Recession: What Role for Policy?

Adele Bergin[1,2], Elish Kelly[1,2] and Seamus McGuinness[1,2,3]

[1]The Economic and Social Research Institute, Whitaker Square, Sir John Rogerson's Quay, Dublin

[2] Ireland. 2 The Department of Economics, Trinity College Dublin, Dublin, Ireland.

[3]National Institute for Labour Studies (NILS), Flinders University, Adelaide, Australia

ABSTRACT

This paper assesses the impact the Great Recession had on individuals' transitions to and from unemployment in Ireland. The rate of transition from unemployment to employment declined between 2006 and 2011, while the rate from employment to unemployment increased. The results indicate that young people are much less likely to exit unemployment but, at the same time, have a lower risk of becoming unemployed. Education has become an increasingly important factor in supporting unemployment exits and reducing the risk of unemployment since the recession. The findings are supportive of current policies aimed at facilitating access to higher education for unemployed people, but they raise questions with regard to the adequacy of the Youth Guarantee.

Keywords: Labour market transitions Great recession Longitudinal data Decomposition techniques Ireland

1 INTRODUCTION

While few countries escaped the adverse impact of the Great Recession, Ireland experienced one of the most severe downturns in the industrialised world. Between 2008 and 2009, the country suffered a cumulative fall in Gross National Product of close to 9 per cent. By 2012 (Q3), real GNP was 8.5 per cent below its 2008 (Q1) level, which is a stark depiction of the rate of contraction experienced within the economy. This collapse in economic activity has had severe knock-on effects on Ireland's labour market. In particular, the unemployment rate increased from 4.6 per cent in 2004 to 15.0 per cent in 2012, while, as one would expect, the employment rate declined – falling from 65.9 per cent in 2004 to 58.8 per cent in 2012 (see Table 1).

Table 1. Irish labour force statistics: 2004 to 2014

	2004 (Q2)	2005 (Q2)	2006 (Q2)	2007 (Q2)	2008 (Q2)	2009 (Q2)	2010 (Q2)	2011 (Q2)	2012 (Q2)	2013 (Q2)	2014 (Q1)
Unemployment rate %	4.6	4.7	4.6	4.8	5.7	12.2	13.9	14.6	15.0	13.9	12.0
Participation rate %	60.5	62.1	63.2	64.1	63.7	62.5	61.1	60.5	60.1	60.5	59.7
Employment rate % (persons aged 15–64)	65.9	67.5	68.5	69.1	67.9	62.2	60.0	59.2	58.8	60.2	60.8

Source: Quarterly National Household Survey, Central Statistics Office.

The collapse in the property sector in Ireland, which was one of the main factors underlining its economic demise, resulted in most job losses occurring in the construction sector, and in particular among males. McGinnity *et al.* (2014) report that the number of people employed in the construction sector fell by just over 61 per cent between 2007 and 2012 – falling from 266,174 to 103,212, with the sector's share in total employment falling from 12.6 per cent in 2007 to 5.5 per cent in 2012. Apart from Information and Communication, Education, Health and the Arts, all other sectors experienced job losses, but none to the extent of the construction sector.

As the downturn progressed, the profile of unemployed people changed, particularly in terms of their educational composition. In 2006, prior to the recession, over two-thirds of those who were unemployed had a second-level qualification or less, with only a fifth having completed third-level. However, over the course of the recession, there has been a striking growth in the number of unemployed individuals with a Post Leaving Cert[1] (PLC) level qualification (which includes apprenticeships), while the proportion of unemployed females with a graduate qualification increased significantly from 22.5 per cent in 2006 to 30.8 per cent in 2011 (Kelly *et al.* 2012).

Existing literature on the impact of the recession on the Irish labour market has found that it has had a differential impact across age groups, with young people in particular being severely affected. Kelly *et al.* (2014) report that total employment among those aged 25 and less fell by almost 60 per cent, from 357,000 in Q3 2007 to 148,000 in Q1 2013. There has been a small increase in the number of employed youths since this time-point, with the figure standing at 160,500 in Q3 2014. The corollary of this fall in employment among young people has been a rapid rise in their unemployment rate, which has grown from 9 per cent in Q3 2007 to almost 30 per cent in Q3 2011, and also a rise in inactivity. Conefrey (2011) found that the majority of young people who exited the labour force after the recession in 2008, and who remained in Ireland, returned to education. However, Kelly *et al.* (2014) found that the rate of transition to employment of those who became unemployed fell considerably, from 38 per cent in 2006 to 17.4 per cent in 2011. Kelly *et al.* (2014) results showed that this fall in the transition rate was not due to changes in the composition of unemployed youths but to adjustments in the external economic environment that resulted in changes in the impact of possessing certain individual characteristics. For example, there was a rise in the marginal impact of education and Irish nationality on the probability of a successful transition from unemployment to employment. The number of young people not in employment, education or training, i.e., NEETs, has also grown since the recession, increasing from 11.8 per cent in 2006 to 24 per cent in 2011 (Eurostat, 2013).[2] Similar to unemployed youths, Kelly and McGuinness (2014) found that NEET individuals' transition rate to employment fell over the course of the recession as well – declining from 21.4 per cent in 2006 to 13.6 per cent in 2011.

Research by Barrett and Kelly (2012) shows that the recession has had a differential nationality effect and, in particular, that immigrants have suffered more than natives. They report that the annual rate of job loss was close to 20 per cent for immigrants in 2009 compared to about 7 per cent for Irish-born. In addition, Barrett and Kelly (2012) found that the employment probabilities of immigrants from the accession states that joined the European Union in May 2004 were particularly negatively affected, especially males from these countries.

In the context of the dramatic changes that have taken place in the Irish labour market since the Great Recession, this paper focuses on identifying the impact that various socio-economic characteristics (e.g., age, gender, marital status, etc.) and job traits (e.g., employment sector, trade union membership, etc.) have on the relative risk of a person losing their job (i.e., transitioning from employment to unemployment) or finding employment (i.e., transitioning from unemployment to employment) and, in particular, assesses how the impact of such characteristics have changed pre and post the Great Recession.[3] In addition to examining the impact of various socio-economic characteristics on individuals' labour market transition patterns, we are also interested in investigating what has driven the change in the unemployment-to-employment and employment-to-unemployment transition rates between 2006 and 2011. This analysis is carried out using decomposition techniques.

The remainder of the paper is structured as follows. Section 2 describes the data that is used in the study. Descriptive statistics are presented in Section 3. The methodology and results are outlined in Sections 4, policy implications are discussed in Section 5, and Section 6 presents the main conclusions.

2 DATA

Newly available longitudinal data from the *Quarterly National Household Survey* (QNHS), which is Ireland's Labour Force Survey,[4] is used to conduct the analyses undertaken in this paper. The objective of the QNHS is to provide quarterly labour force estimates of employment, unemployment, etc. The survey is continuous and targets all private households. Each quarter, approximately 26,000 households are sampled.[5] Households are asked to take part in the survey for five consecutive quarters. In each quarter, one-fifth of the households surveyed are replaced, and the QNHS sample involves an overlap of 80 per cent between consecutive quarters and 20 per cent between the same quarters in consecutive years. While participation in the QNHS is voluntary, the response rate is high (approximately 85 per cent).[6]

One of the main benefits of using the QNHS longitudinal data is that it allowed us to follow the labour market transitions of individuals for up to 5 consecutive quarters. In terms of the periods covered in our study, we focused on comparing individuals' labour market transitions both pre and post the Great Recession. Quarter 2 (Q2) 2006 was selected as the starting point for our pre-recession analysis, which was during the height of the boom in Ireland; and Q2 2011 marked the starting point for the analysis relating to the post-recession period.[7] We selected two unbalanced panels and focused on working age individuals (age 15–64) who remained in the panel for, at least, the consecutive quarter. Within each panel, by following the same individuals over time, we can observe changes in labour market status and determine gross flows between different labour market states. The transition rate for moving into employment (unemployment) is calculated as the percentage of those who were employed (unemployed) in the previous quarter whose labour market status has changed to unemployed (employed) in the current quarter. Given that we only consider individuals who remain in Ireland over the observation periods, those who migrated from Ireland during the time period covered by each panel are excluded from the analysis.

In this paper, we begin by assessing the impact of various socio-economic and employment characteristics on an unemployed person's likelihood of transitioning to employment. We then examine the impact of characteristics on an employed person's likelihood of becoming unemployed. Models are estimated for both 2006 and 2011. The characteristics investigated are as follows: gender, age, nationality, marital status, educational attainment, geographic location, sector of employment, previous unemployment duration, trade union membership, employment contract type, job type (i.e., full-time or part-time), firm size and job search methods.

3 DESCRIPTIVE STATISTICS

Table 2 shows average transition rates over the five waves for 2006 and 2011. In 2006, the pre-crisis period, over 37 per cent of those who were unemployed in the previous quarter transitioned into employment.[8] In 2011, the average unemployment to employment transition rate had fallen by almost 10 percentage points. In 2006, when the economy was essentially at full employment, the transition rate from employment to unemployment was under 2 per cent, and this rate rose to just under 5 per cent in 2011.

Table 2. Transition rates

	2006	2011
Overall:		
Employment to unemployment	1.8%	4.9%
Unemployment to employment	37.3%	27.8%
By age group:		
Employment to unemployment:		
15-19	3.3%	6.3%
20-24	3.4%	9.7%
25-34	2.0%	6.1%
35-44	1.4%	4.3%
45-54	1.2%	3.6%
55 plus	0.8%	2.6%
Unemployment to employment:		
15-19	19.5%	8.5%
20-24	43.4%	23.1%
25-34	43.3%	30.8%
35-44	38.7%	31.4%
45-54	38.8%	31.4%
55 plus	33.5%	26.9%
By education level:		
Employment to unemployment:		
Below leaving certificate	2.1%	6.0%
Leaving cert	1.9%	5.7%
PLC	1.6%	6.8%
Third level non-degree	1.5%	3.6%
Third level degree	1.2%	2.9%
Unemployment to employment:		
Below leaving certificate	24.3%	15.7%
Leaving cert	43.0%	27.5%
PLC	46.9%	27.2%
Third level non-degree	49.1%	40.7%
Third level degree	59.8%	50.0%

Note: Derived from the QNHS micro-data. The base for the employed to unemployed transition rates is employed in the previous quarter, and the base for the unemployed to employed transition rates is unemployed in the previous quarter.

There is an almost linear negative relationship between age and transitioning to unemployment. Apart from the youngest age group (15–19), the employment to unemployment transition rates approximately trebled for each age group in 2011 compared to 2006.

Younger workers have the lowest transition rates from unemployment to employment. The employment transition rates fell for all age groups in 2011, with the largest percentage point falls occurring for those under the age of 35.

Table 2 reveals that those with higher levels of education are less likely to move to unemployment, and this effect is more marked in 2011. There is a strong positive relationship between education level and transitioning into employment. In 2006, 60 per cent of unemployed graduates moved into employment while the comparable figure for those with less than Leaving Certificate education was only 24 per cent. In 2011, the education gradient persisted although the transition rates had fallen somewhat for each education level.

4 Methodology and results

With respect to assessing the link between measures of labour market status in period t and t + 1, we employ a random effects logit model.[9] We estimate separate models for two distinct labour market transitions between the two periods: i) transitions from unemployment to employment and ii) transitions from employment to unemployment, with the equations taking the following general form:

$$Y_{it+1} = X'_{it}\beta + \alpha_i + u_{it} \quad (i = 1, ..., N; t = 1, ..., T), \quad (1)$$

where Y_{it+1} captures a person's labour market status between the previous quarter and the current quarter, X'itXit' is a vector of personal and job characteristics; α_i are the individual random effects; and u_{it} is an error term, which is assumed to be identically and independently distributed. The models are estimated on two unbalanced panels covering Q2 2006 to Q2 2007 and Q2 2011 to Q2 2012.[10]

The main weakness with the random effects model proposed here is that it assumes the explanatory variables are uncorrelated with the error term, suggesting that a fixed effects model, where individual-specific effects are captured through the inclusion of a separate intercept for each individual in the data, might be more appropriate. A conditional fixed effects logit model might have been estimated, but it comes at a huge cost: ii) the loss of many cases, since these models are conditional on changes in the outcome variable being observed, which is a particular problem when using quarterly panel data; and (ii) since most of the explanatory variables will not change over five quarters, most of our controls relating to, for example, education, region and industrial sector will drop out of the models. For these reasons, we are forced to adopt the random effects logit model. Nevertheless, as we are interested in changes in the value of observable characteristics over time, and accepting that any bias relating to unobserved heterogeneity is likely to affect both panels in similar ways, we are less concerned with respect to potential correlations with the error term in our current context.

Table 3 shows the results from models estimating the likelihood of transitioning from unemployment to employment in both 2006 and 2011. The odds ratios for each observable characteristic are reported and a number of notable changes in the importance of certain attributes are apparent pre and post recession. In 2006, relative to the comparison case of individual's aged 15 to 19, older workers had, on average, 4 to 5 times the odds of transitioning into employment, with the effect being relatively constant throughout the age ranges. By 2011, relative to the base case, workers aged 20 to 24 had almost ten times the odds of successfully exiting to employment, while individuals in the older age brackets had between 27 and 45 times the odds of finding a job relative to 15 to 19 year old unemployed individuals. This result highlights the desperate position of youth unemployed and the importance of initiatives, such as the Youth Guarantee, which targets education and training assistance towards younger claimants.

Education was important in securing an exit to employment in both periods, but its importance rose substantially between 2006 and 2011, particularly with respect to third-Level qualifications. Prior to the recession, claimants with third-Level certificates/diplomas and degrees had between 6 and 10 times the odds of finding employment relative to individuals with a Junior Certificate education (lower secondary) or lower, which is quite large. However, by 2011 those with a third-Level certificate/diploma qualification were almost 40 times more likely to find a job relative to those with a Junior Certificate education or lower, while those with a third-Level degree were 126 times more likely to obtain employment. These results suggest that new and replacement labour demand in Ireland post-recession was heavily skewed towards graduates.

Table 3. Odds ratios from random effects logit estimations of transitions from unemployment to employment

	2006		2011	
	Odds ratio	Standard error	Odds ratios	Standard error
Male	1.902***	0.195	0.611***	0.069
Age 20-24	5.063***	0.996	9.888***	3.226
Age 25-34	5.138***	1.013	33.055***	11.267
Age 35-44	4.559***	0.936	37.615***	13.202
Age 45-54	5.541***	1.195	44.614***	16.041
Age 55+	3.821***	0.855	26.761***	9.792
Leaving certificate	4.445***	0.622	10.605***	1.726
Post Leaving Cert level (includes apprenticeships)	4.761***	0.913	6.225***	1.099
Third level: non degree	5.909***	1.211	39.703***	9.365
Third level: degree	10.007***	2.059	125.714***	30.770
Irish	1.652***	0.143	2.857***	0.485
Married	1.245*	0.146	2.581***	0.336
Border	0.628***	0.100	0.660*	0.151
Mid-East	0.937	0.179	0.966	0.211
Midlands	0.703	0.155	1.092	0.264
Mid-West	0.501***	0.089	1.009	0.210
South-East	0.762*	0.125	0.728	0.142
South-West	0.705**	0.108	1.228	0.229
West	0.698*	0.133	0.962	0.200
Prev. unemployed for 3–6 months	0.876	0.111	1.217	0.206
Prev. unemployed for 6–12 months	0.658***	0.084	1.145	0.186
Prev. unemployed for 12+ months	0.368***	0.043	0.908	0.125
Prev. sector: Agriculture	1.402	0.576	1.709	0.813
Prev. sector: Construction	0.967	0.165	1.234	0.225
Prev. sector: Wholesale and retail	1.031	0.182	1.435*	0.298
Prev. sector: Transport and storage	0.862	0.255	1.023	0.327
Prev. sector: Accommodation and food service activities	0.825	0.173	1.121	0.283
Prev. sector: Information and communication	0.731	0.239	0.895	0.361
Prev. sector: Financial, insurance and real estate activities	0.797	0.286	0.790	0.358
Prev. sector: Professional, scientific and technical activities	0.694	0.250	0.817	0.268
Prev. sector: Administrative and support service activities	0.990	0.237	1.248	0.372
Prev. sector: Public Administration and defence	0.703	0.315	0.581	0.295
Prev. sector: Education	1.387	0.410	1.536	0.554
Prev. sector: Health	0.901	0.228	1.093	0.326
Prev. sector: Other	1.247	0.312	1.081	0.316
Prev. sector: No sector information	0.866	0.138	1.426*	0.283
Prev. job search: Contacted public employment office	0.819*	0.090	0.656***	0.073
Prev. job search: Contacted private employment agency	1.075	0.114	1.554***	0.176
Prev. job search: Applied directly to employers	0.973	0.116	1.164	0.154
Prev. job search: Asked friends/relatives/trade unions	0.846	0.103	0.643***	0.107
Prev. job search: Studied ads in newspapers	1.009	0.165	0.593***	0.115
Prev. job search: Inserted/answered ads in newspapers	0.991	0.105	0.977	0.108

Prev. job search: Looked for permits, licences or financial resources	0.526	0.303	1.274	1.064
Prev. job search: Looked for land, premises or equipment	1.317	0.885	0.987	1.073
Pending job decisions: Waiting for call from public employment office	0.866	0.098	1.021	0.126
Pending job decisions: Waiting for public sector competition results	1.306***	0.136	1.540***	0.190
Pending job decisions: Took a test, interview or exam	1.396***	0.146	1.051	0.131
Pending job decisions: Waiting for results from job application	0.956	0.210	0.874	0.288
Constant	0.052***	0.017	0.000***	0.000
Number of observations	8,299		18,488	
Number of people	6,653		13,776	
Log likelihood	−4820.0517		−9450.0625	
Prob > chi2	0.0000		0.0000	

Note: Dependent variable is transitioned from unemployment to employment. Omitted categories are: age 15–19, Junior Certificate or lower education, Dublin, previously unemployed for less than three months and manufacturing.
Note: ***p < .001; **p < .01; *p < .05.

In 2006, we observe the well documented scarring effect of previous unemployment durations on unemployment-to-employment labour market transitions. Relative to individuals who were unemployed for less than three months, those with durations of between 6 to 12 months or more than 12 months had around two-thirds (0.66) and one-third (0.37), respectively, the odds of moving into employment by the following quarter. By 2011, however, we find that previous unemployment duration had no discernible impact on exits to employment. One possible explanation for the disappearance of the scarring effect is that the magnitude, and indiscriminate nature, of the incidence of both unemployment and long-term unemployment over the period eradicated the value of durations as a quality signal to employers. Alternatively, the rapid rise in the population of long-term unemployed individuals over the recession with high levels of labour market attachment may have led to a structural behavioural shift in the intensity of job-search among long-term claimants which will also have dampened the scarring effect.

The QNHS contains a number of variables that capture the extent to which an unemployed individual is awaiting a response on a job application and the nature of any job-search activity undertaken in the previous quarter. In 2006, individuals awaiting the results from a public sector competition or an aptitude test had between 1.3 and 1.4 times the odds of exiting to employment by the following quarter relative to unemployed individuals who were not awaiting a response to one of these two job application activities. In 2006, none of the job search variables had any significant impact on exits from unemployment, with the exception of contact with a public employment office: such individuals had 0.8 times the odds of finding a job relative to unemployed individuals that did not use this type of job search activity.[11,12] Differences in job search activity became somewhat more important in the later period, with individuals who had interacted with a private employment agency having one and a half times the odds of entering employment by the following quarter relative to those who did not engage with a private recruitment group in 2011. The same result emerged for those waiting the results from a public sector employment competition in 2011. On the other hand, unemployed individuals who had engaged with a public employment office, sought work through family or friends or by searching newspaper advertisements all had lower odds of finding a job within three months relative to unemployed people that did not utilise these job search methods.[13]

With respect to gender, males had almost twice the odds of exiting to employment in 2006 relative to females. However, by 2011, the situation had reversed, with males having around two-thirds (0.61) the odds of moving from unemployment to employment than females. In both time periods examined in this study, Irish nationals that were unemployed were more likely to transition out of unemployment than immigrants, with the scale of the advantage rising in 2011. Neither pre nor post the Great Recession did previous industrial sector employment have any importance in explaining transitions into employment. Married individuals were more likely to successfully exit from unemployment in both periods. Finally, while unemployment-to-employment transition rates were generally lower in most regions relative to Dublin in 2006, apart from the Border region, the remaining regional effects had dissipated by the later period.

Table 4 shows the impact of characteristics on the risk of unemployment in both 2006 and 2011. Again, we report the odds ratios associated with a range of attributes for both time periods. It is important to note that we cannot distinguish the extent to which transitions from employment-to-unemployment were as a consequence of involuntary or voluntary separations. Nevertheless, it is reasonable to assume that the majority of separations were involuntary in nature, particularly in 2011 when the Irish economy was still experiencing substantial difficulties. As was the case with unemployment-to-employment transitions, we observe substantial change in the impacts of age and gender over the period. In 2006, relative to 15 to 19-year-olds, employees aged 20 to 34 had a higher risk of unemployment, as measured by higher odds ratios, while those aged 35 and over had

Table 4. Odds ratios from random effects logit estimations of transitions from employment to unemployment

	2006		2011	
	Odds ratio	Standard error	Odds ratio	Standard error
Male	1.448***	0.101	3.178***	0.186
Age 20-24	1.861***	0.237	5.388***	0.712
Age 25-34	1.028	0.129	3.466***	0.427
Age 35-44	0.756**	0.102	2.407***	0.305
Age 45-54	0.659***	0.092	1.604***	0.209
Age 55+	0.271***	0.045	0.745**	0.107
Leaving certificate	0.613***	0.055	0.638***	0.050
Post Leaving Cert Level (includes apprenticeships)	0.640***	0.080	1.134	0.102
Third level: non degree	0.589***	0.076	0.377***	0.038
Third level: degree	0.381***	0.044	0.220***	0.021
Irish	1.038	0.060	0.552***	0.044
Married	0.351***	0.031	0.381***	0.025
Border	1.002	0.118	1.202	0.134
Mid-East	0.558***	0.074	1.313***	0.132
Midlands	0.569***	0.091	1.897***	0.228
Mid-West	0.933	0.120	1.901***	0.190
South-East	0.851	0.102	1.773***	0.175
South-West	0.735***	0.079	1.141	0.101
West	0.801	0.110	1.981***	0.199
Prev. sector: Agriculture	0.432***	0.087	0.520***	0.082
Prev. sector: Construction	1.197	0.140	1.061	0.123
Prev. sector: Wholesale and retail	0.904	0.104	0.940	0.087
Prev. sector: Transport and storage	0.894	0.150	0.947	0.125
Prev. sector: Accommodation and food service activities	1.424**	0.200	0.940	0.108
Prev. sector: Information and communication	0.662**	0.134	1.236	0.175
Prev. sector: Financial, insurance and real estate activities	0.671**	0.120	0.807	0.115
Prev. sector: Professional, scientific and technical activities	0.542***	0.099	0.923	0.125
Prev. sector: Administrative and support service activities	1.509**	0.252	1.105	0.158
Prev. sector: Public Administration and defence	0.553***	0.104	0.724**	0.104
Prev. sector: Education	0.885	0.139	0.983	0.120
Prev. sector: Health	0.975	0.125	1.117	0.110
Prev. sector: Other	1.123	0.179	0.895	0.117
Prev. sector: No sector information	0.715	0.411	0.415	0.291
Prev. Permanent contract	1.100	0.085	1.101	0.068
Prev. Full-time	0.882*	0.057	0.683***	0.035
Prev. Trade union member	0.812**	0.067	0.845**	0.058
Prev. Firm size 11-19	1.088	0.112	1.007	0.089
Prev. Firm size 20-49	0.917	0.092	0.970	0.079
Prev. Firm size 50-99	1.103	0.126	0.865	0.083
Prev. Firm size 100-500	1.018	0.102	0.915	0.077
Prev. Firm size 500+	1.081	0.151	0.823*	0.083
Constant	0.001***	0.000	0.004***	0.001

Number of observations	178,325	104,879
Number of people	91,815	57,862
Log likelihood	−14706.688	−18397.634
Prob > chi2	0.0000	0.0000

Note: Dependent variable is transitioned from employment to unemployment. Omitted categories are: age 15–19, Junior Certificate or lower education, Dublin, manufacturing and firm size 1–10 employees.
Note: ***$p < .001$; **$p < .01$; *$p < .05$.

lower odds of becoming unemployed - with the risk falling with age. In 2011, employees aged between 20 and 54 had between 1.6 and five times the odds of becoming unemployed relative to the younger cohort. Only workers aged 55 and over had a lower risk of unemployment in 2011 compared to those aged 15 to 19. A potential explanation for this result is that firms became more sensitive to the price of labour post-recession, implying that the youngest workers, who also tend to be the least expensive, had the lowest risk of a redundancy arising from any cost rationalisation process. Nevertheless, it must be borne in mind that younger workers, due to their relative lack of experience are also likely to be less productive, suggesting that any substitution for more experienced labour is likely to be restricted to relatively unskilled occupations. Thus, while 15 to 19-year-olds are at the greatest risk of sustained unemployment, they appear to have a relatively low risk of job loss.

With respect to education, we observe a general linear relationship in both periods, with the risk of unemployment declining with higher levels of educational attainment. Relative to 2006, third-level qualifications are of greater importance in deterring unemployment in 2011, which is again consistent with a change in the composition of labour demand in favor of educated workers. Furthermore, by 2011, the Post Leaving Cert (PLC) level qualification, which is typically vocational in nature, no longer afforded workers any advantage relative to those with a Junior Certificate or lower levels of education. In 2006, males had approximately 1.5 times the odds of transitioning to unemployment relative to females. However, by 2011, males had over three times the odds of transitioning into unemployment compared to females. In the earlier period, Irish workers and immigrants had a similar risk of becoming unemployed, but by 2011, Irish natives had approximately half the odds of moving into unemployment relative to immigrants.

In 2006, relative to manufacturing, the risk of moving into unemployment was higher for workers in accommodation and food services as well as administrative and support services; and it was lower for those in the agriculture, public administration, professional, financial, and information and communication sectors. By 2011, only workers in the public administration sector had a lower likelihood of becoming unemployed relative to those working in manufacturing. In both 2006 and 2011, full-time workers, and those who were members of trade unions, had lower odds of unemployment, with the impact relatively constant over time. Finally, with respect to region relative to Dublin, the risk of unemployment was lower in a number of areas in 2006 (e.g., Mid-East and Midlands). However, by 2011, employees located in areas other than Dublin had higher odds of becoming unemployed. This result suggests a greater concentration of economic activity in the capital post-recession.

The random effects logit models gave us a sense of the extent to which the value of certain attributes changed pre and post recession with respect to transitioning from, or falling into, unemployment. It is not clear, however, the extent to which variations in the transition rate over time are being driven by (i) changes in the value of observable characteristics, (ii) changes in the composition of the populations in employment and unemployment, or (iii) unobservables that may relate to either individuals or changes in the external environment. In order gain further insights, we estimated the following non-linear Oaxaca decomposition, on the pooled years of data, of the change in transition rates from 2006 to 2011:

$$\overline{T_{11}}-\overline{T_{06}} = (\overline{X_{11}}-\overline{X_{06}})\hat{\beta}_{1_{11}} + \left(\hat{\beta}_{1_{11}}-\hat{\beta}_{1_{06}}\right)\overline{X_{06}} + (\hat{\alpha}_{11}-\hat{\alpha}_{06}) \qquad (2)$$

The term on the left-hand-side, $\overline{T_{11}}-\overline{T_{06}}$, captures the change in the transition rate between 2006 and 2011. The first term on the right-hand-side is known as the endowment effect: this effect captures the proportion of the change in the transition rate between 2006 and 2011 that is due to differences in the composition of the employed and unemployed populations in both time periods. The second term captures the coefficient effect, which is a measure of the extent to which the 2006 and 2011 employed and unemployed populations holding similar characteristics are treated differently in the labour market. The final term in equation (2) denotes the factors that we cannot control for in our model that will impact on a person's transition rate from employment to unemployment and unemployment to employment. These factors include, for example, social class, previous employment tenure, etc., (i.e., unobservables). The results from this decomposition analysis are shown in Table 5.

Table 5. Decomposition results for changes in transition rates

	Employment to unemployment	Unemployment to employment
Overall difference	0.0311	−0.0921
Endowment effect	−0.0103	0.0277
Coefficient effect:	0.0325	−0.1052
Of which:		
Observables	0.0105	0.0358
Constant	0.0220	−0.1410
Interaction effect	0.0089	−0.0146

Note: The decomposition is one for binary dependent variables proposed by Yun (2004). The analysis uses pooled data for 2006 and 2011 and 2006 is the base year in both decompositions.

The first observation to note is that endowment effects explained very little of the overall change in either transition rate examined, suggesting that changes in the composition of the respective populations over the period mattered little. While the structure of employment will tend to change slowly over time, the lack of an endowment effect on the transition from unemployment-to-employment is somewhat surprising given the well documented rapid growth in the proportions of unemployed claimants with higher levels of education since the onset of the recession.

Dealing firstly with the transitions from unemployment-to-employment, the vast majority of the change in the transition rate can be attributed to changes in the constant coefficient, which will incorporate largely unobserved external factors. Nevertheless, some changes in the value of certain observable characteristics had important impacts on the changing rate of transition. The decline in the impact of being male is the most important single coefficient effect, which resulted in a 6 percentage point reduction in the transition rate from unemployment-to-employment between 2006 and 2011.[14] It is not clear what the gender coefficient effect is picking up, given that the models account for claimants' previous industrial sector. However, it is not necessarily the case that the control for previous sector of employment will reflect the degree to which the human capital of claimants meets the requirements of current labour demand. Given this, the results would suggest that between 2006 and 2011, the demand for labour dramatically switched towards industries and occupations where females were more heavily represented, with little evidence that claimants previously employed in particular sectors of employment heavily affected by the economic downturn were at any particular disadvantage in accessing emerging opportunities. In support of this view, McGinnity *et al.* (2014) show that the Health and Social Work sector, which is heavily female dominated, exhibited the largest absolute level of sectoral employment growth[15] in Ireland over the 2007 to 2012 period.[16]

The rise in the coefficients for older unemployed individuals, which presumably proxies an increase in the value of labour market experience, exerted a positive influence on the change in the transition rate. The very substantial reduction in the scarring impact of long-term unemployment durations also tended to increase transition rates over the period. The elimination of the decline in the relative return to the vocationally orientated PLC qualification had a depressing affect on the transition rate, and it is again likely that the fall in the return to this qualification is correlated with the lack of demand in vocationally orientated sectors such as construction, manufacturing and wholesale and retail.

With respect to the rise in the rate of transitions to unemployment,[17] the increase in the relative exposure of males and older workers were the largest single coefficient effects. In this instance, the age effect may well reflect a rise in the price sensitivity of employers to labour costs post recession.

5 POLICY IMPLICATIONS

From a policy perspective, the results emphasize the importance of higher level credentials in terms of preventing transitions to unemployment and exiting unemployment. The research is suggestive of a rise in demand for graduate labour over time, which would be supportive of a further expansion of higher-education provision. In terms of activation policy, there has been a substantial focus on enabling unemployed claimants to gain third-level qualifications through the Springboard initiative, which currently offers 6,400 free higher education places to jobseekers leading to qualifications at certificate, degree and post-graduate level.

The study also identifies that labour demand is evolving in an uneven pattern with respect to both male and female dominated industries. Over the period in question, employment growth appears to have been particularly skewed towards female dominated sectors, which has resulted in a substantial lowering in the likelihood that males will exit the Live Register[18] in any three-month period. Although no significant sectoral effects were obvious at the one-digit industry-level, the results point to the possible existence of structural unemployment within the male claimant population, with the risk likely to be high for persons previously employed in particular construction occupations. Activation policy has, to date, failed to identify or address the degree to which particular occupations have been disproportionately disadvantaged in terms of re-entering employment, and the results suggest that more action is required in this respect.

With respect to labour market activation and young people, the research highlights the drastic situation faced by unemployed youths. Thus, the findings emphasise the importance of implementing the Youth Guarantee. Nevertheless, the scale of the unemployment problem in Ireland and the associated strain on resources implies that a much more scaled down version of the Guarantee will be implemented to what was initially envisaged. Specifically, claimants under the age of 18 who leave school without formal qualifications will be offered a "second chance" education place outside the school system; however, this aspect of the Guarantee will not be fully operational until the end of 2015. Claimants aged between 18 and 24 will be categorised as high and low risk on the basis of the country's profiling system. Under this system, each new claimant is asked a series of questions on making a claim for unemployment benefit, and a probability of exit to the labour market (PEX) score is calculated. Individuals with a low PEX will be deemed high risk. High risk claimants will only receive an intervention after four months on the Live Register, while the waiting time for medium- to high-risk claimants will be nine months. It is likely that such relatively low intensity interventions will have limited impact on the transition rates of young claimants to unemployment.

Finally, the apparent reduction of the scarring effect associated with long-term unemployment suggests that activation policy need not be so heavily focused around durations, but instead should attempt to ensure that the claimants are equipped with the right skills and provided with the appropriate advice and training that would enable them to re-enter employment irrespective of their length of time spent in unemployment.

Table 6. Oaxaca individual coefficient effects for the change in the unemployment to employment transition rate between 2006 and 2011

	Coefficient	Standard error
Male	−0.060***	(0.007)
Age 20-24	−0.004	(0.004)
Age 25-34	0.012*	(0.007)
Age 35-44	0.014**	(0.006)
Age 45-54	0.011**	(0.005)
Age 55+	0.008**	(0.003)
Leaving certificate	−0.004	(0.004)
Post leaving cert level (includes apprenticeships)	−0.008**	(0.003)
Third level: non degree	0.004	(0.002)
Third level: degree	0.006**	(0.003)
Irish	−0.019	(0.012)
Married	0.011**	(0.006)
Border	0.002	(0.002)
Mid-East	0.001	(0.002)
Midlands	0.002	(0.002)
Mid-West	0.008***	(0.003)
South-East	0.001	(0.003)
South-West	0.008**	(0.003)
West	0.003	(0.003)
Prev. unemployed for 3–6 months	0.003*	(0.002)
Prev. unemployed for 6–12 months	0.006**	(0.003)
Prev. unemployed for 12+ months	0.051***	(0.009)
Prev. sector: Agriculture	0.000	(0.001)
Prev. sector: Construction	0.001	(0.005)
Prev. sector: Wholesale and retail	0.001	(0.003)
Prev. sector: Transport and storage	0.001	(0.001)
Prev. sector: Accommodation and food service activities	0.002	(0.002)
Prev. sector: Information and communication	0.000	(0.001)
Prev. sector: Financial, insurance and real estate activities	0.000	(0.001)
Prev. sector: Professional, scientific and technical activities	0.000	(0.001)
Prev. sector: Administrative and support service activities	0.000	(0.001)
Prev. sector: Public Administration and defence	0.000	(0.001)
Prev. sector: Education	−0.001	(0.001)
Prev. sector: Health	0.000	(0.001)
Prev. sector: Other	−0.001	(0.001)
Prev. sector: No sector information	0.005	(0.004)
Prev. job search: Contacted public employment office	−0.006	(0.008)
Prev. job search: Contacted private employment agency	[illegible]	[illegible]
Prev. job search: Applied directly to employers	0.014	(0.013)
Prev. job search: Asked friends/relatives/trade unions	−0.008	(0.016)
Prev. job search: Studied ads in newspapers	−0.030	(0.021)
Prev. job search: Inserted/answered ads in newspapers	−0.002	(0.004)
Pending job decisions: Waiting for call from public employment office	0.004	(0.004)

Pending job decisions: Waiting for results from job application	0.000	(0.001)
Prev. job search: Looked for permits, licences or financial resources	0.000	(0.000)
Prev. job search: Looked for land, premises or equipment	0.000	(0.000)
Pending job decisions: Waiting for public sector competition results	0.002	(0.003)
Pending job decisions: Took a test, interview or exam	−0.007**	(0.003)
Constant	−0.141***	(0.040)

Note: ***p < .001; **p < .01; *p < .05.

6 CONCLUSIONS

This paper assesses the impact of the Irish recession on transitions to and from unemployment.[19] We find, not surprisingly, that the rate of transition from unemployment to employment declined over the period, while the transition rate from employment to unemployment increased.

In terms of the factors contributing to the likelihood of a transition taking place, some important changes appear to have occurred over the 2006 to 2011 period. The results show that young people are much less likely to exit unemployment while simultaneously having a lower risk of becoming unemployed. Education has become an increasingly important factor post recession in both securing an exit from unemployment and preventing transitions to unemployment, with the impact most pronounced for the transition from unemployment-to-employment. We find that the scarring effect of long-term unemployment has fallen substantially post-recession, suggesting that either (i) the rapid and indiscriminate rise in the incidence of long-term durations has eradicated the signalling value of the attribute, or (ii) structural shifts in the population of long-term claimants has led to a rise in the job-search intensity causing a decline in the relationship between unemployment durations and exits to employment.

Despite the rapid changes in the structure of the unemployed population, results from a decomposition analysis show that compositional changes are largely unimportant in explaining the fall in the transition rate from unemployment to employment between 2006 and 2011. While most of the change is, not surprisingly, attributable to unobserved changes in the external environment, variations in the value of certain attributes also explained some of the movement in transition rates. In particular, we find that the fall in the return of being male over time contributed to a decline in the transition rate from unemployment to employment, with the gender effect indicating that labour demand

Table 7. Oaxaca individual coefficient effects for the change in the employment to unemployment transition rate between 2006 and 2011

	Coefficient	Standard error
Male	0.007***	(0.001)
Age 20-24	0.001***	(0.000)
Age 25-34	0.005***	(0.001)
Age 35-44	0.004***	(0.001)
Age 45-54	0.003***	(0.001)
Age 55+	0.002***	(0.001)
Leaving Certificate	0.000	(0.001)
Post Leaving Cert Level (includes apprenticeships)	0.001***	(0.000)
Third level: non degree	−0.001***	(0.000)
Third level: degree	−0.003***	(0.001)
Irish	−0.013***	(0.002)
Married	0.000	(0.001)
Border	0.000	(0.000)
Mid-East	0.002***	(0.000)
Midlands	0.001***	(0.000)
Mid-West	0.001***	(0.000)
South-East	0.002***	(0.000)
South-West	0.002***	(0.000)
West	0.002***	(0.000)
Prev. sector: Agriculture	0.000	(0.000)
Prev. sector: Construction	0.000	(0.000)
Prev. sector: Wholesale and retail	0.000	(0.000)
Prev. sector: Transport and storage	0.000	(0.000)
Prev. sector: Accommodation and food service activities	−0.001***	(0.000)
Prev. sector: Information and communication	0.000***	(0.000)
Prev. sector: Financial, insurance and real estate activities	0.000	(0.000)
Prev. sector: Professional, scientific and technical activities	0.000*	(0.000)
Prev. sector: Administrative and support service activities	0.000	(0.000)
Prev. sector: Public Administration and defence	0.000	(0.000)
Prev. sector: Education	0.000	(0.000)
Prev. sector: Health	0.000	(0.000)
Prev. sector: Other	0.000	(0.000)
Prev. sector: No sector information	0.000	(0.000)
Prev. Permanent contract	−0.001	(0.001)
Prev. Full-time	−0.003***	(0.001)
Prev. Trade union member	0.000	(0.001)
Prev. Firm size 11-19	0.000	(0.000)
Prev. Firm size 20-49	0.000	(0.000)
Prev. Firm size 50-99	0.000	(0.000)
Prev. Firm size 100-500	0.000	(0.000)
Prev. Firm size 500+	0.000	(0.000)
Constant	0.022***	(0.004)

Note: ***p < .001; **p < .01; *p < .05.

was more heavily skewed towards female dominated sectors over the 2006 to 2011 period. The decline in the scarring effect of long-term unemployment and the relative rise in the return to labour market experience, proxied by age, exerted a positive influence on the transition rate to employment over the period.

From a policy perspective, the study highlights the importance of initiatives that focus on equipping claimants with educational credentials: while existing programmes that provide routes into third-level schooling, such as Springboard, appear fit for purpose, aspects of the Youth Guarantee appear under-resourced relative to the scale of the problem. Finally, the apparent reduction of the scarring effect associated with long-term unemployment suggests that activation policy need not be so heavily focused around targeting durations but, instead, should concentrate on ensuring claimants are properly equipped with the correct information and skills that will facilitate re-entry to employment. As Ireland continues to grow, it is crucial that the county's Public Employment Services are underpinned by accurate labour market intelligence that identifies areas of emerging employment growth and that existing training and education programmes are sufficiently flexible to respond the changing needs of the economy.

7 ENDNOTES

[1]This is a post-secondary, mainly vocational, qualification.

[2]Eurostat, March 2013: http://appsso.eurostat.ec.europa.eu/nui/show.do?dataset=edat_lfse_20&lang=en.

[3]Our analysis does not include inactivity either in the transition to or from unemployment. While there was a marked increase in the rate of inactivity over the Great Recession, the focus of this paper is solely on movements from and into unemployment given the dramatic increase in unemployment following the downturn.

[4]The QNHS is carried out by the Central Statistics Office (CSO), Ireland's national statistical collection organisation.

[5]The CSO introduced a new sample in Quarter 4 2012 as a result of the 2011 Census of Population. This new sample was introduced on an incremental basis across each quarter from Quarter 4 2012 to Quarter 4

2013. Thus, the new sample has only been fully effective since Quarter 4 2013.

[6]Information provided by the CSO.

[7]The two time-points considered in the analysis broadly approximate peak to trough activity in the labour market. Of course, there could also be rapid changes within the two time periods considered here. However, this analysis is concerned with how the nature of transitions changed from peak to trough activity in Ireland's labour market.

[8]Ward-Warmedinger and Macchiarelli (2014) examined labour market transition patterns across a range of EU regions (Central Eastern, Nordics, Continental and Mediterranean) over the period 2004 to 2008: overall (see Table 2) and broken down by gender, age and educational attainment (see Table 4). Their results are not directly comparable with those derived in this paper due to variations in the time periods examined and the use of different employment and unemployment definitional measures (ILO versus subjective measures). Nevertheless, a loose comparison of the results suggests that the employment-to-unemployment transition rate in Ireland in 2006, which would be similar to the pre-recessionary period of 2004–2008 examined by Ward-Warmedinger and Macchiarelli (2014), was lower than the EU regional rates identified by Ward-Warmedinger and Macchiarelli (2014): the average rate for the regions examined was 2.7 per cent, which compares with 1.8 per cent for Ireland. For the same time periods (2006 compared to 2004–2008), the unemployment-to-employment transition rate in Ireland was higher (37.3 per cent) for all the EU areas examined by Ward-Warmedinger and Macchiarelli (2014), apart from the Nordic region's rate (39.7 per cent). The age and educational attainment labour market transition rate results derived by Ward-Warmedinger and Macchiarelli (2014) are again not directly comparable with those derived in this paper due to the reasons outlined previously, and also because different age and educational attainment definitions were employed in both studies.

[9]The data in our analysis spans a relatively short time period; individuals can only be included in the panels for a maximum of five quarters. As such, alternative techniques such as duration models, which generally require longer panels of data with lower attrition rates, are not suitable for this analysis.

[10]Although our models allow for individuals to be in the analysis for up to five quarters, on average, individuals are present in the unemployment to employment transition models in 2006 and 2011 for

1.2 and 1.3 quarters respectively, and for 1.9 and 1.8 quarters in the employment to unemployment transitions models in 2006 and 2011 respectively. This minimises the possibility that our results are affected by individuals making multiple transitions over the five-quarter periods; in fact, excluding individuals who make multiple transitions has no material impact on the model results. These results are available on request from the authors.

[11]This finding is consistent with the work of McGuinness et al. (2011) who report that the activation system in force at the time (2006), the National Employment Action Plan (NEAP), actively reduced exits from the Live Register to employment.

[12]In addition, to serve as a proxy for job-search intensity, a variable was created that sums the number of different job search activites undertaken by an individual. However, the estimated odds ratio was close to one in both models and insignificant.

[13]With respect to the public employment office, while the NEAP was in the process of being replaced in 2011, the scale of the unemployment problem at that time meant that existing resources were severely stretched in their ability to deal with the unemployment crisis that existed in the country at that time.

[14]See Table 6.

[15]Sectoral employment increased by 23,585 (10.6 per cent).

[16]Over the period, total employment fell by 303,091 (14.1 per cent).

[17]See Table 7.

[18]Ireland's national register of all individuals in receipt of unemployment benefits.

[19]For an assessment of the income distributional impact of the recession in Ireland, see Callan et al. (2014).

DECLARATIONS

Acknowledgements

We would like to thank the Central Statistics Office (CSO) for making the Quarterly National Household Survey (QNHS) data available to us and, in particular, Brian Ring (CSO) for his assistance with data queries. The authors would like to thank the anonymous referee.

Responsible editor: Martin Kahanec

Competing interests

The IZA Journal of European Labor Studies is committed to the IZA Guiding Principles of Research Integrity. The authors declare that they have observed these principles.

REFERENCES

1. Barrett A, Kelly E (2012) The impact of Ireland's recession on the labour market outcomes of its immigrants. Eur J Popul 28(1):99–111
2. Callan T, Nolan B, Keane C, Savage M (2014) Walsh JR (2014) Crisis, response and distributional impact: the case of Ireland. IZA J Eur Labor Stud 3:9
3. Conefrey T (2011) Unemployment and Labour Force Participation During the Recession, Economic Letter Series from Central Bank of Ireland. 4
4. Kelly E, McGuinness S (2014) The impact of the recession on the structure and labour market success of NEET youth in Ireland. Intereconomics 48(4):196–235
5. Kelly E, McGuinness S, O'Connell PJ (2012) Submission to the Joint Committee on Jobs, Social Protection and Education on unemployment and youth unemployment
6. Kelly E, McGuinness S, O'Connell PJ, Haugh D (2014) Pandiella González A (2014) Transitions in and out of unemployment among young people in the Irish recession. Comp Econ Stud 56:616–634
7. McGinnity F, Russell H, Watson D, Kingston G, Kelly E (2014) Winners and losers? The equality impact of the great recession in Ireland. The Equality Authority and the Economic and Social Research Institute, Dublin

8. McGuinness S, O'Connell PJ, Kelly E, Walsh JR (2011) Activation in Ireland: An Evaluation of the National Employment Action Plan. ESRI Research Series No. 20. Economic and Social Research Institute, Dublin

9. Ward-Warmedinger M, Macchiarelli C (2014) Transitions in labour market status in EU labour markets. IZA J Eur Labor Stud 3:17

10. Yun MS (2004) Decomposing differences in the first moment. Econ Lett 82:275–280

9

CHAPTER

Economic Difficulties and Common Mental Disorders among Finnish and British White-collar Employees: The Contribution of Social and Behavioural Factors

Elina Laaksonen[1], Pekka Martikainen[2], Tea Lallukka[1], Eero Lahelma[1], Jane Ferrie[3], Ossi Rahkonen[1], Michael Marmot[3], and Jenny Head[3]

[1]*Department of Public Health, University of Helsinki, Finland*

[2]*Department of Sociology, University of Helsinki, Finland*

[3]*Department of Epidemiology and Public Health, University College London, UK*

ABSTRACT

Background

In addition to conventional indicators of socioeconomic position, material conditions such as economic difficulties are associated with mental health. However, there has been little effort to investigate explanations for these associations. This study aims to examine the association of current economic difficulties with common mental disorders (CMD) and the contribution of social and behavioural factors to this association in two cohorts of Finnish and British white-collar employees.

Methods

We used comparable survey data from the Finnish Helsinki Health Study (n=3949) and the British Whitehall II Study (n=3116). CMD were measured with the GHQ-12. Inequality indices from logistic regression analysis were used to examine the association between current economic difficulties and CMD, and the contribution of other past and present socioeconomic circumstances, health behaviours, living arrangements and work-family conflicts to this association. Inequality indices show the average change in ill-health for each step up in the level of economic difficulties. Analyses were conducted separately for men and women in each cohort.

Results

Clear associations between current economic difficulties and CMD were found. Adjusting for work-family conflicts attenuated the associations. Adjusting for indicators of past and present socioeconomic circumstances, health behaviours and living arrangements had generally negligible effects on the associations. The results were very similar among both sexes in the two cohorts.

Conclusions

Conflicts between work and family contribute to the association between economic difficulties and CMD in both Finland and Britain. Supporting people to cope not only with everyday economic difficulties but also with work-family conflicts may be important for reducing inequalities in mental health.

INTRODUCTION

Background

Studies on socioeconomic inequalities in health have typically examined the conventional dimensions of socioeconomic circumstances i.e. education, occupational class and income. Home and car ownership and other measures of wealth have been used to reflect the material resources dimension of socioeconomic circumstances.[1] Less attention has been paid to the importance of economic difficulties and to their associations with health. Economic difficulties are a domain of the multidimensional construct of socioeconomic circumstances, but they are not fully captured by income or other standard socioeconomic measures. They indicate immediate material hardship, but are not related to low income only. Daily life economic difficulties can exist at all income levels,[2] being caused for example by excessive consumption habits and debt[3, 4] or emerging because of adverse life events and circumstances.

In our previous study comparing cohorts of middle-aged Finnish and British employees, economic difficulties, i.e. difficulties in paying bills and affording food and clothes that the family needs, were associated with common mental disorders (CMD) independent of other past and present socioeconomic circumstances.[2] Such association was not found for other socioeconomic circumstances, e.g. income or occupational class. Other studies have also documented associations between economic difficulties and CMD.[3-7] Furthermore, associations have been demonstrated between economic difficulties and other health outcomes including severe physical conditions. An analysis of the Whitehall II Study data confirmed an association between economic difficulties and incident of coronary heart disease, and this was not explained by other socioeconomic circumstances, early life factors, working conditions or health behaviours.[10] Economic difficulties have also been associated with physical functioning[11] and self-rated health[12] in the Helsinki Health Study.

Potential explanations for the association of economic difficulties with mental health include material and perceived deprivation, physical hardship, economic uncertainty, and impaired social relationships, which can act as acute or chronic exposures and stressors.[8, 13-15] Thus, in addition to acting as a stressor in itself and having a direct effect on health, economic difficulties can affect health through mediating factors such as diminished possibilities for healthy behavioural and lifestyle choices, as well as difficulties in other areas of life [6] such as family. The effects of economic difficulties on health can also be either strengthened or weakened by other factors. For example, other simultaneous problems can further increase the overall stressfulness of the problematic situation.[16, 17]

Aims and context of the study

We aim to examine factors contributing to the associations between current economic difficulties and CMD in white-collar employee cohorts from Finland and Britain. We have previously found strong associations between current economic difficulties and CMD which were very similar in these two cohorts.[2] We now aim to compare possible explanations for these associations in the two cohorts. Although Finland and Britain are both affluent western European countries, there are also dissimilarities between them and it is thus possible that the explanations for these associations vary between these countries. The countries differ for example in their patterns of welfare provision and allocation, labour markets, social and family structures, and income distributions.[18, 19] There is a higher employment rate among women, a more universal welfare coverage and smaller income differences in Finland than in Britain.

A range of factors which may contribute to the associations between current economic difficulties and CMD are included in the analyses. These include social factors, i.e. past and present socioeconomic circumstances, living arrangements and work-family conflicts, and behavioural factors, i.e. health behaviours. Although the causal order can not be examined in this cross-sectional study, we assume a tentative temporal order as a basis of our analysis. In our simplified framework, we assume socioeconomic circumstances such as education and subsequent occupational class to precede economic difficulties and act as explanatory factors, i.e. influencing economic difficulties which in turn influence CMD. Also living arrangements, i.e. living alone or with partner and/or children, might influence the experience of economic difficulties. We consider work-family conflicts as potential mediators, i.e. economic difficulties influencing work-family conflicts which would further influence CMD. Health behaviours occupy an intermediate role in this framework. On one hand, they can precede economic difficulties as they are often adopted set at a relatively early age. On the other hand, maintaining and adopting unhealthy behaviours may also be a way of coping with economic difficulties. We further assess whether the associations of economic difficulties with CMD are modified, i.e. whether there is an interaction, by household income or conflicts experienced between work and family.

DATA AND METHODS

Data

The data used in this study derived from surveys conducted among public sector employees in Finland and Britain. The Finnish data derived from the Helsinki Health Study which is a longitudinal prospective cohort study of male and female employees of the City of Helsinki. The baseline surveys were conducted in 2000, 2001 and 2002, and 67% responded (N=8960).[20] Each year a questionnaire was posted to male and female employees reaching the age of 40, 45, 50, 55 and 60 years. We used data from years 2001 and 2002 (N=5819) as data from year 2000 did not include information on work-family conflicts.

The British data derived from the Whitehall II Study which is a longitudinal prospective cohort study of male and female civil servants aged 35-55 years at the time of recruitment, working in the London offices of twenty National Government Civil Service departments. The study includes data from seven postal surveys and four screening examinations conducted in years 1985-2004. At baseline 73% responded (N=10308).[21, 22] We used data mainly from the postal survey at phase 5 (1997) (N=7830, response rate 76%), as the earlier phases do not include all the measures needed, and to be more comparable with the Helsinki Health Study time frame.

The Helsinki Health Study data collection largely followed the Whitehall II Study protocol and the data were further harmonised as much as possible. To make the two cohorts as comparable as possible, we included respondents according to three criteria: 1) Being aged 45-60 years so that similar age-groups were formed for both cohorts; 40-year-olds (N=1135) from Helsinki and 61-65 year-olds (N=2036) from London were excluded. 2) Being a white-collar employee; thus manual workers (N=705 in age groups 45-60) were excluded from the Helsinki cohort. 3) Being in current employment in the civil service; those who had left civil service in the London cohort were excluded (N=2397 in age-groups 45-60). The final number of participants who met these criteria and had information on the outcome measure was 3949 (713 men and 3236 women) in Helsinki and 3116 (2241 men and 875 women) in London.

The Helsinki Health Study has been approved by ethical committees at the Department of Public Health, University of Helsinki, and at the City of Helsinki health authorities. The Whitehall II Study has been approved by the University College London ethics committee.

Measurements

Common mental disorders (CMD) were measured by the 12-item version of the General Health Questionnaire (GHQ-12). The GHQ indicates primarily disorders that are recent, general and non-psychotic,[23, 24] as well as context free, i.e. not related to a specific context such as work or family[25]. The GHQ has been well validated and also predicts more severe mental disorders.[23, 24, 26] The Helsinki Health Study data included the 12-item version of the GHQ. The Whitehall II Study data included the 30-item version from which the 12-item version was extracted. Different versions of the GHQ have been shown to be equally valid and the validity is unlikely to be affected by the language of the questionnaire.[24] Total score of the GHQ-12 ranges from 0 to 12. In this study, a recommended cut-off point of three or more symptoms was used to indicate CMD.[23, 24, 26]

The measure of current economic difficulties was constructed from two questions from Pearlin's list of chronic strains.[27] (1) "How much difficulty do you have in meeting the payment of bills?"; the response categories were scored as 0 'very little', 1 'slight', 2 'some', 3 'great' and 4 'very great'. (2) "How often does it happen that you do not have enough money to afford the kind of food or clothing you/your family should have?" (London) and "How often do you have enough money to buy the food or clothing you or your family need?" (Helsinki); the response categories were scored as 0 'never', 1 'seldom', 2 'sometimes', 3 'often' and 4 'always' in London, and vice versa in Helsinki. The scores of the two variables were summed up to yield a total score of economic difficulties ranging from 0 to 8. This score was used as a continuous variable in which a higher score indicated a higher level of difficulties. In descriptive analyses the variable was divided into three categories (0, 1-3, 4+) which approximately correspond to those used in our previous study.[2]

Six measures of socioeconomic circumstances and a measure of living arrangements were included. Parental education was based on information about both mother's and father's education, of which the higher one was chosen. Childhood economic difficulties were measured by asking whether the respondent's childhood family had faced serious (Helsinki) or continuing (London) financial problems before the respondent was aged 16. Own education and occupational class were included to indicate adult socioeconomic position. Household income was divided by the household size and weighted using the modified OECD equivalence scale.[28] Housing tenure was dichotomised into owner-occupiers and renters. Living arrangements were categorised into five groups: living alone, living with spouse/partner, living alone with children, living with spouse/partner and children, and others. More details on the socioeconomic measures can be found in our previous publication.[2]

Four measures of health behaviours were used. Smoking was divided into two categories: current smokers and non-smokers. Alcohol consumption was based on reported units of alcoholic beverages consumed during an average week (Helsinki) or the previous week (London). Units were converted into grams. Consumption exceeding 280 grams/week among men and 140 grams/week among women was considered as heavy drinking. Measure of physical activity was combined from questions asking about weekly and monthly frequency of physical activity on different levels of strenuousness. The least active quintile was classified as inactive. BMI was calculated from self-reported (Helsinki) or measured (London) height and weight, and obesity was classified as BMI of 30 or higher.

Work-to-family and family-to-work conflicts were measured with four items each.[29] The work-to-family question was: To what extent do your job responsibilities interfere with your family life? The response statements were: (1) Your job reduces the amount of time you can spend with the family, (2) Problems at work make you irritable at home, (3) Your work involves a lot of travel away from home, and (4) Your job takes so much energy you do not feel up to doing things that need attention at home. The family-to-work question was: To what extent does your family life and family responsibilities interfere with your performance on your job in any of the following ways? The response statements were: (1) Family matters reduce the time you can devote to your job (2) Family worries or problems distract you from your work (3) Family activities stop you getting the amount of sleep (4) family obligations reduce the time you need to relax or be yourself. For each item, there were four response categories: 'not at all', 'to some extent', 'a great deal', 'not applicable'/'I don't have a family'. The responses were summed to form separate scales from 4 to 12 for work-to-family and family-to-work conflict. The sum scores were grouped into three categories, i.e. 'low' (4), 'average' (5-7) and 'high' (8+) conflicts.

Correlations between current economic difficulties and other variables ranged between r=-0.01 and r=0.32 in both cohorts. In Helsinki the highest correlation was between economic difficulties and household income (r=0.28) and the lowest between economic difficulties and parental education (r=0.03). In London the highest correlation was between economic difficulties and household income (r=0.31) and the lowest between economic difficulties and heavy drinking (r=0.003). The proportion of missing values in the variables was generally small in Helsinki. In London the proportion of missing values was larger, particularly in household income (16% in women, 14% in men). However, approximately half of the missing values in household income could be replaced with information on individual income; the criterion was that the respondent was living alone or reported that no others contributed to the household income. Further treatment of missing values is described below.

Statistical methods

Analyses were conducted separately for men and women in each cohort. For descriptive purposes, age-adjusted prevalence for CMD with 95% confidence intervals (CI) were calculated by each independent variable. Inequality indices with 95% CI for CMD were calculated with logistic regression analysis using economic difficulties as a continuous variable. The inequality index is interpreted as the average change in ill-health (in terms of the odds ratio) for each step up in the level of economic difficulties. Age-adjusted indices were first calculated. In the subsequent multivariate models the socioeconomic variables were first adjusted for. After this, living arrangements, health behaviours and work-family conflicts were added, one variable group at a time. In the final model all variables were simultaneously adjusted for. Interactions of household income and work-to-family as well as family-to-work conflicts with economic difficulties were also examined.

Treatment of item missing was carried out with multiple imputation using ICE (Imputation by Chained Equations) method in STATA.[30] Five copies of the data were formed in the imputation process, each with missing values imputed on the basis of the variables used in the analyses of this study. These copies were independently analysed in the logistic regression analyses, and estimates of parameters were averaged across the copies to obtain mean estimates and their 95% CI. Using ICE, the results were practically identical with those obtained with a complete case analysis (N=2626, Helsinki; N=1921, London), but the precision of the estimations was improved.

RESULTS

The overall prevalence of CMD was 27% among women and 23% among men in Helsinki (Table2). The corresponding figures were 29% and 23% in London (Table3). The prevalence of CMD was higher among respondents with current economic difficulties among women and men in both cohorts (Table 1), with Helsinki women having the largest difference.

Table 1. Number of participants (N), age-adjusted prevalence (%) and odds ratio (OR) with 95% confidence intervals (CI) of GHQ-12 3+ by current economic difficulties, Helsinki and London

	Helsinki women N	Prevalence % of GHQ-12 3+	OR (CI)	Helsinki men N	Prevalence % of GHQ-12 3+	OR (CI)
Current economic difficulties						
0	1851	22	1.00	441	20	1.00
1-3	1080	30	1.57 (1.32-1.86)	217	26	1.41 (0.95-2.09)
4+	305	45	2.98 (2.31-3.85)	55	33	1.96 (1.06-3.62)
	London women N	Prevalence % of GHQ-12 3+	OR (CI)	**London men** N	Prevalence % of GHQ-12 3+	OR (CI)
Current economic difficulties						
0	478	26	1.00	1278	20	1.00
1-3	327	32	1.29 (0.94-1.78)	804	26	1.41 (1.15-1.75)
4+	71	36	1.64 (0.96-2.81)	160	36	2.05 (1.41-2.98)

There were large variations in CMD by work-to-family and family-to-work conflicts and childhood economic difficulties in both cohorts and sexes (Tables 2 and and3).3). Variations in CMD were less consistent by other variables, and only among Helsinki men and to a lesser degree among women current smoking and physical inactivity were associated with CMD. In both cohorts, economic difficulties were more common in lower position groups by all socioeconomic variables except parental education. They were also more common among those living with children, having conflicts between work and family, and reporting unhealthy behaviours, except heavy drinking among women (no results shown).

Table 2. Number of participants (N), age-adjusted prevalence (%) and odds ratio (OR) with 95% confidence intervals (CI) of GHQ-12 3+ by explanatory and mediating variables, Helsinki.

	Helsinki women N	Prevalence % of GHQ-12 3+	OR (CI)	Helsinki men N	Prevalence % of GHQ-12 3+	OR (CI)
Total	3236	27		713	23	
Parental education						
Higher	678	30	1.00	206	23	1.00
Intermediate	823	26	0.82 (0.65-1.03)	182	21	0.86 (0.52-1.42)
Basic	1735	26	0.81 (0.66-0.98)	326	24	1.05 (0.69-1.59)
Childhood economic difficulties						
No difficulties	2635	25	1.00	601	21	1.00
Difficulties	601	34	1.56 (1.28-1.90)	112	31	1.72 (1.09-2.72)
Own education						
Higher	878	27	1.00	305	23	1.00
Intermediate	1106	29	1.11 (0.91-1.35)	225	22	0.93 (0.61-1.41)
Basic	1251	25	0.93 (0.76-1.13)	183	23	0.95 (0.61-1.48)
Occupational class						
Administrative/managerial	247	28	1.00	187	23	1.00
Professional/semi-professional	1407	27	0.93 (0.68-1.26)	439	23	1.06 (0.70-1.61)
Clerical	1582	26	0.87 (0.65-1.18)	87	18	0.81 (0.42-1.55)
Household income						
Highest group	677	23	1.00	168	24	1.00
2nd	928	26	1.16 (0.91-1.47)	190	23	1.00 (0.60-1.65)
3rd	796	27	1.22 (0.95-1.56)	198	21	0.84 (0.50-1.40)
Lowest group	835	29	1.34 (1.05-1.70)	157	25	1.12 (0.66-1.90)
Housing tenure						
Owner-occupier	2275	26	1.00	550	22	1.00
Renter	961	27	1.06 (0.89-1.26)	163	25	1.15 (0.76-1.75)
Living arrangements						
Alone	805	29	1.00	166	26	1.00
With spouse/partner	820	24	0.77 (0.62-0.96)	197	23	0.76 (0.45-1.28)
Alone with children	214	33	1.02 (0.71-1.46)	19	32	1.49 (0.53-4.21)
With spouse/partner and children	706	24	0.82 (0.63-1.06)	212	19	0.71 (0.42-1.17)
Other	691	28	0.94 (0.74-1.19)	118	25	0.99 (0.56-1.74)
Current smoking						
No	2553	26	1.00	543	20	1.00
Yes	683	31	1.29 (1.07-1.56)	170	30	1.70 (1.15-2.52)
Heavy drinking						
No	3026	26	1.00	666	23	1.00
Yes	210	32	1.33 (0.98-1.81)	47	22	1.03 (0.50-2.11)
Physical inactivity						
No	2592	26	1.00	573	20	1.00
Yes	644	30	1.21 (1.00-1.46)	140	31	1.81 (1.19-2.75)
Obesity						
No	2768	26	1.00	613	22	1.00
Yes	468	32	1.24 (1.00-1.54)	100	26	1.27 (0.78-2.07)
Family-to-work conflict						
Low	1581	18	1.00	376	14	1.00
Average	1188	32	2.18 (1.82-2.63)	245	25	2.07 (1.37-3.13)
High	257	56	6.40 (0.48-8.55)	55	55	7.48 (4.05-13.80)
Not applicable/ no family	211	32	1.99 (1.45-2.74)	37	34	2.46 (1.14-5.33)
Work-to-family conflict						
Low	595	12	1.00	142	8	1.00
Average	1899	24	2.46 (1.84-3.28)	403	18	2.36 (1.24-4.51)
High	530	52	8.21 (5.97-11.30)	131	48	9.91 (4.97-19.74)
Not applicable/ no family	211	32	3.35 (2.26-4.96)	37	34	4.38 (1.73-11.08)

The age-adjusted logistic regression analysis confirmed a clear association between economic difficulties and CMD among women and men in Helsinki (Table 4, Model 0). Adjusting for socioeconomic circumstances (Model 1) had no effect on the association between economic difficulties and CMD. Further adjustment for living arrangements (Model 2) and health behaviours (Model 3) had mostly small or negligible effects on the association between economic difficulties and CMD. Only adjusting for health behaviours caused some attenuation among men. Adjusting for work-family conflicts (Model 4) clearly attenuated the association among both sexes. This attenuation was slightly more due to family-to-work conflict (OR=1.20, women; OR=1.09, men) than work-to-family conflict (OR=1.24, women; OR=1.15, men) among both women and men (no results shown). Overall, adjusting for conflicts between work and family (Model 4) attenuated the inequality index value of the basel model (Model 1) by

27% (100*(1.26-1.19)/(1.26-1) among women and 50% (100*(1.18-1.09)/(1.18-1)) among men in Helsinki.

Table 3. Number of participants (N), age-adjusted prevalence (%) and odds ratio (OR) of GHQ-12 3+ by explanatory and mediating variables, London.

	London women N	Prevalence % of GHQ-12 3+	OR (CI)	London men N	Prevalence % of GHQ-12 3+	OR (CI)
Total	875	29		2241	23	
Parental education						
Higher	221	30	1.00	505	25	1.00
Intermediate	155	30	1.11 (0.69-1.80)	545	22	0.83 (0.62-1.16)
Basic	500	28	0.91 (0.62-1.34)	1191	23	0.88 (0.68-1.15)
Childhood economic difficulties						
No difficulties	617	27	1.00	1672	21	1.00
Difficulties	258	36	1.54 (1.11-2.13)	569	31	1.78 (1.43-2.22)
Own education						
Higher	289	32	1.00	918	23	1.00
Intermediate	177	30	0.90 (0.58-1.41)	698	24	1.06 (0.83-1.35)
Basic	409	29	0.83 (0.59-1.18	625	24	1.08 (0.85-1.39)
Occupational class						
Administrative/managerial	208	28	1.00	1120	22	1.00
Professional/semi-professional	405	33	1.18 (0.82-1.70)	989	25	1.15 (0.94-1.41)
Clerical	262	23	0.70 (0.45-1.07)	132	16	0.68 (0.41-1.10)
Household income						
Highest group	261	28	1.00	772	23	1.00
2nd	167	27	0.93 (0.60-1.45)	314	25	1.09 (0.80-1.49)
3rd	199	29	1.03 (0.67-1.59)	569	23	0.96 (0.74-1.26)
Lowest group	248	31	1.13 (0.76-1.68)	586	24	1.04 (0.80-1.34)
Housing tenure						
Owner-occupier	800	30	1.00	2128	23	1.00
Renter	75	20	0.56 (0.31-1.03)	113	24	1.04 (0.66-1.64)
Living arrangements						
Alone	231	49	1.00	360	23	1.00
With spouse/partner	311	39	0.87 (0.60-1.27)	548	22	0.92 (0.67-1.28)
Alone with children	22	14	0.61 (0.22-1.64)	60	24	1.03 (0.54-1.94)
With spouse/partner and children	61	25	0.98 (0.53-1.80)	474	23	0.97 (0.70-1.34)
Other	250	45	0.83 (0.56-1.24)	799	25	1.07 (0.80-1.44)
Current smoking						
No	763	29	1.00	1852	23	1.00
Yes	112	29	1.00 (0.64-1.55)	389	24	1.05 (0.81-1.36)
Heavy drinking						
No	761	28	1.00	1969	23	1.00
Physical inactivity						
No	704	29	1.00	1806	23	1.00
Yes	171	29	0.95 (0.65-1.38)	435	24	1.06 (0.82-1.359
Obesity						
No	707	29	1.00	1952	23	1.00
Yes	168	30	1.08 (0.73-1.59)	289	26	1.17 (0.87-1.58)
Family-to-work conflict						
Low	310	22	1.00	738	13	1.00
Average	337	30	1.58 (1.09-2.27)	1060	24	2.17 (1.67-2.81)
High	107	50	3.67 (2.28-5.93)	286	46	5.62 (4.07-7.75)
Not applicable/ no family	121	31	1.70 (1.05-2.75)	157	23	2.09 (1.36-3.21)
Work-to-family conflict						
Low	146	19	1.00	261	10	1.00
Average	421	41	2.41 (1.12-5.19)	1062	18	1.97 (1.22-3.16)
High	187	65	7.08 (3.36-14.92)	761	35	4.83 (2.99-7.78)
Not applicable/ no family	121	31	3.23 (1.42-7.36)	157	23	2.78 (1.56-4.98)

Table 4. Associations of current economic difficulties with common mental disorders (GHQ-12 3+) and the contribution of socioeconomic circumstances, living arrangements, health behaviours and work-family conflicts. Inequality index values[a] from logistic regression ...

	Inequality indices (95 % confidence intervals)					
	MODEL 0 Age-adjusted	**MODEL 1** 0+ Socio-economic circumstances[b]	**MODEL 2** 1+ Living arrangements	**MODEL 3** 1+ Health behaviours[c]	**MODEL 4** 1+ Work-family conflicts[d]	**MODEL 5** Fully adjusted
Helsinki						
Men	1.18 (1.05-1.33)	1.18 (1.04-1.33)	1.18 (1.04-1.34)	1.15 (1.01-1.30)	1.09 (0.95-1.25)	1.07 (0.92-1.23)
Women	1.26 (1.20-1.32)	1.27 (1.20-1.34)	1.27 (1.20-1.34)	1.26 (1.20-1.33)	1.19 (1.13-1.26)	1.17 (1.11-1.24)
London						
Men	1.18 (1.11-1.27)	1.19 (1.11-1.28)	1.19 (1.11-1.29)	1.19 (1.10-1.28)	1.11 (1.03-1.20)	1.11 (1.03-1.21)
Women	1.10 (1.00-1.22)	1.11 (0.99-1.24)	1.12 (1.00-1.25)	1.11 (0.99-1.24)	1.03 (0.91-1.16)	1.04 (0.92-1.17)

[a] Current economic difficulties score 0-8 is used as a continuous variable. Inequality index is the OR for each one point increase in economic difficulties.

[b] Parental education, childhood economic difficulties, own education, occupational class, household income, housing tenure

[c] Current smoking, heavy drinking, physical inactivity, obesity

[d] Family-to-work and work-to-family conflict

As in Helsinki, also in London the age-adjusted models showed a clear association between economic difficulties and CMD in both sexes (Table 4, Model 0). Similarly in London, the adjustments for other socioeconomic circumstances (Model 1) and for living arrangements (Model 2) and health behaviours (Model 3) had practically no effects on the association between economic difficulties and CMD. Adjusting for work-family conflicts (Model 4) clearly attenuated the association among both sexes. Similarly to Helsinki women and men, among London women adjusting for work-to-family conflict (OR=1.04) had a somewhat stronger effect on the association than family-to-work conflict (OR=1.07), whereas among London men work-to-family conflict (OR=1.15) was slightly less important than family-to-work conflict (OR=1.13) (no results shown). After adjusting for work-to-family and family-to-work conflicts (Model 4) the inequality index value of the base model (Model 1) was reduced by 73% among women and 42% among men in London.

Interactions of household income, family-to-work conflict and work-to-family conflict with current economic difficulties were examined (no results shown). No interactions were found for family-to-work and work-to-family conflict. For household income, a stronger association between economic difficulties and CMD in lower income groups (age-adjusted inequality index OR=0.77 in the highest and OR=1.39 in the lowest income group) was found in Helsinki men (no results shown). In London and in Helsinki women, there was a similar tendency but it did not reach statistical significance.

DISCUSSION

Main results

We have previously found current economic difficulties to be strongly associated with CMD.[2] In this study we sought to improve our understanding of this association by examining the contribution of a range of social and behavioural factors, i.e. past and present socioeconomic circumstances, living arrangements, health behaviours and work-family conflicts, to this association. We also sought to compare employee cohorts including women and men from two countries, Finland and Britain.

Our first main finding was that adjusting for conflicts between work and family attenuated the associations of economic difficulties with CMD (adjusted for age and socioeconomic circumstances) by approximately 30-70%. First of all, these conflicts might act as mediators between economic difficulties and CMD, i.e. economic difficulties would contribute to conflicts between work and family which in turn would contribute to mental health. As the attenuation of the association between economic difficulties and CMD was slightly more due to the adjustment for the variable 'family-to-work conflict' than for the variable 'work-to-family conflict', it is possible that the same family problems that impede work are the ones leading to economic difficulties. Thus, for example a large number of dependants or family members' health problems might cause both the economic difficulties and the conflicts between family and work. Furthermore, it is possible that there is some conceptual overlap between work-family conflicts and economic difficulties, and they might reflect partly similar phenomena. This kind of overlap might also be possible between work-family conflicts and the GHQ, although the correlations between these were not very high, ranging between r=0.13 and r=0.26 (results not shown). Finally, the strong contribution of work-family conflicts to the association between economic difficulties and CMD might also derive from a situation in which several simultaneous problems, such as economic difficulties and work-family conflicts, increase the overall mental strain and contribute to CMD.[16, 17]

Our second main finding was that other past and present socioeconomic circumstances, living arrangements and health behaviours did not generally affect the association between economic difficulties and CMD. This has been previously observed in the Whitehall cohort for severe physical health problems, i.e. coronary events, which is a medically confirmed health outcome free of self-report bias.[10] It is particularly notable that in our study, there were generally no clear mediating or explanatory effects of health-related behaviours, although unhealthy behaviours have tended to be associated with poorer mental health[31, 32] and been shown to vary by other socioeconomic circumstances[33, 34]. Overall, these results suggest that economic difficulties may differ from other socioeconomic circumstances, at least among white-collar employees.

According to our third main finding, patterning of CMD by the studied variables was very similar in the two cohorts. Thus, the associations of economic difficulties with CMD and the effects of contributing factors appear not to be affected by the differences Finnish and British societies have between them for example in working life, social policies and welfare regimes in general[18] and in the income distributions[19]. It is possible that the similarity of the two employee cohorts was more important than the cultural and social differences between the countries. This may suggest a better generalisability of these results to similar employee groups also in other western European societies.

Methodological considerations

An advantage of our study was the availability of comparable employee cohorts using largely identical measurements. However, some limitations need to be considered when interpreting the results. Firstly, as our samples were relatively homogeneous consisting of middle-aged white-collar employees only, the results cannot be generalised to all employees or the general population. Secondly, due to the cross-sectional design, causal interpretations of the found associations should be made with caution. There is a possibility of health-related selection, i.e. that low socioeconomic position and economic difficulties in particular, as well as work-family conflicts, are influenced by prior poor mental health. However, previous studies suggest that the causal direction is mainly from socioeconomic position to health.[35, 36] It has also been shown that among the respondents of the Whitehall II Study health affects the social position much less than vice versa.[37] Thirdly, as the data were self-reported, the possibility of reporting bias has to be considered: the respondents' common mental disorders might influence their responses to questions about socioeconomic circumstances and economic difficulties. Negative affectivity, i.e. a disposition to respond negatively in surveys, might equally affect the results.[38] However, we were able to test this in the London cohort and further adjusting for negative affectivity in the logistic regression models did not affect the main findings. Fourthly, non-response bias may affect the results of surveys. In the Helsinki cohort, women and higher social classes had a higher response rate. However, the effects of non-response on the results concerning relative socioeconomic differences in health appear to be negligible.[39, 40] Also attrition between the Whitehall II Study baseline (1985-88) and phase 5 (1997) may have affected the results. Despite attrition, we used data from the phase 5 as the earlier phases did not include all the measures needed for this study. Furthermore, we have checked that in phases 1 and 3 the associations of economic difficulties and other available socioeconomic indicators with CMD are practically similar to those in phase 5. Fifthly, the Helsinki Health Study year 2000 data was excluded from the analysis. However, the results for economic difficulties and CMD were similar to those in data from all three years 2000-2002.[2]

CONCLUSIONS

The associations between economic difficulties and CMD were in a large part dependent on conflicts between work and family, but not on other socioeconomic circumstances, living arrangements or health behaviours. This held true for women and men from the Finnish and the British cohorts. However, factors contributing to the associations between economic difficulties and CMD still remain partly open, and analyses focusing on other possible contributory factors are needed. In the light of our results, supporting people to cope with everyday economic difficulties as well as efforts to improve the balance between work and family life may help employees to maintain good mental health.

What is already known on this topic

- Current economic difficulties are associated with common mental disorders but the explanations for this association are unclear.

What this study adds

- Work-family conflicts explained a large part of the associations between current economic difficulties and common mental disorders in the Finnish and British employee cohorts.
- Other socioeconomic circumstances, living arrangements, and health behaviours had negligible effects on the associations between economic difficulties and common mental disorders.
- Work-family conflicts and economic difficulties should be considered in efforts to reduce inequalities in mental health.

ACKNOWLEDGMENTS

We thank all participating employees in Helsinki and London and all members of the Helsinki Health Study group and the Whitehall II Study team.

Funding

The Helsinki Health Study is supported by Academy of Finland (#205588, #121748). The Whitehall II study has been supported by grants from the Medical Research Council; British Heart Foundation; Health and Safety Executive; Department of Health; National Heart Lung and Blood Institute (HL36310), US, NIH: National Institute on Aging (AG13196), US, NIH; Agency for Health Care Policy Research (HS06516); and the John D and Catherine T MacArthur Foundation Research Networks on Successful Midlife Development and Socio-economic Status and Health. The first author is supported by the Finnish Cultural Foundation. PM (#70631 and 48600) and OR (#210435) are supported by the Academy of Finland. MM is supported by an MRC Research Professorship.

FOOTNOTES

The published version of this paper 'Economic difficulties and common mental disorders among Finnish and British white-collar employees: the contribution of social and behavioural factors. Laaksonen E, Martikainen P, Lallukka T, Lahelma E, Ferrie J, Rahkonen O, Marmot M, Head J J Epidemiol Community Health. 2009 Jun;63(6):439-46. Epub 2009 Feb 15' can be found at http://jech.bmj.com /cgi/content/full/63/6/439

REFERENCES

1. Braveman PA, Cubbin C, Egerter S, et al. Socioeconomic status in health research. One size does not fit all. J Am Med Assoc. 2005;294:2879–2888.
2. Laaksonen E, Martikainen P, Lahelma E, Lallukka T, Rahkonen O, Head J, et al. Socioeconomic circumstances and common mental disorders among Finnish and British public sector employees: Evidence from the Helsinki Health Study and the Whitehall II Study. Int J Epidemiol. 2007;36:776–786.
3. Drentea P, Lavrakas PJ. Over the limit: the association among health, race and debt. Soc Sci Med. 2000;50:517–29.
4. Zimmermann FJ, Katon W. Socioeconomic status, depression disparities, and financial strain: what lies behind the income-depression relationship? Health Econ. 2005;14:1197–1215.
5. Cheng YH, Chi I, Boey KW, Ko LS, Chou KL. Self-rated economic conditions and the health of elderly persons in Hong Kong. Soc Sci Med. 2002;55:1415–24.
6. Viinamäki H, Kontula O, Niskanen L, Koskela K. The association between economic and social factors and mental health in Finland. Acta Psychiatr Scand. 1995;92:208–13.
7. Weich S, Lewis G. Poverty, unemployment, and common mental disorders: population based cohort study. BMJ. 1998;317:115–19. A.
8. Pudrovska T, Schieman S, Pearlin LI. The sense of mastery as a mediator and moderator in the association between economic hardship and health in late life. J Aging Health. 2005;17:634–60.
9. Skapinakis P, Weich S, Lewis G, Singleton N, Araya R. Socio-economic position and common mental disorders: Longitudinal study in the general population in the UK. Br J Psychiatry. 2006;189:109–17.
10. Ferrie JE, Martikainen P, Shipley MJ, Marmot M. Self-reported economic difficulties and coronary events in men: evidence from the Whitehall II Study. Int J Epidemiol. 2005;34:640–48.
11. Laaksonen E, Martikainen P, Head J, Rahkonen O, Marmot M, Lahelma E. Associations of multiple socioeconomic

circumstances with physical functioning among Finnish and British employees. Submitted.

12. Laaksonen M, Rahkonen O, Martikainen P, Lahelma E. Multiple dimensions of socioeconomic position and self-rated health. The contribution of childhood socioeconomic circumstances, adult socioeconomic status and material resources. Am J Public Health. 2005;95:1403–1409.

13. Pearlin LI. The sociological study of stress. J Health Soc Behav. 1989;30:241–56.

14. Elstad JI. The psycho-social perspective on social inequalities in health. Sociol Health Illn. 1998;20:598–618.

15. Weich S, Lewis G. Material standard of living, social class, and the prevalence of the common mental disorders in Great Britain. J Epidemiol Community Health. 1998;52:8–14. B.

16. Kahn JR, Pearlin LI. Financial strain over the life course and health among older adults. J Health Soc Behav. 2006;47:17–31.

17. Pearlin LI, Aneshensel CS, LeBlanc AJ. The forms and mechanisms of stress proliferation: The case of AIDS caregivers. J Health Soc Behav. 1997;38:223–36.

18. Esping-Andersen G. Three Worlds of Welfare Capitalism. Oxford: Polity Press; 1990.

19. Gottschlak P, Schmeeding TM. Cross-national comparisons of earnings and income inequality. J Econ Lit. 1997;35:633–87.

20. Lahelma E, Martikainen P, Rahkonen O, Roos E, Saastamoinen P. Occupational class inequalities across key domains of health: results from the Helsinki Health Study. Eur J Public Health. 2005;15:504–10.

21. Marmot M, Davey Smith G, Stansfeld S, et al. Health inequalities among British Civil Servants: the Whitehall Study. Lancet. 1991;337:1387–93.

22. Marmot M, Brunner E. Cohort Profile: The Whitehall II Study. Int J Epidemiol. 2005;34:251–56.

23. Goldberg DP. The Detection of Psychiatric Illness by a Questionnaire Maudsley Monograph no 21. Oxford; Oxford University Press; 1972.

24. Goldberg DP, Gater R, Sartorius N, et al. The validity of two versions of the GHQ in the WHO study of mental illness in general health care. Psychol Med. 1997;27:191–97.

25. Warr P. Work, Unemployment and Mental Health. Oxford: Clarendon; 1987.

26. Makowska Z, Merecz D, Moscicka A, Kolasa W. The validity of General Health Questionnaires, GHQ-12 and GHQ-28, in mental health studies of working people. Int J Occup Med Environ Health. 2002;15:353–62.

27. Pearlin LI, Schooler C. The structure of coping. J Health Soc Behav. 1978;19:2–21.

28. Hagenaars A, de Vos K, Zaidi MA. Poverty Statistics in the Late 1980s: Research Based on Micro-Data. Luxembourg: Office for Official Publications of the European Communities; 1994.

29. Grzywacz J, Marks N. Reconceptualizing the work–family interface: an ecological perspective on the correlates of positive and negative spillover between work and family. J Occup Health Psychol. 2000;5:111–16.

30. Royston P. Multiple imputation of missing values. Stata Journal. 2004;4:227–41.

31. Rohrer JE, Pierce JR, Jr, Blackburn C. Lifestyle and mental health. Prev Med. 2005;40:438–43.

32. Strine TW, Balluz L, Chapman DP, Morarity DG, Owens M, Mokdad AH. Risk behaviors and healthcare coverage among adults by frequent mental distress status, 2001. Am J Prev Med. 2004;26:213–6.

33. Lynch JW, Kaplan GA, Salonen JT. Why do poor people behave poorly? Variation in adult health behaviours and psychosocial characteristics by stages of the socioeconomic lifecourse. Soc Sci Med. 1997;44:809–19.

34. Power C, Graham H, Due P, Hallqvist J, Joung I, Kuh D, Lynch J. The contribution of childhood and adult socioeconomic position to adult obesity and smoking behaviour: an international comparison. Int J Epidemiol. 2005;34:335–44.

35. Benzeval M, Judge K. Income and health: the time dimension. Soc Sci Med. 2001;52:1371–90.

36. Blane D, Davey-Smith G, Bartley M. Social selection: what does it contribute to social class differences in health? Sociol Health Illn. 1993;15:1–15.

37. Chandola T, Bartley M, Sacker A, Jenkinson C, Marmot M. Health selection in the Whitehall II study, UK. Soc Sci Med. 2003;56:2059–72.

38. Watson D. Intraindividual and interindividual analyses of positive and negative affect: their relation to health complaints, perceived stress, and daily activities. J Pers Soc Psychol. 1988;54:1020–30.

39. Martikainen P, Laaksonen M, Piha K, Lallukka T. Does survey non-response bias the association between occupational social class and health? Scand J Public Health. 2007;35:212–15.

40. Laaksonen M, Aittomäki A, Lallukka T, Rahkonen O, Saastamoinen P, Silventoinen K, Lahelma E. Register-based study among employees showed small nonparticipation bias in health surveys and check-ups. J Clin Epidemiol. 2008 d

CHAPTER 10

A Narrative Review on the Effect of Economic Downturns on the Nursing Labour Market: Implications for Policy and Planning

Mohamad Alameddine[1], Andrea Baumann[2], Audrey Laporte[3] and Raisa Deber[3]

[1]*Faculty of Health Sciences, Department of Health Management and Policy, American University of Beirut, Riad El-Solh, Beirut 1107 2020, Lebanon.*

[2]*Faculty of Health Sciences International Health, Michael G. DeGroote Centre for Learning, McMaster University, Hamilton, ON L8S 4K1, Canada.*

[3]*Faculty of Medicine, Institute of Health Policy Management and Evaluation, University of Toronto, Health Sciences Building, 155 College Street, Suite 425, Toronto, ON M5T 3M6, Canada.*

ABSTRACT

Economic downturns and recession lead to budget cuts and service reductions in the healthcare sector which often precipitate layoffs and hiring freezes. Nurses, being the largest professional group in healthcare, are strongly affected by cost reductions. Economic downturns destabilize the nursing labour market with potential negative outcomes, including serious shortages, extending beyond the recessionary period. The objectives of this manuscript are to provide an overview of the potential short- and long-run impact of economic downturns on the supply and demand of nurses, and present healthcare decision makers with a framework to enhance their ability to strategically manage their human resources through economic cycles.

A narrative review of the literature on the effects of economic downturns on the nursing labour market in developed countries was carried out with a special focus on studies offering a longitudinal examination of labour force trends. Analysis indicates that economic downturns limit the ability of public payers and institutions to finance their existing health workforce. As salaried healthcare workers, nurses are especially susceptible to institutional budget cuts. In the short run, economic downturns may temporarily reduce the demand for and increase the supply of nurses, thereby influencing nursing wages and turnover rates. These effects may destabilise the nursing labour market in the long run. After economic downturns, the market would quickly display the pre-recessionary trends and there may be serious demand–supply imbalances resulting in severe shortages. Potential long-term effects of recession on the nursing labour market may include a downsized active workforce, difficulty in retaining younger nurses, a decreased supply of nurses and workforce casualisation.

Lack of understanding of labour market dynamics and trends might mislead policy makers into making misinformed workforce downsizing decisions that are often difficult and expensive to reverse. In the aftermath of an economic downturn, the costs of attracting nurses back often outweigh the short term cost savings. Effective management should support the nursing workforce by creating attractive and stable work environments to retain nurses at a manageable cost.

PREFACE

Economic downturns affect all sectors of the economy including healthcare [1-3]. They may escalate into a recession, defined broadly as a self-reinforcing reduction in economic activity characterized by persistent job losses precipitating increased unemployment [4]. Many countries around the globe are currently in the midst of economic downturns, which are anticipated to grow into a global recession [5].

Nurses, being the largest professional group in the healthcare sector, are strongly affected by budget balancing attempts. For many institutions, the easiest and fastest means to balance the books is to cut back the nursing workforce as institutions restructure, downsize, merge or actively shift care from hospital to community [6,7]. Such restructuring may precipitate detrimental and difficult to reverse consequences in the longer run [8-10].

Now that the economy of many countries around the globe is undergoing turbulent times, it is important that the recessionary trends in the healthcare sector do not drive policy and decision makers to take decisions that may destabilise the nursing labour market for years to come. In this manuscript, we attempt to examine the effects of economic downturns and recession on the supply and demand of nurses and provide a framework to help healthcare decision makers understand and manage their valuable nursing resources during tough economic times.

The supply and demand for nurses: a brief overview

Projecting nurses' supply in a labour market traditionally uses a stock and flow model [11] (Figure (Figure1).1). This model measures total workers' involvement in a labour market using full-time equivalents (FTE). One FTE indicates that a worker is putting the number of work hours of a full-time worker.

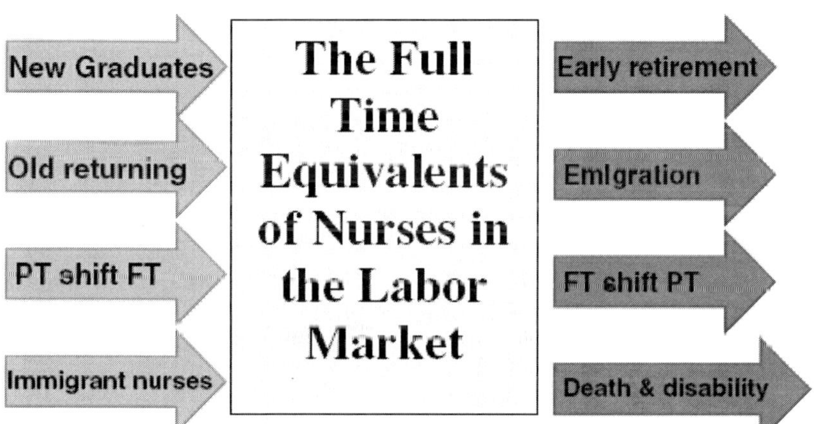

Figure 1. A Stock and Flow Model for the supply of nurses into the labour market.

In a stable fiscal environment, the total number of nurse FTEs in a labour market is replenished through various sources. These include graduates of nursing training programmes, inactive nurses returning into the labour market, recruitment of foreign-trained nurses (immigrant) into the labour market and an increased proportion of part-time/casual nurses enhancing their labour force participation by increasing the total number of hours worked. Conversely, nurse FTEs are subtracted from the labour market through death, retirement, emigration, disability and decreased labour force participation (shifting from full-time to part-time employment). Policy makers use policy levers to project and optimise the number of nursing FTEs required to address current and future anticipated needs of the population. This optimisation is a complex task compounded by many issues, such as the lag time needed to train specialised human resources and the importance of maintaining surge capacity to deal with unexpected emergencies (e.g., emerging diseases and global epidemics) [12,13].

On the demand side of the nursing labour market there is an array of potential employers (e.g., hospitals, long-term care facilities, homecare, etc.) competing for the employment of nurses with various specialties and skills. The demand for nurses thus depends on their productivity in different tasks, their skills and the degree to which they could be replaced by other employees.

REVIEW

In order to review and analyse the effect of economic downturns on the nursing workforce a combination of a narrative review and expert opinion were utilised. The two methods were combined towards the development of an analytical framework that could guide the human resource decisions of health decision makers and stakeholders in tough economic times.

Narrative reviews are invaluable in theory development/evaluation, problem identification or in surveying the state of knowledge on a particular topic [14,15]. A narrative review of published manuscripts on the effect of economic downturns and recession on the nursing labour market was conducted using PubMed, the Cumulative Index to Nursing and Allied Health Literature (CINAHL) and the Institute for Scientific Information (ISI) library databases. A special focus was placed on studies offering a longitudinal examination of labour force trends in developed countries. Key words used to search the title and abstract included various combinations of: recession, economic downturn and nurse(s), nursing and labor/labour market, workforce trends and employment. The search was not meant to be exhaustive but rather purposeful to help shape a clearer understanding of the effect of economic downturns on the nursing labour market.

Although the search was not limited by year of publication, the focus was on the most recent economic downturn beginning in 2007–2008 in many developed countries around the globe. The original search yielded a large number of articles that were reduced to 42 unique manuscripts after a review of the abstract for relevance. The 42 manuscripts were fully reviewed by two members of the research team to judge their type, general focus and the means through which they addressed the question of interest. After this review, nineteen manuscripts were excluded from the analysis because their main focus was not on the analysis of economic downturns, workforce trends or because they did not focus on the nursing workforce. The remaining 23 manuscripts were thoroughly reviewed by two members of the research team. Each member individually read all the articles and identified main themes relating to the effect of economic downturns on the nursing workforce. The two reviewers met and consolidated the identified themes into five main themes (demand, supply, salary, turnover and shortages) in order to enhance the clarity of analysis. The five themes were reviewed and approved by all authors and are reported in this manuscript, with reference to the articles when necessary.

This search was supplemented by the authors' experience with analysing and deciphering nursing labour market trends within the Canadian context. Note that the multi-disciplinary authorship team has had several decades of research experience in investigating the training, recruitment and retention of nurses, human resources policy analyses, labour economics and human resources management.

Budget cuts and economic downturns: why are nurses susceptible?

Economic downturns and recessions force governments to restrict their overall public spending. The budget for healthcare programmes, constituting a sizable proportion of the gross domestic product (GDP; e.g., 11% of Canada's GDP in 2011), is inevitably affected [1,3].

Human resources consume a sizeable proportion of health expenditures with considerable variability in how these workers are paid. This, in turn, means that an important impact of economic downturns is on the ability of governments to maintain and pay for the health workforce. Attempts to decrease healthcare expenditures might also include downsizing of institutions and consequently the size of the workforce. Such a strategy has a strong impact on the nursing workforce for two main reasons. Firstly, nursing is often the largest professional group in the healthcare sector; thus any workforce downsizing attempt will disproportionally affect them. Secondly, an overwhelming majority of nurses are salaried employees in healthcare organisations (as compared to physicians who are self-employed professionals working on a fee-for-a service or capitation basis). Strategies to cope with fiscal pressures may have a direct effect on nurses if institutions opt to balance their budgets by downsizing their nurse workforce or an indirect effect if institutions downsize services and decrease the number of hospital beds [16,17].

The effect of economic downturns on the nursing labour market

The reviewed literature reports five key indicators measuring the effect of economic downturns on the nursing labour market: demand, supply, salary, turnover and shortages. To facilitate stakeholders' assimilation of the short-term and long-term effects of economic downturns on the nursing labour market, we propose a simplified framework in Table Table1.1. This framework could serve as a convenient reference guide for nursing and human resources managers, leaders and planners on potential nursing labour force dynamics during and after an economic downturn. It is based on evidence compiled from the literature coupled with the authors' experience in workforce planning and their analyses of nursing labour market trends.

Economic downturns and the demand for nurses

Economic downturns and recessions impact the healthcare sector with varying effects on the demand, supply and other labour market indicators for nurses depending on the jurisdiction (Table (Table1)1) [2,18]. On the demand side, they are likely to decrease the demand for nurses as well as the need for nursing services. Restricted availability of public and private funds in the healthcare sector might push healthcare organizations to downsize their operations and consequently the size of their nursing workforce [6,7,19].

Table 1. Analytical framework on the short-term and strategic impact of economic downturns on the nursing labour market

Labor market indicator	Temporary/ short term		Strategic/ long term	
	During an economic downturn	Potential reasons	Post economic downturn	Potential reasons
Demand for nurses	**Decrease**	- Downsizing of institutional operations	**Increase**	- Need to recoup lost nursing jobs
		- Budgetary constraints	(Slowly if jobless recovery & fast under full recovery)	- Services restored or expanded
		- Service reductions		- Need to replace retiring baby boomers
Supply of nurses	**Increase**	- Nurses increase number of hours worked	**Decrease**	- Decreased enrollment in & graduation from nursing programs at time of recession
		- Inactive nurses return to the labor market		Decreased labor force participation
		- Multiple job holdings for some		- Increased nursing dropouts from nursing labor market
				- Difficulty in attracting nurses working in other industries or those that sought early retirement
Nursing Salaries	Frozen or decreased	- Increased supply coupled with decreased demand	**Increasing**	- Decreased supply & increased demand
				- Need to attract inactive nurses back
Nursing turnover	Decreased	- Need for work with decreased family earnings	**Increased**	- More jobs available in the market
		- lack of job vacancies		- decreased need for work with increased family earning
		- Reduced likelihood that nurses leave their job		- Stress and burnout
Nursing shortages	Temporary perception of surpluses rather than shortages	- Disturbed labor market dynamic	**Aggravated**	- Supply-demand imbalances
		- More supply less demand		- Increased population needs
				- Decreased proportion of active nurses
				- Retiring baby boomers

Recent evidence from the current economic downturns suggests that the health systems in many European countries are contracting or freezing the size of their nursing workforce. For example, despite the estimated shortage of 60,000 nurses in Italy, the Italian government recommended that institutions revisit nursing workforce standards and freeze the recruitment of healthcare workers [20]. Note that younger nurses are disproportionally affected by workforce downsizing since job cuts usually start from the bottom in a unionized environment [21].

Similarly, the Spanish economic crisis has resulted in reductions in the public financing of the healthcare sector which precipitated salary decreases and job freezes in the nursing workforce. This is quite disconcerting since Spain has a lower nurse-to-population ratio compared to other Organization for Economic Cooperation and Development (OECD) countries (7.5 per 1000 population, compared to an average of 9.6 in other OECD countries) [22]. Furthermore, Greece continues to experience a shortage of nurses because of the aging population, the demands of integrating new technology and rising consumer expectations, but has limited ability to meet these needs given its current economic crisis [23].

The need for nursing services might also affect the demand for nurses in other ways. On the one hand, there may be a decrease in occupational injuries due to the contraction in the size of the active workforce. On the other hand, since poverty and unemployment are associated with poorer health, need might increase particularly for those who become unemployed [24-27]. Yet, such demand might be mitigated by the unwillingness of people to pay out of pocket should they lose their insurance coverage [20].

In addition, demand for nurses might be focused on specific sectors/sub-sectors of employment as care shifts from (costly) institutions to the (more affordable) community [28]. The demand for nurses might also be focused on less costly nurses (e.g., practical nurses within the Canadian context) possessing a narrower scope of practice or cheaper non-nursing substitutes (e.g., personal support workers, nursing aides, etc.) [29]. The implications of this skill mix change might extend beyond affecting nurses to affecting the outcomes of patient care [30-32].

Economic downturns and the supply of nurses

Economic downturns may cause an unanticipated increase in the supply of nurses in the healthcare market. Decreased family earnings coupled with concerns about job security may push nurses to reintegrate into the labour market and to remain in their current jobs [33]. Thus, increased supply may result from an increased number of inactive nurses returning to the active workforce, increasing the number of working-hours or holding multiple jobs [18,34].

Economic downturns and nursing wages

Increased supply and decreased demand for nurses may push nursing wages down over time. Under publically financed healthcare systems and unionized environments, nurses might be shielded from the wage effects of economic downturns in the short-run. However, if economic troubles prevail for longer periods, nurse wages may eventually decline. In addition, if labour agreements curtail the ability to adjust wages downward, the employers may reduce staff numbers via layoff or via service cuts.

This wage effect is currently observed in some countries where the effect of economic downturns is more pronounced. For example, Spain recently passed a law that aims to reduce healthcare spending by introducing a 5% cut in salaries [22]. Similarly, wage decreases have been reported in other troubled economies [22,35,36]. Interestingly, a recent salary survey of nurses in the US revealed a decrease in nurse leaders' wages at a rate that is comparable to that of their Spanish counterparts (5.2%), but decreases only influenced female workers [35]. Such findings bring to question the influence of economic downturns on the gender equity of wages in a professional workforce.

Such wage decreases might precipitate increased financial burdens on the nursing workforce with an increased number of nurses in financial hardship [37].

Economic downturns and nurses' turnover

Under normal circumstances, nurses dissatisfied with aspects of their work environment would leave their work setting and seek employment elsewhere (or perhaps become unemployed). Economic downturns might prevent this from happening due to the decreased job vacancies and increased financial pressures for families [18]. For example, a recent survey of US nurses reports that the majority of nurses believed they were inappropriately compensated. However, many nurses consider themselves privileged to be still working under a serious economic downturn [35].

Economic downturns and nursing shortages

The aforementioned effects of economic downturns on the labour market may provide temporary relief of previously reported nursing shortages. With more nurses rejoining or increasing participation in the nursing labour market, some of the existing nursing vacancies are filled. Similar influences of recessionary trends on nursing shortages were recently reported in the US [2], with increased employment of returning nurses and new nursing graduates [2,38]. Nursing shortages may also decrease because of the cancellation of vacancies due to lack of funds to hire new nurses. Indeed, it is not uncommon to observe hiring freezes in the market during economic downturns [20].

What happens to the nursing labour market post economic downturns?

The framework outlined in Table Table11 highlights some of the anticipated nursing labour market trends in the aftermath of an economic downturn. With respect to the demand for nurses, it is anticipated that the restoration, expansion and improvement of patient care would necessitate the quick hiring of nurses, which would increase the demand for nurses in the market. In practice, the nature of the recovery would dictate what could happen on the demand side of the nursing labour market. Should recovery be jobless, the growth in the demand for nurses will be slow. However, if the recovery leads to job creation, the demand for nurses would increase considerably [39].

On the supply side, the longer-run effect of economic downturns might be a decrease in the supply of nurses. The supply of new nurse graduates decreases due to space constraints in educational institutions, shortages in the number of faculty members, fewer nursing preceptors at healthcare organizations and diminished scholarships available for students [22,40]. For example, recent analyses reveal that budget cutbacks to educational institutions in Ireland reduced the nursing students' acceptance by up to 1200 in 2009 [41].

Increased turnover is anticipated with improved economic conditions. This also contributes to a decrease in the supply of nurses with decreased labour force participation for some nurses (with increased family earnings), especially those with small children and older nurses who are closer to retirement [3]). Some nurses might also drop out of the labour market due to accumulated stress and burnout precipitated by the heavy workloads and poor work environment during economic downturns [39,42,43]. As mentioned above, economic recovery might also increase the number of jobs available in the healthcare market and other markets.

Reduced supply coupled with increased demand for nurses will eventually push nursing wages up when the economy recovers [21]. Again, wage agreements that are binding for a number of years may delay these wage adjustments and thus impact the ability of institutions to quickly replenish their nursing labour force.

Implication for policy and planning

Economic downturns place healthcare planners and decision makers under tremendous pressure to balance budgets and cut expenses. Under economic downturns, difficult decisions have to be made in a short period with little opportunity to consult with concerned stakeholders (i.e., patients, nurses, analysts). A clearer understanding of nursing labour market dynamics will help policy makers take decisions that would help them overcome the economic downturn while protecting the strategic interests of the healthcare system.

Despite observing a decrease in the demand for nurses in the labour market during economic downturns, nursing stakeholders should keep in mind that the demand for nurses will eventually increase upon economic recovery. Additional nurses will also need to be hired to address growing population needs, recoup jobs lost during economic downturns, and replace retiring nurses in an aging workforce [44,45]. With respect to the supply of nurses, nursing planners and stakeholders should refrain from eroding the training capacity for nurses during an economic downturn. Such a risky policy option could lead to serious demand–supply imbalances in the nursing labour market in the long-run.

Nursing managers, leaders, planners and policy makers are cautioned against adopting staff layoffs as a strategy to balance their budgets. Layoffs will increase the workload and decrease the morale and productivity of working nurses [8,30,46] and rehiring nurses back will be a costly and time-consuming process [47,48]. Furthermore, the reintegration of inactive nurses into the labour market will necessitate additional investments in a targeted and timely recruitment strategy [49]. A combination of decreased demand and increased layoffs for younger nurses will eventually aggravate the aging workforce problem [50].

At the institutional level, hospitals should prepare for intense recruitment and retention efforts to recover from the job losses caused by the recession, and potentially aggravated by the retirement of baby boomers from the nurse workforce. Avoiding this shortfall requires targeted interventions on the system and institutional levels [2,34]. At the system level, it is essential to maintain adequate funding for nurses training and professional development programs. Institutions should be incentivised to cut expenses through improving efficiency and performance rather than lay off staff. Furthermore, particular attention should be dedicated to the integration of younger nurses into the workforce. One good example is the Nursing Graduate Guarantee in Ontario, Canada. This initiative of the Ontario Ministry of Health and Long-Term Care is intended to ensure that every new nursing graduate will have the opportunity to find a full-time job upon graduation [51].

Interventions at the institutional level may include job-sharing as a way to enhance nurse retention amid budgetary constraints [52]. Other retention initiatives focus on good nursing management during difficult times, including improved nurse recognition, enhanced transparency and communication opportunities, decentralised decision-making, enhanced nurse-physician relationships and improved group cohesion [43,53,54]. Particular attention should be dedicated to providing nurses with professional development opportunities, which have a high impact on retention [55,56].

A number of shortcomings in this manuscript are worth mentioning. First, the literature search supporting the findings in this manuscript might have missed some of the published or grey literature on the topic. Second, some of the reported labour market dynamics in the proposed framework may not be applicable to some jurisdictions or may not account for certain local market specificities. Finally, although some of the discussions and findings of this manuscript are global in nature, most will be more relevant to developed contexts. Note that lack of primary and secondary workforce data might be a barrier to observing workforce trends in developing contexts.

CONCLUSIONS

Healthcare human resources leadership entails seeing beyond the temporary trends by investing in the nursing workforce despite economic turbulence. We argue that this is the optimal means to achieve efficiency and effectiveness, while enhancing patient safety and protecting one of the most valuable assets in a healthcare system–nurses.

Lack of understanding of labour market dynamics and trends might mislead policy makers to make misinformed workforce downsizing decisions that are often difficult and expensive to reverse. Leadership and sound decision making dictates that policy-makers look beyond the temporary relief that might be achieved from staff downsizing decisions and consider the long-term strategic interests of the healthcare system. In the aftermath of an economic downturn, the costs of attracting nurses back often outweigh the short-term cost savings. Effective management would support the nursing workforce by creating attractive and stable work environments to retain nurses at a manageable cost.

COMPETING INTERESTS

The authors declare that they have no competing interests.

AUTHORS' CONTRIBUTIONS

MA conceptualised the topic, carried out the literature analysis and wrote the first draft of the manuscript. AB helped with the conceptualisation of the topic and reviewed the manuscript providing valuable advice. AL helped conceptualise the labour market implications and thoroughly reviewed the manuscript. RD reviewed and edited the manuscript enhancing its rigor and intellectual content. All authors read and approved the final manuscript.

REFERENCES

1. Houston M, Day M, de Lago M, Zarocostas J. Health services across Europe face cuts as debt crisis begins to bite. BMJ. 2011;343:d5266.
2. Buerhaus PI, Auerbach DI. The recession's effect on hospital registered nurse employment growth. Nurs Econ. 2011;29:163–167.
3. Sussman JB, Halasyamani LK, Davis MM. Hospitals during recession and recovery: vulnerable institutions and quality at risk. J Hosp Med. 2010;5:302–305.
4. Leamer E. What's a Recession, Anyway? National Bureau of Economic Research Working Paper Series. 2008;14221:1–36.
5. OECD calls for urgent action to boost ailing global economy. OECD calls for urgent action to boost ailing global economy.http://www.oecd.org/document/47/0,3746,en_2157 1361_44315115_49095919_1_1_1_1,00.html.

6. Duffield C, Kearin M, Johnston J, Leonard J. The impact of hospital structure and restructuring on the nursing workforce. Aust J Adv Nurs. 2007;24:42–46.

7. Lineweaver LA, Battle CE, Schilling RM, Nall CM. Six hospitals describe decentralization, cost containment, and downsizing. J Nurses Staff Dev. 1999;15:198–204.

8. Kalimo R, Taris TW, Schaufeli WB. The effects of past and anticipated future downsizing on survivor well-being: an equity perspective. J Occup Health Psychol. 2003;8:91–109.

9. Greenglass ER, Burke RJ. Hospital restructuring and burnout. J Health Hum Serv Adm. 2002;25:89–114.

10. Hertting A, Theorell T. Physiological changes associated with downsizing of personnel and reorganisation in the health care sector. Psychother Psychosom. 2002;71:117–122.

11. Maynard A. Medical workforce planning: some forecasting challenges. Aust Econ Rev. 2006;39:323–329.

12. Cooper RA, Getzen TE, Laud P. Economic expansion is a major determinant of physician supply and utilization. Health Serv Res. 2003;38:675–696.

13. Baumann AO, Blythe JM, Underwood JM. Surge capacity and casualization: Human resource issues in the post-SARS health system. Can J Public Health. 2006;97:230–232.

14. Baumeister R, Leary M. Writing narrative literature reviews. Rev Gen Psych. 1997;1:311–320.

15. Riessman C. Narrative analysis. Thousand Oaks, CA, London: Sage Publications; 1993.

16. Blythe J, Baumann A, Giovannetti P. Nurses' experiences of restructuring in three Ontario hospitals. J Nurs Scholarsh. 2001;33:61–68.

17. Baumann A, Blythe J. Restructuring, reconsidering, reconstructing: implications for health human resources. Int J Public Adm. 2003;26:1561.

18. Brewer S. Landing a job in a tough economy. Nursing. 2010;40(Suppl):18–19.

19. Hertting A, Nilsson K, Theorell T, Larsson US. Downsizing and reorganization: demands, challenges and ambiguity for registered nurses. J Adv Nurs. 2004;45:145–154.

20. Bortoluzzi G, Palese A. The Italian economic crisis and its impact on nursing services and education: hard and challenging times. J Nurs Manag. 2010;18:515–519.

21. Benjamin D, Gunderson M, Riddel W. Labour Market Economics. Toronto: McGraw-Hill Ryerson; 2002.

22. Zabalegui A, Cabrera E. Economic crisis and nursing in Spain. J Nurs Manag. 2010;18:505–508.

23. Notara V, Koupidis SA, Vaga E, Grammatikopoulos IA. Economic crisis and challenges for the Greek healthcare system: the emergent role of nursing management. J Nurs Manag. 2010;18:501–504.

24. Gallo WT, Teng HM, Falba TA, Kasl SV, Krumholz HM, Bradley EH. The impact of late career job loss on myocardial infarction and stroke: a 10 year follow up using the health and retirement survey. Occup Environ Med. 2006;63:683–687.

25. Strully KW. Job loss and health in the U.S. labor market. Demography. 2009;46:221–246.

26. Puig-Barrachina V, Malmusi D, Martenez JM, Benach J. Monitoring social determinants of health inequalities: the impact of unemployment among vulnerable groups. Int J Health Serv. 2011;41:459–482.

27. Jin RL, Shah CP, Svoboda TJ. The impact of unemployment on health: a review of the evidence. CMAJ. 1995;153:529–540.

28. Alameddine M, Laporte A, Baumann A, O'Brien-Pallas L, Croxford R, Mildon B, Wang S, Milburn B, Deber R. Where are nurses working? employment patterns by sub-sector in Ontario, Canada. Healthc Policy. 2006;1:65–86.

29. Heitlinger A. The paradoxical impact of health care restructuring in Canada on nursing as a profession. Int J Health Serv. 2003;33:37–54.

30. Aiken LH, Clarke SP, Sloane DM. Hospital restructuring: does it adversely affect care and outcomes? J Health Hum Serv Adm. 2001;23:416–442.

31. Aiken LH, Clarke SP, Silber JH, Sloane D. Hospital nurse staffing, education, and patient mortality. LDI Issue Brief. 2003;9:1–4.

32. Needleman J, Buerhaus P, Mattke S, Stewart M, Zelevinsky K. Nurse-staffing levels and the quality of care in hospitals. N Engl J Med. 2002;346:1715–1722.

33. Link CR, Settle RF. Wage incentives and married professional nurses: a case of backward-bending supply? Econ Inq. 1981;19:144–156.

34. Buerhaus P. The recession and the nursing shortage. OR Manager. 2009;25:5–6.

35. Hader R. The compensation tumble. Nurs Manage. 2010;41:26–31.

36. Yang BM, Prescott N, Bae EY. The impact of economic crisis on health-care consumption in Korea. Health Policy Plan. 2001;16:372–385.

37. Staines R. Recession forces nurses to seek financial rescue. Nurs Times. 2009;105:1.

38. Auerbach D, Buerhaus P, Staiger D. Registered nurse supply grows faster than projected amid surge in new entrants ages 23–26. Health Aff. 2011;30:2286–2292.

39. Buerhaus PI. The shape of the recovery: economic implications for the nursing workforce. Nurs Econ. 2009;27:338–340. 336.

40. Broome ME. At what cost? Stewardship of our most important resources. Nurs Outlook. 2010;58:1–2.

41. Carney M. Challenges in healthcare delivery in an economic downturn, in the Republic of Ireland. J Nurs Manag. 2010;18:509–514.

42. Cohen J, Stuenkel D, Nguyen Q. Providing a healthy work environment for nurses: the influence on retention. J Nurs Care Qual. 2009;24:308–315.

43. Christmas K. How work environment impacts retention. Nurs Econ. 2008;26:316–318.

44. International Centre for Human Resources in Nursing: An Ageing Nursing Workforce. 2007.

45. CanadianNurses Association. http://www.cna-aiic.ca/

46. Alameddine M, Baumann A, Laporte A, O'Brien-Pallas L, Levinton C, Onate K, Deber R. Career trajectories of nurses leaving the hospital sector in Ontario, Canada (1993–2004) J Adv Nurs. 2009;65:1044–1053.

47. Jones CB. The costs of nurse turnover, part 2: application of the Nursing Turnover Cost Calculation Methodology. J Nurs Adm. 2005;35:41–49.

48. Jones CB. Revisiting nurse turnover costs: adjusting for inflation. J Nurs Adm. 2008;38:11–18.

49. Alameddine M, Baumann A, Onate K, Deber R. Career transitions of inactive nurses: a registration database analysis (1993–2006) Int J Nurs Stud. 2011;48:184–192.

50. O'Brien-Pallas L, Duffield C, Alksnis C. Who will be there to nurse? Retention of nurses nearing retirement. J Nurs Adm. 2004;34:298–302.

51. Nursing Graduate Guarantee for New Ontario Graduate Nurses.http://www.healthforceontario.ca/Work/InsideOntario/OntarioNurses/NursingGradGuarantee.aspx.

52. Kane D. Job sharing: a retention strategy for nurses. Can J Nurs Leadersh. 1999;12:16–22.

53. Cameron S, Armstrong-Stassen M, Bergeron S, Out J. Recruitment and retention of nurses: challenges facing hospital and community employers. Nurs Leadersh (Tor Ont) 2004;17:79–92.

54. Lcurer MD, Donnelly G, Domm E. Nurse retention strategies: advice from experienced registered nurses. J Health Organ Manag. 2007;21:307–319.

55. Shields MA, Ward M. Improving nurse retention in the National Health Service in England: the impact of job satisfaction on intentions to quit. J Health Econ. 2001;20:677–701.

56. Hayes LJ, O'Brien-Pallas L, Duffield C, Shamian J, Buchan J, Hughes F, Laschinger HK, North N. Nurse turnover: A literature review - An update. Int J Nurs Stud. 2012;49:887–905.

11
CHAPTER

Differential Effects of Graduating During a Recession Across Gender and Race

Ayako Kondo

Yokohama National University, Yokohama, Japan

ABSTRACT

This study examines the differential effects of the unemployment rate at labor market entry, defined as the time of leaving school, on subsequent wages across gender and race using the National Longitudinal Survey of Youth 79. Results suggest that the negative effect of a recession at entry on wages is weaker for women. The differences between blacks and whites are not statistically significant for both genders. These results are robust to controlling for the endogenous timing and location of entry, using an instrumental variable based on the predicted year of graduation and the state of residence at age 14.

Keywords: Gender Race Recession at entry

1 INTRODUCTION

Recent studies have established that entering the labor market during a recession has long-term negative effects on subsequent wages and career paths for white male college graduates (Genda et al. 2010; Kahn 2010; Oreopoulos et al. 2012). It is also known that, in the United Sates, the initial impact of a recession at entry on earnings immediately after graduation is stronger for high school graduates than for college graduates, but this negative effect diminishes quickly (Genda et al. 2010; Speer 2015). However, there is limited evidence regarding the long-term consequences of shocks at entry for women, and similar evidence for any racial minority is even scarcer. Compared to white men, women have a weaker attachment to the labor force, and blacks are more vulnerable to contemporaneous labor market conditions. Therefore, the effects of the early labor market experience may be quite different for women and blacks than for white men.

Economic theories predict that the negative effect of a recession at entry to the labor market on subsequent wages is more persistent for demographic groups who have strong labor force attachment and are less likely to be dismissed. This is because the advantage of obtaining a high-wage job at entry is lost when the worker quits due to exogenous reasons or is dismissed. Since women are more likely to quit for family reasons, the negative effect of a recession at entry is expected to be weaker and less persistent for women than for men. In addition, since blacks are more likely to become unemployed in recessions after entry,[1] the negative effect of entering the labor market during such periods may be less persistent for them, although the initial impact of a recession is expected to be stronger.

Motivated by these theoretical predictions, I examine how the effect of the unemployment rate at entry to the labor market on subsequent wages differs across race and gender. Specifically, I compare the effect for the following four demographic groups: white men, white women, black men, and black women. The main data source is the National Longitudinal Survey of Youth 79 (NLSY79). To control for nation-wide cohort effects, I exploit variations in unemployment rates across states, with controls for state-fixed effects. I also address the endogenous determination of time and location of entry by using an instrumental variable based on the predicted timing of entry and the state of residence at age 14.[2] I find a weaker effect of a recession at entry for women than for men. However, I do not find strong evidence for the differential effect across race.

To the best of my knowledge, this is the first study to analyze the differential effect of labor market conditions at entry across race. However, it is not the first study to examine the effect of labor market conditions experienced at youth for women.[3] Hershbein (2012) compares high school-educated men and women in the United States. He finds that the long-term effects of graduating high school in a recession on wages are minimal for women and that young women who face adverse labor market conditions temporarily reduce labor supply and substitute into home production.[4] I believe this study complements that of Hershbein (2012) because my approach is different from his. First, while Hershbein (2012) focuses on the effect of the unemployment rate at high school graduation for all individuals including those who proceed to college, I focus on the effect of the unemployment rate in the last year of enrollment. Furthermore, I measure differences across and within racial groups. In addition, methodologically, Hershbein (2012) uses the national unemployment rate as the explanatory variable, whereas I use the state unemployment rate and control for state fixed effects and nationwide year effects.

The comparison between whites and blacks is closely related to the literature on the differential effects of a recession at entry across groups with different skill levels and educational backgrounds. In particular, Kahn (2010); Speer (2015) are most relevant in that both studies use the same dataset and an empirical strategy very similar to this study. Kahn (2010) shows a persistent negative effect of the unemployment rate at graduation on wages for white male college graduates. In contrast, Speer (2015) shows that the initial impact of a recession at graduation on employment and wages is substantial for high school graduates, but these effects diminish quickly. A similar pattern is observed by Genda et al. (2010) using the Current Population Survey (CPS). Blacks are on average less educated than whites are, and racial minorities and less-skilled workers share a similar vulnerability to business cycle conditions. Therefore, theoretically, it is possible that the effect of a recession at entry for blacks and whites is similar to that for high school graduates and college graduates, respectively. However, I do not find as clear a difference between blacks and whites as the existing studies found between college and high school graduates. At the same time, despite the statistical insignificance, the pattern of black-white difference depicted by the point estimates resembles the difference between high school and college graduates to some extent.

It is important to keep in mind that whether the effect of labor market conditions at entry is weaker for disadvantaged workers depends on the institutional settings. For example, Genda et al. (2010) show that the effect of high unemployment at graduation is more negative and persistent for high school graduates than for college graduates in Japan. Furthermore, Brunner and Kuhn (2014) show a more negative and persistent effect for blue-collar workers than for white-collar workers in Austria. On the other hand, Raaum and Røed (2006) find that the effects of the unemployment rate experienced in youth tend to be more persistent for those with advantaged backgrounds in Norway. Moreover, a recession at entry could increase the incidence of non-employment in subsequent years without affecting the wage rate for less-educated men in countries with a rigid labor market structure such as Belgium (Cockx and Ghirelli 2015) and Spain (Fernández-Kranz and Rodríguez-Planas 2015). Therefore, my findings may not be generalizable to minorities in countries with rigid labor market structures. However, these findings provide useful insights for countries with flexible labor market structures similar to those in the United States.

Lastly, this study relates to the broader literature of differential effects of labor market conditions across different demographic groups. Although it is controversial whether an economic upturn benefits economically disadvantaged people as much as the more advantaged,[5] there is little doubt that the costs of a downturn are borne disproportionately by the disadvantaged (Clark and Summers 1981; Cutler and Katz 1991; Hines et al. 2001; Hoynes et al. 2012). Studies on cyclical upgrading of the labor force (Devereux 2004; Okun 1973) also suggest that less-skilled workers tend to lose their jobs in recessions, while more-skilled workers tend to move upward to higher-paying jobs in booms. Since the contemporaneous labor market conditions affect blacks significantly (Altonji and Blank 1999), the initial impact of a recession at entry is expected to be stronger for them. On the other hand, however, the vulnerability to aggregate shocks after entry to the labor market may reduce the persistence of a negative shock at entry.

2 PREDICTIONS FROM ECONOMIC THEORIES

Several confounding factors can produce persistent negative effects of a recession at entry to the labor market on subsequent employment and wages. First, search frictions prolong the process to resolve the initial worker-job mismatch. That is, it takes time and money to find a good job under incomplete information about available job opportunities. Oreopoulos et al. (2012) find that the job turnover rate remains high for 8–10 years for cohorts that graduated from college during a recession, suggesting that the matching process takes longer for them.

Furthermore, the nominal wage rigidity may prevent firms from reducing incumbent workers' wages even during a recession. Thus, an individual lucky enough to have entered the labor market during a boom may be able to maintain a relatively high-paying job. Indeed,

Beaudry and DiNardo (1991) find that incumbent workers' wages do not fall during recessions as long as the workers remain employed, and they explain this by implicit long-term wage contracts with mobile workers.

These advantages of obtaining a high-wage job at entry disappear when the worker leaves the job without moving to a better position. Thus, the effect of obtaining a high-wage job at entry is less persistent for workers who tend to quit because of exogenous reasons. Since women are more likely to quit jobs for childcare and other household needs, the effect of recessions at entry is expected to be less persistent for women than for men.

The initial impact of a recession is stronger for groups more sensitive to temporary fluctuations of labor demand in the entry-level labor market. Since unemployment rates for blacks are more sensitive to business cycle conditions (Altonji and Blank 1999; Hoynes et al. 2012),[6] the initial impact is expected to be stronger for blacks. However, it is unclear whether this negative shock at entry persists for them, because they are more vulnerable to fluctuations in labor demand later in their career, and thus, blacks who entered labor market during a boom may not able to maintain a good job obtained at entry.

In addition, missing opportunities for on-the-job training due to a poor match can aggravate the negative effect of entering the labor market during a recession. Although it is ambiguous whether the loss of training opportunities matters more to blacks than to whites, women's weaker labor force attachment implies less incentive for firms to invest in human capital for them. Thus, this result predicts a weaker effect of a recession at entry on subsequent wages for women than for men.

3 DATA: NLSY79

My primary data source is the National Longitudinal Survey of Youth 1979 (NLSY79), which consists of a representative sample of the noninstitutionalized U.S. civilian segment of population aged 14–22 in 1979, interviewed annually from 1979 to 1994 and biennially from 1996 to the present. For this study, I use data from 1979 to 2000 and limit my sample to the cross-sectional sample of whites and blacks and the supplemental samples of blacks.[7] I drop observations that have missing information necessary to define the year and the state of entry;

the detailed sample restrictions are described in the appendix. Finally, 5387 individuals remain in the sample.

3.1 Definition of the year and state of entry

The year of labor market entry is defined as the last year of enrollment. The cases of enrollment for up to two years in colleges after not being enrolled at least for a year and enrollment after the age of 30 are not considered.[8] The survey variables used to define the last year of enrollment is the enrollment status of respondents as of May 1 in each year, and the last month and year in school asked in 1979 for those who were not enrolled in 1979. Note that I do *not* use the highest grade completed here, and the year of entry is defined not only for those who graduated from a school but also for those who did not complete the degree or grade after enrollment. For example, if an individual was in 12th grade in 1980 and was not enrolled for years after 1980, the year of entry for the individual is 1980, regardless of his/her age at that time or whether this individual completed the high school diploma.

The state of entry is defined as the state of residence in the year of entry for those whose entry year is 1979 or later. For those who entered before 1979, I use the state of residence in 1979 because data pertaining to the state of residence prior to 1979 is not available. This definition is the same as that in Maclean (2014, 2015).

Table 1 summarizes the number of individuals of each race-gender group and average state unemployment rates by the year of labor market entry. Approximately 90% of the sample entered the labor market during the 12 years between 1975 and 1986, the period including the recessions in 1975 and 1982–83.

3.2 Outcome variables

The main outcome variable is the log real hourly wages. The real wages are deflated by the consumer price index normalized to the price level in 1982–1984. The hourly wages in the NLSY are defined as "hourly rates of pay at the current or most recent job." I dropped observations with nominal hourly wages exceeding 1000 dollars. This variable is available for anyone who reported that he or she was employed since the last interview. Thus, jobs include not only full-time jobs, but also part-time ones.

Table 1. Number of individuals and mean unemployment rate by year of entry

Year of entry	U. rates	White men	White women	Black men	Black women	Total
1973	4.88	3	5	3	1	12
1974	5.97	12	16	9	10	47
1975	10.90	57	79	35	41	212
1976	7.39	86	116	46	48	296
1977	6.84	103	138	62	62	365
1978	6.03	116	133	76	101	426
1979	5.81	155	202	94	117	568
1980	7.41	151	183	103	121	558
1981	7.89	174	185	87	125	571
1982	10.26	155	182	94	132	563
1983	10.12	124	126	61	83	394
1984	7.61	97	110	56	66	329
1985	7.34	92	95	34	49	270
1986	7.15	81	98	28	34	241
1987	6.43	55	65	16	34	170
1988	5.67	34	41	9	17	101
1989	5.27	31	25	9	15	80
1990	5.96	16	23	8	14	61
1991	6.83	15	17	3	9	44
1992	7.61	9	8	4	6	27
1993	6.66	3	7	3	0	13
Total	7.64	1569	1854	840	1085	5348

I allow for college enrollment up to 2 years after entry to the labor market, and if the respondents worked while in college, I include them in the wage data. I find that 2.86% of the observations with valid wages and within 12 years since entry are enrolled in college. Furthermore, a recession at entry to the labor market may induce some workers to return to college, thus leading to part-time employment. If so, the estimated effect on wages may include such an effect through college enrollment after entry. Card and Lemieux (2000) show that the positive effect of unemployment rate at age 17 on obtaining college education is stronger for women than for men, implying that women may be more likely to be enrolled later in response to initial labor market conditions.

If the respondents did not work at all since the last interview, their hourly wages are missing. At the same time, about 3% respondents are currently employed but lack wages for some unknown reason.

Table 2 shows the number of observations with valid (positive) hourly wages, missing wages due to non-employment, and missing wages for other reasons for each race-gender-potential experience cell.

Table 2. Number of observations with and without valid wages (% of total number of observations in the corresponding race-sex-potential experience category)

	Exp.	White men	Black men	White women	Black women
With valid wages	1–3	3715 (88.7%)	1666 (75.4%)	3962 (81.6%)	1853 (63.3%)
	4–6	4248 (93.2%)	2101 (85.4%)	4418 (81.8%)	2220 (70.0%)
	7–9	4110 (94.7%)	2066 (86.2%)	4147 (80.6%)	2288 (74.8%)
	10–12	3603 (94.5%)	1824 (84.8%)	3588 (78.0%)	2054 (74.7%)
Missing wages due to non-employment	1–3	330 (7.9%)	466 (21.1%)	744 (15.3%)	1002 (34.2%)
	4–6	171 (3.8%)	293 (11.9%)	820 (15.2%)	885 (27.9%)
	7–9	97 (2.2%)	258 (10.8%)	854 (16.6%)	716 (23.4%)
	10–12	81 (2.1%)	255 (11.9%)	872 (19.0%)	629 (22.9%)
Missing wages though being employed	1–3	145 (3.5%)	78 (3.5%)	151 (3.1%)	71 (2.4%)
	4–6	140 (3.1%)	65 (2.6%)	161 (3.0%)	65 (2.1%)
	7–9	131 (3.0%)	74 (3.1%)	145 (2.8%)	55 (1.8%)
	10–12	130 (3.4%)	72 (3.3%)	140 (3.0%)	68 (2.5%)

The proportion with missing wages due to non-employment varies across gender and race: women and blacks are less likely to have valid wages. Moreover, labor supply patterns of white women over potential experience are opposite to that of black women. Since the unemployment rate at entry is expected to have a negative effect on subsequent wages, there might be a negative effect on subsequent employment as well. If the likelihood of having a valid wage were affected by the unemployment rate at entry, it would cause a sample selection bias. Thus, I also examine the effects on employment and the likelihood of having a valid wage. As shown later, the unemployment rate at entry does not have a statistically significant negative effect on the likelihood of having a valid wage.

Since data on hourly wages prior to 1978 are not available, the estimates for the short-run impact are based only on cohorts who left school in 1978 or later. This implies that the current data do not allow measurement of the short-term impact of labor market entry around the recession of 1975. Furthermore, those who left school before 1978 tend to be less educated. Thus, the sample with 1–3 years of potential experience underrepresent less-educated individuals.

3.3 Explanatory variables

The main explanatory variable is the state unemployment rate at entry. The state unemployment rates based on the CPS are available only from 1976. However, dropping individuals who entered the labor market before 1975 may unbalance the composition of birth-year cohorts by making older cohorts more educated on average. Thus, I use the state unemployment rates based on the Unemployment Insurance (UI) records for 1973–1975. Since the UI series tends to be lower than the CPS series, I rescale it, multiplying by the coefficient of the CPS series in a regression of the UI series between 1976 and 1982 on the CPS series of the same year and constant. Details are described in the appendix. Both the CPS- and the UI-based unemployment rates are annual averages.

I also control for the state unemployment rate of the current residence, the years of schooling, and the age-adjusted Armed Forces Qualification Test (AFQT) score. The variable for the years of schooling is "highest grade completed as of May 1." The AFQT score is the percentile score of the test, which was attached to the NLSY in 1981 and is often used as a measure of ability in studies using the NLSY79. I adjust the score to the age at which the respondent took the test by taking a z-score of the raw percentile score within each birth-year cohort.[9]

4 DESCRIPTIVE STATISTICS

Figure 1 plots the average log real hourly wages over potential experience (years since entry) for the four demographic groups: white men, black men, white women, and black women. To see how the observed average wage profiles vary with labor market conditions at entry, I split each demographic group into two subgroups: one with unemployment rate at entry higher than the median and the other with that lower than the median. First, the upper left panel shows a gradually fading wage gap for white men. This pattern is consistent with the results by Kahn (2010); Oreopoulos et al. (2012). For black men, the lower left panel shows a substantial wage gap in the first few years, which disappears by the fifth year.

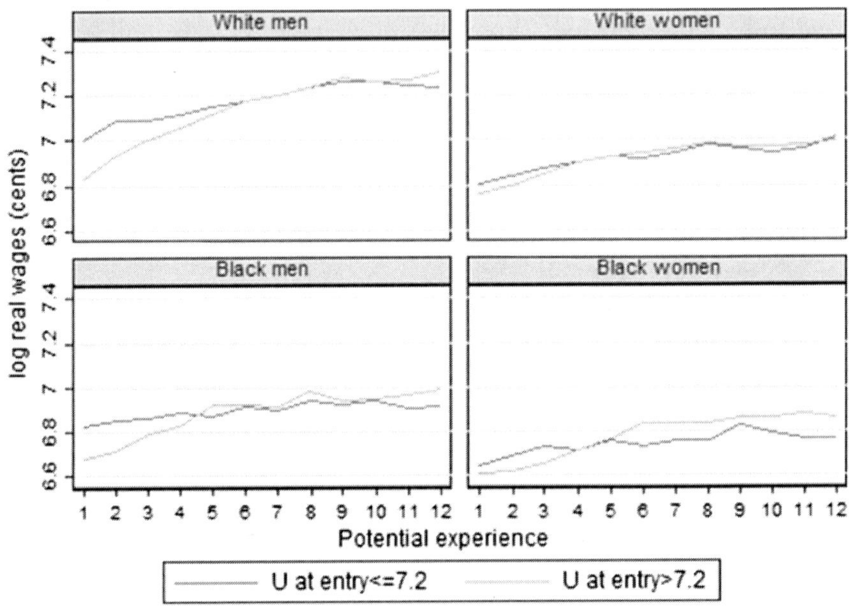

Figure 1. Average wage profiles (no control for state/year). The average of log real wages is normalized to 1982–84 prices, by a single-year potential experience. 7.2% is the median of the unemployment rates at entry into the labor market for the entire sample (based on the number of individuals)

Regarding women, the upper right panel shows a very small gap among white women. The smaller gaps for women than men are consistent with the theories that predict a weak effect on those with weak labor force attachment. Surprisingly, black women who left school during recessions earn more in their fifth year and later. However, this may be spurious due to accidental positive selection on educational background, as shown in Table 3, or a state-specific component that happened to correlate with the unemployment rates.

Table 3 shows summary statistics of educational background and the age-adjusted AFQT scores by gender, race, and unemployment rate at entry. The highest grades completed are almost equal among those who entered the labor market during recessions and booms, except that black women who entered during recessions are slightly more educated than those who entered during booms. The age-adjusted AFQT score is also slightly higher for black women with higher unemployment rates at entry. Except for this, there is little difference between the groups with higher and lower unemployment across gender and race. At least, people who left school during recessions are not negatively selected on the basis of education or pre-market human capital measured by the AFQT.

Table 3. Means of explanatory variables by race, gender and unemployment rate at entry

		White men	Black men	White women	Black women
Highest grades completed	U<=7.2%	13.4	12.4	13.4	12.7
	U>7.2%	13.4	12.3	13.4	13.0
	Total	13.4	12.4	13.4	12.8
Age adjusted AFQT score	U<=7.2%	0.25	−0.93	0.16	−0.93
	U>7.2%	0.27	−0.95	0.19	−0.82
	Total	0.26	−0.94	0.17	−0.88
Number of individuals	U<=7.2%	778	442	938	593
	U>7.2%	791	398	916	492
	Total	1569	840	1854	1085

Note: 7.2% is the median of the unemployment rates at entry among all individuals in the sample

The bottom row of Table 3 shows that the numbers of white men and women in the groups with unemployment rate at entry higher and lower than the median are approximately equal and that black men and women are more likely to have graduated when the unemployment rate was low. This difference mainly comes from the difference in race compositions across states, suggesting that it is essential to control for the entry-state fixed effects. Furthermore, the timing and location of entry may be endogenous because people may try to avoid entering the labor market during recessions. The next section describes the strategies to deal with these issues.

5 EMPIRICAL STRATEGY

5.1 Baseline model

My primary objective in this study is to identify the effect of the unemployment rate at labor market entry on subsequent wages for each gender and race group. To observe the differences in persistence, I also allow the effect of the unemployment rate at entry to vary with potential experience (years since leaving school).

Since the state unemployment rate may correlate with unobserved characteristics of each state, which in turn may affect young workers' wages, it is essential to control for the entry-state fixed effects. This is especially crucial for the comparison of blacks and whites given the considerably different racial composition across states. In addition, since less-educated people entered the labor market earlier than the others within the same birth-year cohort, temporary macro shocks in the year of entry can correlate with the years of schooling and cause bias. In particular, it is important to keep in mind that the majority of the sample who graduated from school during the recession in 1982–1983 are college graduates.

To control for state fixed effects and entry year effects, I include dummy variables for the state and year of entry, respectively. The identification of the effect of high unemployment at entry relies on the variations in unemployment rates at the year- and state- level net of those fixed components. Given the strong auto-correlation of unemployment rates, I also need to control for the current unemployment rate so that the estimated coefficients are not affected by business cycle fluctuations.

If the sample size was large enough, I could allow state fixed effects to vary with both gender and race. However, some states have too few blacks to include entry-state dummies if I limit the sample to blacks. Therefore, I employ a parsimonious specification that pools blacks and whites together, while I run separate regressions for men and women. To incorporate the difference in racial wage gaps across regions, I include dummy variables for the 10 BEA regions of residence in the school-leaving year interacted with a dummy variable for blacks.

Specifically, I consider the following wage function:

$$\log w_{it\tilde{s}ysg} = \alpha_{(t-y),g} + \beta_{(t-y),g} u_{ys} + \gamma_{(t-y),g} u_{t\tilde{s}} + \delta' X_{it} + \phi_t + \eta_s + \theta_{rg} + \mu_y + \varepsilon_{itysg} \tag{1}$$

where $w_{it\tilde{s}ysg}$ is the real hourly wage of individual i belonging to demographic group g, who left school in year y and in state s observed in calendar year t and state $\tilde{s}$. $\alpha_{(t-y),g}$ is a coefficient of potential experience dummy, u_{ys} is the unemployment rate of the year and the state of entry into the labor market, $u_{t\tilde{s}}$ is the current unemployment rate in the state of current residence, and X_{it} represents other control variables including potential experience, the highest grade completed, and the age-adjusted AFQT score.

To take into account the differences in the wage-experience profiles and sensitivity to aggregate labor market conditions across race groups, I allow the intercept, $\alpha_{(t-y),g}$, and the coefficients of unemployment rates, $\beta_{(t-y),g}$ and $\gamma_{(t-y),g}$, to vary across race and with potential experience. Note that each coefficient represents the effect for each demographic group, not the difference from a reference group (there is no "reference group"). Equation (1) is estimated separately for men and women.

Unobserved error components are decomposed into a calendar year fixed effect ϕ_t, an entry-state fixed effect η_s, a region-specific black-white gap θ_{rg}, an entry-year fixed effect μ_y, and the remaining error ε_{itys}. Since the time-variant error term, ε_{itys}, can be correlated within states across years, the standard errors are clustered at the state level. Sampling weights are not used for any regressions.[10]

5.2 Endogenous determination of timing and location of entry

Even after controlling for state-fixed effects and nation-wide entry year effects, a potential source of bias remains if the timing and location of labor market entry are endogenous and affected by business cycle conditions. In particular, people may determine their timing and location of entry accordingly to avoid entry during recessions. Existing studies show that a high unemployment rate may increase enrollment to schools for two reasons: the relatively low opportunity cost of not working and avoidance of entering the slack labor market. Concerned mainly with the first aspect, Card and Lemieux (2000) have shown that a temporary rise of the local unemployment rate increases high school enrollment for ages 15–17, using the CPS. In contrast, the effect on college enrollment is weak, indecisive for men and slightly negative for women. A similar concern applies to the geographical mobility. Using the Census data, Wozniak (2010) reports that college graduates tend to move to states with high labor demand when they enter the labor market, although less-educated people do not move as often.

To address the endogeneity issue regarding the timing and location of college graduation, Kahn (2010) uses the unemployment rate in the year when an individual turned 22 and the state of residence at age 14.

Following this approach, I use the unemployment rate in the year of predicted entry and state of residence at age 14 as an instrument for the state unemployment rate in the actual year and state of entry. Specifically, I define the year of predicted entry based on the highest degree/diploma attained as follows: year of birth +18 for those without any degree/diploma and those with high-school diploma or equivalent, year of birth +20 for those with associate degrees and year of birth +22 for those with bachelor or graduate degrees.[11] Although the highest degree/diploma attained is a choice variable, from a practical viewpoint, it would be difficult to define entry using a single age for everyone. The unemployment rates at age 18 and younger do not have predictive power strong enough to work as an instrument for college graduates. The unemployment rates at older ages are unlikely to be independent of the error term, since the business cycle conditions in the first few years after entry may affect subsequent wages for high school graduates. Maclean (2014, 2015) uses the same data and similar instrumental variables.

The key assumption here is that the highest degree/diploma attained and the state of residence at age 14 are independent from the state unemployment rate in the year of predicted entry. While the state of residence at age 14 is plausibly exogenous, theoretically, it is not clear whether the highest diploma/degree attained is affected by business cycle conditions. In theory, the decision to attain a degree is a choice and those who proceed to college during a recession might be different from those who proceed to college during a boom. Empirically, however, Kahn (2010) shows that the correlations between characteristics of college graduates and the unemployment rate at age 18 are weak for white men in the NLSY79, suggesting that such endogeneity may be practically negligible. Using the CPS, Genda et al. (2010) also show that the future earnings of college graduates, which they use as a proxy for potential productivity, are not correlated with the unemployment rate at age 18. Furthermore, Card and Lemieux (2000) find that the effect of the local unemployment rate at around high school graduation on college enrollment is weak, although they find a statistically significant effect on high school enrollment.

Note that what matters here is the enrollment behavior of young people who have just graduated from high school. It is true that the enrollment of community college is countercyclical (Betts and McFarland 1995), and the 2-year college enrollment of people who have some labor market experience is quite sensitive to labor market conditions and policies (Barr and Turner 2015). Since I define the year of entry as the last year of enrollment, excluding college enrollment for less than two years after more than a year out of school, this cyclical enrollment of community college does not affect the year of entry used in this study.

Hence, I use age 18, 20, or 22 as the age of predicted entry, depending on the highest degree attained. Later in this section, I confirm that a high unemployment rate does not induce people to earn an additional undergraduate degree in college, although it seems to induce some people to continue in college. Note that the information on college degree is not based on the years of schooling, but is directly obtained from the respondents.[12] Thus, it is not affected by respondents' continuity in college without obtaining additional degrees. I assign the year of birth +18 to high school drop-outs because Card and Lemieux (2000) find positive effects of the unemployment rate on high school completion. Likewise, I ignore graduate degrees because Kahn (2010) reports that a recession at graduation from college slightly increases the likelihood of attaining a graduate degree.

To know if the unemployment rate at actual or predicted entry or that at age 18 affects the year and state of entry, I estimate several regressions on the entire sample (not multiple observations per person) in the following form:

$$Dept.\mathrm{var}_i = \beta_g u_i + \delta' X_i + FEs + \varepsilon_i \quad (2)$$

The results are summarized in Table 4. The first column of Table 4 indicates the dependent variables, and the second column indicates what u_i stands for: the unemployment rate at actual entry, at age 18, or at predicted entry. X_i includes the race dummy and the age-adjusted AFQT score, and *FEs* represent a set of fixed effects appropriate for the corresponding u_i (see the notes below Table 4). The dependent variables in rows (2)–(4) are discrete choice indices, and the estimates reported in Table 4 are from the linear probability model for the sake of intuitive grasp.[13]

Row (1) suggests weak positive effects of the unemployment rates on years of schooling, which is consistent with the findings by Card and Lemieux (2000), although the effect of the unemployment rates at age 18 is not statistically significant probably due to the large standard errors. However, the effect on the likelihood of having a college degree (row (2)) is not statistically significant either and seems to be economically small as well: a 1 percentage-point rise in the unemployment rate changes the likelihood of proceeding to college at most by 1 percentage-point.[14] Even if some people avoid entering the labor market by continuing in school, this does not affect the final degree attainment, perhaps because they can postpone or hasten completion of the degree without changing the targeted degree itself. Rows (3) and (4) show no strong evidence that people avoid graduating during a recession.

Table 4. Correlation with unemployment rates at entry or age 18 and options upon graduation

Dependent var.	U at	White men	Black men	White women	Black women
(1) Years of schooling	Actual entry	0.024 [0.027]	−0.009 [0.033]	0.059 [0.026]**	0.062 [0.030]**
	Age 18	0.047 [0.045]	0.027 [0.047]	−0.006 [0.039]	0.008 [0.040]
(2) Having a college degree (AA, BA, BS)	Age 18	0.013 [0.009]	0.007 [0.009]	−0.003 [0.009]	−0.006 [0.009]
(3) Actual entry is later than predicted entry	Predicted entry	0.011 [0.014]	0.009 [0.014]	0.013 [0.014]	0.021 [0.015]
(4) Having changed state of residence	Actual entry	−0.003 [0.006]	0.004 [0.007]	−0.004 [0.005]	−0.002 [0.006]

Note: OLS regressions (the linear probability model for rows (2)–(4)). The regressions on the unemployment rate at actual entry include dummies for year of entry and state of residence at entry. The regressions on the unemployment rate at age 18 include dummies for year of birth and state of residence at age 14. The regression on the unemployment rate at predicted entry includes dummies for year of predicted entry and state of residence at age 14. Standard errors are in brackets, clustered by the relevant pair of the year and the state. ** indicates statistically significant at the 5% level

Overall, the unemployment rates at actual entry is correlated with the years of schooling, but the correlation between labor market conditions at age 18 and options upon graduation is very weak for this sample. Therefore, I correct for this potential endogeneity of entry by instrumenting for u_{ys} with the unemployment rate in the predicted year of graduation based on the highest degree attained and the state of residence at age 14.[15]

Since the unemployment rate at entry is interacted with the four race-gender groups and the four 3-year potential experience brackets, there are 16 pairs of endogenous variables and corresponding instruments. Therefore, there are 16 separate first-stage regressions. For easier grasp of the correlation between the unemployment rates at actual entry and at predicted entry, I also estimate the following collapsed regression:

$$u_{ys} = \beta_g u_{\tilde{y}\tilde{s}} + \delta' X_i + \eta_{\tilde{s}} + \theta_{rg} + \mu_{\tilde{y}} + \varepsilon_i \qquad (3)$$

where $\tilde{y}$ is the year of predicted entry and $\tilde{s}$ is the state of residence at age 14. Equation (3) is estimated separately for men and women. $\beta_{,g}$ varies across race. X_i includes the race dummy, the age-adjusted AFQT score, and years of schooling. \({\eta}_{\tilde{s}} \) θ_{rg} $\mu_{\tilde{y}}$ are the fixed effects corresponding to the subscripts. The dataset consists of persons, not multiple observations per person.

The upper panel of Table 5 reports estimated β_g: they are in the range of 0.37–0.51, and the value of t-statistics is approximately 10. The correlation between the endogenous variable and the instrument is strong enough for all four race-gender groups. The lower panel of Table 5 reports the coefficient of the instrument in the actual first stage regressions common to the IV estimates reported in Tables 6, 7 and 8. It shows only the coefficient of the instrument corresponding to the endogenous variable in each regression. For example, the upper right cell implies that a unit increase of the instrument is associated with an increase of the unemployment rate at actual entry by 0.454 for white men with 1–3 years of potential experience. The differences over potential experience are probably due to change in the composition of the sample caused by entry before 1979, which affect the group with 1–3 years of experience the most.

Table 5. Coefficients of instruments in the first stage regressions

	White men	Black men	White women	Black women
Collapsed regressions	0.503 [0.042]***	0.455 [0.054]***	0.508 [0.043]***	0.378 [0.047]***
Actual first stage (16 separate regressions)				
Potential Exp = 1–3	0.454 [0.006]***	0.441 [0.006]***	0.455 [0.006]***	0.316 [0.006]***
Potential Exp = 4–6	0.574 [0.007]***	0.523 [0.007]***	0.589 [0.006]***	0.404 [0.006]***
Potential Exp = 7–9	0.562 [0.007]***	0.508 [0.007]***	0.588 [0.006]***	0.428 [0.006]***
Potential Exp = 10–12	0.557 [0.006]***	0.534 [0.006]***	0.589 [0.006]***	0.454 [0.006]***

Note: Each coefficient is taken from a different regression, see the text for detail. Standard errors are in brackets, clustered by the year of predicted entry and the state of residence at age 14. *** indicates statistically significant at the 1% level

6 RESULTS

The first two columns of Table 6 reports the OLS estimates of $\beta_{(t-y),g}$ in equation (1), the coefficients of the unemployment rate at entry interacted with race and potential experience, estimated by separate OLS regressions for men and women. Not surprisingly, there are negative effects immediately after entry for all demographic groups except for white women. However, the size and persistence of the effects differ across demographic groups. For white men, the initial

Table 6. The effect of the unemployment rate at entry on wages

	OLS		IV	
	Men	Women	Men	Women
U at entry				
White exp = 1–3	–0.016 [0.006]**	–0.008 [0.006]	–0.030 [0.016]*	0.006 [0.015]
White exp = 4–6	–0.011 [0.006]*	–0.006 [0.006]	–0.027 [0.011]**	–0.002 [0.011]
White exp = 7–9	–0.008 [0.006]	–0.003 [0.006]	–0.019 [0.012]	–0.002 [0.011]
White exp = 10–12	–0.007 [0.006]	–0.005 [0.007]	–0.029 [0.012]**	–0.004 [0.014]
Black exp = 1–3	–0.019 [0.008]**	–0.025 [0.007]***	–0.051 [0.023]**	–0.034 [0.028]
Black exp = 4–6	–0.013 [0.009]	–0.014 [0.007]**	–0.049 [0.019]**	–0.015 [0.019]
Black exp = 7–9	0.000 [0.009]	–0.007 [0.007]	–0.034 [0.020]*	0.003 [0.018]
Black exp = 10–12	0.008 [0.009]	–0.001 [0.007]	–0.028 [0.023]	0.024 [0.018]
Highest grade completed	0.062 [0.005]***	0.080 [0.004]***	0.057 [0.005]***	0.077 [0.005]***
Age adjusted AFQT score	0.104 [0.010]***	0.105 [0.010]***	0.108 [0.010]***	0.108 [0.011]***
Observations	22,947	24,233	22,333	23,404
R-squared	0.30	0.30	0.30	0.29

Note: The dependent variable is log real hourly wages (cents). Constant, current unemployment rates interacted with race and the 3-year experience brackets, a race dummy, non-linear controls for potential experience differentiated by race are also included in the regressions though omitted from the table. OLS regressions include dummies for year of entry, state of residence at entry and year of the survey; IV regressions include dummies for year of predicted entry, state of residence at age 14 and year of the survey. Standard errors are in brackets, clustered by the year and the state of entry (predicted entry for IV). ***, **, * indicate statistically significant at the 1% , 5% and 10% level, respectively

Table 7. The effect of the unemployment rate at entry on employment

	OLS		IV	
	Men	Women	Men	Women
U at entry				
White exp = 1–3	0.000 [0.005]	0.009 [0.004]*	–0.002 [0.011]	0.003 [0.012]
White exp = 4–6	0.000 [0.004]	0.002 [0.004]	0.002 [0.007]	0.004 [0.009]
White exp = 7–9	0.003 [0.004]	0.005 [0.005]	0.006 [0.007]	0.007 [0.009]
White exp = 10–12	0.004 [0.004]	0.005 [0.005]	0.001 [0.008]	0.008 [0.010]
Black exp = 1–3	0.002 [0.007]	0.001 [0.007]	–0.003 [0.017]	0.033 [0.022]
Black exp = 4–6	0.005 [0.006]	–0.001 [0.007]	0.005 [0.013]	0.010 [0.015]
Black exp = 7–9	0.010 [0.006]	0.005 [0.006]	0.003 [0.014]	–0.003 [0.016]
Black exp = 10–12	0.012 [0.006]*	0.011 [0.007]	–0.008 [0.015]	–0.011 [0.016]
Highest grade completed	0.023 [0.002]***	0.045 [0.003]***	0.023 [0.003]***	0.047 [0.003]***
Age adjusted AFQT score	0.035 [0.006]***	0.043 [0.008]***	0.037 [0.006]***	0.051 [0.008]***
Observations	25,688	31,460	24,992	30,430
R-squared	0.13	0.13	0.13	0.13

Notes: The dependent variable takes one if the respondent is employed. Linear probability model with the same right hand side variables as the OLS regressions in Table 6; see notes for Table 6 *** and * indicate statistically significant at the 1% and 10% level, respectively

Table 8. The effect of the unemployment rate at entry on likelihood of having a valid wage

	OLS		IV	
	Men	Women	Men	Women
U at entry				
White exp = 1–3	0.002 [0.004]	0.004 [0.004]	0.008 [0.009]	−0.002 [0.011]
White exp = 4–6	0.000 [0.003]	0.005 [0.004]	0.004 [0.006]	0.007 [0.008]
White exp = 7–9	0.002 [0.003]	0.007 [0.004]*	0.005 [0.006]	0.009 [0.008]
White exp = 10–12	−0.001 [0.003]	0.006 [0.005]	0.004 [0.006]	0.007 [0.009]
Black exp = 1–3	0.000 [0.006]	0.009 [0.007]	−0.01 [0.016]	0.047 [0.021]**
Black exp = 4–6	0.002 [0.005]	0.009 [0.007]	0.002 [0.011]	0.016 [0.014]
Black exp = 7–9	0.008 [0.005]	0.008 [0.006]	0.000 [0.011]	0.008 [0.014]
Black exp = 10–12	0.004 [0.005]	0.008 [0.006]	−0.015 [0.012]	−0.015 [0.015]
Highest grade completed	0.007 [0.002]***	0.034 [0.003]***	0.007 [0.003]***	0.035 [0.003]***
Age adjusted AFQT score	0.026 [0.005]***	0.035 [0.007]***	0.026 [0.005]***	0.041 [0.008]***
Observations	25,688	31,460	24,992	30,430
R-squared	0.09	0.13	0.09	0.13

Notes: The dependent variable takes one if the observation has a valid (positive) wage. Linear probability model with the same right hand side variables as the OLS regressions in Table 6; see notes for Table 6 ***, ** and * indicate statistically significant at the 1%, 5% and 10% level, respectively

impact is slightly weaker than for black men, but the negative effect remains statistically significant up to 6 years after entry. Furthermore, though statistically nonsignificant, a one percentage point rise in unemployment rate at entry lowers hourly wages by 0.7% after 10–12 years. For black men, the effect in fourth to sixth year after entry is not statistically significant, but the size is similar to that for white men. After the first six years, the effect disappears. The effect for white women is not statistically significant even in the first 3 years, and the size of the coefficient is closer to zero. In contrast, the initial impact of a recession at entry for black women is strongest among the four demographic groups, and it remains statistically significant for 6 years. Except that the effect for black women is significantly negative, these observations are essentially the same as what Fig. 1 suggested.

The last two columns of Table 6 report the IV estimates in the same manner as the OLS results. Here, the unemployment rate in the state and the year of actual entry is instrumented by the unemployment rate that the person would have experienced if he/she had stayed in the same state since he/she was 14 years old and had attained his/her final degree on time. This instrumental variable should correct the biases from endogenous choice of timing and location of graduation conditional on the highest degree attained. The endogeneity of entry seems to bias the OLS estimates toward zero for men. Note that IV estimators in general have larger standard errors than the corresponding OLS estimators; in fact, the standard errors in the last two columns in Table 6 are much larger than those in the first two columns. In particular, the negative effect for black women is not statistically significant, but this is mainly caused by the boosted standard errors.

Table 6 also reports the coefficients of years of schooling and the age-adjusted AFQT score for a comparative analysis. Although not reported in the table, the coefficients of the contemporaneous unemployment rate are not statistically significant, except that those for black men are significantly negative. This confirms that black men are the group most affected by the contemporaneous labor market conditions. Each set of fixed effects is jointly statistically significant.

To display the result more intuitively, Fig. 2 plots the coefficients of the unemployment rate at entry from the IV estimates over years since leaving school. Each of the four panels compares men and women of the same race, or blacks and whites of the same gender. Dotted lines show the 95% confidence intervals.

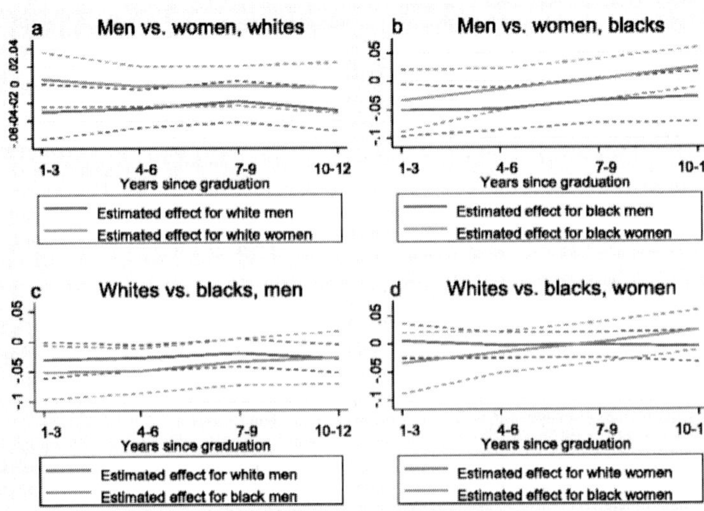

Figure 2. Pairwise comparison of the coefficients of unemployment at entry. Plot of the coefficients of unemployment rate at entry, obtained by IV estimates shown in Table 6. Dotted lines show 5% confidence intervals of the estimated coefficients

Panel a compares white men and white women. It confirms that the effect for men is significantly negative, while the effect for women is almost zero. Although the 95% confidence intervals overlap, the difference between white men and white women looks marginally significant. Furthermore, Appendix C shows that $\beta_{(t-y),g}$ are jointly significant at the 10% level for white men but not significant for white women. These findings are consistent with the theoretical prediction that the effect of the unemployment rate at entry is weaker and less persistent for those with weaker labor force attachment.

Panel b compares black men and black women. For blacks, the confidence intervals are wider than for whites. Although standard errors are quite large in the first 3 years, the effect for black men tends to be more negative than for black women, like the comparison between white men and women. However, unlike whites, $\beta_{(t-y),g}$ are jointly significant for both black men and women.

Panels c and d compare black and whites of each gender. For both men and women, the confidence intervals for blacks and whites overlap widely. Statistical tests reported in Appendix C also show that $\beta_{(t-y),g}$ are not statically significantly different between blacks and whites, except for the first 3 years after entry for women. However, the differences in point estimates of $\beta_{(t-y),g}$ are not economically negligible. For example, a one percentage point rise in the unemployment at entry can lower hourly wages of black and white men by 5 and 3%, respectively. Furthermore, the pattern depicted by the point estimates appears to be consistent with the theoretical prediction: the initial impact is stronger for blacks, but they catch up quickly. Therefore, it is hard to conclude whether the effect of a recession at entry differs across race from these results.

If the unemployment rate at entry has a negative effect on wages, it may well have a negative effect on employment. Therefore, I estimate the effect on employment by replacing the dependent variable in equation (1). Table 7 reports the results from the linear probability model.[16] Surprisingly, the estimated coefficients are mostly *positive*, although statistically insignificant. If those who were not employed were negatively selected based on their potential wages, this positive effect would cause an upward bias on the estimated effect. Assuming that those with low potential wages are less likely to be employed when there is a negative shock to wages at the cohort level, my estimates are unlikely to be biased downward. Furthermore, the estimates tend to be larger for women, suggesting that decisions on marriages and fertility may matter. Thus, the direction of potential biases is ambiguous.

In any case, recall that non-employment does not necessarily imply missing wages because respondents who have worked since the last interview report wages even if they are not employed in the week of survey. Thus, to examine this issue more directly, Table 8 reports the effect on the likelihood of having a valid wage. The estimated coefficients are still positive but on average smaller and noisier. Moreover, except for the IV estimates of black women, the estimated effects are economically small compared to the effects of years of schooling and the AFQT score. Further, I replace the missing wage data with imputed wages based on several slightly different versions of wage equations with individual fixed effects, and find little differences in the estimated coefficients in the wage regressions. This leads me to believe that, even if there are biases from non-random selection of those lacking valid wages, they will not alter the qualitative conclusions.

7 CONCLUSION

By examining the effect of unemployment rate in the year and state of school-leaving, I have found that the negative effect of a recession at entry is weaker for women than for men. In particular, white women do not seem to be affected by a recession at entry, at least in terms of hourly wages and employment. In addition, the endogeneity of entry seems to cause underestimation of the effect for men. These findings are consistent with the economic theories reviewed in Section 2: the effect of a recession at entry will be stronger for people with stronger labor force attachment.

However, whether the effect differs across race remains unclear. On the one hand, statistical tests cannot reject that the effects for whites and blacks are the same. On the other hand, the differences in point estimates are economically non-negligible. The difference between blacks and whites are somewhat similar but not as clear as the differences between high school graduates and college graduates in previous studies (Kahn 2010; Speer 2015; Genda et al. 2010), although I use the same dataset and similar methodology to Kahn (2010); Speer (2015).

Admittedly, the cohorts covered by the NLSY79 entered the labor market a few decades ago, and the labor market structure may have changed since then. Nonetheless, the differences in the sensitivity to contemporaneous labor market conditions across demographic groups have been fairly stable between the 1982 recession and the Great Recession that began in 2008 (Hoynes et al. 2012). Furthermore, the female labor force participation rate has not increased much in the United States since the 1990s,[17] implying that women still quit jobs for exogenous reasons more often than men do. Thus, I expect that similar patterns across gender and race will be observed for cohorts who graduated around the Great Recession. Whether this expectation is supported empirically needs to be assessed in the future.

It is difficult to distinguish one theory from the others. Note that skill level matters for both access to stable employment in high-paying jobs and returns to training. In theory, once a worker finds a good job after entry, a recession prior to the job change no longer matters in absence of human capital accumulation through the past on-the-job training. Therefore, controlling for labor demand at the beginning of the current job will cancel out the effect of a recession at entry if the loss of training opportunity does not matter. However, it is very difficult to include unemployment rates in the year of leaving school and in the year of beginning of the current job simultaneously, because they are highly collinear. Since this collinearity amplifies the bias caused by misspecification of the effect of tenure and experience, it is necessary to include many interaction terms in the regression. To do so, the required sample size needs to be far larger than the NLSY; this remains for future research.

8 ENDNOTES

[1]Altonji and Blank (1999) show that the unemployment rate for blacks is more sensitive to business cycle conditions. Hoynes et al. (2012) also confirm that the employment rate of blacks is more sensitive to the state unemployment rate.

[2] This instrument is used in existing studies using the NLSY79, such as Kahn (2010); Speer (2015); Maclean (2014); Maclean (2015); Maclean et al. (2015).

[3] Relatedly, Gregg (2001) examines the long-term effect on an individual's own experience of unemployment at youth and finds that the effect is weaker for women than that for men, using British data.

[4] Relatedly, Kondo (2012) finds that women who face worse labor market conditions at youth tend to marry earlier, but this is just a temporary shift, and the probability of having married by the age of 30 does not change. Using the NLSY79, the same dataset used in this study, Maclean et al. (2015) also find that a recession at entry has a positive effect on fertility among women.

[5] While Cutler and Katz (1991) argue that the expansion in the mid-late 80s did not benefit the disadvantaged, Hines et al. (2001) view the 1980s as an exception and conclude that the benefits from strong economic growth for the disadvantaged are at least as great as they are for the more advantaged, using data spanning from the 1970s to the 2000s.

[6] Fig. 4 in Hoynes et al. (2012) shows that a one percentage point increase in the state unemployment rate increases the unemployment rate of white men by one percentage point and that of black men by nearly two percentage point; in this sense, the latter group is twice as sensitive to local labor market conditions than the former one. Moreover, women are less responsive to local labor market conditions, while the racial differences among women are similar to that among men: a 1-percentage point increase in the state unemployment rate increases white women's unemployment rate by about 0.8 percentage point, and black women's unemployment rate by about 1.6 percentage point.

[7] I drop the military subsample because it covers only cohorts born between 1957 and 1961. I do not consider the supplemental sample of poor whites because they are excluded from the survey after 1991. I also drop Hispanics because the sample size is too small for a separate analysis.

[8]This definition follows Neumark (2002), who also used the NLSY to identify the effect of early job mobility on adult wages.

[9] This process follows Kahn (2010) and other existing studies using the NLSY79.

[10] Some existing studies use sampling weights (Maclean 2014, 2015), but others do not (Kahn 2010; Hershbein 2012; Speer 2015). Since the unemployment rate at entry is unlikely to be correlated with the sampling weights, using the sampling weights would not change the results much.

[11] The estimated effects from this instrumental variable can be interpreted as the Local Average Treatment Effect (LATE) among people

who graduate on time and do not move across states between age 14 and the school-leaving year.

[12] Information on the highest degree/diploma attained is not based on the years of schooling completed, but on the following two questions: "What is the highest degree you ever received" and "Do you have a high school diploma or equivalent?"

[13]The results from the probit model are similar in terms of both statistical significance and marginal effects measured at the mean of the explanatory variables.

[14] My estimates are smaller than those in Table 6 in Kahn (2010), which also reported the effect of unemployment rate at age 18 for white men in the NLSY79. This is probably because of differences in sample selection; while Kahn (2010) dropped 1957 cohorts, I dropped those who disappeared from the data by age 30. Card and Lemieux (2000) also report that the effects of the unemployment rate on the likelihood of proceeding to college for students in the 12th grade are statistically insignificant and variable in sign.

[15] Note that the information on college degree is not based on the years of schooling, but is directly asked obtained from the respondents; thus, it does not reflect some people staying more than a year without obtaining additional degrees. I assign the year of birth +18 to high school drop-outs because Card and Lemieux (2000) find positive effects of the unemployment rate on high school completion; likewise, I ignore graduate degrees because Kahn (2010) reports that a recession at graduation from college slightly increases the likelihood of attaining a graduate degree.

[16] The probit estimates are similar to the corresponding OLS estimates in Tables 7 and 8, with regard to both statistical significance and marginal effects evaluated at the mean of explanatory variables.

[17]The labor force participation rate for women older than 20 years stays around 55–60% for white women and 60–65% for black women, according to the Current Population Survey available from the BLS website.

DECLARATIONS

Acknowledgments

This study was funded by the Japan Society for the Promotion of Science (grant number 15K17072). I would like to thank Janet Currie and Till von Wachter for their helpful suggestions on earlier draft. I also appreciate the valuable comments from the editor and three anonymous reviewers, Brendan O'Flaherty, Claudia Olivetti, Tomohiro Machikita, and participants of Applied Micro Lunch Seminar at Columbia University. Access to the geo-code data of NLSY79 requires an approval from the Bureau of Labor Statistics and is limited to researchers located in the United States. All the data analyses were conducted when the author was at Columbia University.

REFERENCES

1. Altonji JG, Blank RM (1999) Race and gender in the labor market. Handbook of Labor Economics vol.3, Ch48
2. Beaudry P, DiNardo J (1991) The effect of implicit contracts on the movement of wages over the business cycle: evidence form micro data. J Polit Econ 99(4):665–688
3. Barr A, Turner S (2015) Out of work and into school: labor market policies and college enrollment during the Great Recession. J Public Econ 124:63–73
4. Betts J, McFarland L (1995) Safe port in a storm: the impact of labor market conditions on community college enrollments. J Hum Resour 30:741–765
5. Brunner B, Kuhn A (2014) The impact of labor market entry conditions on initial job assignment and wages. J Popul Econ 27:705–738
6. Card D, Lemieux T (2000) Dropout and enrollment trends in the post-war period: what went wrong in the 1970s? Working Paper no. 7658. National Bureau of Economic Research, Cambridge
7. Clark K, Summers LH (1981) Demographic differences in cyclical employment variation. J Hum Resour 16(1):61–79

8. Cockx B, Ghirelli C (2015) Scars of recessions in a rigid labor market, IZA Discussion Paper No. 8889

9. Cutler DM, Katz L (1991) Macroeconomic performance of the disadvantaged. Brook Pap Econ Act 2:285–239

10. Fernández-Kranz D, Rodríguez-Planas N (2015) The perfect storm: graduating in a recession in a segmented labor market, Presentation at SOLE/EALE 4th World Meeting

11. Devereux PJ (2004) Cyclical quality adjustment in the labor market. South Econ J 70(3):600–615

12. Genda Y, Kondo A, Ohta S (2010) Long term effects of a recession at entry in Japan and the United States. J Hum Resour 45(1):157–196

13. Gregg P (2001) The impact of youth unemployment on adult unemployment in the NCDS. Econ J 111:F626–F653

14. Hershbein BJ (2012) Graduating high school in a recession: work, education, and home production. B E J Econom Anal Policy 12:1–32**Google Scholar**

15. Hines JR Jr, Hoynes H, Krueger AB (2001) Another look at whether a rising tide lifts all boats, Working Paper, no. 8412. National Bureau of Economic Research, Cambridge

16. Hoynes H, Miller DL, Schaller J (2012) Who suffers during recessions? J Econ Perspect 26(3):27–48

17. Kahn LB (2010) The long-term labor market consequences of graduating college in a bad economy. Labour Econ 17(2):303–316

18. Kondo A (2012) Gender-specific labor market conditions and family formation. J Popul Econ 25:151–174

19. Maclean J (2014) Does leaving school in an economic downturn impact access to employer-sponsored health insurance? IZA J Labor Policy 3:19

20. Maclean J (2015) The lasting effects of leaving school in an economic downturn on alcohol use. Ind Labor Relat Rev 68:120–152

21. Maclean J, Covington R, Kessler AS (2015) Labor market conditions at school-leaving: long-run effects on marriage and fertility. Contemp Econ Policy, forth coming

22. Neumark D (2002) Youth labor markets in the United States: shopping around vs. staying put. Rev Econ Stat 84(3):462–482

23. Okun A (1973) Upward mobility in a high-pressure economy. Brook Pap Econ Act 1973(1):207–261

24. Oreopoulos P, von Wachter T, Heisz A (2012) The short-and long-term career effects of graduating in a recession. Am Econ J Appl Econ 4(1):1–29

25. Raaum O, Røed K (2006) Do business cycle conditions at the time of labor market entry affect future employment prospects? Rev Econ Stat 88(2):193–210

26. Speer JD (2015) Wages, hours, and the school-to-work transition: the consequences of leaving school in a recession for less-educated men. B E J Econom Anal Policy, forth coming

27. Wozniak A (2010) Are College graduates more responsive to distant labor market opportunities? J Hum Resour 45(4):944–97

12

CHAPTER

The Impact of the 2008 Economic Crisis on Substance Use Patterns in the Countries of the European Union

Geert Dom[1], Jerzy Samochowiec[2], Sara Evans-Lacko[3] , Kristian Wahlbeck[4], Guido Van Hal[5] and David McDaid[6]

[1]*Collaborative Antwerp Psychiatric Research Institute (CAPRI), Antwerp University, Antwerp 2640, Belgium*

[2]*Department of Psychiatry, Pomeranian Medical University, Szczecin 71-460, Poland;*

[3]*Health Service and Population Research Department, Institute of Psychiatry, King's College London, SE5 8AF, UK;*

[4]*The Finnish Association for Mental Health, Helsinki 00240, Finland;*

[5]*Medical Sociology and Health Policy, Antwerp University, Antwerp 2640, Belgium;*

[6]*Personal Social Services Research Unit, London School of Economics and Political Science, London WC2A 2AE, UK*

ABSTRACT

From 2008 on, a severe economic crisis (EC) has characterized the European Union (E.U.). However, changes in substance use behavioral patterns as a result of the economic crisis in Europe, have been poorly reflected upon, and underlying mechanisms remain to be identified;: In this review we explore and systematize the available data on the effect of the 2008 economic crisis on patterns of substance use and related disorders, within the E.U. countries;: The results show that effects of the recession need to be differentiated. A number of studies point to reductions in population's overall substance use. In contrast, an increase in harmful use and negative effects is found within specific subgroups within the society. Risk factors include job-loss and long-term unemployment, and pre-existing vulnerabilities. Finally, our findings point to differences between types of substances in their response on economic crisis periods;: the effects of the 2008 economic crisis on substance use patterns within countries of the European Union are two-sided. Next to a reduction in a population's overall substance use, a number of vulnerable subgroups experience serious negative effects. These groups are in need of specific attention and support, given that there is a real risk that they will continue to suffer negative health effects long after the economic downfall has formally been ended.

1. INTRODUCTION

Since 2008, a severe economic crisis (EC) has characterized the European Union (E.U.). The countries most severely impacted were those countries whose banking systems have been most exposed to the economic crisis; *i.e.*, Cyprus, Greece, Ireland, Italy, Portugal and Spain [1]. However, there is growing evidence that the effects are seen well beyond these countries impacting a broad set of social, economic and health domains [2]. It is within this context that the 2010 European Monitoring Centre for Drugs and Drug Addiction (EMCDDA) Annual Report noted that economic slowdown has produced "fears that this may be accompanied by an increase in problematic forms of drug use".

However, until now a systematic overview of the E.U. data that substantiate these fears has not been done. Indeed, although a sizeable number of studies have explored the relationship between (earlier) economic crises and changes in substance use patterns, throughout many countries in the world, the European context has been as yet been poorly explored [3]. An additional complicating factor is that the E.U. context is characterized by great differences between countries in a number of dimensions, *i.e.*, the impact of the crisis, traditional substance use patterns, and legal regulation systems.

In addition to systematize epidemiological data there is a strong need to find explanatory mechanisms that mediate the relation between EC and changes in substance use patterns within a population. Identifying specific mechanisms is important in developing more targeted interventions to decrease the effect of EC on substance use. Based upon the findings in their systematic review, including studies worldwide, de Goeij *et al.* suggest two mechanisms. First, the psychological distress triggered by EC's consequences explains an increase of harmful substance use, specifically in those subgroups most affected by the EC. The second mechanism, suggests that due to tighter budget constraints, less money is spent on psychoactive substances such as alcohol or nicotine [3]. However, many other mechanisms may play a role [4,5].

Taken together, changes in substance use behavioral patterns as a result of the economic crisis in Europe, which started in 2008, have been poorly reflected upon, and underlying mechanisms remain to be identified. This represents a serious caveat, especially within the context of the current ongoing processes in which the E.U. is developing joint action plans and policies on alcohol, tobacco and drug-related issues as well as on broader mental health domains.

Therefore, the aim of the current review is to explore the relationship between the "Great Recession" and changes in patterns of substance use and related disorders, within the European Union countries. In addition we explored whether the E.U. data give support to the dual effects of the EC, *i.e.*, reduction of substance use within the general population and increase of harmful substance use patterns within vulnerable subgroups, as suggested by de Goeij *et al.* [3].

2. METHOD

We used the Pubmed database with the search terms (alcohol or drugs or nicotine or smoking) or (alcohol or drugs or nicotine) abuse or dependence and (economic crisis or business cycles) AND Europe, within the title or abstract. Limitations were set on studies published from 1 January 2008 to 31 May 2015. This search procured 75 hits.

All abstracts of the articles were screened (by first author Geert Dom) to identify literature relating to our specific focus: the European Union, the 2008 economic crisis and its aftermath in relation to changes in alcohol, drug, or smoking behaviors within the general population. Review articles (n = 8) and articles not having as primary focus data on alcohol, illicit drug, or smoking behaviors in relation to economic crisis were excluded (n = 50). We limited our search to original research studies providing data in countries belonging to the European Union and candidate countries. References of the selected articles were screened for additional literature (n = 0). The corresponding Prisma flowchart is shown in Figure 1.

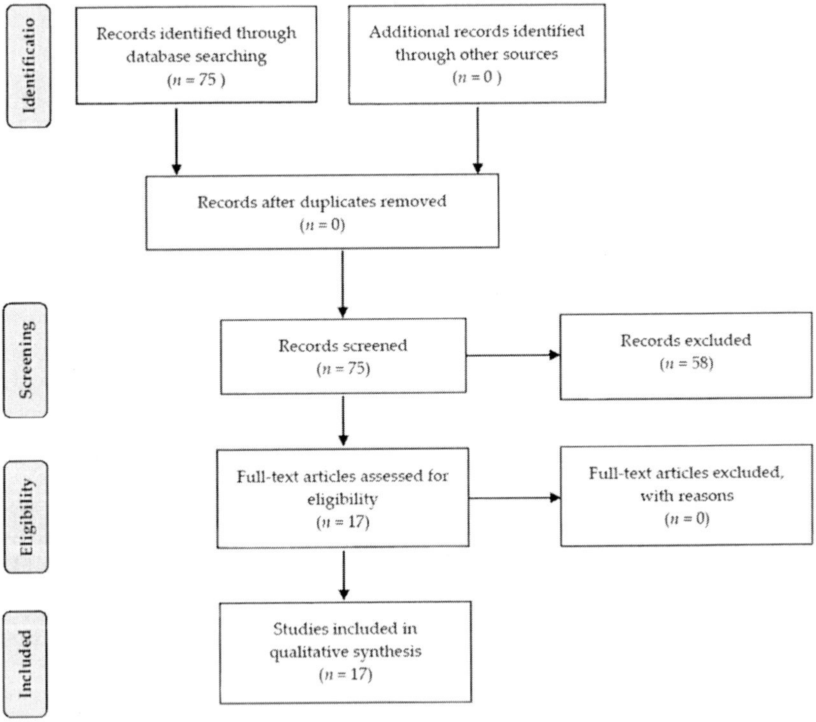

Figure 1. Prisma flow diagram.

3. RESULTS

Ultimately 17 original research articles were included, 11 on alcohol, three on drugs, and three on cigarette smoking.

3.1. Alcohol

We found eleven studies on alcohol and related disorders (Table 1). Two show a decrease in the general population's alcohol consumption and related harm during EC periods. Six studies report negative effects of economic crisis periods on alcohol consumption, most frequently associated with unemployment status. Three studies showed mixed results, *i.e.*, a reduction of heavy drinking patterns but increases in binge drinking.

Table 1. Studies on alcohol and alcohol use disorders during and after the economic crisis in European Union countries.

Author [Reference]	Sample	Period Survey	Country	Outcome
Mattei *et al.*, 2014 [6]	Data from Italian government agencies	2000 *vs.* 2010	Italy	Increased population alcohol consumption in 2009.
Harray *et al.*, 2014 [7]	Nationally representative sample of non-institutionalized white persons aged 20–60 years from seven waves of the Health Survey for England, 2004–2010 (*n* = 36,525)	2004 *vs.* 2010	UK	Decreased frequent (hazardous) drinking in 2008/2009 and rise of binge drinking among unemployed drinkers.
Gili *et al.*, 2013 [9]	Samples of patients attending primary care centers representing Spain's consulting populations (*n* = 7940)	2006/2007 *vs.* 2010/2011	Spain	4.6% rise of alcohol dependence and related disorders, specifically within those with severe economic losses
Garcy and Vagero, 2012 [10]	All Swedish men and women (*n* = 3,392,169) born between 1931 and 1965, and who were still alive on 31 December 1996. (Data: The Work and Mortality Database, WMD)	1997 *vs.* 2002	Sweden	Increased hazard alcohol-related mortality associated with duration unemployment
Eliason *et al.*, 2014 [11]	Employee-employer data merged with information on alcohol-attributable deaths and hospital admissions from the Causes of Death Register and the National Patient Register	Employee-employer data were used to identify all establishment closures during 1990–1999. Follow-up for 12 years	Sweden	Job-loss associated with increased alcohol-related mortality and morbidity
Herttua *et al.*, 2007 [12]	A register-based follow-up study of all over 15-year-old Finnish men and women.	1975 *vs.* 2001	Finland	Improvement of macroeconomic conditions associated with decreased alcohol-related mortality
Johansson *et al.*, 2006 [13]	Cross-sectional population survey "health 2000 in Finland" (*n* = 10,000) carried out in 2000	1975 *vs.* 2001	Finland	Decreased alcohol-related mortality in the early 1990's
Stuckler *et al.*, 2009 [14]	Age-standardized and age-specific mortality data from the WHO European Health for All Database	1970–2007	26 European countries	Rise of unemployment associated with excess alcohol-related mortality
Toffolutti and Suhrcke, 2014 [15]	Unemployment rate as the main indicator for the macroeconomic fluctuation. Health indicator the overall mortality rate, selected cause-specific mortality rates, as well as health behavior proxies.	2003 *vs.* 2010	23 European countries	Short-term effects arising decreased total rate alcohol consumption and mortality due to liver disease
Colell *et al.*, 2015 [8]	Cross-sectional data from four editions of the Spanish Household Survey on Alcohol and Drugs, economically active individuals aged 16–64 years (total sample = 62,440).	2005/2007 (P1) *vs.* 2009/2011 (P2)	Spain	During P2: Heavy drinking (daily average >40 g. for men and 24 g. for women) decreased for both men and women. Increased binge drinking (>5 units/2 h) in both men and women

In Italy, although all-cause mortality remained stable during economic fluctuations, alcohol consumption increased in 2009, the year with the worst real GDP decrease (−5.1%) [6]. In England, comparing data between 2004 and 2010, there was a remarkable decrease in frequent (hazardous) drinking following the onset of the banking crisis in 2008/2009 [7]. However, in this study there was a notable rise of binge drinking among a smaller high-risk group of unemployed drinkers [7]. These findings are in line with a recent Spanish study showing that during the period of economic recession in Spain heavy drinking decreased and binge drinking increased [8]. In another, Spanish study comparing the pre- and post-crisis years 2006 and 2010, a significant rise in alcohol dependence and related disorders was found, specifically among those who experienced severe economic losses, e.g., unemployment [9].

In the Nordic countries such as Sweden a deep recession occurred earlier (1992–1996). Some of the adverse effects of the recession persisted long after the crisis had ended. Between 1997 and 2002 there was an increase in the hazard of alcohol disease-related mortality, in line with the duration of unemployment for women, while for men mortality peaked with middle-level of unemployment duration [10]. The importance of job-loss was underlined in another longitudinal Swedish study, where job-loss was associated with an excess risk of both alcohol-related hospitalization and mortality among both displaced men and women. For women, alcohol-attributable health problems were mainly limited to alcohol use disorders, whereas men also had an increased risk of hospitalization from poisoning and alcohol-induced liver disease and pancreatitis [11]. In Finland, a worsening alcohol-related mortality was associated with improvement in macro-economic conditions [12,13].

Overall there seems to be an association between alcohol use related morbidity and unemployment. In a large study in 26 European countries, a 3% increase in unemployment was associated with excess deaths from alcohol abuse during the economic downfall (excess deaths E.U.-wide) [14].

This is consistent with a recent study on the short-term health effects of the economic crisis using data from 23 European countries, which reported an overall decrease in the total rate of alcohol consumption and mortality due to chronic liver diseases [15].

3.2. Smoking

Only three studies on smoking and economic crisis could be found (Table 2). In Italy, comparing 2009 (the height of the Italian crisis) with 2008 data, a significant increase of smoking prevalence in both women and men was reported. Of interest, there was no change in the number of never smokers in this study, leading the authors to believe that former smokers relapsed in their old smoking patterns [16].

Table 2. Studies on cigarette smoking during and after the economic crisis in European Union countries.

Author [Reference]	Sample	Period Survey	Country	Outcome
Gallus *et al.*, 2011 [16]	Representative general population survey ($n_{(2008)}$ = 3085, $n_{(2009)}$ = 3213)	2008 *vs.* 2009	Italy	Compared to 2008 significantly increased smoking prevalence in 2009; 22.0% to 25.4%, in both men and women. Number of never smokers remained the same
Tarantilis *et al.*, 2015 [17]	Econometric modeling of cigarette consumption with different cigarette price and gross domestic product fluctuation scenarios	1994–2012	Greece	Decreased cigarette consumption
Schoretsaniti *et al.*, 2014 [18]	Trend analysis of three representative national and cross-sectional surveys	2006–2010, 2011	Greece	Increased number people with intention to quit smoking. Quit attempts more frequent in people with high socioeconomic status.

Although Tarantelli *et al.* [17] report in their study a sharp drop in overall cigarette consumption during the last decades, this study does not provide original data but rather gives an econometric estimation of changes of cigarette consumption in function of changes in taxation rates and incomes. Also in Greece, and in part probably due to a combination of tobacco control policies and austerity measures, the intention to quit smoking has increased, although actual quit attempts were higher among those less disadvantaged potentially widening inequalities between socio-economic groups [18]. Taken together, only one study provides data on changes in smoking prevalence's [16], with two studies providing information on smoking proxy-variables [17,18].

3.3. Illicit Drugs

Although it might be expected that any economic downturn could potentially have a great effect on changes in drug use patterns, the number of studies within the European context is remarkably limited (Table 3). Between 2008 and 2010 there was a substantial increase in the number of persons with problematic drug use in Greece. The increase was most notable among older persons [19]. Taking into account that in 2010 the average age in Greece for initiation of injection drug use was estimated at 22.4 years old the authors suggest that the sharp increase of older heroin users in Greece indicates probable relapses rather than new cases, presumably associated with the ongoing economic downturn. Analysis of wastewater in two North-Italian cities showed a decrease in use of more expensive drugs (*i.e.*, heroin and cocaine) and an increase in cheaper drugs (cannabis and amphetamine) [20]. In Spain a recent study reported that sporadic cannabis use increased among older unemployed men and women [8].

Table 3. Studies on drug use and drug use disorders during and after the economic crisis in European Union countries.

Author [Reference]	Sample	Period Survey	Country	Outcome
Zuccato *et al.*, 2012 [20]	Urban wastewater analysis in two cities	2005 *vs.* 2009	Italy Wastewater analysis in two cities	Decrease of expensive drugs and increase cheap drugs in wastewater analyses.
Kondilis *et al.*, 2013 [19]	Based upon national statistic health data	Data EMCDDA 2008 *vs.* 2010	Greece	Number of persons with problematic drug use rose by 11.6% between 2008 and 2010. Among those aged 35 to 64 years, the increase was far more intense at 88.2%.
Colell *et al.*, 2015 [8]	Data from the Spanish Household Survey on Alcohol and Drugs (EDADES). Representative population survey age 15–64 (n = 62,440)	2005/2007 (P1) *vs.* 2009/2011(P2)	Spain	Unemployed men and women increased sporadic use cannabis *vs.* employed.

4. DISCUSSION

Although substance use and related disorders are a major public health problem only a surprisingly low number of studies explored the impact of the recent economic crisis on substance use patterns in E.U. countries. In addition the wide variability in the used methodology and sample choices provide mostly fragmented information on the topic chosen and make interpretation of results difficult.

Most studies focused on alcohol. The results show that effects of the recession need to be differentiated, and give some support for a bidirectional effect. On the one hand a number of studies point to reductions in population's overall substance use. On the other hand an increase in harmful use and negative effects is found within specific subgroups within the society. Risk factors include job-loss and long-term unemployment, and pre-existing vulnerabilities. Finally, our findings point to differences between types of substances in their response on economic crisis periods.

Overall a majority of the studies included in this review provide indications that within different European countries the economic crisis has been paralleled with a reduction of use and heavy use in the general population. This accounts specifically for drinking alcohol and cigarette smoking but interestingly not for illicit drugs. These findings are consistent with findings in other non-E.U. countries and different crisis time periods. The EC in Iceland led to large and significant reductions in health behaviors such as alcohol consumption and cigarette smoking [21]. In the U.S. there was a tendency during economic crisis periods for a large part of the population to buy and use less alcoholic beverages [22,23]. This was reflected in market reductions and decreases in hazardous drinking and drink-driving prevalence (although this latter relationship may be biased by an overall reduction in car-possession and driving due to economic hard-ships) [7,24]. The findings are also consistent with a Canadian study comparing data between 2003 and 2010. Canada experienced substantial negative economic growth in 2009 and a one-point increase in the unemployment rate was associated with 0.15% fewer drinks consumed in the past month and a 0.14% decrease in past-month heavy drinking, specifically in men [25].

Taken together, economic crisis periods seem to have a down regulatory effect on the use of alcohol and tobacco in the population, which affect the populations health positively. Price regulation and budget restriction are probably the main driving mechanisms [26]. However, we need to take into account that the number of studies in support of these hypotheses remains low, so studies in more (European) countries with different social systems are clearly needed.

In contrast to these general population's positive effects the findings in this overview show that specific subgroups are very negatively affected by the EC. In current review this was most consistently documented for alcohol use in association with people suffering from job-loss or unemployment [7,9,10,11,14,27], and to a lesser degree regarding tobacco [18], and illicit drug use [8]. The findings on the alcohol-unemployment association were very recently confirmed in a multi-country European study published after closing time of our review [28].

Most studies in this overview highlight the negative effect of job loss and unemployment on substance use patterns; more risky use (binge drinking), alcohol-related hospitalization and mortality, and illicit drug use. The increase in binge-drinking patterns that is reported in many studies is important. Indeed, binge-drinking patterns have been associated with a higher risk on medical, mental health, and social adversities [29,30].

Overall, these findings are consistent with other non-E.U. countries reporting increases in alcohol use, alcohol use disorders, and alcohol-related morbidity and mortality, associated with unemployment within a substantial part of the population [14,22,31,32,33].

The economic crisis has affected employment rates on a major scale. Stuckler *et al.* [34] found that in 26 European countries, job loss increased above the 2007 level after 2009. Unemployment appears to be a major driver of increased mental health problems, both during "economic normal" and economic crisis periods. Some authors have suggested a dose-response effect [24]. Our findings on substance use patterns point in the same dose-response direction. In the largest study included in the review, over 26 European countries, a 3% increase in unemployment was associated with excess deaths from alcohol abuse during the economic downfall (excess deaths E.U.-wide) [14]. Of importance, not only the population prevalence but also the individual duration of the unemployment may be a risk factor for developing heavy drinking patterns [35]. Also, the relationship between substance use and unemployment is likely to be influenced not only by the duration of the unemployment but also by the overall employment rate for the area [22,36]. Indeed, becoming unemployed at a time of strong economic growth may have substantially different psychological and social implications than losing one's job in times of recession [22]. Of importance within this context is that having a (pre-existing) history of mental health problems increases the vulnerability to suffer more severe consequences, *i.e.*, losing a job and becoming unemployed during economic crisis periods [37]. Indeed people suffering from mental illness are among the first to lose jobs during periods of economic downfall. Effects are especially harmful since having meaningful employment is one of the most important factors related to the sustained recovery of people with mental illness and/or substance use disorders. Overall, one of the consequences of the recession in Europe is that the gap in employment between individuals with and without mental health problems has widened significantly. These findings suggest that times of economic hardship may intensify social exclusion; in particular men and individuals with lower education seem to be affected most negatively [37].

Taken together, economic hardship undoubtedly increases the number and intensity of different sources of stress people have to deal with. Specifically subgroups that are vulnerable due to job-loss, unemployment or mental health problems experience a disproportional excess of stress. Independent of the type of stressor, an abundance of literature illustrates the intimate relationship between stress and a variety of substance use related consequences. Basically, stress seems to increase the risk of initiating substance use, of transitioning to regular (excessive) use, and ultimately the development of substance use disorders [38]. This may also explain that former addicts relapse back into their smoking or drug behavior during EC, as suggested by the findings of Gallus *et al.*, 2011 [16] and Kondilis *et al.*, 2013 [19]. Overall findings suggest that the effect of EC can compound existing socio-economic disadvantage and lead to an increase in societal inequity, including substance use effects.

Finally, we found remarkable differences between types of drugs of abuse. For alcohol and cigarette smoking, the economic crisis was associated with an overall decrease in the population, largely through an income effect. In contrast, the limited number of studies on drugs shows a consistent increase of use during the EC. It is interesting that these studies point to a change in the drug market, *i.e.*, more drug use, less use of expensive drugs like cocaine and an increase in cheaper laboratory made drugs such as amphetamines [20]. This is consistent with earlier U.S. studies showing that increases in poverty are associated with both an increase in illicit drugs use and an expansion of the illegal economy, *i.e.*, crime, sex work and drug dealing [22,33]. Indeed, in a U.S. study, Arkes *et al.* [39] provided evidence that a weaker economy led to greater teenage use of marijuana as well as hard-drug use. They found that teenagers were more likely to sell drugs in weaker economies, and suggested one mechanism for counter-cyclical drug use—that access to illicit drugs is easier when the economy is weaker. Apparently, in contrast with legal substances, the illicit drug market is much more flexible. The downward trend in the price of illicit drugs during the last decade in both the U.S. and E.U. can be interpreted as an adaption to the economic downturn [40]. In addition, compared to alcohol use the relationship between unemployment and increases in illicit drug use is much more consistent. Experiencing unemployment was associated with increased hazard of starting cannabis use in a U.S. study [41].

Finally, our findings on tobacco smoking suggest a dual pattern, *i.e.*, reduction of smoking for large parts of the populations and difficulties to quit in people who are disproportionally affected by the crisis (e.g., unemployment) [18]. The acute effects of losing a job have been earlier associated with relapse in smoking behavior within the U.S. [42]. These findings are consistent with a recent U.S. study, showing that the 2008 financial crisis had a weak effect on overall smoking prevalence. The pro-cyclical relationship (*i.e.*, the crisis results in a lower number of smokers) found among the employed is offset by the counter-cyclical relationship (*i.e.*, the crisis results in a higher number of smokers) found among unemployed individuals [43]. Importantly, within the U.S., teenagers and young adults increase cigarette use when the economy is weaker [44]. Thus, from this (US) context, public health interventions should specifically target both teenagers and those in unemployment, particularly in times of economic downfall. Whether this accounts for the European situation remains to be explored. Indeed, the scarce number of studies found within the current review and the fragmented information they offer, do not allow drawing, at this point, any conclusions. However, a recent Spanish study, published after the closing date of our review, showing unemployment in young (16–24 years) men associated with increased tobacco consumption, consistent with the U.S. findings [27,44].

Our review has several limitations. Foremost we need to acknowledge that the number of studies on this topic within the E.U. countries is very limited and methodology and sample choice varies widely. Although we think that the most relevant literature has been covered within our search the low number of studies found may be in part due to the fact we limited our search to Pubmed database. Overall, we need to acknowledge that the findings provide a fragmented information pattern that, although important and indicative in support of some hypotheses, warrants prudent interpretation. Next, we limited ourselves to traditional substances of abuse, leaving out important others, e.g., prescription drugs, legal highs and behavioral addiction. Although this is a limitation, we do think that alcohol, nicotine and to a lesser degree the more traditional illicit drugs account by far for the largest portion of burden due to substance use patterns in our society. In addition, many causal pathways may be involved that connect economic hardship experiences with different health behaviors [41]. Not many studies included in this review take this complexity into account; even when they do they may use only one measure or a limited number of variables, e.g., unemployment, leaving ample room for many confounding factors. Thus, findings need to be seen as indicative rather than conclusive. Finally, we limited the review to E.U. countries. Of importance, the E.U. is developing its own alcohol- and drug policies for the E.U. member states, so information based upon studies within these countries is highly relevant in this context. However this choice implicates that many other regions, e.g., U.S. and eastern European countries such as Russia were not included. These countries have often a different substance use culture so our findings need to be interpreted carefully when comparing with these countries.

5. CONCLUSIONS

Taken together, the results of the current overview illustrate that the effects of the economic crisis on changes in substance use patterns and their subsequent consequences are not unequivocal and are mediated by different factors. Identification of these factors may allow for identification of population subgroups, which are more vulnerable to the effects of economic hardship. Specifically, young men confronted with enduring longer standing unemployment may be at higher risk for substance use disorders and related problems during economic crises. Targeted interventions may help to reduce risks and alleviate potential negative consequences. In addition, and on a broader scale, interventions to combat economic exclusion and to promote social participation of individuals with mental health problems are key in times of economic crisis [37,45].

Finally, it is the strong opinion of the authors that interventions are not only important during, but even more so during the aftermath of economic crisis periods. Indeed, it is to be feared that during economic revival (as currently is happening in some parts of Europe though on a very modest scale) a substantial portion of the population may continue to suffer the (social) consequences of the crisis, being left behind and unable to benefit from economic growth. For these people continuing debt and unemployment can potentially make them especially vulnerable to developing new problems. This can in turn be a further barrier to alleviating existing mental health and substance use problems. These people are at risk of becoming a forgotten group, when the wave of attention for the effects of the economic crisis has waned (e.g., dramatic reduction of publication on the topic). So we, as professionals in mental health and substance use disorders, have an obligation to keep focused and continue to raise awareness, especially in the periods of economic recovery following any economic crisis.

ACKNOWLEDGMENTS

No funding was used for this study.

AUTHOR CONTRIBUTIONS

The first author, Geert Dom, did the primary literature search. Geert Dom, Jerzy Samochowiec, Sara Evans-Lacko, Kristian Wahlbeck, Guido van Hal, and David McDaid contributed equally in controlling the literature search, critically analyzing the findings and discussing the results.

CONFLICTS OF INTEREST

The authors declare no conflict of interest.

REFERENCES

1. Quaglio G., Karapiperis T., van Woensel L., Arnold E., McDaid D. Austerity and health in Europe. Health Policy. 2013;113:13–19.
2. Karanikolos M., Mladovsky P., Cylus J., Thomson S., Basu S., Stuckler D., Mackenbach J.P., McKee M. Financial crisis, austerity, and health in Europe. Lancet. 2013;381:1323–1331.
3. De Goeij M.C., Suhrcke M., Toffolutti V., van de Mheen D., Schoenmakers T.M., Kunst A.E. How economic crises affect alcohol consumption and alcohol-related health problems: A realist systematic review. Soc. Sci. Med. 2015;131:131–146.
4. Fountoulakis K.N., Kawohl W., Theodorakis P.N., Kerkhof A.J., Navickas A., Hoschl C., Lecic-Tosevski D., Sorel E., Rancans E., Palova E., et al. Relationship of suicide rates to economic variables in Europe: 2000–2011. Br. J. Psychiatry. 2014;205:486–496.
5. Dalglish S.L., Melchior M., Younes N., Surkan P.J. Work characteristics and suicidal ideation in young adults in France. Soc. Psychiatry Psychiatr. Epidemiol. 2014;50:613–620.
6. Mattei G., Ferrari S., Pingani L., Rigatelli M. Short-term effects of the 2008 Great Recession on the health of the Italian population: An ecological study. Soc. Psychiatry Psychiatr. Epidemiol. 2014;49:851–858.

7. Harhay M.O., Bor J., Basu S., McKee M., Mindell J.S., Shelton N.J., Stuckler D. Differential impact of the economic recession on alcohol use among white British adults, 2004–2010. Eur. J. Public Health. 2014;24:410–415.

8. Colell E., Sanchez-Niubo A., Delclos G.L., Benavides F.G., Domingo-Salvany A. Economic crisis and changes in drug use in the Spanish economically-active population. Addiction. 2015;10:1129–1137.

9. Gili M., Roca M., Basu S., McKee M., Stuckler D. The mental health risks of economic crisis in Spain: Evidence from primary care centres, 2006 and 2010. Eur. J. Public Health. 2013;23:103–108.

10. Garcy A.M., Vagero D. The length of unemployment predicts mortality, differently in men and women, and by cause of death: A six year mortality follow-up of the Swedish 1992–1996 recession. Soc. Sci. Med. 2012;74:1911–1920.

11. Eliason M. Alcohol-related morbidity and mortality following involuntary job loss: Evidence from Swedish register data. J. Stud. Alcohol Drugs. 2014;75:35–46.

12. Herttua K., Makela P., Martikainen P. Differential trends in alcohol-related mortality: A register-based follow-up study in Finland in 1987–2003. Alcohol Alcohol. 2007;42:456–464.

13. Johansson E., Bockerman P., Prattala R., Uutela A. Alcohol-related mortality, drinking behavior, and business cycles: Are slumps really dry seasons? Eur. J. Health Econ. 2006;7:215–220.

14. Stuckler D., Basu S., Suhrcke M., Coutts A., McKee M. The public health effect of economic crises and alternative policy responses in Europe: An empirical analysis. Lancet. 2009;374:315–323.

15. Toffolutti V., Suhrcke M. Assessing the short term health impact of the Great Recession in the European Union: A cross-country panel analysis. Prev. Med. 2014;64:54–62.

16. Gallus S., Tramacere I., Pacifici R., Zuccaro P., Colombo P., Ghislandi S., La Vecchia C. Smoking in Italy 2008–2009: A rise in prevalence related to the economic crisis? Prev. Med. 2011;52:182–183.

17. Tarantilis F., Athanasakis K., Zavras D., Vozikis A., Kyriopoulos I. Estimates of price and income elasticity in Greece. Greek debt

crisis transforming cigarettes into a luxury good: An econometric approach. BMJ Open. 2015;5

18. Schoretsaniti S., Filippidis F.T., Vardavas C.I., Dimitrakaki C., Behrakis P., Connolly G.N., Tountas Y. 5-Year trends in the intention to quit smoking amidst the economic crisis and after recently implemented tobacco control measures in Greece. Addict. Behav. 2014;39:140–145.

19. Kondilis E., Giannakopoulos S., Gavana M., Ierodiakonou I., Waitzkin H., Benos A. Economic crisis, restrictive policies, and the population's health and health care: The Greek case. Am. J. Public Health. 2013;103:973–979.

20. Zuccato E., Castiglioni S., Tettamanti M., Olandese R., Bagnati R., Melis M., Fanelli R. Changes in illicit drug consumption patterns in 2009 detected by wastewater analysis. Drug Alcohol Depend. 2011;118:464–469.

21. Asgeirsdottir T.L., Corman H., Noonan K., Olafsdottir T., Reichman N.E. Was the economic crisis of 2008 good for Icelanders? Impact on health behaviors. Econ. Hum. Biol. 2014;13:1–19.

22. Ritter A., Chalmers J. The relationship between economic conditions and substance use and harm. Drug Alcohol Rev. 2011;30:1–3.

23. Mulia N., Ye Y., Zemore S.E., Greenfield T.K. Social disadvantage, stress, and alcohol use among black, Hispanic, and white Americans: Findings from the 2005 U.S. National Alcohol Survey. J. Stud. Alcohol Drugs. 2008;69:824–833.

24. Van Hal G. The true cost of the economic crisis on psychological well-being: A review. Psychol. Res. Behav. Manag. 2015;8:17–25.

25. Nandi A., Charters T.J., Strumpf E.C., Heymann J., Harper S. Economic conditions and health behaviours during the "Great Recession" J. Epidemiol. Commun. Health. 2013;67:1038–1046.

26. Olafsdottir T., Hrafnkelsson B., Asgeirsdottir T.L. The Icelandic economic collapse, smoking, and the role of labor-market changes. Eur. J. Health Econ. 2014;16:391–405.

27. Aguilar-Palacio I., Carrera-Lasfuentes P., Rabanaque M.J. Youth unemployment and economic recession in Spain: Influence on

health and lifestyles in young people (16–24 years old) Int. J. Public Health. 2015;60:427–435.

28. Bosque-Prous M., Espelt A., Sordo L., Guitart A.M., Brugal M.T., Bravo M.J. Job Loss, Unemployment and the incidence of hazardous drinking during the late 2000s recession in Europe among adults aged 50–64 Years. PLoS ONE. 2015;10

29. Popovici I., French M.T. Binge drinking and sleep problems among young adults. Drug Alcohol Depend. 2013;132:207–215.

30. Czapla M., Simon J.J., Friederich H.C., Herpertz S.C., Zimmermann P., Loeber S. Is binge drinking in young adults associated with an alcohol-specific impairment of response inhibition? Eur. Addict. Res. 2015;21:105–113.

31. Luoto R., Poikolainen K., Uutela A. Unemployment, sociodemographic background and consumption of alcohol before and during the economic recession of the 1990s in Finland. Int. J. Epidemiol. 1998;27:623–629.

32. Midanik L.T., Clark W.B. Drinking-related problems in the United States: Description and trends, 1984–1990. J. Stud. Alcohol. 1995;56:395–402.

33. Cooper B. Economic recession and mental health: An overview. Neuropsychiatry. 2011;25:113–117.

34. Stuckler D., Basu S., Suhrcke M., Coutts A., McKee M. Effects of the 2008 recession on health: A first look at European data. Lancet. 2011;378:124–125.

35. Mossakowski K.N. Is the duration of poverty and unemployment a risk factor for heavy drinking? Soc. Sci. Med. 2008;67:947–955.

36. Khan S., Murray R.P., Barnes G.E. A structural equation model of the effect of poverty and unemployment on alcohol abuse. Addict. Behav. 2002;27:405–423.

37. Evans-Lacko S., Knapp M., McCrone P., Thornicroft G., Mojtabai R. The mental health consequences of the recession: Economic hardship and employment of people with mental health problems in 27 European countries. PloS ONE. 2013;8

38. Lijffijt M., Hu K., Swann A.C. Stress modulates illness-course of substance use disorders: A translational review. Front. Psychiatry. 2014;5

39. Arkes J. Does the economy affect teenage substance use? Health Econ. 2007;16:19–36.

40. Bretteville-Jensen A.L. Illegal drug use and the economic recession—What can we learn from the existing research? Int. J. Drug Policy. 2011;22:353–359.

41. Kalousova L., Burgard S.A. Unemployment, measured and perceived decline of economic resources: Contrasting three measures of recessionary hardships and their implications for adopting negative health behaviors. Soc. Sci. Med. 2014;106:28–34.

42. Falba T., Teng H.M., Sindelar J.L., Gallo W.T. The effect of involuntary job loss on smoking intensity and relapse. Addiction. 2005;100:1330–1339.

43. Gallus S., Ghislandi S., Muttarak R. Effects of the economic crisis on smoking prevalence and number of smokers in the USA. Tob. Control. 2015;24:82–88.

44. Arkes J. How does youth cigarette use respond to weak economic periods? Implications for the current economic crisis. Subst. Use Misuse. 2012;47:375–382.

45. Wahlbeck K., McDaid D. Actions to alleviate the mental health impact of the economic crisis. World Psychiatry. 2012;11:139–145.

13

CHAPTER

Organizational Downsizing and Depressive Symptoms in the European Recession: The Experience of Workers in France, Hungary, Sweden and the United Kingdom

M. Harvey Brenner[1,2], Elena Andreeva[2], To¨ res Theorell[3], Marcel Goldberg[4,5], Hugo Westerlund[3], Constanze Leineweber[3], Linda L. Magnusson Hanson[3], Ellen Imbernon[6], Sophie Bonnaud[4,5]

[1]*Department of Behavioral and Community Health, School of Public Health, University of North Texas Health Science Center, Fort Worth, Texas, United States of America,*

[2]*FG Epidemiologie, Fakulta¨t VII, Technische Universita¨t Berlin, Berlin, Germany,*

[3]*Institute for Stress Research, Stockholm University, Stockholm, Sweden,*

[4]*Inserm, Centre for Research in Epidemiology and Population Health, U1018, Population-based Cohorts Research Platform, F-94807, Villejuif, France,*

[5]*Public Health Department, Universite´ de Versailles Saint Quentin, Villejuif, France,*

[6]*De´partement Sante´ Travail, Institut de veille sanitaire, Saint Maurice, France*

ABSTRACT

Background

Organizational downsizing has become highly common during the global recession of the late 2000s with severe repercussions on employment. We examine whether the severity of the downsizing process is associated with a greater likelihood of depressive symptoms among displaced workers, internally redeployed workers and lay-off survivors.

Methods

A cross-sectional survey involving telephone interviews was carried out in France, Hungary, Sweden and the United Kingdom. The study analyzes data from 758 workers affected by medium- and large-scale downsizing, using multiple logistic regression.

Main Results

Both unemployment and surviving layoffs were significantly associated with depressive symptoms, as compared to reemployment, but the perceived procedural justice of a socially responsible downsizing process considerably mitigated the odds of symptoms. Perception of high versus low justice was assessed along several downsizing dimensions. In the overall sample, chances to have depressive symptoms were significantly reduced if respondents perceived the process as transparent and understandable, fair and unbiased, well planned and democratic; if they trusted the employer's veracity and agreed with the necessity for downsizing. The burden of symptoms was significantly greater if the process was perceived to be chaotic. We further tested whether perceived justice differently affects the likelihood of depressive symptoms among distinct groups of workers. Findings were that the odds of symptoms largely followed the same patterns of effects across all groups of workers. Redeploying and supporting surplus employees through the career change process–rather than forcing them to become unemployed–makes a substantial difference as to whether they will suffer from depressive symptoms.

Conclusions

While depressive symptoms affect both unemployed and survivors, a just and socially responsible downsizing process is important for the emotional health of workers.

INTRODUCTION

Organizational downsizing has become highly common during the global recession of the late 2000s, with severe repercussions on employment. Between 2007 and 2009, global unemployment increased by almost 34 million [1]. In economically difficult times, layoff decisions are often driven by the logic of business survival and competitiveness. Yet even when the downturn subsides, downsizing for structural reasons will hardly disappear from the list of strategies aimed at improving the efficiency of firms [2]. It is a continuous situation of business life in which jobs are both created and destroyed. These processes are often intended as an adjustment of companies to changes in the global market. Meanwhile, growing research evidence suggests adverse effects of downsizing on workers' health [3]. Depression is one of the most common health conditions in the workforce. It is ranked as the leading cause of disability worldwide [4]. Recent studies considered a variety of pathways by which downsizing may increase depression risks. They include changes in the major category of employment status, such as job displacement (i.e., involving the unemployed and reemployed) [5]–[8], specifically, unemployment or underemployment [9]–[13] and surviving layoffs (i.e., remaining at work after organizational downsizing) [14]–[17]. Further risk factors are closely linked with the threat of such changes [18], their stressful consequences [19]–[21] and maladaptive health behaviors used to cope with the stress [14]; [22].

Virtually all research on downsizing and depression has been dominated by the focus on outcomes of the personnel reduction in the post-layoff period. The downsizing process itself has undeservedly received little attention by occupational health researchers. Published papers report descriptive and qualitative results [23]–[26]. These results indicate that workers' morale and productivity are directly affected by the way layoffs are implemented. The mismanagement of the downsizing process was perceived by workers as a major source of emotional distress and depression. Employees consistently articulated painful feelings stemming from an unfair process, poor communication of layoff plans and lack of involvement in organizational decision-making. Furthermore, the manner in which terminations are handled can apparently be more traumatic than the terminations themselves [27]. However, no attempts have yet been made to analyze these effects. It is unknown whether the subjective perception of the process differs in displaced–i.e., unemployed "victims", internally redeployed workers or "survivors" who remained at their workplace. We wish to understand which aspects of the process will be significantly associated with depressive symptoms when altered employment status is taken into account.

Employees' perception of fairness and justice at the workplace is conceptualized in the framework of organizational justice [28]–[30]. Researchers have most widely tested three dimensions of this concept. Procedural justice is fostered when decision making rules followed in organizations are fair. This implies the accuracy of information collected for making decisions, suppression of bias and representativeness of viewpoints from all affected parties [31]. Distributive justice refers to the fairness of decision outcomes and resource allocation [32]. Finally, relational justice describes equity, politeness and fairness in the interpersonal treatment of employees by supervisors [33]. Associations between justice and psychological health have been consistently documented [34]–[37]. Findings from several well-designed prospective studies suggest that depressive symptoms could represent the consequence of perceived injustice [38]–[41]. We contribute to this literature theoretically and empirically, by proposing and testing new measures of organizational justice in the context of downsizing. Specifically, perceptions of procedural justice are recognized as most important to employees during times of large-scale organizational changes [30].

The aim of the present study is to fill the gap in the knowledge concerning relationships between various aspects of the downsizing process and depressive symptoms. We investigated perceptions of affected workers along multiple dimensions: advance notification; communication of impending redundancies; clarity, fairness and transparency of the downsizing process; the degree to which the downsizing is perceived as well planned or chaotic; extent of democracy in decision-making and opportunity to influence the process; impact of personal factors on dismissals; trust in the truthfulness of the employer; and agreement with the necessity of downsizing. In the situation of workers threatened by involuntary unemployment, we studied perceived support in terms of financial compensation, retraining or any other help by employers for smoothing the transition to new employment. These dimensions have been widely discussed in theoretical and policy-oriented papers focused on the idea of responsible restructuring [27]; [42]–[45]. While this idea is in keeping with the organizational justice approach, it is largely concerned with the policies and practices of organizational change, and with planning and managing their strategic aspects in a humane and resource-efficient manner. This focus recognizes that people are the source of innovation and renewal; workers should be treated as assets to be developed rather than costs to be eliminated. Therefore, redundancies should be used by firms as a last resort, when a wide range of measures fail to produce expected financial viability [42]. Yet if layoffs are unavoidable, downsizing in a socially responsible way foresees strategies to mitigate the negative impact on affected workers. The pre-layoff support in the form of retraining programs and early warning has been identified as crucial for the post-layoff adjustment of "victims" [43];[44]. The optimal management of downsizing should involve workers in the process of organizational change, open and honest communication, clear and fair criteria for terminations and assistance to departing employees [43]; [45]. In sum, responsible restructuring should be aimed at implementing the procedural, relational and distributive aspects of organizational justice. The main research hypothesis of our epidemiological study was formulated in advance. We assumed that the downsizing process carried out in a socially responsible way will mitigate the likelihood of depressive symptoms in affected workers.

METHODS

Ethics Statement

Our cross-sectional survey was carried out in four European countries: France, Hungary, Sweden, and United Kingdom. The national parts of the study have been approved by the respective research ethics committees: in Hungary, the approval has been received from the Scientific Research Ethics Committee of the Medical Research Council, Budapest (Ref.no: TUKEB 187/2008), in Sweden, the Restructuring Survey has been approved by the Regional Research Ethics Committee, Stockholm (Ref.no: 2009/337-32) and London (Kingston University, approval from January 22, 2010). The French part of the survey received approval from the "Comité Consultatif sur le Traitement de l'Information en matière de Recherches dans le domaine de la Santé (CCTIRS)" of the Ministry of Research (March 12, 2009) and the legal authorization of the "Commission Nationale de l'Informatique et des Libertés (CNIL)" on April 23, 2009. All participants provided their written informed consent. They received an invitation letter with information about the study.

Study Sample

The Restructuring Survey was designed to address some of the major gaps in research on organizational practices for mitigating the negative impact of downsizing on workers' health. The study settings were chosen according to specified criteria relevant to downsizing and its aftermath for workers. Specifically, there are different models of social protection, health systems and flexibility of labor markets. The conditions shaped by these models are likely to affect flexibility and security of transitions between jobs in cases of downsizing. Hungary, Sweden, France and the UK represent, respectively, the Eastern European, Nordic, Mediterranean-Continental and Anglo-Saxon models. Included in each country were respondents who worked in small, medium and large organizations with 10 or more employees. Data were collected in telephone interviews between April 2009 and mid-May 2011 from two groups of respondents: (1) employees who have never experienced downsizing and (2) workers from recently downsized companies. A downsizing event was considered to be recent if it happened in the last two years preceding the interview. We focused only on larger scale events with cuts in at least 10% of the workforce, because they are less individually selective: general economic requirements are responsible for layoffs, rather than personal characteristics of workers [46]. The downsized group consisted of displaced workers still unemployed or already reemployed at interview, layoff survivors and internally redeployed employees in occupational transitions. We excluded farmers, the self-employed, workers in micro-businesses and those notified of downsizing who retired, quit or found another job before becoming unemployed. Additionally excluded were non-working persons with no experience of downsizing, as well as people who sustained a non-recent or small-scale downsizing.

Given the strict inclusion criteria, we used a targeted selection of respondents from a variety of sources. The Hungarian sample was drawn from the Hungarostudy 2006, a follow-up of the nationwide representative survey Hungarostudy 2002 [47]; [48]. In order to achieve a sufficient number of interviews, the Hungarian research team derived an additional random sample from the public telephone book. Two successive waves of the nationally representative Swedish Longitudinal Occupational Survey of Health [49]–[52], 2008 and 2010, included data on downsizing and thus served as a basis for the selection of the Restructuring Survey participants. In France, employed respondents were recruited through occupational physicians in the regions of Franche-Comté and Lyon and the health screening centers located in Brittany and South-West regions. These centers and physicians provide regular free health screenings for salaried employees. The recruitment of unemployed persons was done through the public employment agencies in the suburbs of Paris and Lyon, as well as by running an advertisement in a free public newspaper. This newspaper with a large circulation nationwide announces vacancies for job seekers. In the UK, the study participants were enrolled at the BT, a large international telecommunications company. At the time of our survey, BT employed some 128 000 full time workers including contractors in over 170 countries. In 2009, the company reported massive losses and restructured the work process in large parts of the business with total expected job cuts up to 30 000 within two years [53].

BT sought to retain its permanent workforce through redeployment and retraining in a "transition center". The purpose of the transition center is to support the surplus employees through the career change process. The redeployed workers consider a number of options, such as secondment (i.e., temporary assignment) outside BT, or even leaving the company, or finding a new role in BT but doing something totally different from what they have done before. According to the statistics provided by the BT Group health adviser, 86% of cases are resolved in the transition center within 6 months, and 96% of redeployed workers stay in BT. The advantage of using the BT sample was that we could study the health effects of redeployment which, to our knowledge, have not yet been analyzed in the civilian labor force. Employees who have never experienced downsizing were enrolled in the survey from units and business lines not affected by job cuts. The group exposed to downsizing consisted of persons redeployed in the transition center, reemployed workers and the downsizing survivors. The employer had no knowledge of who decided to participate in the survey.

In each country, we planned to include a minimum of 292 participants. This sample size was calculated under the following assumptions: the downsized group will be compared with employees who have never experienced downsizing, and the expected prevalence of symptoms will be 25% and 10%, respectively, in order to obtain results with statistical significance of alpha 0.05 (two-sided) and power 0.90. This sample size was adjusted upward up to a maximum of 400 participants in order to account for potential nonresponse or exclusion. We used prevalence data for major health outcomes from occupational health studies as a guide for these assumptions [54]; [55].

Telephone interviews were carried out with preselected persons whose telephone numbers were available. All participants were informed about the aim, scope and duration of the survey and the strict confidentiality in handling personal data. Figure 1 shows how the sample of the Restructuring Survey was created. The participation rates vary by country with nearly 90% for Sweden, 82% for the UK, 62% for France and 19% for Hungary. These rates take into account all refusals and break-offs by respondents, as well as non-interviews due to incorrect telephone numbers, respondents' never being available or being unavailable during the fieldwork. The lower response rate in the Hungarian sample is caused by the high rate of refusals: nearly 64% of preselected persons declined participation. Interviewers reported a high level of distrust in this population, probably as a result of the socioeconomic situation during the recession of the late 2000s [56]. In all countries, we collected 1456 usable surveys from 681 employees in the non-downsized group and 775 workers exposed to downsizing.

In this report, we analyze data including 758 workers exposed to downsizing with complete responses on all depressive symptoms. Table 1 shows socio-demographic characteristics of these workers and their health habits.

Questionnaire and Measures

The study questionnaire was designed for use in telephone interviews with a maximum length of 20 minutes. The interview contained two sections: the basic questionnaire which collected demographic and health-related information and the part on downsizing for displaced workers, layoff survivors and redeployed employees.

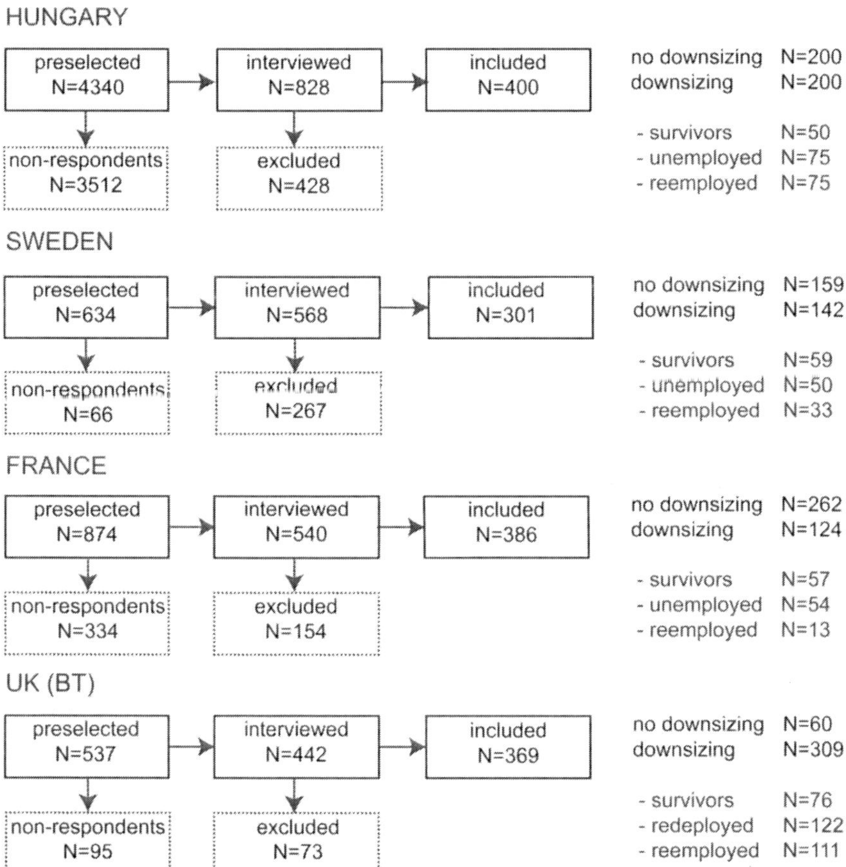

Figure 1. Flow chart showing selection and participation in Restructuring Survey.

Depressive Symptoms

Health-related questions included a brief subscale of depressive symptoms from the Hopkins Symptom Checklist (SCL-90). This subscale has been validated and found to have comparable psychometric properties to longer epidemiological self-report instruments, such as Center for Epidemiological Studies Depression scale (CES-D), but to have superior unidimensionality and consequently more suitable as a

Table 1. Characteristics of study participants who experienced downsizing, data are mean (SD) and number (%).

Characteristic	Description	Respondents (N = 758)
Sex	men	452 (59.6%)
	women	306 (40.4%)
Age	years: mean ± SD	46 ± 9.8
Education	university	309 (40.8%)
	any lower education	449 (59.2%)
Country	Hungary	187 (24.7%)
	Sweden	141 (18.6%)
	France	122 (16.1%)
	UK	308 (40.6%)
Employment status	reemployed	225 (29.7%)
	redeployed	121 (16.0%)
	survivor	239 (31.5%)
	unemployed	173 (22.8%)
Smoking	daily or occasional smoker	163 (21.5)
	non-smoker	595 (78.5%)
Frequency of alcohol drinking	"never" (abstainer)	91 (12.0%)
	"once a month or less"	161 (21.2%)
	"2–4 times a month"	208 (27.4%)
	"2–3 times a week"	200 (26.4%)
	"4 times a week or more"	96 (12.7%)
	"don't know" (non-abstainer)	2 (0.3%)
Sum score for depressive symptoms	mean ± SD	7 ± 5.9

Abbreviations: N (%), number and percent; mean (SD), mean value and standard deviation.

dimensional measure of depression severity [57]. It estimates one-week prevalence and consists of six items covering the core symptoms of depression: melancholic mood ("feeling blue"), anhedonia ("feeling no interest in things"), reduced energy and increased fatigability ("feeling lethargy and lack of energy"), excessive worries ("worrying too much"), self-accusation ("blaming yourself for things") and feeling that "everything is an effort" [58]. Respondents rated how much they have been troubled by each symptom on a five-point Likert scale from "not at all" to "very much". We computed a sum score ranging from 0 to 24. For the present analysis, the responses were dichotomously categorized (0="low level of depressive symptoms", 1="high level of depressive symptoms") based on the sum score indicating depression severity. Respondents were regarded to have high level of depressive symptoms if their score exceeded the mean plus the standard deviation of the total Restructuring Survey sample. The clinical significance of high-level symptoms was not further assessed in our respondents. However, the subscale used here was examined before in the Swedish population with reference to the DSM-IV diagnosis of major depression. High-level symptoms (score 17 and above) were predictive of the subsequent antidepressant use and hospitalizations with a depressive episode [57].

Aspects of the Downsizing Process

The questionnaire section on downsizing was constructed on the basis of relevant scientific literature [27]; [42]; [43]. Downsizing was defined as a process whereby an organization reduces its personnel [46]. In this report, we examined 17 aspects of this process for their potential to affect the likelihood of high-level depressive symptoms. These aspects are listed in Table 2. Unless noted otherwise, workers reported their responses in yes-or-no format. The responses were coded as 1=yes and 0=no. First, workers were asked whether they would describe the process of downsizing to be transparent and understandable, fair and unbiased, chaotic or disorganized, well planned and democratic. For this, respondents were requested to think about how decisions were made, no matter if they liked the outcome or not. Second, participants indicated whether they agree that it was necessary to downsize the organization. Third, workers were asked about their influence on downsizing "Did you feel that you could influence how the downsizing was carried out?" and early warning about downsizing "Did your employer give you notification in advance regarding the plans for downsizing?".

Table 2. Responses for experienced downsizing and related conditions, data are number (%).

Aspects of the downsizing process	yes	no	don't know, refuse	not applicable
Downsizing transparent and understandable	351 (46%)	387 (51%)	20 (<3%)	
Downsizing fair and unbiased	299 (39%)	403 (53%)	56 (7%)	
Downsizing chaotic/disorganized	381 (50%)	353 (47%)	24 (3%)	
Downsizing well planned	298 (39%)	416 (55%)	44 (6%)	
Downsizing democratic	158 (21%)	325 (43%)	43 (6%)	232 (31%)
Agreement with downsizing necessity	359 (47%)	335 (44%)	64 (8%)	
Employee influence on downsizing	81 (11%)	667 (88%)	10 (1%)	
Early warning about downsizing	507 (67%)	249 (33%)	2 (<0.3%)	
Trust in the veracity of employer's statements	470 (62%)	222 (29%)	66 (9%)	
Influence of personal factors on dismissals	327 (43%)	333 (44%)	98 (13%)	
Manager responsible for staff	188 (25%)	569 (75%)	1 (<0.2%)	
Forced to lay-off personnel	84 (11%)	103 (14%)	1 (<0.2%)	570 (75%)
Financial compensation	149 (20%)	142 (19%)	58 (7%)	409 (54%)
Retraining	194 (26%)	355 (47%)	38 (5%)	171 (22%)
Other help	256 (34%)	293 (39%)	38 (5%)	171 (22%)
Decreased income and benefits after downsizing	220 (29%)	423 (56%)	115 (15%)	
Large-scale downsizing (≥20% laid off)	273 (36%)	229 (30%)	24 (3%)	232 (31%)

Trust in the veracity of the employer's statements was assessed by the question "Did you think the main reason for downsizing stated by the employer was the true motive?" Interviewees were also queried about the impact of personal factors on dismissals: "Did personal factors influence which employees were dismissed?" The involvement of respondents in laying-off workers was studied in managers responsible for staff. All participants were asked "Were you a manager responsible for staff?" If they answered in the affirmative, they were guided to the question "Were you yourself forced to lay off personnel?" In workers threatened by redundancy, we evaluated support in terms of financial compensation, retraining or any other help by their employers: "Was financial compensation offered in the case of your losing your job?", "Were you offered re-training to increase your likelihood of getting a new job?", "Did you receive any other type of help by your company to prepare yourself to find new work?".

We also included a measure of income loss for all participants who experienced downsizing: "Is your current level of income and benefits: equal to or higher than before the downsizing? ... Lower than before the downsizing? ... Substantially lower than before the downsizing?" We coded this variable dichotomously indicating 1 for those with decreased income and benefits and 0 for others. Finally, we explored the impact of the downsizing scale: "How large a proportion of the employees were made redundant during downsizing?" The scale included the options "less than 10%", "between 10% and 20%" and "20% or more." In workers from recently downsized companies with cuts in at least 10% of the personnel, the variable was coded as 1 for a large-scale downsizing exceeding 20% of staff and 0 for the moderate extent of 10%–20%.

Employment Status at Interview

We addressed the possibility that the individual outcome of downsizing – employment status at interview – can affect both the perception of the downsizing process and the likelihood of depressive symptoms. Participants from recently downsized companies were asked how they were affected by the downsizing. Workers were classified as displaced if they "were laid off and became unemployed". This group was further subdivided into those still unemployed or already reemployed at interview, based on yes-or-no responses to the question "Have you got a new job yet?". The group of layoff survivors consists of workers who stayed in employment in their downsized organizations. Of 239 survivors, 177 (74%) kept their workplaces despite having been notified of possible layoff. In the BT sample, redeployed workers stated that they are "currently in the transition center". Those who "have been in the transition center for any time during the last two years" but "now have a new job or role which is not a temporary assignment" were classified as reemployed. Employment status is coded as 1=reemployed (reference group), 2=redeployed at BT transition center, 3=layoff survivor and 4=unemployed at interview. Appendices S1 and S2 show the distribution of responses by employment status for all variables included in the analyses.

Covariates

Age (in years), gender, education, smoking, alcohol consumption and country-specific effects were examined as potential covariates. Self-reported education included two categories: "university or equivalent degree" versus "any lower education". For smoking, the dichotomous variable combined daily and occasional smokers versus current nonsmokers. Alcohol consumption was assessed by the question "How often do you drink alcohol?" with the response alternatives coded as 1="never" (abstainers, reference group), 2="once a month or less", 3="2–4 times a month", 4="2–3 times a week", 5="4 times a week or more". Four country-specific indicator variables were used to control for unobservable effects, particularly due to national differences in social protection, health systems and flexibility of labor markets. These variables were coded 1 or 0 to denote the country of respondents' residence. For example, the indicator variable for France equated to 1 in French respondents and 0 in participants from other countries.

Data Availability

Group level data, statistical code and full details of the explanatory analyses are available from the study research coordinator (-ed.nilreb ut@aveerdna.anele) to all interested researchers upon request, on condition that the European Commission provides its written authorization prior to any distribution of this information. Individual level data of study participants are not available for public data deposition or sharing: the research study is compliant with the ethics and legislation of the data protection in the United Kingdom, France, Hungary and Sweden, according to which necessary arrangements should be met to ensure confidentiality of such data.

Statistical Analysis

We analyze four sets of questions with multiple logistic regression. First, we examine the relationships between the employment status at interview and depressive symptoms. The rationale for this analysis is based on the previous findings of increased risks of depressive symptoms in unemployed workers [9]–[13] and layoff survivors [14]–[17]. Our study extends the prior literature by including these groups from several countries and adding a new group of internally redeployed civilian workers, which to our knowledge has never been investigated before. Reemployed respondents represent the reference category, since we assumed their status to be most secure and stable in the downsized group, at least in the short term.

Second, we explore the relationships between the employment status at interview and the aspects of the downsizing process. The latter are treated as dependent variables, while employment status is used as a key explanatory variable. We try to shed light on the peculiarities of downsizing in distinct groups of workers. The aim is to examine whether the groups of workers differ with respect to (a) extent of downsizing or income losses, (b) early warning and degree of support in terms of financial compensation, retraining or any other help, and (c) perceptions of the process. Perceptions might vary across groups depending on how closely the individuals were personally affected by downsizing. However, the lack of significant impact of employment status would suggest that perceptions are uniform and unrelated to the current (in)security of employment.

The first two sets of analyses are shown in Table 3. The results are simultaneously adjusted for age, gender, education, smoking, frequency of alcohol drinking and country-specific effects. The measures are modeled as dichotomous variables, except for age (in years), the ordinal frequency of drinking (reference group abstainers) and the categorical "employment status", which was included in all models as a set of virtual indicator variables.

Table 3. Odds ratios and 95% confidence intervals for the associations between employment status, depressive symptoms and dimensions of the downsizing process.

referent: reemployed (OR = 1)		redeployed		survivors		unemployed	
Dependent variables	**N**	**OR (95% CI)**	**p val.**	**OR (95% CI)**	**p val.**	**OR (95% CI)**	**p val.**
Depressive symptoms	756	1.13 (0.63 to 2.02)	0.684	2.04 (1.26 to 3.31)	0.004	2.85 (1.61 to 5.06)	<0.001
Downsizing transparent, understandable	736	0.75 (0.46 to 1.23)	0.260	1.02 (0.69 to 1.52)	0.906	0.73 (0.46 to 1.15)	0.176
Downsizing fair and unbiased	700	1.06 (0.64 to 1.77)	0.821	1.42 (0.95 to 2.12)	0.086	0.65 (0.40 to 1.06)	0.083
Downsizing chaotic/disorganized	732	1.01 (0.61 to 1.67)	0.961	1.05 (0.71 to 1.56)	0.796	1.12 (0.70 to 1.77)	0.637
Downsizing well planned	712	1.29 (0.77 to 2.16)	0.339	1.01 (0.67 to 1.52)	0.964	1.24 (0.77 to 2.00)	0.376
Downsizing democratic	483	n.a.	n.a.	1.28 (0.70 to 2.33)	0.421	0.89 (0.49 to 1.61)	0.698
Agreement with downsizing necessity	693	1.16 (0.68 to 1.97)	0.581	1.04 (0.69 to 1.58)	0.839	0.52 (0.32 to 0.86)	0.011
Employee influence on downsizing	746	0.93 (0.37 to 2.29)	0.869	1.96 (1.00 to 3.83)	0.050	1.78 (0.80 to 3.99)	0.160
Early warning about downsizing	754	0.89 (0.53 to 1.50)	0.659	2.46 (1.59 to 3.80)	<0.001	1.39 (0.87 to 2.23)	0.169
Trust in the employer's veracity	690	1.05 (0.61 to 1.82)	0.853	1.27 (0.82 to 1.99)	0.289	0.84 (0.50 to 1.41)	0.516
Influence of personal factors	658	0.93 (0.54 to 1.60)	0.805	0.87 (0.58 to 1.31)	0.515	1.27 (0.79 to 2.06)	0.326
Manager responsible for staff	755	0.93 (0.54 to 1.62)	0.809	1.02 (0.64 to 1.61)	0.940	1.30 (0.75 to 2.26)	0.342
Forced to lay-off personnel	187	0.90 (0.35 to 2.35)	0.835	1.08 (0.48 to 2.45)	0.852	2.35 (0.87 to 6.37)	0.094
Financial compensation	291	n.a.	n.a.	0.66 (0.17 to 2.52)	0.542	1.08 (0.65 to 1.82)	0.772
Retraining	547	0.79 (0.47 to 1.33)	0.372	1.54 (0.60 to 3.99)	0.372	1.16 (0.58 to 2.40)	0.647
Other help	547	1.14 (0.64 to 2.02)	0.655	0.25 (0.10 to 0.62)	0.003	0.87 (0.49 to 1.53)	0.622
Decreased income and benefits	641	1.27 (0.73 to 2.22)	0.404	0.34 (0.21 to 0.55)	<0.001	4.18 (1.99 to 8.77)	<0.001
Large-scale downsizing	144	n.a.	n.a.	0.41 (0.23 to 0.70)	0.001	0.92 (0.55 to 1.55)	0.758

Results from multiple logistic regression analysis.
Variables included in the equations but not shown in the table were age (in years), sex, education, smoking, frequency of alcohol drinking (ordinal variable, referent: abstainer, OR = 1) and country-specific effects.
Abbreviations. N, number of respondents; OR, odds ratio; 95% CI, 95% confidence interval; p val., p value; n.a., not appropriate.

In the third set of analyses, aspects of the downsizing process are treated as key "predictors". We estimate whether the downsizing process, when carried out in a socially responsible way, mitigates the likelihood of high-level depressive symptoms in affected workers. In Model 1 of Table 4, the adjustment is limited to country-specific effects. Model 2 of Table 4 additionally includes employment status, demographic (age, sex and education) and health-related variables (smoking, frequency of alcohol drinking). Model 3 is further adjusted for decreased income and benefits.

Fourth, to examine whether the effects of the downsizing process differently affect the likelihood of high-level symptoms among distinct groups of workers, we re-fitted Models 2 and 3 with interaction terms as Models 2a and 3a, respectively. A summary of these analyses is shown in Appendix S3. The interaction terms were generated between the dichotomously coded dimensions of the downsizing process and employment status (reference group reemployed). We computed odds ratios (ORs) for the impact of downsizing by employment status as point estimates for linear combinations of coefficients after regressions with interaction terms [59];[60]. For each employment status, the odds ratios compare workers who responded to all questions on the dimensions of the downsizing process with "no" (reference, OR=1) with the persons who answered the respective questions in the affirmative.

Table 4. Odds ratios and 95% confidence intervals for the associations between the dimensions of the downsizing process and depressive symptoms.

Downsizing process	Model 1			Model 2			Model 3		
referent: no (OR = 1)	**N**	**OR (95% CI)**	**p value**	**N**	**OR (95% CI)**	**p value**	**N**	**OR (95% CI)**	**p value**
Downsizing transparent	738	0.60 (0.42 to 0.86)	0.005	736	0.61 (0.42 to 0.88)	0.008	626	0.63 (0.42 to 0.96)	0.026
Downsizing fair and unbiased	702	0.41 (0.28 to 0.60)	<0.001	700	0.40 (0.27 to 0.60)	<0.001	599	0.42 (0.27 to 0.65)	<0.001
Downsizing chaotic	734	2.53 (1.74 to 3.67)	<0.001	732	2.53 (1.73 to 3.69)	<0.001	625	2.79 (1.81 to 4.30)	<0.001
Downsizing well planned	714	0.47 (0.32 to 0.69)	<0.001	712	0.45 (0.30 to 0.67)	<0.001	608	0.40 (0.25 to 0.64)	<0.001
Downsizing democratic	483	0.48 (0.29 to 0.82)	0.006	483	0.50 (0.29 to 0.85)	0.010	380	0.60 (0.33 to 1.08)	0.088
Agreement with downsizing	694	0.51 (0.35 to 0.75)	0.001	693	0.53 (0.36 to 0.79)	0.002	590	0.55 (0.36 to 0.85)	0.007
Employee influence	748	0.78 (0.43 to 1.43)	0.426	746	0.75 (0.41 to 1.39)	0.366	632	0.85 (0.45 to 1.61)	0.617
Early warning	756	0.82 (0.57 to 1.17)	0.274	754	0.76 (0.52 to 1.10)	0.147	641	0.54 (0.36 to 0.82)	0.004
Trust in the employer's veracity	692	0.49 (0.34 to 0.72)	<0.001	690	0.48 (0.33 to 0.71)	<0.001	589	0.42 (0.27 to 0.65)	<0.001
Influence of personal factors	660	1.50 (1.04 to 2.18)	0.031	658	1.49 (1.02 to 2.17)	0.040	560	1.42 (0.94 to 2.16)	0.099
Manager responsible for staff	757	0.90 (0.60 to 1.35)	0.612	755	0.88 (0.58 to 1.33)	0.543	641	0.89 (0.56 to 1.40)	0.607
Forced to lay-off personnel	187	1.06 (0.52 to 2.16)	0.864	187	1.08 (0.50 to 2.31)	0.843	160	1.47 (0.60 to 3.56)	0.400
Financial compensation	291	0.69 (0.39 to 1.21)	0.196	291	0.60 (0.32 to 1.12)	0.106	183	0.23 (0.08 to 0.64)	0.005
Retraining	549	0.89 (0.55 to 1.44)	0.641	547	0.88 (0.54 to 1.43)	0.595	439	0.80 (0.47 to 1.37)	0.420
Other help	549	0.87 (0.54 to 1.38)	0.545	547	0.91 (0.56 to 1.47)	0.690	437	0.73 (0.41 to 1.28)	0.268
Decreased income/benefits	643	1.40 (0.93 to 2.11)	0.109	641	1.74 (1.12 to 2.71)	0.014		n.a.	n.a.
Large-scale downsizing	502	0.92 (0.60 to 1.42)	0.718	502	0.95 (0.61 to 1.48)	0.806	389	0.86 (0.50 to 1.48)	0.394

Results from multiple logistic regression analysis (dependent variable: depressive symptoms).
Variables included in the equations but not shown in the table were:
Model 1: country-specific effects.
Model 2 = Model 1 plus age (in years), sex, education, smoking, frequency of alcohol drinking (ordinal variable, referent: abstainer, OR = 1) and employment status (referent: reemployed, OR = 1).
Model 3 = Model 2 plus decreased income and benefits (actual responses).
Abbreviations: N, number of respondents; OR, odds ratio; 95% CI, 95% confidence interval; n.a., not appropriate.

We used the Wald test to examine whether the interaction terms have a significant contribution in models in addition to the main effects of employment status and the downsizing process [61]. The Wald test explores whether all coefficients of the interaction terms are jointly zero, respectively, OR=1. For the test statistics, a value of $p<0.05$ indicates that the interaction terms are jointly significant, consistent with the hypothesis that the impact of the downsizing process on depressive symptoms differs by employment status.

For all analyses, we used Stata/SE 11.2 for Windows. Results are presented in terms of odds ratios (ORs) with 95% confidence intervals (95% CI).

RESULTS

Our descriptive data in Table 2 show that workers have frequently perceived downsizing as a painful process. Less than half of them felt that it was transparent, understandable, fair, unbiased and well planned. Half of the respondents believed that the process was chaotic. The question about democratic downsizing was omitted in the subsample from the BT transition center due to sensitivities within the business and specific conditions of restructuring in the company: these workers were not involved in the decision making about balancing resources across the business. In other subsamples, more than two-thirds indicated undemocratic downsizing (325 of 483 persons).

Downsizing was experienced by many respondents as an "out of control" process. The vast majority of participants felt they had no influence on how it was carried out. A substantial proportion (44%) disagreed that it was necessary to downsize their organizations. Nearly the same percentage of workers felt that personal factors influenced which employees were dismissed or redeployed. More than one-quarter doubted the veracity of employer's statements about the main reason for downsizing; an additional 9% were uncertain that their employers revealed their true motives.

Very frequently, workers perceived insufficient support from their employers prior to downsizing. One-third of respondents stated no early warning. Only a minority of Hungarian, French and Swedish participants received retraining or any other help. Such programs were, however, offered to the majority of UK employees in occupational transitions. Nearly 41% of the displaced workers indicated no financial compensation. Many workers experienced decreased income and benefits after the downsizing.

Large-scale downsizing was very common. Massive cuts of ≥20% of the personnel were reported by more than a half of the respondents who were aware of the scale of downsizing in their companies. A question about the proportion of redundancies was omitted in the subsample from the BT transition center due to sensitivities within the organization and a policy of "no compulsory redundancy".

Depressive Symptoms, Peculiarities Of Downsizing And Perception Of The Downsizing Process By Employment Status

Table 3 shows associations between the employment status and depressive symptoms. It also presents associations between the employment status and the aspects of the downsizing process. Elevated odds of suffering from a high level of depressive symptoms were observed in persons unemployed at interview ($OR=2.85$, $p<0.001$) and in layoff survivors ($OR=2.04$, $p=0.004$), as compared to the reemployed group. The BT workers in occupational transitions did not differ from employees with a more stable status with respect to their odds of high-level symptoms.

The results concerning the extent of downsizing and income losses suggest that layoff survivors were less likely to work in organizations with massive job cuts. This is indicated by circa 60% lower odds for the large-scale downsizing in survivors versus reemployed (OR=0.41, p=0.001). Remaining in the workplace resulted in lower chances to experience income losses (OR=0.34, p<0.001). In contrast, unemployment was strongly associated with decreased income and benefits (OR=4.18, p<0.001).

The group of layoff survivors had a significantly greater probability of early warning (OR=2.46, p<0.001), but employers were less likely to support survivors with "any other help" for finding a new job (OR=0.25, p=0.003). For support in terms of retraining, there were no statistically significant associations with employment status. Similarly, no significant differences were observed in the odds of reporting financial compensation. One group of workers – the BT redeployees in occupational transitions – did not receive financial compensation, because the employer continued paying their salaries.

Regarding perceptions of the downsizing process, employment status showed no statistically significant relationships with trust in the employer's veracity or influence of personal factors. Furthermore, employment status was not associated with the likelihood of perceiving downsizing as transparent and understandable, chaotic or disorganized, well planned and democratic. However, survivors were more likely to experience the process as fair and unbiased (OR=1.42, p=0.086), while this association was reversed in the unemployed (OR=0.65, p=0.083); the relationship was almost significant in both groups. Unemployed persons were significantly less likely to agree with the necessity of downsizing in their organizations (OR=0.52, p=0.011), as compared to reemployed workers. Layoff survivors were more likely than reemployed to feel that they could influence how the downsizing was carried out; the association was nearly significant (OR=1.96, p=0.050).

Downsizing Process And Perceived Burden Of Depressive Symptoms

Table 4 presents associations between the aspects of the downsizing process and depressive symptoms. After adjustment for country-specific effects, the perception of process as transparent and understandable, fair and unbiased, well planned and democratic was strongly associated with a lower likelihood of depressive symptoms (Model 1). These associations remained significant after additional adjustment for employment status, demographic and health-related variables (Model 2). Odds ratios for reporting high-level depressive symptoms vary in this model from 0.4 for the process perceived as fair and unbiased ($p<0.001$) to 0.61 for downsizing transparent and understandable ($p=0.008$). Workers who perceived downsizing as chaotic had a circa 2.5-fold increase in odds of depressive symptoms ($p<0.001$).

If workers agreed that it was necessary to downsize their organizations, they had a significantly lower probability of depressive symptoms. In these workers, the odds were reduced approximately twofold ($p=0.002$). An even larger reduction was observed for trust in the employer's veracity ($p<0.001$). Inversely, the belief of our respondents that personal factors influenced which employees were dismissed or redeployed was strongly associated with a roughly 1.5-fold greater likelihood to score poorly on the scale of depressive symptoms ($p=0.040$).

Diminished income and benefits were significantly related to depressive symptoms ($OR=1.74$, $p=0.014$). However, we encountered a problem of selective item-nonresponse: unemployed participants from Hungary and Sweden had a strong tendency to withhold information about relative changes in their income and benefit levels, despite the interviewers' assurances of confidentiality. We have therefore checked whether the revealed association is due to limitations in our data; we performed a sensitivity analysis, based on the assumption of decreased income and benefits in the unemployed who failed to provide answers to this question. The results were only marginally affected, with a slight increase in the odds ratio for depressive symptoms ($OR=1.77$, $p=0.010$).

Displaced workers who were offered financial compensation were less likely to report depressive symptoms. This relationship, however, was statistically non-significant. Small and also insignificant reduction in odds was revealed in respondents who could influence how the downsizing was managed and in those who received a forewarning regarding the employer's plans for downsizing. We observed no effects of significant magnitude for retraining, other help, managerial position, large-scale downsizing and personal involvement of respondents in laying-off workers.

Estimators were only slightly affected in terms of statistical significance by additional adjustment for decreased income and benefits (Model 3). The associations were somewhat weakened for democratic process ($OR=0.60$, $p=0.088$) and influence of personal factors ($OR=1.42$, p=0.099) but ameliorated for early warning (OR=0.54, p=0.004) and financial compensation (OR=0.23, p=0.005). No considerable changes were observed for other variables. The introduction of decreased income and benefits in the model led to a large reduction in the size of our analytic sample due to selective item-nonresponse. We therefore conducted a sensitivity analysis based on the assumption of income loss in all unemployed (not shown). This reversed the majority of changes observed after adjustment for income loss based on actual responses, except for the influence of personal factors, which remained non-significant (OR=1.42, p=0.069).

We performed further analyses to test possible interaction effects on depressive symptoms (Appendix S3). The odds ratios in Model 2a indicate some variation in the likelihood of depressive symptoms by employment status depending on the effects of the downsizing process. However, the Wald test shows that the interaction terms are jointly significant only for the early warning (p=0.013). Early warning appears to decrease the probability of depressive symptoms in the reemployed (OR=0.68, p=0.293), redeployed (OR=0.43, p=0.053) and layoff survivors (OR=0.46, p=0.031), yet the association was reversed in the unemployed respondents (OR=2.13, p=0.053). When the results are further adjusted for decreased income and benefits based on the actual responses (Model 3a), there is no evidence of interactions for either dimension of the downsizing process with the employment status. The sensitivity analysis (not shown) assuming income losses in all unemployed revealed jointly significant coefficients of the interaction terms for early warning (p=0.017 for the Wald test statistics) and elevated nearly significant odds of depressive symptoms in warned unemployed (OR=2.14, p=0.053). These results suggest no protective impact of early warning in the unemployed group. For the other dimensions of the downsizing process, odds of depressive symptoms followed the same patterns of effects across employment groups. Thus, odds were reduced if the process was perceived as transparent and understandable, fair and unbiased (significant in survivors and unemployed), well planned (significant in redeployed and survivors) and democratic (mostly significant in unemployed). In contrast, the likelihood of symptoms was elevated in relation to perception of a chaotic process, with the largest significant increase in odds for redeployed and surviving workers. Further comparisons within each status group suggest that our respondents were less likely to suffer from depressive symptoms if they agreed with downsizing necessity. These results were significant in survivors and unemployed. Likewise, trust in the employer's veracity mitigated odds of symptoms, statistically significant in survivors. Finally, influence of personal factors was linked to high-level symptoms, with significant relationships in the unemployed group.

DISCUSSION

This is apparently the first multi-country study focusing on a comprehensive assessment of various aspects of downsizing from the standpoint of employees in relation to depressive symptoms. The results indicate that downsizing was frequently perceived as a painful process: non-transparent and poorly understandable, unfair and biased, chaotic or disorganized, poorly planned and undemocratic. Workers have often believed that personal factors influenced dismissals or redeployment. Further, findings demonstrate that the subjective perception of the process is not completely determined by the downsizing outcomes in terms of employment status: the perceptions appear largely uniform and unrelated to the current (in)security of employment. When the process experience is painful, it seems to be emotionally wrenching, and the perceived burden of depressive symptoms is larger. In contrast, workers are less likely to have a higher level of symptoms if the process is experienced as positive. We found a strong association between the perceived influence of personal factors and depressive symptoms in unemployed respondents; this association failed to reach statistical significance in layoff survivors, reemployed and redeployed persons, yet the odds of symptoms followed the same pattern across all employment groups. These results were expected given the earlier findings. In the qualitative research literature, both layoff victims and survivors were outspoken about their bitter feelings if termination decisions appeared arbitrary to them and the process was harsh [27]. Our findings are consistent with the theoretical perspective of procedural justice emphasizing the idea of fair process, fair and consistent decision-making, suppression of bias, accuracy of information and representativeness of the opinions of workers affected [31]. Recent epidemiological studies revealed associations between measures of procedural (in)justice and mental health outcomes among employees, both on a longitudinal basis [36];[38]–[41];[62] and in cross-sectional analysis [35]. However, to our knowledge, this survey is the first to document these relationships with the new measures in the context of the downsizing process.

Another implication of our study is that many workers view the downsizing decisions negatively. There are attitudes of disagreement with the downsizing necessity and distrust in the truthfulness of the employer. Unemployed persons were the least likely to support the idea of downsizing necessity, while trust in the truthfulness of the employer was not significantly related to any of the employment status groups. After adjustment for the employment status and other covariates, the odds for depressive symptoms were reduced more than twofold in workers who trusted their employers regarding the truthfulness of the downsizing reasons stated. A similar effect size was observed in respondents who agreed with the downsizing necessity. These results indicate the importance of the organizational climate during downsizing for the emotional health of workers. The management literature suggests that growing job insecurity due to an accelerated pace of organizational changes can result in a crisis of trust across persons at differential levels of hierarchy in the work setting. This crisis did not exist even a generation ago [63]. Distrust is engendered by opaque decision-making processes [63]. In turn, lack of trust and reciprocity between employers and employees is regarded as a risk factor for depression [64].

Losing a job and remaining unemployed at interview was strongly associated with a reduction in income. Unexpectedly, we observed a strong tendency in unemployed respondents from Hungary and Sweden to deny any information about relative changes in their income and benefit levels. This behavior may be partially explained by the reluctance of the unemployed to raise any issues about "black" (i.e., unreported) income they may earn [56]. Possible concerns about threats to privacy in telephone surveys could also affect their willingness to respond to this question [65]. After adjustment for employment status and covariates, we observed that workers with decreased income and benefits are more likely to score poorly on the scale of depressive symptoms. These findings are well in line with those of prior research: employees with poor financial security are most at risk for poor health during downsizing [66].

Financial compensation was, logically, expected to be inversely associated with depressive symptoms. Our results indicate a tendency towards a lower burden of symptoms in workers who were offered this sort of safety net to temper the income loss inherent in redundancies, but statistical significance was not universally reached. It should however be cautioned that the small numbers of departing employees in our sample (N=291) could affect the power of these analyses. On an aggregate population basis, the effects of financial compensation may be potentially important. No sizeable associations with depressive symptoms were observed in workers with a managerial position, most specifically, in managers who laid off personnel.

Contrary to expectations based on prior research [22];[66], the scale of downsizing had no association with depressive symptoms. This could be due to a number of factors. First, downsizing scale may not be precisely measured through self-reports of workers. The ideal source would include employer data on redundancies captured at the end of the downsizing event and linked with individual-level data from employees. However, a perfect data source does not exist at present. The earlier studies used employer-based data on downsizing in Finland covering the period of national economic decline in the 1990s. The scale of that decline and the magnitude of job insecurity were almost unequalled in the post war period, yet job loss was experienced only by employees without permanent contracts [22]. Our data were collected during the global recession of late 2000s, when virtually no job was truly secure. It should also be noted that the earlier studies treated respondents involved in a minor downsizing (<8% of the workforce) as the reference group. Our focus on larger scale events resulted in a more homogeneous sample in terms of respondents being heavily affected by the organizational changes. It is also possible that the global recession was substantially responsible for enlarging the massiveness of downsizing in our sample. Finally, the pervasive nature of recent downsizing might have resulted in increased resilience of workers. There are few publications on this topic, and the hypothesis is not supported by evidence so far: workers showed no increased resilience as they experienced more layoff events [17]. In fact, both employed and non-employed population groups reported more depressed feelings during recession with large-scale layoffs, as indicated by the findings from northern Sweden [67].

In line with much of the recent research, we expected an increased burden of depressive symptoms among the unemployed victims of downsizing and layoff survivors [5]–[17]. The odds of symptoms associated with unemployment in our work is comparable with the average effect size of OR=2.0 [10] reported in the review of well designed prospective studies on job loss and distress or emotional ill health [68]–[71]. Becoming unemployed appeared to more than double the risk of depression in the analysis of panel data from Epidemiologic Catchment Area [11]. Null findings in survivors [72] or young unemployed [69] were by and large less frequent. The empirical evidence showed that layoff victims and survivors are exposed to psychosocial adversities with assumed depression-generating effects. These adversities usually include a sequence of stressful events from anticipation of downsizing, through the layoff itself, to adaptation to the altered circumstances. Publications of the last two decades identified sets of stressors typical for each employment status. The risk profile of layoff survivors is characterized by continuous job insecurity due to repeated rounds of downsizing [18], adverse changes in work characteristics [3];[19];[22] and destabilization of the psychosocial climate at work [23]–[25]. These risks can probably outweigh the advantages associated with the status of layoff survivor. In our study, those who kept their jobs had a greater burden of depressive symptoms despite being the lucky ones – somewhat more influential and better informed about the prospect of downsizing, less affected by income losses and massive job cuts. The risks of harm to unemployed layoff victims are not limited to financial strain, disruption to social role, difficulties of reemployment, loss of social support and damage to self-esteem [9];[73];[74]. Our analysis adds that unemployed victims did not feel well prepared for downsizing and job loss. This is indicated by their lack of agreement with the necessity of downsizing. In fact, poor preparedness for downsizing could result from the abrupt nature of layoff events or from insufficient pre-layoff support.

Our results indicate that the strategy of keeping and supporting surplus employees through the career change process – rather than forcing them to become unemployed – makes a substantial difference as to whether they will suffer from a high level of depressive symptoms. In the case of redeployed BT workers, we found no significant increase in the likelihood of depressive symptoms relative to employees with a more secure status. We can thus assume considerable savings in health costs and a good maintenance of worker capacity if organizations could utilize redeployment policies as exemplified by the BT. This study is probably the first to analyze the effects of redeployment in the civilian labor force. Our data suggest that redeployed workers are protected from major risks faced by those displaced. Indeed, maintenance of income level was reported by the vast majority of workers who are or were formerly redeployed in the BT transition center. By contrast, income level deteriorated in the majority of workers with the experience of job loss in the population samples from Hungary, Sweden and France. Skill upgrading and other help was indicated much more frequently by the BT redeployees than by displaced workers.

Contrary to our expectations, no statistically significant protective effects on depressive symptoms were found for retraining, other help and employee influence on downsizing [27];[42]–[45];[73]. Early warning showed an inconsistent pattern of relationships. On closer inspection in models with interaction terms, early warning was linked to a decreased likelihood of symptoms in all groups employed at interview, with significant odds ratios in survivors, but no beneficial effects could be confirmed in those unemployed. These variables were hypothesized to denote the pre-layoff support and the involvement of workers in the process of organizational change. It should however be noted that we analyzed the short-term impact of these strategies. Significant beneficial effects may become visible in a longer term context, while the immediate stage of transition to new employment may place a great strain on the affected workers. Despite bringing better opportunities of new employment, the pre-layoff support does not resolve the question of what the future holds. In particular, many workers might be nervous about entering a retraining program; they may lack confidence in their abilities to acquire new skills and compete in the new world of work [44]. The cross-sectional design could therefore make the protective effects of such programs difficult to detect.

Due to the cross-sectional nature of our data, causal inferences cannot be made. Studying causal relationships between the dimensions of the downsizing process and depressive symptoms would require a longitudinal extension to this study. The main aim of the Restructuring Survey was to provide a detailed snapshot of medium- to large-scale downsizing as perceived by workers in different European economies and to check whether some of the downsizing dimensions are the likely determinants of depressive symptoms. A high level of these symptoms does not necessarily reflect the presence of a clinically significant depressive disorder. Focusing on clinically significant illness only would require a larger sample size to have adequate power. Our results should therefore be interpreted in relation to an increased or decreased risk of depressive morbidity [57]. Existing literature suggests that relationships between the nature of the downsizing process and depressive symptoms, observed in this study, might have occurred because the perception of procedural (in)justice or (dis)trust in organizations led to subsequent emotional health problems. However, research on the affective nature of perception can imply reverse causality [75]: poor emotional health can influence the perception of downsizing. Contrasting both theoretical perspectives by, for example, controlling for negative affectivity and emotional ill health prior to downsizing and testing the longitudinal health effects would be the next research step. Understanding the adverse effects of the downsizing process is important for identifying strategies that can mitigate its negative impact on workers' health and productivity.

The data collection took place during the most severe recession since the Great Depression. Probably, the need of firms to quickly react to emergencies in the economic crisis could have altered the institutional practices of enacting the downsizing procedures, and our study illustrates the perception of these practices in affected workers. How these trends affected the generalizability of our main findings across time is not clear. The observed relationships may be weaker or stronger during periods of relatively low unemployment. Given the pervasiveness of downsizing practices even in stable times, researchers should continue to study the effects of the downsizing dimensions when the economic conditions are significantly improved.

Further limitations of the study include a potential for selection bias. The UK sample of the BT employees is highly selective due to practices of staff retraining and redeployment [76] which are likely to be beneficial for the mental health of employees, as our results show. Furthermore, it is possible that the most disadvantaged workers in Hungary, Sweden and France – for instance, migrants with insufficient language skills or the working poor without telephone lines – could not participate in the telephone interviews. This could cause the strength of the associations observed in our analysis to be attenuated, since these workers are most likely to suffer from harsh layoff processes and their health consequences.

This multi-country study contributes to the identification of a broad spectrum of possible risk factors related to the process of downsizing. Our results underline the importance of just and socially responsible downsizing processes for the emotional health of workers. We find it reasonable to believe that our study sample is representative in terms of variations in downsizing strategies applied in European organizations with medium- to large-scale reduction in personnel. The BT was selected as an example of a company which uses redeployment rather than redundancy for dealing with surplus employees. However, the results presented here are not necessarily valid outside the European Union. They are also not necessarily generalizable to the population of all European workers. Due to the strict selection criteria applied in this study, our attention was focused on labor market participants who could not withdraw from the downsizing situation. It should be kept in mind that workers exposed to downsizing often have a variety of responses: some can choose withdrawal from the situation through early retirement, while others would find another job before becoming unemployed. Therefore, future research should investigate the generalizability of the findings to the groups of workers beyond the scope of this study. In particular, the health effects of downsizing should be clearly differentiated in potentially healthier and better educated workers who find it easier to obtain new employment before the actual job loss, and in older workers for whom it might be extremely difficult to find new jobs.

ACKNOWLEDGMENTS

We would like to thank all researchers and contributors to the study: Dr. Mária Kopp (Semmelweis University, Budapest, Hungary), Dr. András Székely (office for research groups attached to universities and other institutions of Hungarian Academy of Sciences), Dr. Thomas Cox (Nottingham University, UK), Dr. Peter Totterdill (UK Work Organisation Network), Dr. Catherine Kilfedder, Joanne Anderson and Simon Allan (BT, UK), Stephen Goldberg (Institut de veille sanitaire, Paris, France), Sophie Launay (INSERM, Paris, France), Teresa McGarry, Beryl Wall and Rob Sheldon (Accent, UK), Dr. Anette Schade, Silke Hönert and Simone Ludwig (Technische Universität Berlin, Germany). We also wish to gratefully acknowledge the participation of all respondents of the Restructuring Survey.

FUNDING STATEMENT

The data collection was financially supported by the European Community Program for Employment and Social Solidarity (2007–2013), service contract #VC/2007/0482. The authors and investigators do not belong to the European public service. The results and opinions presented in this paper do not represent the official position of the European Commission.

REFERENCES

1. ILO (2010) Global employment trends, January 2010. Geneva: ILO International Labour Office. 9–10.
2. Kets de Vries M, Balazs K (1996) The human side of downsizing. European Management Journal 14: 111–120
3. Quinlan M, Bohle P (2009) Overstretched and unreciprocated commitment: reviewing research on the occupational health and safety effects of downsizing and job insecurity. Int J Health Serv 39: 1–44
4. Mathers CD, Bernard C, Iburg KM, Inoue M, Ma Fat D, et al. . (2003) Global burden of disease in 2002: data sources, methods and results. Global programme on evidence for health policy discussion paper No. 54. Geneva: World Health Organization. 52–54.
5. Dew MA, Bromet EJ, Penkower L (1992) Mental health effects of job loss in women. Psychol Med 22: 751–764
6. Gallo WT, Bradley EH, Dubin JA, Jones RN, Falba TA, et al. (2006) The persistence of depressive symptoms in older workers who experience involuntary job loss: results from the health and retirement survey. J Gerontol B Psychol Sci Soc Sci 61: S221–228
7. Mandal B, Roe B (2008) Job loss, retirement and the mental health of older Americans. J Ment Health Policy Econ 11: 167–176
8. Brand JE, Levy BR, Gallo WT (2008) Effects of layoffs and plant closings on depression among older workers. Res Aging 30: 701–721
9. Dooley D, Fielding J, Levi L (1996) Health and unemployment. Annu Rev Public Health 17: 449–465
10. Catalano R, Goldman-Mellor S, Saxton K, Margerison-Zilko C, Subbaraman M, et al. (2011) The health effects of economic decline. Annu Rev Public Health 32: 431–450
11. Dooley D, Catalano R, Wilson G (1994) Depression and unemployment: panel findings from the Epidemiologic Catchment Area study. Am J Community Psychol 22: 745–765

12. Dooley D, Prause J, Ham-Rowbottom KA (2000) Underemployment and depression: longitudinal relationships. J Health Soc Behav 41: 421–436

13. Kasl SV, Jones BA (2000) The impact of job loss and retirement on health. In: Berkman L, Kawachi I, editors. Social epidemiology. Oxford: Oxford University Press. 118–136.

14. Grunberg L, Moore SY, Greenberg E (2001) Differences in psychological and physical health among layoff survivors: the effect of layoff contact. J Occup Health Psychol 6: 15–25

15. Tsutsumi A, Kayaba K, Theorell T, Siegrist J (2001) Association between job stress and depression among Japanese employees threatened by job loss in a comparison between two complementary job-stress models. Scand J Work Environ Health 27: 146–153

16. Greubel J, Kecklund G (2011) The impact of organizational changes on work stress, sleep, recovery and health. Ind Health 49: 353–364

17. Moore S, Grunberg L, Greenberg E (2004) Repeated downsizing contact: the effects of similar and dissimilar layoff experiences on work and well-being outcomes. J Occup Health Psychol 9: 247–257

18. Ferrie JE, Shipley MJ, Stansfeld SA, Marmot MG (2002) Effects of chronic job insecurity and change in job security on self-reported health, minor psychiatric morbidity, physiological measures, and health related behaviours in British civil servants: the Whitehall II study. J Epidemiol Community Health 56: 450–454

19. Dragano N, Verde PE, Siegrist J (2005) Organisational downsizing and work stress: testing synergistic health effects in employed men and women. J Epidemiol Community Health 59: 694–699

20. Devine K, Reay T, Stainton L, Collins-Nakai R (2003) Downsizing outcomes: better a victim than a survivor? Human Resource Management 42: 109–124

21. Quinlan M (2007) Organisational restructuring/downsizing, OHS regulation and worker health and wellbeing. Int J Law Psychiatry 30: 385–399

22. Kivimäki M, Vahtera J, Pentti J, Ferrie JE (2000) Factors underlying the effect of organisational downsizing on health of employees: longitudinal cohort study. BMJ 320: 971–975

23. Noer D (1993) Healing the wounds: overcoming the trauma of layoffs and revitalizing downsized organizations. San Francisco: Jossey-Bass. 272 p.

24. Pepper L, Messinger M, Weinberg J, Campbell R (2003) Downsizing and health at the United States Department of Energy. Am J Ind Med 44: 481–491

25. Campbell R, Pepper L (2002) Organizational downsizing: implications for the health of survivors. New Solut 12: 177–194

26. Farley JE (1991) Responses of mental health professionals to lay-offs. Hosp Community Psychiatry 42: 624–627

27. Schweiger DM, Ivancevich JM, Power FR (1987) Executive actions for managing human resources before and after acquisition. The Academy of Management Executive 1: 127–138

28. Colquitt JA (2001) On the dimensionality of organizational justice: a construct validation of a measure. J Appl Psychol 86: 386–400

29. Cropanzano R, Byrne ZS, Bobocel DR, Rupp DE (2001) Moral virtues, fairness heuristics, social entities, and other denizens of organizational justice. J Vocat Behav 58: 164–209

30. Cascio WF (2002) Responsible restructuring: What to do and what not to do. In: Cascio WF. Responsible restructuring: Creative and profitable alternatives to layoffs. San Francisco, CA: Berrett-Koehler Publishers. 91–106.

31. Leventhal GS, Karuza J, Fry WR (1980) Beyond fairness: a theory of allocation preferences. In: Mikula G, editor. Justice in social interaction. New York: Springer. 167–218.

32. Leventhal GS (1976) The distribution of rewards and resources in groups and organizations. Adv Exp Soc Psychol 9: 91–131

33. Tyler TR, Lind EA (1992) A relational model of authority in groups. Adv Exp Soc Psychol 25: 115–191

34. Elovainio M, Kivimäki M, Vahtera J (2002) Organizational justice: evidence of a new psychosocial predictor of health. Am J Public Health 92: 105–108

35. Laaksonen M, Rahkonen O, Martikainen P, Lahelma E (2006) Associations of psychosocial working conditions with self-rated general health and mental health among municipal employees. Int Arch Occup Environ Health 79: 205–212

36. Kivimäki M, Elovainio M, Vahtera J, Ferrie JE (2003) Organisational justice and health of employees: prospective cohort study. Occup Environ Med 60: 27–33

37. Lang J, Bliese PD, Lang JW, Adler AB (2011) Work gets unfair for the depressed: cross-lagged relations between organizational justice perceptions and depressive symptoms. J Appl Psychol 96: 602–618

38. Ylipaavalniemi J, Kivimäki M, Elovainio M, Virtanen M, Keltikangas-Järvinen L, et al. (2005) Psychosocial work characteristics and incidence of newly diagnosed depression: a prospective cohort study of three different models. Soc Sci Med 61: 111–122

39. Kivimäki M, Vahtera J, Elovainio M, Virtanen M, Siegrist J (2007) Effort-reward imbalance, procedural injustice and relational injustice as psychosocial predictors of health: complementary or redundant models? Occup Environ Med 64: 659–665

40. Ybema JF, van den Bos K (2010) Effects of organizational justice on depressive symptoms and sickness absence: a longitudinal perspective. Soc Sci Med 70: 1609–1617

41. Grynderup MB, Mors O, Hansen ÅM, Andersen JH, Bonde JP, et al. (2013) Work-unit measures of organisational justice and risk of depression-a 2-year cohort study. Occup Environ Med 70: 380–385

42. Cascio WF (2005) Strategies for responsible restructuring. The Academy of Management Executive 19: 39–50

43. Appelbaum SH, Delage C, Labib N, Gault G (1997) The survivor syndrome: aftermath of downsizing. Career Development International 2: 278–286

44. Hansen GB (2009) A guide to worker displacement: Some tools for reducing the impact on workers, communities and enterprises. (Second ed.). Geneva: ILO International Labour Office. 77 p.

45. European Commission (2012) Restructuring in Europe 2011. Luxembourg: Publication office of the European Union. 241 p.

46. Bartley M, Ferrie J (2001) Glossary: unemployment, job insecurity, and health. J Epidemiol Community Health 55: 776–781

47. Susánszky É, Székely A, Szabó G, Szántó Zs, Klinger A, et al. (2007) A Hungarostudy Egészség Panel (HEP) felmérés módszertani leírása. [Methodological description of the Hungarian epidemiological panel (HEP) survey]. Mentálhigiéné és Pszichoszomatika 8: 259–276

48. Pilling J, Thege BK, Demetrovics Z, Kopp MS (2012) Alcohol use in the first three years of bereavement: a national representative survey. Subst Abuse Treat Prev Policy 7: 3.

49. Kinsten A, Magnusson Hanson LL, Hyde M, Oxenstierna G, Westerlund H, et al. . (2007) Swedish Longitudinal Occupational Survey of Health (SLOSH) – a nationally representative psychosocial survey of the Swedish working population. Stockholm: Stress Research Institute, Stockholm University. 139 p.

50. Magnusson Hanson LL, Theorell T, Bech P, Rugulies R, Burr H, et al. (2009) Psychosocial working conditions and depressive symptoms among Swedish employees. Int Arch Occup Environ Health 82: 951–960

51. Hasson D, Theorell T, Westerlund H, Canlon B (2010) Prevalence and characteristics of hearing problems in a working and non-working Swedish population. J Epidemiol Community Health 64: 453–460

52. Leineweber C, Baltzer M, Magnusson Hanson LL, Westerlund H (2012) Work-family conflict and health in Swedish working women and men: a 2-year prospective analysis (the SLOSH study). Eur J Public Health

53. Jones A, Evans G (2009) BT doubles job cuts to 30,000. The Independent. Thursday 14 May 2009. Available: http://www.independent.co.uk/news/business/news/bt-doubles-job-cuts-to-30000-1684727.html Accessed 2013 January 25.

54. Jenkins R, Harvey S, Butler T, Thomas RL (1996) Minor psychiatric morbidity, its prevalence and outcome in a cohort of civil servants–a seven-year follow-up study. Occup Med (Lond) 46: 209–215

55. Sanderson K, Nicholson J, Graves N, Tilse E, Oldenburg B (2008) Mental health in the workplace: using the ICF to model the prospective associations between symptoms, activities, participation and environmental factors. Disabil Rehabil 30: 1289–1297

56. Horváth B (2010) On the nature of nonresponse and interviewer effects in the Hungarian Labour Force Survey. Hungarian Statistical Review 88: 125–147

57. Magnusson Hanson LL, Westerlund H, Leineweber C, Rugulies R, Osika W, et al. . (2013) The Symptom Checklist-core depression (SCL-CD6) scale: Psychometric properties of a brief six item scale for the assessment of depression. Scand J Public Health Aug 27, [Epub ahead of print].

58. Bech P (2011) Klinisk psykometri/Clinical psychometrics. København: Gyldendal Akademisk. 206 p.

59. Hosmer DW, Lemeshow S (2000) Applied logistic regression. (Second ed.). New York: Wiley. 74–79.

60. Juul S (2006) An introduction to Stata for health researchers. College Station, Texas: Stata Press. 198–202.

61. Judge GG, Griffiths WE, Hill RC, Lütkepohl H, Lee TC (1985) The theory and practice of econometrics. (Second ed.). New York: Wiley. 25–28.

62. Kivimäki M, Elovainio M, Vahtera J, Virtanen M, Stansfeld SA (2003) Association between organizational inequity and incidence of psychiatric disorders in female employees. Psychol Med 33: 319–326

63. Hurley RF (2006) The decision to trust. Harv Bus Rev 84: 55–62, 156.

64. Oksanen T, Kouvonen A, Vahtera J, Virtanen M, Kivimäki M (2010) Prospective study of workplace social capital and depression: are vertical and horizontal components equally important? J Epidemiol Community Health 64: 684–689

65. Groves RM (1990) Theories and methods of telephone surveys. Annu Rev Sociol 16: 221–240

66. Kivimäki M, Vahtera J, Thomson L, Griffiths A, Cox T, et al. (1997) Psychosocial factors predicting employee sickness absence during economic decline. J Appl Psychol 82: 858–872

67. Novo M, Hammarström A, Janlert U (2001) Do high levels of unemployment influence the health of those who are not unemployed? A gendered comparison of young men and women during boom and recession. Soc Sci Med 53: 293–303

68. Catalano R, Aldrete E, Vega W, Kolody B, Aguilar-Gaxiola S (2000) Job loss and major depression among Mexican Americans. Soc Sci Q 81: 477–487

69. Breslin FC, Mustard C (2003) Factors influencing the impact of unemployment on mental health among young and older adults in a longitudinal, population-based survey. Scand J Work Environ Health 29: 5–14

70. Thomas C, Benzeval M, Stansfeld SA (2005) Employment transitions and mental health: an analysis from the British household panel survey. J Epidemiol Community Health 59: 243–249

71. Gallo WT, Bradley EH, Teng HM, Kasl SV (2006) The effect of recurrent involuntary job loss on the depressive symptoms of older US workers. Int Arch Occup Environ Health 80: 109–116

72. Østhus S (2012) Health effects of downsizing survival and job loss in Norway. Soc Sci Med 75: 946–953

73. Wilson SH, Walker GM (1993) Unemployment and health: a review. Public Health 107: 153–162

74. Kessler RC, Turner JB, House JS (1987) Intervening processes in the relationship between unemployment and health. Psychol Med 17: 949–961

75. Lang J, Bliese PD, Lang JW, Adler AB (2011) Work gets unfair for the depressed: cross-lagged relations between organizational justice perceptions and depressive symptoms. J Appl Psychol 96: 602–618

76. Wallington D, Jefferys S, Moore S (2009) Health policy in BT under continuous restructuring. In: Kieselbach T, et al. ., editors. Health in restructuring: innovative approaches and policy recommendations (HIRES). München: Rainer Hampp Verlag. 154–160.

Index